T0293180

University President's Crisis Handbook

University President's Crisis Handbook

How a Non-Traditional Leader
Took His Alma Mater from
Insolvency to Sustainable Success

C. Scott Green
Temple Kinyon

WILEY

Published by John Wiley & Sons, Inc., Hoboken, New Jersey.
Published simultaneously in Canada.

For general information on our other products and services or for technical support, please contact our Customer Care Department within the United States at (800) 762-2974, outside the United States at (317) 572-3993 or fax (317) 572-4002.

Wiley also publishes its books in a variety of electronic formats. Some content that appears in print may not be available in electronic formats. For more information about Wiley products, visit our web site at www.wiley.com.

Library of Congress Cataloging-in-Publication Data:

Names: Green, Scott, 1962- author. | Kinyon, Temple, author.
Title: University president's crisis handbook / Scott Green, Temple Kinyon.
Description: Hoboken, New Jersey : Wiley, [2024] | Includes bibliographical references and index.
Identifiers: LCCN 2023028795 (print) | LCCN 2023028796 (ebook) | ISBN 9781394219957 (cloth) | ISBN 9781394219971 (adobe pdf) | ISBN 9781394219964 (epub)
Subjects: LCSH: University of Idaho. | Crisis management—Idaho. | College presidents—Idaho.
Classification: LCC HD49 .G74 2024 (print) | LCC HD49 (ebook) | DDC 658.4/05609796—dc23/eng/20231003
LC record available at https://lccn.loc.gov/2023028795
LC ebook record available at https://lccn.loc.gov/2023028796

Cover Design: Wiley
Cover Image: © 2023 by University of Idaho

We dedicate this book to
the University of Idaho faculty, staff, alumni, and
state-wide partners,
along with our Regents,
who assisted the university in avoiding insolvency and
remaining safely open during a pandemic.
These caring individuals also, without question or pause,
helped the campus heal after tremendous loss.
Brave. Bold. Unstoppable.

Contents

Timeline of Events

The timeline of events allows readers a reference as the story progresses. Management insights provided by President Scott Green are included at the end of every chapter to summarize key takeaways, and "Smart Collaborations" are woven throughout to provide in-depth examples of how the University of Idaho community and stakeholders partnered to achieve milestones for the institution. Scott also shares "Scott's Third Rail" content, which takes a deeper dive into essential concepts faced in higher education, including lawsuits, athletics, politics, and accreditation.

Fall 2018
- Scott receives texts from Chandra Zenner Ford and Clint Marshall about applying to become the U of I president.
- Scott applies for the U of I president position.

March 2019
- SBOE unanimously approves the U of I to commence with the bidding and construction phase for new arena contingent on project approval by the SBOE executive director and new U of I president when named.

April 2019
- The U of I officially announces Scott as its 19th president; Scott begins a non-paid consultantship contract with the U of I.

June 2019
- The U of I celebrates the groundbreaking for ICCU Arena.
- Scott travels from Long Island to Moscow to begin his new job as president; a large social media following tracks his progress via Scott's posts with Joe Vandal.

July 2019
- Scott officially starts as the U of I president.
- Scott meets with campus executives to discuss the financial crisis and tasks them with targets for cutting the FY20 budget.
- Scott begins his goal of visiting every College of Agricultural and Life Sciences extension office and research center located in 42 of Idaho's 44 counties.

October 2019
- Scott establishes the Financial Model Working Group to produce a whitepaper and suggest a new, sustainable financial model.

January 2020
- Scott establishes the R1-2026 Research Initiative Working Group to move the university toward R1 Carnegie Classification.
- Scott and Provost John Wiencek host an All-Staff Town Hall Meeting outlining optional retirement, voluntary separation, and other separation options to reduce headcount, along with potential furloughs.
- Administration holds first meeting/discussions as it pertains to COVID-19, international students, and support response.

February 2020
- The Lionel Hampton Jazz Festival brings a potential COVID-19 exposure.

March 2020
- The U of I employees present Scott with their $22 million in cuts for FY21.
- Matt Freeman (SBOE) reaches out to the U of I, BSU, ISU, and LCSC to take a coordinated approach to COVID-19 preparedness and protocols; institutions agree to meet as a COVID-19 group with representatives from around the state.

- SBOE hosts the Presidents Leadership Council with all eight presidents from Idaho's higher education public institutions; Idaho Governor Brad Little attends and emphasizes each needs a COVID-19 plan for the remainder of the spring 2020 semester.
- Scott meets in Boise with other Big Sky Conference university presidents, and in a split vote, the Conference cancels the rest of the Big Sky basketball tournament.
- Scott and Provost Wiencek email faculty, staff, and students that the SBOE supports indefinite online/remote instruction; all events planned with more than 100 attendees are also canceled, including UIdaho Bound recruiting events and spring commencements.
- Scott adopts FSH 6990 COVID-19 Virus Emergency Response.
- Scott sends an email asking all employees who can work from home starting the end of day on March 25, effectively closing the university.
- Governor Little officially declares a 21-day statewide stay-at-home order; state educational systems are deemed essential, but Little reiterates that employees who can work at home do so.
- Scott appoints Torrey Lawrence as interim provost.
- Matt Freeman (SBOE) announces the first tranche of CARES Act funding for students to cover expenses related to the disruption of campus operations due to coronavirus.

April 2020
- Latah County reports the first COVID-19 cases, with three U of I students and one resident testing positive.
- The R1-2026 Research Initiative Working Group presents its whitepaper to Scott.

May 2020
- Toni Broyles, Kara Besst, and Kane Francetich begin officially planning to establish a CLIA-approved COVID-19 testing lab at Gritman Medical Center in collaboration with the U of I.
- Scott commissions the Online Education Working Group.

June 2020
- The U of I records a small operating surplus for FY20.
- Gritman Medical Center begins coordinating lab setup with the U of I.
- The U of I encourages all employees to return to standard work locations for the first time since March 25.

- Gritman staff conduct the first COVID-19 swabbing/testing trial run on the U of I campus.
- Scott receives a petition signed by 250 faculty members stating their position regarding in-person education during COVID-19 as ethically troubling and pedagogically challenging.

August 2020
- The U of I Marketing and Creative Services deploys the "We're Closer Than You Think" campaign to increase recruitment and enrollment, taking advantage of California's decision to stay closed and online during the fall 2020 semester; Marketing and Creative Services uses techniques to appeal to a tech-savvy demographic.
- Scott receives a letter and petition from the community of Moscow and the Palouse (also sent to Change.org) with 1552 signatures asking the U of I to go entirely online.
- The U of I/Gritman CLIA-approved COVID-19 testing lab produces its first two batches of testing results.
- The Online Education Working Group finalizes its whitepaper draft with Scott.
- The U of I offers live, in-class learning with a Hyflex model; all students are required to receive a COVID-19 test to attend in-person classes.
- The university opens its infirmary in Targhee Hall.

September 2020
- The U of I campus closes and cancels all events for one week due to smoke from regional forest fires creating poor air quality and clogging HVAC filters.

October 2020
- *US News & World Report* names the U of I the best value of any public university in the West and third nationally, behind the University of Virginia and the University of North Carolina.

November 2020
- The U of I chooses to go entirely online with classes and finals after Thanksgiving break to ensure safety for the remainder of the semester.

December 2020
- Torrey Lawrence is named Provost for the U of I.
- Gritman begins front-line worker COVID-19 vaccinations.

- The U of I and Plenary Americas USA Ltd., Sacyr Infrastructure USA LLC, and McKinstry finalize the steam plant P3 transaction, which results in the single largest financial transaction in the institution's history; a $225 million up-front payment allowed for an endowment that generates over $6 million annually to invest in strategic growth.

January 2021
- All U of I Moscow-based students must show proof of COVID-19 testing or exemption by this date to attend in-person classes (Hyflex) for the spring 2021 semester.

February 2021
- Idaho announces COVID-19 vaccines are available for those over the age of 65.
- The U of I Vandal football spring season opens at the Kibbie Dome against Eastern Washington University.

March 2021
- Idaho announces COVID-19 vaccines are available to those over the age of 35.
- Vandal Hybrid Budget Model presented to campus to begin implementation for FY22.

April 2021
- Idaho announces those over the age of 16 are eligible for the COVID-19 vaccine.
- Idaho Legislature votes to cut $500,000 from the U of I FY22 budget to address indoctrination allegations from the Idaho Freedom Foundation (IFF).

May 2021
- Six in-person commencement ceremonies take place at the Kibbie Dome for both 2020 and 2021 graduates.
- Scott allocates $3 million of P3 funds to the R1-2026 research initiative and $2 million to student success and scholarship initiatives.
- Scott awards the Pandemic Response Teams from the U of I and Gritman the newly designed President's Medallion.

June 2021
- For FY21, the university attains its second annual financial surplus in a row.

July 2021
- All employees who have not returned to their pre-COVID-19 workspace or without an ongoing approved flex place agreement are expected to return to their university-provided workspace.
- The Idaho Center for Plant and Soil Health in Parma, ID, hosts its groundbreaking ceremonies.
- Scott hires Ken Udas as Vice Provost for Digital Learning Initiatives to advance student success initiatives through remote learning.

August 2021
- The U of I sees the largest incoming freshman class since 2016.

October 2021
- The U of I hosts its official ribbon cutting for the ICCU Arena and the kick-off of "Brave. Bold. A Promise to Idaho Students" campaign.

January 2022
- The U of I signs and executes an MOU with the other Idaho universities in an agreement with Idaho National Laboratory (INL) to transfer the decommissioned Falcon supercomputer to the management of the U of I, Idaho State University, and Boise State University.
- In front of the Idaho JFAC committee, Scott rejects the Idaho Freedom Foundation's claims of indoctrinating programs at the U of I and releases an independent report compiled by the law firm of Hawley Troxell dismissing the claims as unfounded.

March 2022
- The U of I Seed Potato Germplasm Laboratory opens.

April 2022
- Scott completes his quest to visit every College of Agricultural and Life Sciences extension office and research center.

June 2022
- The university attains its third annual financial surplus in a row in FY22.
- The U of I hosts the Center for Agriculture, Food, and Environment (CAFE) project groundbreaking; construction of the nation's largest research dairy and experimental farm begins.

August 2022
- The U of I sees its largest incoming freshman classes in university history; the university puts up 117 students in a local hotel due to housing constraints.
- The university reports its largest annual fundraising total ever at $64 million.

September 2022
- The U of I receives a $55 million grant, the largest research award in its history, to address climate-smart agriculture.

November 2022
- The U of I responds to the brutal killings of four students and coordinates communications and enhanced campus safety and security measures.

December 2022
- Police arrest a suspect for the murders of four U of I students.

The Vandal Tribe
of Contributors

The University of Idaho fight song, "Go, Vandals, Go!" by J. Morris O'Donnell, U of I Class of 1933, starts with the line, "Came a Tribe from the North, brave and bold" (University of Idaho 1933). This verse serves as a lifelong mantra for the institution's students, faculty, staff, alumni, and friends. They are proud Vandals and part of an everlasting tribe and family, always brave, always bold. These particular individuals are a small but mighty part of the Vandal tribe who banded together to help the coauthors write this incredible piece to the U of I's story.

Listed in alphabetical order by last name (with U of I degree, if applicable) and position title or affiliation to the university.

Kathy Barnard, BS 1981, Assistant Vice President for Alumni Relations and Advancement Communications, University of Idaho

John Barnhart, Senior Director of Marketing and Creative Services, University of Idaho

Dr. Dennis R. Becker, PhD 2002, Dean, College of Natural Resources, University of Idaho

Kara Besst, BS 1994, CEO, Gritman Medical Center

Danielle Breed, Administrative Chief of Staff, Gritman Medical Center

Toni Broyles, BS 2001, MS 2010, Special Assistant, Strategic Initiatives, University of Idaho

Donald "Don" Burnett, Dean, College of Law, 2002–2013, Interim President, 2013–2014, Professor of Law Emeritus, University of Idaho

Linda C. Campos, Associate Vice President for Finance, University of Idaho

Dr. Ginger E. Carney, Dean, College of Science, Professor, Biological Sciences, University of Idaho

Dr. Marc Chopin, Dean, College of Business and Economics, September 2016–June 2022, University of Idaho

Dr. Shauna Corry, Dean, College of Art and Architecture, University of Idaho

Dr. John Crepeau, Interim Dean, College of Engineering, June 2021–June 2022, Professor, Mechanical Engineering, University of Idaho

Dr. Blaine Eckles, PhD 2011, Vice Provost of Student Affairs and Dean of Students, University of Idaho

Ms. Frances Ellsworth, BS 1983, U of I Foundation Board, University of Idaho

Lee Espey, Division Operations Officer, Division of Finance and Administration, University of Idaho

Daniel "Dan" Ewart, Vice President for Information Technology and Chief Information Officer, University of Idaho

Brian Foisy, Vice President, Division of Finance and Administration, University of Idaho

Kane Francetich, Chief Information Officer, Gritman Medical Center

Matt Freeman, JD 1995, Executive Director, Idaho State Board of Education (SBOE)

Terry L. Gawlik, Director of Athletics, University of Idaho

Scott Green, BS 1984, President, University of Idaho

Dr. Terrance "Terry" Grieb, Professor of Finance, Faculty Senate Chair, 2019–2020, University of Idaho

Brenda Helbling, BA 2014, Chief of Staff, Office of the President, University of Idaho

Angela Helmke, BS 1996, Associate Director of Campus Visits and Events, University of Idaho

Stephen "Steve" Immelt, CEO, Hogan Lovells

Dr. Dean R. Kahler, Vice Provost for Strategic Enrollment Management (SEM), University of Idaho

Johanna Kalb, Dean, College of Law, University of Idaho

Barbara Kirchmeier, BS 2000, MEd 2003, MA 2005, Director of First Year Composition, Faculty Chair, 2020–2021, University of Idaho

Katy Lawler, Design and Marketing Coordinator, Institute for Interdisciplinary Data Sciences, University of Idaho

Dr. Torrey Lawrence, DMA, Provost and Executive Vice President, 2020–Present, Vice Provost for Faculty, 2018–2020, Professor of Music, University of Idaho

William "Bill" Lee, Co-Managing Partner, WilmerHale

Jacob Lockhart, BS 2020, ASUI President, Fall 2019–Spring 2020, University of Idaho

Trina Mahoney, Assistant Vice President University Budget and Planning, University of Idaho

Clint Marshall, BS 1997, U of I Foundation President, 2016

Wesley McClintick, BS 2001, MA 2010, MA 2014, Director for Institutional Research, University of Idaho

Mary Kay McFadden, BA 1980, Vice President for University Advancement, University of Idaho

Dr. Jerry McMurtry, Dean, College of Graduate Studies, University of Idaho

Gary Michael, BS 1962, HON 2003, Interim President, 2002–2003, University of Idaho

Dr. Christopher "Chris" Nomura, Vice President for Research and Economic Development, University of Idaho

Connie Osborn, Nurse, Gritman Medical Center

Dr. Michael P. Parrella, Dean, College of Agricultural and Life Sciences, University of Idaho

Dr. Sean M. Quinlan, Dean, College of Letters, Arts, and Social Sciences, University of Idaho

Bradley Ritts, Interim Vice President for Research and Economic Development, 2019–2020, Senior Associate Vice President for Research, University of Idaho

Dr. Barrie Robison, MS 1995, Senior Associate Vice President for Research and Director of Institute for Bioinformatics and Evolutionary Studies (IBEST), University of Idaho

Kimberly "Kim" Salisbury, BS 1999, MAcc 2004, Associate Vice President for Budget and Planning, University of Idaho

Karla Scharbach, BFA 1987, Graphic Designer, Creative Services, University of Idaho

Dr. Philip Scruggs, Interim Dean, College of Education, Health, and Human Sciences, June 2020–June 2022, Department Chair, Associate Professor, Movement Sciences, University of Idaho

Nicole Skinner, BA 2019, ASUI President, Fall 2018–Spring 2019, University of Idaho

Kimlye Stager, BS, 2021, Multimedia Reporter, Casa Grande Valley Newspapers, Inc.

Dr. Larry A. Stauffer, Dean, College of Engineering, 2011–2021, Acting Center Executive Officer, U of I Coeur d'Alene, University of Idaho

Jeff Stoddard, BS 1975, 1976, Buie Stoddard Group

Lydia Stucki, BA, 1995, Office Manager, Division of Finance and Administration, University of Idaho

Brandi Terwilliger, Director of Human Resources, University of Idaho

Seth Vieux, COVID-19 Project Manager, Special Projects Manager, Office of the President, University of Idaho

Chris Walsh, Associate Athletic Director, University of Idaho

Dr. John M. Wiencek, Provost and Executive Vice President, July 2014 – June 2020, University of Idaho

Chandra Zenner Ford, BS 1988, MS 1995, CEO SW Idaho and Special Advisor, Office of the President, University of Idaho

Foreword

Having spent the past 15 years researching and advising global organizations on "smart collaboration," I can say with confidence that President Scott Green is a true exemplar of the concept. From my first time working with him and his leadership team several years ago, I witnessed firsthand his commitment to effective collaboration *and* its successful execution. This was key in the University of Idaho emerging stronger from financial insolvency, a global pandemic, and a senseless tragedy involving four students.

My teaching and research at Harvard University (both the Business and Law Schools) have revealed that top leaders typically value collaboration, but they often don't know how to do it right. This costs them highly in terms of lost revenue, slower innovation, poor employee and customer engagement, and more.[1]

Scott is an exception.

As shown time and time again in the *University President's Crisis Handbook* (by Scott and his coauthor Temple Kinyon), he has the skill and will to collaborate smarter to achieve his top goals. And the "top goals" piece is crucial. One of the first tenets of smarter collaboration is to start with the end in mind. Throughout the book, Scott reiterates his three strategic pillars: student success, the path to R1 Carnegie research classification, and controlling the narrative by telling the U of I's story.

Scott never loses sight of these pillars, viewing every challenge and opportunity through the lens of these objectives. Not only do they shape his priorities, but they guide him when deciding whom to tap for associated projects. Let's take soil research as an example. When College of Agricultural and Life Sciences (CALS) Dean Michael Parrella applied for a highly competitive $18.9 million grant to build a center for deep soil research, Scott and Special Assistant Toni Broyles became heavily involved. They made the grant proposal a "presidential priority," which aligned the provost, vice provosts, vice presidents, Office of Research and Economic Development, and Office of Sponsored Programs with CALS. Working closely with experts from these different key areas was crucial for landing the grant. Now, researchers from across the world will come to the Moscow campus to study deep soil carbon capture, water quality, and variables impacting health. This can help industry adapt to warmer temperatures in a sustainable way.

In addition to starting with the end (such as research excellence) in mind, Scott knows how to bring in the right perspectives—from both inside and outside the university. In fact, his network is so vast and ever growing that he repeatedly thinks of someone nontraditional yet highly beneficial to consult with. We'll take his decision to become university president as an example. To make the most informed choice possible, he met with alumni and longtime U of I supporters, his current boss (the CEO at Hogan Lovells), and his former boss (comanaging partner at WilmerHale)—among others. Using their collective knowledge of both the university and his strengths helped him realize the position was a good fit. And sometimes, these ties boosted his prospects. For example, after meeting with Scott, one influential contact shared with an Idaho board regent that the new president should have business, marketing, communications, fundraising, and political expertise (which Scott had)—not necessarily a PhD—and provost and land-grant experience (which Scott didn't have). If Scott hadn't cultivated and leveraged these connections, who knows what would have happened?

It's clear that Scott's networking savvy extends to his colleagues. For example, when the U of I needed more space for its Boise law school, and a property went up for sale, President's Office Special Advisor Chandra Zenner Ford stepped in. She met with the listing agent for the property, an old friend she typically saw once a year, to catch up. She let him know of the university's interest in the building; while the sales price was too high, a connection of this agent (and U of I alumnus) agreed to purchase and lease it to the university for a fair amount.

Smart collaborators also embrace conflict, knowing that a diversity of perspectives makes for a better end result. Whether it relates to budget cutting (e.g. $14 million in FY20) or new policies (e.g. the return to in-person instruction in the fall of 2020), differing viewpoints have helped Scott and his team formulate the best plan forward. For example, for the return to face-to-face classes, the university required masks, and online learning was available for those uncomfortable being physically close to others.

When things got heated during the pandemic and beyond, Scott made it a point of staying calm and continuing to work with others. His mantra, "Stay Calm and Vandal On," has been used by faculty, staff, and students throughout his tenure and supported by the use of data and facts. When faculty expressed fear or hysteria during budget cutting, for example, he worked to keep his cool and share relevant statistics. In one case, he countered the perception the university was understaffed with stats on the student/faculty ratio at the U of I (1:14) versus its most comparable peers (1:16). This knowledge helped Scott and his leadership team determine where to make cuts, and his composed explanation earned him broader support. This kind of behavior aligns with our research on smarter collaboration: times of stress can cause people to withdraw, but this is exactly when purposeful, outcome-focused collaboration is most needed.

Transparent, clear, and regular communication also helps build interpersonal and competence trust, two key ingredients for effective collaboration and its strategic outcomes. Whether it's with students, faculty, staff, alumni, partners, or the public, Scott consistently re-shares the U of I's three pillars, its new developments and protocols, and the connection between priorities and decisions made. As fantasy and sci-fi author Alex Irvine has so wisely written, *"Overcommunicate. It's better to tell someone something they already know than to not tell them something they needed to hear."* This was the approach Scott took following the brutal murder of four students, sending 18 email communications to students, faculty, and alumni in the weeks that followed.

Scott understands that to drive real change, it takes a combination of mindsets, behaviors, structures, and cultural elements. Whether it's standardizing financial reporting structures across colleges and units, investing in research capabilities to boost student learning, or marketing the research/academic accolades of the university to prospective students, these kinds of efforts support the strategic pillars *and* require smart collaboration from pertinent parties. Luckily, Scott and his team have this down pat.

I highly encourage university presidents, as well as leaders from any kind of organization, to read the *University President's Crisis Handbook*. It provides a blueprint for identifying your top goals, collaborating the right way to accomplish them, and handling crises and day-to-day challenges that get in your way. Like me, you'll surely be impressed by the progress that the U of I has made over the last four years—under President Scott Green's collaborative leadership. But Scott makes it clear it was a team effort: As you'll read in this book, *"The teamwork and dedication displayed by faculty and staff stood out to him. The institution persevered through incredibly difficult and stressful situations because of its collaborative efforts."* Read on and prepare to be wowed.

Dr. Heidi K. Gardner, Distinguished Fellow,
Harvard Law School

Note

1. For more on this topic, see my latest book *Smarter Collaboration: A New Approach to Breaking Down Barriers and Transforming Work*

Preface

University President's Crisis Handbook offers a chronological account of Scott Green's path to becoming the University of Idaho's 19th president and his first four years in that position, beginning in July 2019. Readers have a front-row seat to how Scott worked to win over faculty and staff while having to make deep financial cuts to keep the university solvent. The book also provides in-depth managerial insights into how he, along with the university staff and faculty—the Vandal tribe—recovered from years of profound deficits despite the potentially severe impacts of the COVID-19 pandemic. Scott's three strategic pillars (student success, the path to R1 Carnegie research classification, and controlling the narrative by telling the U of I's story), along with guidance from industry experts, focused the institution on charting its course. The collaborative efforts of the Vandal tribe along with external experts resulted in the university's financial solvency, soaring enrollments, record research awards, and record fundraising within Scott's four years as president.

However, amid the momentum, the university faced one of the most heinous crimes in the area and state's history against four U of I students. This book shares how the university responded to the tragic loss while keeping the needs of the families and campus community forefront.

The university community's collaboration and collective efforts through the three monumental crises helped strengthen the University of Idaho and position it as a leading national teaching and research institution.

Acknowledgments

From the authors:

Telling the story of the State of Idaho's land-grant institution takes a lot of people. We'd like to thank the following individuals for believing in the importance of telling the story of how University of Idaho Vandals faced three significant crises in three and a half years, rose to the challenge, pulled together, and came out stronger, braver, and bolder. We couldn't have done it without you.

Thank you to the 57 Vandal tribe contributors listed in the book. We appreciate your time, insight, honesty, and enthusiasm for the project. Woven together, your contributions created a rich story with in-depth and detailed examples of how collaboration can achieve incredible success even in the worst of times. Your challenges and triumphs, highs and lows, wins and losses assembled a handbook for other universities, corporations, and businesses on how to do hard things and defeat unprecedented foes. You never gave up on the University of Idaho or your Vandal tribe and family.

We are grateful for the supportive individuals "behind the scenes" who made the magic happen. Without your assistance, we couldn't have mastered the challenge of coauthoring this book: Cindy Barnhart, Yolanda Bisbee, Christine Dunn, Tom English, Joana Espinoza, Heidi Gardner, Alisa Goolsby, Lea Haggerty, Margo Holthaus, Dee L. Hunter, Ben Hunter,

Patricia Huth, Dulce Kersting-Lark, Katy Lawler, Kurt Liebich, Florence Lince, Chris Lynne, Tricia Maxey, Sean McIlraith, Todd Mordhorst, Kent Nelson, Edith Pacillo, Joe Pallen, Ray Pankopf, Erik Peterson, David Pittsley, Megan Pratt, Michelle Reagan, Larry Rouse, Kim Rytter, Mahmood Sheikh, Michael Strickland, Lisa Snyder, Donna Stolaroff, DeLaina Storhok, Mary Stout, Gina Taruscio, Kayla Thrall, and Nichole Vietz.

This is my (Scott's) third book published by John Wiley & Sons, and Sheck Cho has served as acquisition editor on all three books. We appreciate his guidance and good judgment navigating the early stages of the publishing process. He is supportive of telling our story and the mission of the nation's higher education system. It's an important story, and we thank him for that. Thank you also goes to Stacey Rivera, Aruna Pragasam, and Kevin Harreld at Wiley for taking the reins when Sheck retired, and to Lori Martinsek at Adept Content Solutions for managing the copy-editing process.

Tina Morlock, thank you for your expert developmental edit on the book. Your enthusiasm for the project and positive approach made the editing process enjoyable and fun. Your insights and suggestions took the manuscript to a higher level.

Scott Gipson, a fellow Vandal, thank you for taking the time and care to read the manuscript and offer insightful, in-depth comments to enhance and improve it. Your expertise is invaluable.

Idaho Governor Brad Little, another fellow Vandal, thank you for your strong leadership and support through the U of I's various crises.

From Scott:

I have been fortunate to have a number of mentors over the years that helped me develop my managerial toolkit. First, I would like to recognize two of them who contributed to this book. Bill Lee is the former co-managing partner of WilmerHale and, as you will read, gave me pivotal advice at exactly the right time. I learned much just by watching how Bill operated, building teams, interacting with them as colleagues, and providing young attorneys with real responsibility, getting the best out of each one. I learned different, more organizational and political skills from his Co-Managing Partner Bill Perlstein. Together, they made a great team.

The second mentor/contributor is Steve Immelt, the former CEO of Hogan Lovells. Steve was a master at breaking down silos and getting his Management Committee to work together, not an easy thing to do when you have far-flung operations across the world. He introduced Heidi Gardner, the author of *Smart Collaboration: How Professionals and Their*

Firms Succeed by Breaking Down Silos (and her new book, *Smarter Collaboration: A New Approach to Breaking Down Barriers and Transforming Work)*, to the firm, and I saw first-hand how that made for a better, more effective, and profitable organization. I am grateful that Heidi agreed to work with our team at the University of Idaho, as well.

David Hudd, the deputy CEO of the Hogan's London office, was also a great mentor, who had broad experience with cultures around the world. I grew exponentially under his leadership.

Other mentors I would like to mention, even though they are not included in the book, include David Allocco from Goldman Sachs and Kevin Curtin from Weil, Gotshal, and Manges, both of whom have long passed, but their counsel stays with me to this day.

I would be remiss not to mention former FBI Director, the Honorable Louie Freeh, who served as executive committee chair at Pepper Hamilton. I learned from Louie that there is plenty of room for empathy in the boardroom and the office.

Finally, while I did not work for him, Gary Michael, the former CEO of the national grocery chain Albertsons, has been an incredible confidant. He served a short time as the U of I president during a time of crisis. I continue to benefit from his sage advice.

There are too many friends and colleagues to mention that have contributed to this book—just know I am grateful. And to Clint Marshall, Chandra Zenner Ford, and Francis Ellsworth, thank you for convincing me to take this job. It would not have happened without your support and your work behind the scenes.

Finally, thanks to my wife for following me out to Idaho so I could take this job. She was looking forward to my early retirement, so we all owe her a debt of gratitude for supporting a change of plans.

From Temple:

I'm incredibly proud to be a lifelong Vandal (BS 1993). When Scott emailed me in May 2021 to ask if I was interested in helping tell the U of I's story in book form, I humbly and ecstatically accepted. Scott, thank you for your insight to know that sharing the U of I's story is imperative to its success. Others will learn and appreciate what the Vandal tribe and family faced and overcame during your first three and a half years as president. Thank you for trusting that I was the one to help you tell this invaluable account and for the opportunity for me to give something back to my alma mater that has given me so much my entire life.

To my husband, Chad, your listening ear and honesty (even when you knew it would sting) were invaluable during this project. You knew it was a labor of love; thank you for understanding whenever the wheels started falling off the Kinyon Family Bus because I was in the "writing zone" or under a deadline. Thank you for being that strong shoulder of support.

My amazing parents, Joe and Pam Anderson (that's "Potlatch" Joe to some of you), have steadfastly stood by me and helped guide me through life's adventures. They instilled that special Vandal pride from the earliest years; the homecomings, basketball games, summer theatre at the Hartung, and drives through campus to see the College of Ag building left an indelible impression on my heart for the U of I. Thank you. You are exceptional humans.

To my sister-in-law, Wendy Vineyard, a huge thank you for the "sho-cean workations." Everyone said we were goofing off, but amid the beach walks and treasure searching, I helped Scott write a book. Wish rocks really do work! Your support and sense of adventure (and work ethic) fueled my creative soul. Thank you for *all* the things.

Lance McPeak, thank you for offering your Casa Grande house for my two shut-me-away-from-the-world marathon writing retreats. I wrote the bulk of the financial and COVID-19 sections during those precious stretches of solitude. I find it hard to express precisely what all that means to me, but your thoughtfulness offered the perfect creative environment to make the book come to life. Incidentally, your neighbor across the street, Gloria Holapa, had a grandson, Charlie, attending the U of I at the time (2021). The significance of that "chance" Vandal meeting when she came to check on you but found me instead, was fate showing me I was and am friends with the right guy who put me in the right place at the right time to help write the U of I's story. Again, I offer you my deepest gratitude.

My most profound appreciation also goes to: Tracy and Cary Dixon, Kris and Cody Anderson, Angela Helmke, Roger and Diane Kinyon, Heather Niccoli, Ken and Mary Beth Howell, Bridgette Ollenberger, Scot Strehlow, Anne Peterson, Brian Rouff, Angela Lenssen, Laurie Fortier, Jodi Pavkov, Lori Piotrowski, Vicki-Ann Bush, Cynthia DeBoer, Gabriella Green, Doll-Hands, Debi Bonds, Linda Sanborn, Penny Yazzie, Beth Parker, Joy Bellis, Nabila Kahnam, Christine Cutler, Cameron Crain, and Susie Johnson. To you and the rest of my spectacular family and friends, thank you for putting up with my immersion in the project over the past two years. I said "no" and "sorry" a lot to many of you, yet you all stuck with me. That didn't go unnoticed or unappreciated.

Introduction

"This is a place where young curiosity and deep intellectual capability formulate research, outreach, and education into a shared experience. This is a place where there is an opportunity for everyone across the state to come together and support educating all our citizens to benefit the economy, industry, and well-being of the people of Idaho. And this is a place where each of us can personally grow, assure ourselves a better future, and develop the foundation for our life story."

—*C. Scott Green*

The young boy ran with enthusiasm at full speed toward his target. The majestic red brick structure loomed ahead, standing proudly, and nestled among manicured grounds and other collegiate buildings. Four stained-glass windows crowned the massive three-part door framed by Tudor-like ivory cement arches. The architecture drew the eye up the five-story buttressed towers toward the heavens above. To an untrained observer, taking in the edifice at face value might elicit feelings of a grand old church, but it wasn't a church. Rather, it held reverence with some as a living memorial, a homage to those who gave their life serving a higher purpose. Erected in November 1928, Memorial Gymnasium honored heroes from the state who gave their lives in service to their country. It may have been christened as a gymnasium, but within the rich red bricks and architectural features hummed an environment of education and collaboration.

Memorial Gym, University of Idaho Media Library.
SOURCE: Reproduced with permission from University of Idaho.

The young boy didn't pause to admire the building's unique and exquisite style or intended purpose. He'd seen it so many times that, although he loved it, the beautiful structure was like a comfortable old friend who didn't need attention or compliments every time they saw each other.

One feature, however, did demand his attention every visit. Without fail, the boy would stop to look at the attribute as if to say, "Hello, I see you and respect you." Huddled under an outcropping on the two pillars making up the three-part entryway were the objects of the boy's affection. Gargoyles. But not just any gargoyles, Vandal gargoyles. And not just any Vandal gargoyles. These weren't the Germanic Vandals known for sacking Rome and battling the Huns and Goths. No, these were *Idaho* Vandals. The tiny yet ferocious chiseled football players tucked themselves under cement outcroppings, valiantly holding the pigskin, strong and steadfast with the weight of the building resting upon their shoulders. No matter if he was in a hurry, the youngster paused to look up at the protectors of this majestic place. They weren't like the scary monster gargoyles on old English castles and manors, ghastly and frightening to stave off unwanted visitors. No, the football gargoyles, brave and bold, were there to welcome anyone to their northern Vandal tribe—anyone but foes.

Every time he took in the magnificent stone figures, vivid memories sparked, and a wash of deeply rooted feelings and fierce loyalty overcame

Memorial Gym Football Gargoyle, University of Idaho Media Library.
SOURCE: Reproduced with permission from University of Idaho.

him. He'd spent hours in this beloved behemoth during summer breaks and every other visit to Moscow, Idaho. His grandfather Leon worked there in those hallowed halls and enjoyed legendary status on the campus, serving at the helm of the Physical Education and Athletic Departments. The football gargoyles protected his grandfather and all Vandals, near and far.

The elder knew offering a task to his grandson, washing and folding towels in the basement for a whopping dollar a day, would instill work ethic and appreciation for a job well done, along with eternally planting the seed that would root itself into the boy's heart and soul for this special place. He joined his grandson and turned his gaze toward the fierce cement footballers. The two stood silently for a tick, then looked at each other.

"Ready to go to work?" the grandfather asked with a smile.

"Ready!" the young boy enthusiastically replied.

The two walked through the doors of the towering building, ready to face whatever the day brought them, together, protected by the gargoyles surrounding the gymnasium fortress.

He didn't know it then, but the young boy's lifelong love affair with this old institution began with those gargoyles and many sessions sweeping the gymnasium floor and folding all those towels. Throughout his life, the boy would return, over and over, acknowledging the inexplicable tug on his heart elicited by this resplendent place. Destiny would reveal its hand

over 40 years later with the opportunity for him to return to the prestigious academy in an unexpected and unplanned capacity. That moment in
time would present a pivotal life change for him at the exact moment the
institution hung on a precipice, facing financial insolvency, buried under
a broken culture, with leadership lacking the desire to make the hard decisions to save it.

This treasured place was the University of Idaho. The young boy was
C. Scott Green.

* * *

This is a story about Scott's return to Idaho and the leadership and management tools he used to guide the state's land-grant university through
turbulent times. It's a story about the institution's shift in culture, the path
to financial health, the fight against unprecedented foes, and the strategic direction that returned the University of Idaho to one of the best in
the country.

Scott's Management Insight

As is often said, find something you love to do, and you will never work
another day in your life. Find a connection to the institution that will provide your source of energy, build your credibility with the faculty, staff, students, local community, and alumni, and success will follow. The university
and I had a history, one much deeper than most. I was highly motivated to
answer the call and return to help when I learned how tenuous things had
become at my alma mater. It has not been easy, but I am proud, along with
an incredibly talented Vandal family, to lead this institution back to financial health and prominence. Whenever things get tough, I remind myself
why I am here. It is not about me but about the University of Idaho. Joy in
performing the job flows naturally from that relationship.

Part I

Chapter 1
The Road Home
June 24, 2019

"It'll be a crazy long shot."

—Chandra Zenner Ford

Scott glanced at the rearview mirror, his house getting smaller and smaller in the reflection. Smiling, he turned his gaze forward as he started this new journey. He wasn't driving away from something but rather, toward a new venture, an extraordinary, full-circle, life-changing event. He might be alone in his car with a stuffed Joe Vandal in the passenger seat, but he didn't feel alone. In fact, he'd never felt more embraced by a loyal group of individuals than he did at that moment. His family was anxious about the move, but they understood the pull of tens of thousands who eagerly awaited Scott's arrival in Moscow, Idaho. He was heading toward his Vandal family, toward a new chapter in his life and theirs. As of July 1, 2019, C. Scott Green would officially step into the role of the University of Idaho president.

He started his 2700-mile trek west on I-80. He would cruise through eastern Pennsylvania, the hardwood mountains and valleys of western Pennsylvania, and then the hills in Ohio dotted with barns. Other routes existed, but this course seemed faster and more comfortable to drive. He'd packed enough clothes and personal items to cover a week, plenty of time for the moving truck to arrive at University House with the rest of his possessions. The moving truck was well on its way from Long Island, and by the looks of it, he was making excellent time to beat them there.

His mind wandered as the vast landscape he typically viewed at 30,000 feet from an airplane zipped by in shades of lush summer greens. Yes, he was speeding, anxious to log as many miles as possible on his first day traveling west. Dozens of things raced through his brain, but for whatever reason, he settled on dissecting how he'd arrived at this spot, not only on the road but in his life.

He still couldn't quite believe how he got here, but in every fiber of his body, Scott knew he'd made the right decision. Leaving his wife, Gabriella, at their home in Glen Head, New York, where they'd made their life together with the kids and dogs for 23 years, was the hardest thing he'd ever done. But she and their kids were with him, maybe not physically, but in spirit. He smiled, knowing they each would dive deep into their lives and activities, and the next time they all got together, the four of them would have countless stories to share.

He'd been laser-focused as global chief financial and operations officer at the international law firm Hogan Lovells, comfortable in that role even though each day brought new challenges and experiences spanning four continents. He entrenched himself in the plan of working in this capacity for a few more years and then retiring at a modest age to enjoy the fruits of his hard work. After closing that life chapter, he would relish time with his beautiful wife and adult children and enjoy *not* commuting or putting in long hours unless he chose that. It was all set.

The smile on his face widened as he thought about the eight-word text that sent his well-planned future spinning on a new trajectory, one he'd never imagined. Ever. Not even once.

It had been a typical day at the office in August 2018. Scott's focus at the time involved meeting with all his direct reports—the senior management team—to go through their finances and how they'd dealt with the recent implementation of a new finance system.

"We asked our team in London if all our offices in various countries had cleared their billing templates because we knew the new system's templates would be very different," Scott explained. "They claimed inside out they had. As it turns out, they hadn't. That created some problems for us. My deputy COO, Darren Mitchell, and I traveled around, collected data, and worked on those billing templates to get them fixed. It wasn't smooth, and the partners were understandably not happy with the billing issues we encountered. Still, at the end of the day, we systematically resolved those problems and had the program up quicker than any other law firm installing that system."

Just business as usual.

Scott's phone buzzed daily with constant texts, emails, and voicemails. When his cell dinged or chimed, he always glanced at the screen to see who was reaching out. This particular day brought a text from his friend Chandra Zenner Ford. It wasn't unusual to hear from her; they'd been friends for years. Chandra and Scott were both alumni of the University of Idaho. When Scott served on the advisory board for the College of Business and Economics (CBE), Chandra was the college's assistant dean for external relations (she would later become CEO, SW Idaho and Special Advisor, Office of the President, University of Idaho).

"I met Scott through CBE and observed his commitment to the U of I firsthand," Chandra conveyed. "Despite his responsibilities managing international professional firms, he never wavered in his commitment to the U of I as a volunteer and benefactor. He and his wife, Gabriella, established the Scott and Gabriella Green Scholarship in CBE and made leadership gifts to the College of Education, Health, and Human Sciences in honor of his grandfather. He also had received numerous awards. He moved on from the advisory board to the Foundation Board of Directors about the time I left the U of I in 2015 to become the director of philanthropy for the City of Boise, Idaho."

Scott was knee-deep in work that day but felt compelled to take a moment and read Chandra's text. Maybe she was headed to New York on business and wanted to connect. It was a short message, but it took a beat for the eight words to register. He blinked, shook his head, and reread the text to ensure he saw it correctly.

You should be the next president of UI. . .

His incredulous laugh punched the air in his office. Never in a million years had he pictured himself as a university president. The closest thing he'd come was working as an adjunct instructor in finance at Hofstra University on Long Island. He'd enjoyed teaching a few semesters, especially when the students lit up when he explained something in a way they could understand. At Hofstra, he'd gotten involved with legal panels on campus, published an article for their annual legal journal, and met great people, including Marty Lipton, the prominent mergers and acquisitions attorney at Wachtell, Lipton, Rosen & Katz who created the "poison pill" defense against hostile takeovers. But never once did he hold any inkling or desire to become president of a university.

His phone dinged again, bringing him out of his reverie—another text from Chandra.

It'll be a crazy long shot.

He sat back in his chair, completely sidetracked from the business at hand. His mind flew in all directions, but all thoughts led to his beloved alma mater, the University of Idaho. Memories flooded his mind, from childhood when his grandfather Leon worked as the athletic director to his treasured college days. He'd joined the Kappa Sigma fraternity, been ASUI president, reveled in Don Monson basketball and Dennis Erickson football, and received his undergraduate degree in 1984.

Earning his bachelor of science in accounting prepared him to drive away from Idaho in his Dodge Omni hatchback toward Boston to attend Harvard Business School for his MBA. In his wildest imagination, he never thought he'd drive back to the university—his university—35 years later to serve as its president.

Sure, Scott had stayed involved with his alma mater over those three-plus decades, never forgetting his roots and always giving back to the place that had given him so much. He'd set up a scholarship endowment, served on boards, and given time and treasure as a proud alumnus. And, like any loyal Vandal, his blood ran silver and gold, but he'd never entertained any thoughts about working at the university in any capacity.

He wasn't an academic. He didn't have a terminal degree. Even as an adjunct instructor at Hofstra, he'd only considered himself an educated, successful person willing to share and teach everything he knew about finance. He *had* authored two books about the Sarbanes-Oxley Act of 2002, offering a deep dive into his dedicated research and knowledge of the subject.

He knew enough to understand that a nontraditional president—even a published author and expert in his field—would never be entirely accepted by some at any university or college, regardless of a stellar resume. Chandra's texts bordered on ludicrous.

The University of Idaho had seen its share of troubles the past few decades. It had witnessed turnover at the top; there had been six presidents since 2003. It bothered Scott that his alma mater served as a steppingstone for some of those folks, equating to their tenure only lasting a few years. He completely understood the drive to advance in one's career—he'd done it himself. But even as human as it was to do that, a university couldn't handle turnover at the top and maintain its strategic mission and growth. It couldn't sustain any respectable standing in national polls, which affected enrollment and everything else. It also affected the U of I's relationship with the State Board of Education (SBOE).

The lack of continuity, stability, and leadership at the university constricted the ability to make meaningful progress on the institution's strategic priorities. This frustrated SBOE members because they knew the university had so much more potential to serve the students and employers in the state, but it was just caught in a cycle of churn at the top.

Turnover wasn't just occurring at the top position on campus, either. Over decades, a surge of new deans and provosts, right along with presidents, left the institution without long-term vision or continuity. Even the division responsible for recruitment, enrollment, and retention had seen turnover at the top.

He was in no position to judge, but he had been concerned about the U of I for a while. He knew his beloved institution was struggling but wasn't privy to *why*. When he served on the U of I Foundation Board after his stint on the CBE advisory board, he'd seen things that left him scratching his head. For example, a proposal for all first-year students to live in the dorms showed a complete disconnect from one of the cornerstones of the university—the Greek system. A decision like that would have an immense impact on the sororities and fraternities, not to mention upset the U of I's significant Greek alumni base.

While serving on the Foundation Board, he'd also witnessed turmoil around the planning and construction of the new president's residence on campus, University House, involving costs and design. During the initial process of updating the showcase campus building, Scott glimpsed signs of a disconnect between the university and its decision-makers and stakeholders.

Scott pointed out, "The people always had the will to keep things going and potentially fix problems—like financial issues—but they just didn't have the propensity to make the tough decisions, formulate the right ideas, or create any solutions."

Maybe Chandra was on to something.

"So what's the meaning of this text," he threw out as soon as she answered his call that fateful day. He'd opted to call her because this conversation was too important to conduct via text.

"Well, Scott," Chandra laughed, "you have the leadership skills. You have some academic credentials. You have a passion for the place. That makes you a strong candidate even though you're not a traditional academic."

Scott let the words hang in silence for a moment.

"I've never envisioned myself as an academic and certainly not as a university president," he finally answered.

"Not just *a* president, Scott," Chandra retorted. "The *University of Idaho* president. There's a difference. A huge difference. That place is part of you, and you're a part of it. I stand by my original statement. It should be you."

Over the next several days, Scott and Chandra had volleyed the idea back and forth in texts and phone calls. At first, he didn't seriously consider her suggestion; becoming the U of I president was just a fun idea to discuss in a what-if way. They both agreed that even if he did throw his name into the applicant pool, he would be the longest shot since Buster Douglas knocked out Mike Tyson in Vegas in 1990.

But Scott's self-confidence wouldn't let him think he was an underdog. He knew he had strong credentials to bring to the table. But did he *want* the job?

Chandra had continued to urge Scott to apply. "After twenty-five years of seeing the U of I presidents come and go, I had a decent idea for what the university needed at the time," she articulated. "The problem? Scott had an amazing career on the East Coast, and this job was not exactly a promotion. I knew he would only do it because of his passion for the place."

She also knew he had the work ethic, big brain, leadership experience, and, maybe most importantly, intense loyalty to the university. "Then you throw in the fact that he was already planning to retire in Idaho, and he had nothing else to prove beyond this last capstone job; it all added up to one fact. Scott Green was the best person on the planet to be the U of I's next president."

Within the same week of Chandra's text, Scott received another pivotal message from his longtime friend and fellow Vandal, Clint Marshall. Scott and Clint served on the CBE advisory board from 2009 to 2015.

"One of the first things that struck me about Scott was he obviously had an impressive background," Clint shared. "He was traveling all over the world. One time, at an advisory board meeting, I asked him, 'Where were you yesterday?' and he answered, 'Vietnam,' and I answered, 'And you're in Moscow today?!'"

Of course, Clint was joking, but he knew Scott's bond with the U of I ran deep like his. Clint was a first-generation Vandal, committed to giving back to his alma mater. "Attending the University of Idaho was an incredible, life-changing thing for me," he expressed. "And anything I can do, over time, to repay that debt, I'm going to try to do. I was impressed by Scott's passion, intensity, commitment, and like-minded dedication to the university. So we struck up a friendship."

Clint was aware of the university's quest for a new president—at that time, he held a seat on the U of I Foundation Board. In Spring 2018, he'd had coffee with then U of I president, Dr. Charles "Chuck" Staben. The lengthy and detailed conversation left Clint wondering, *Is my university in peril?*

Clint had seen enrollment decline and costs grow at "an alarming clip." As a businessperson, he'd witnessed academic institutions lose their sense of economic reality. "The U of I had seen years of bloat," he said. "I left that meeting with President Staben worried but thinking, *What the heck can I do?*"

When the SBOE announced in May 2018 that they would not renew President Staben's contract and that he would step down as president in spring 2019, the wheels started turning in Clint's head. He began to ponder the appetite for a nontraditional candidate for the U of I president.

"I kind of had Scott in the back of my mind but thought there's no way in the world he'd do it," Clint laughed. "But with his love for the university and his experience, he could serve as a prototype for a candidate."

Scott and Clint ended up in Las Vegas at the same time in the fall of 2018 and got together to catch up before they had to jump on their respective flights home. Clint took the opportunity to pick his friend's brain about the U of I's search for a new president.

"So, Scott, there's an opening at the University of Idaho," he'd nonchalantly posed. "Is that something you would ever at all be interested in? Because you would be amazing."

A second person—unsolicited and independent of Chandra's quest to head-hunt Scott—voiced the opinion that Scott should be the next president at their alma mater. Scott had sat dumbfounded.

What the hell was happening?

"Yeah, I'm aware," he'd hesitantly responded.

The two talked in depth over the next few hours before they departed Vegas.

"And I could just tell by his reaction that it was something he would consider," Clint smiled.

After Clint and Chandra independently approached Scott about considering applying for the position, the two Vandals, unbeknownst to Scott, started casually asking their connections to determine if support existed for a nontraditional candidate for the U of I president.

"I started putting feelers out and talking to my network," Clint recalled. "It was pretty clear to me there was frustration and concern about the U of I's direction. I sensed an overwhelming willingness to consider a nontraditional. I never mentioned Scott's name. I was just feeling it out in general. To me, two major pillars had to fall. One, was SBOE willing to hire a nontraditional candidate, and two, was Scott willing to do it?"

As Scott stared through his windshield at the gray asphalt of I-80 stretched out ahead, he smiled at the recollection of those life-changing interactions with Chandra and Clint. He'd always believed that certain people were in one's life for a purpose beyond being a colleague or friend. It wasn't a coincidence that two of his trusted allies had channeled the same belief that Scott could be the next U of I president. Fate had played its hand, and Scott was on his way to Moscow, Idaho, to shake hands with Destiny.

Scott's Management Insight

Don't take the journey alone when operating outside your field of expertise. Identify a trusted colleague, a Sherpa (or two), who will help you understand the political landscape and avoid mistakes. Chandra and Clint became my Sherpas—they spent hundreds of hours of their own time preparing the ground and leading the way.

You must also do your homework to get the job and sketch out how you will add value and improve the institution. The more I learned about the challenges the U of I faced, particularly the financial issues, the more concerned I became. But I also knew I could help. I had improved financial performance at every place I worked as a senior executive. I knew I could do the same for my alma mater.

Gabby, Sam, Zeus, Scott, Nick (Scott and Gabby's son), and Joe Vandal take one last photo at their house in Glen Head, New York, the evening before Scott drives cross-country to Moscow, Idaho.

SOURCE: Reproduced with permission of Scott Green (Book Author).

Chapter 2
Would You Rather?
June 24, 2019, later that day

"The one thing the University of Idaho always had was momentum."
—*Gary Michael*

Scott flipped on his blinker and slowed to exit for his first pitstop in Western Pennsylvania. He was making good time; he'd left his Long Island house at 4:30 a.m., clearing New Jersey and NYC before the rush hour. The climb of nearly 2,000 feet through the Delaware Water Gap to the Poconos offered him a nice 12-degree temperature drop. He hopped out and stretched his legs, making sure to snap a picture with his copilot, Joe Vandal. Eyes on social media were tracking his progress toward his new home. He'd shared a photo taken at his house the day before and then another shot as he made his way through Chicago. He enjoyed reaching out to his fellow Vandals, some of whom he knew and some he would meet for the first time as President Scott Green.

He still couldn't believe he held that prestigious title. The long-shot, nonacademic-guy-who-had-it-all-in-New-York-and-the-world was stepping up to the plate to hit as many homeruns for his university as possible. And he would.

He and Joe climbed back into his cockpit on wheels and sped off toward Wisconsin, with thoughts continuing to flood his mind about how he got into this incredible opportunity.

Throughout Scott's life, he never made decisions without researching the facts. And the decision to change the entire course of his life was no different. Before he applied for the job as president, he needed facts about the status of the university. Were the concerns he'd felt over the past decade rooted in reality? Was his alma mater facing trouble? He knew what he knew, but he needed more. And who better to ask but those involved?

Scott needed to conduct massive due diligence, researching everything he could about the U of I. He began asking trusted friends and colleagues their take on the status of the university and their thoughts about him applying for the job. He wouldn't dive into the applicant pool until he knew the university needed his skill set and that *he* was the best candidate for the job. His investigation revealed a university still nationally ranked and conducting state-of-the-art research but with potential dire straits looming.

As Scott cruised along, his thoughts settled on his most worrisome issue—the U of I's dismal financial situation. He didn't know the entire picture but knew enough to cause serious concern. He'd examined facts, ruminated over them several times in his head, and broke them down to three unsettling points.

1. The U of I had operational and unrestricted net position deficits that, due to employee contracts, could not be fully addressed in one fiscal year.
2. The U of I was burning through cash at an alarming rate and running out of time before it was gone.
3. The U of I had no plan to address the fundamental reasons for the declines.

Scott's life revolved around numbers, and the numbers didn't lie. He surmised that the problems had gradually happened—maybe because of bad policies and financial structure, maybe because of turnover at the top. Regardless, the financial state of affairs had reached a point of no return if something didn't change quickly and drastically. The fiscal situation alone had bothered him enough to seriously consider Chandra and Clint's suggestion to apply for the job. He'd seen enough to know that the U of I's spending was far outpacing the declining tuition revenue, which was Scott's second major concern. Enrollment was the primary revenue driver, and if it was waning, the resulting consequences could be catastrophic.

Scott also presumed the upper administration's steppingstone mentality resulted in low morale among staff and faculty over the years. He couldn't fault leadership who exited the U of I after only serving a short time. Still, he knew continual personnel changes usually shook any organization's foundation, mission, and culture, and the U of I was no different.

Scott's numerous conversations with people like Chandra and Clint convinced him that the U of I's turnover was tied directly to the financial woes and enrollment declines his alma mater faced. He needed to determine if he possessed the right combination of personal and professional experiences and talent to help the seemingly distressed and depressed university. He had to get "boots on the ground," so he booked a trip to Boise to meet personally with some of Idaho's most loyal and trusted Vandals.

His first discussions took place with Chandra. They strategically dissected the pros and cons of Scott's application for the president position. At dinner one night, she was frank with Scott.

"When I left the university, I did not have very much faith in leadership," she admitted. She had known and worked with, to some capacity, every U of I president since Richard Gibb, who started as president in 1977. President Gibb helped Chandra get her first job in higher education after graduating from the U of I in 1988 by calling the president of Washington State University.

"I witnessed all the leadership throughout those years going through the good, the bad, the ugly, and observed what worked and didn't work," she continued. "The U of I people just kept getting let down. Leadership was always sincere in what they wanted to do for the university, but it was an example of the churn of higher education where presidents were just going from one institution to the next."

Scott also thought discussing the state of the university with Frances Ellsworth, an alumna who also boasted a long track record of supporting the U of I, would be a good idea. He knew Frances through their shared activities at the university, including serving on the U of I Foundation Board. Frances was a board member from 2002 to 2019 and was chair from 2008 to 2010.

During his Boise recon mission, they met over lunch to dig deeper into their alma mater's structure, culture, and mission. "I was just so enthused about him thinking about this job," Frances conveyed. "But I was concerned, and we talked about that because many people thought the university needed someone who was a provost, had a PhD, and had land grant experience. Scott didn't have those things, but he had a PhD in life and learning, a universal experience. I did nothing but encourage him. The U of I needed a gutsy guy, and certainly for him to consider applying was big-time gutsy."

Frances expressed her belief to Scott that he was the right person at the right time to get the U of I back on course. "He had managed large international law firms and would have seen a lot of strong people with big egos," she observed, "so he would be able to work with all kinds of people, keep his own ego in check, listen to the people, and continue to see the big picture for the university, which wasn't always the case with university presidents. I knew Scott was smart, loyal, and dedicated, and he understood the

University of Idaho. These qualities, along with his financial, development, and political knowledge, I felt, would make him an excellent president."

After the meeting, Frances sprang into action, again, unbeknownst to Scott. "Because of an earlier conversation with a state board regent, I had been meaning to send an email with my thoughts about the presidential search, and meeting with Scott got me on the stick," she explained. On October 12, 2018, with no mention of Scott, she sent an email saying (Ellsworth, F., personal communication):

> I keep thinking about a short conversation we had about the U of I president search, where you said we needed someone with land-grant experience. I meant to say that I don't think that is necessarily true, because that can be learned, and we shouldn't limit ourselves that much. Too often we look for a PhD, provost, and land-grant experience, and I'm afraid, if those qualities are in the job requirements, it limits our pool. We've had these qualities in past presidents, not always with the best results—let's try something new. What we need is someone with business, marketing, communication, fundraising, and political expertise, and he, or she, doesn't need a PhD, provost, and land-grant experience. The right president will hire a good provost and acquire the land-grant knowledge needed. These abilities will take the University of Idaho boldly into the future, and then everyone, and everywhere, will understand what the University of Idaho is all about.

On the same day, she received an email thanking her for her wisdom and a positive answer about the presidential qualities needed but expressing that some still held the desire for land-grant experience.

Scott's next stop in Boise was to meet with one of the U of I's long-standing supporters, Gary Michael. Gary's resume included serving on the boards or working for powerhouse companies like Albertson's, Caesar's Entertainment, Boise Cascade, The Clorox Company, Idaho Power, and the Idaho Lottery. He received his BS in accounting from the U of I in 1962 and served in several capacities with the institution over the decades, including a stint as a nontraditional interim president from 2003 to 2004.

"The interim president job was a fairly easy job, but it was the most time-consuming professional commitment I've ever had," Gary shared. "The one thing the University of Idaho always had was momentum. There have been a lot of competent people working at the university, but for a long time, it ran with poor leadership."

Gary advised Scott that if he applied and became president, he would have to separate himself from the pack to be the true leader the university desperately needed. "I told him he would have to stay on the deans and department heads and ask what they wanted things to look like in their area in the next five years."

Scott shared a few more morsels of advice that Gary offered him that day. "Gary told me to watch out for the silo mentality, which I already knew existed," Scott recalled. "He also emphasized that I would have to adapt."

"Scott, you know when to shut up," Gary had bluntly stated during their meeting. "But you have high awareness, so you also know when to speak up. And one more thing, don't cross the street alone."

Gary meant Scott would have to get everyone together to move as a herd, not independently.

Feeling energized by his information gathering from insightful Vandals, Scott had decided to get input from the people who knew him best in his current line of work. His boss at the time and CEO at Hogan Lovells, Steve Immelt, had several conversations with Scott about the job opening at the university. When Scott first approached him, Steve offered sound advice.

"There are similarities between a law firm and a university in the sense that partners were not unlike tenured faculty," Steve pointed out. "A tenured faculty member had a bit more legal protection. But working in a law firm environment for a long time, Scott had developed a sense of how to move organizations forward."

Steve had conducted a bit of independent research regarding the U of I after his initial conversation with Scott about the job; it was then he realized the university was in turmoil.

"Scott, this is going to be frustrating," he'd stated during another one of their conversations. He knew Scott well and that he liked to move things forward. His concern was whether Scott would feel hampered if he couldn't do that.

"I've represented a lot of universities, Scott, and somebody once joked that a university faculty is a collection of highly intelligent, highly contentious people organized around a common grievance about the parking on campus," Steve had remarked. "They could get caught up in some pretty petty stuff that people would go to the mat over. They may fight you over everything because they're passionate about whatever it is they believe in. So beware."

After numerous phone calls, emails, texts, and in-person conversations with a long list of confidants and U of I stakeholders, the consensus for Scott to apply was a resounding yes for various reasons, the main one being consistency.

Idaho needed a leader who wanted to stay longer than a few years. The steppingstone mentality of the previous presidents had left the U of I on shaky financial ground and left the faculty and staff needing a renewed sense of trust in the administration. The Vandal population needed someone who knew the U of I and would put the institution first. A few of his Vandal mentors told Scott they felt Idaho hadn't had a dedicated president since Robert "Bob" Hoover in the late 1990s. Many who graduated from the U of I in the mid-1970s felt the U of I was uncontested as *the* place in the state to get a degree. Those nostalgic feelings allowed the U of I to enjoy support and loyalty from its alumni base, who held those fond memories close to their hearts. That equated to contributions of time and treasure and a fierce competitive spirit with Boise State University and Idaho State University. Usually, the competitive nature spilled out through athletics, especially football. For many years, Idaho held its own against the two in-state foes on the courts and fields and maintained its stronghold in higher education as Idaho's premier land-grant institution. But a change started to happen during the late 1980s and early 1990s. Boise began to evolve and proliferate.

The U of I had several alumni in powerful positions in the state and Boise, and when Bob Hoover became president in 1996, one of his priorities was to utilize those connections and increase the university's presence in the Boise market. From a strategic standpoint, it made sense. The U of I needed to be where the people were and have a foot in that market.

The university's presence in Southwest Idaho dates back to 1910 with the College of Agricultural and Life Sciences (CALS) extension programs. But eight decades later, Bob Hoover wanted more U of I offerings in the state's largest and fastest-growing market. The university couldn't ignore the tremendous impact of the demographic changes in Boise relative to the rest of the state, so as the U of I president, Bob Hoover teamed up with an outside firm to create that presence.

Some said the combination of that strategy, a certain amount of arrogance, and a lack of business acumen on the part of people at the university led to a crisis situation.

Bob Hoover's goal led to conversations about where to house the eventual programs the university would offer in Boise. His discussions regarding constructing a new building evolved into legislators, stakeholders, and even the governor lending their opinion that the U of I needed to expand in the state capitol. At the time, a project was underway in Boise around the Front Street and Broadway Avenue area—a highly visible corridor—that included the Ada County Courthouse. The location on Front Street would be the perfect spot for the U of I's expansion. The programs housed in the new building would pull together state and federal entities to focus on natural resources—mainly water—which was Idaho's number-one resource. The project became known as the Idaho Water Center.

According to Gary, who stepped in as the U of I's interim president after Bob Hoover's departure in June 2003, the U of I Foundation had asked to purchase a piece of property on Front Street. The developer agreed to sell the land for $136 million, which would become home to the Idaho Water Center.

The U of I Foundation incurred $28 million in preconstruction costs, including an $8 million loan from the U of I. When the Foundation set up the financing for the project, the Idaho Housing and Finance Association agreed to back the project but not the $28 million of preconstruction costs.

"They said those were sunk costs and the Foundation's responsibility," Gary continued.

"The Foundation had borrowed the $8 million from the U of I, thinking they would pay it back as part of the financing package. But since the state didn't agree to finance those sunk costs, the Foundation sat holding the bag, which included the $8 million it owed to the U of I."

Controversy surrounded the deal, including how it ever happened in the first place. At that time, the CFO (U of I vice president for Finance and Administration) was also the CFO of the Foundation, and that person was moving money back and forth with few checks and balances in place. The university loaning state taxpayer funds to the Foundation—which was a not-for-profit 501(c)3 corporation separate from the U of I—was technically legal but became a hot button of debate due to the optics and the trouble that ensued.

"It was all about the execution," Scott emphasized.

The Foundation scrambled to pay the money back, but the damage was done; the deal left a permanent scar on the U of I's reputation with all its stakeholders, including the state government and Idahoans. Bob Hoover took full responsibility and resigned.

The Foundation covered the deficit, and in the process, the SBOE established new policies to prevent the situation from ever happening again. The structure now doesn't allow the Foundation's CFO to be the same person as the U of I's vice president for Finance and Administration.

"Even so, the U of I made many decisions after the Water Center issue that were far too influenced by what happened," Chandra Zenner Ford emphasized. "The U of I was still in this skewed mode of being so conservative because of the Water Center. We have continued to have challenges in how we operate in Southwest Idaho. We need to become less risk averse."

After completion in 2004, the Idaho Water Center project became the home of the University of Idaho Boise. The building housed programs, research, and outreach to the growing population in that area, along with collaborations with other institutions of higher education. The U of I face in Boise that Bob Hoover looked to establish became a reality, but not without the long-lasting residue of questionable financial actions.

Kathy Barnard, assistant vice president for Alumni Relations and Advancement Communications, shared how other negative episodes added to the U of I's somewhat soiled reputation after the Water Center fiasco. "Other than Bob Hoover, there was not one president at the institution who understood anything about the value of marketing. If you don't invest in producing a constant, positive drumbeat of good stories, you are at the mercy of your headlines. And if your headlines are bad, guess what? You're going to suffer."

The U of I's headlines were making the U of I vs. Boise State University (BSU) rivalry into more than just competition in sports. BSU was enjoying positive headlines under its president, Bob Kustra, who started in 2003, while Idaho's headlines were attention-grabbing for the wrong reasons (ESPN 2010). There weren't just one or two negative headlines, and they were starting to erode the university's public perception and financial footing. "People weren't cheering about all the good things going on at the U of I," Toni Broyles, who was a Vandal alumnus and U of I special assistant, strategic initiatives, summed up.

Some of the more worrisome incidents (including the Water Center) left long-lasting stains on the university's reputation with the state government, SBOE, and the U of I stakeholders.

1. The murder of a psychology student, 22-year-old Katie Benoit, occurred at the hands of her former U of I professor and romantic partner, Ernesto Bustamante. Bustamante committed suicide after killing Benoit in August 2011.

2. U of I student-athlete Mairin Jameson filed a lawsuit in October 2018 against the university for mishandling her sexual assault in 2013 at the hands of another student-athlete.

3. The announcement in April 2016 by U of I President Staben that the university's football program would move to the Big Sky conference beginning in Fall 2018 took them out of the FBS (Football Bowl Series) competition and placed them with FCS (Football Championship Subdivision). That move created a massive division between alumni, friends, and Vandal fans and severely impacted the financial and cultural support for the U of I Athletic Department.

4. Three students, over multiple years, fell out of upper-story windows at residence halls and Greek residences, resulting in lawsuits. Those accidents only heightened the ever-present spotlight on the perceived Greek and residence hall life of drinking and partying, creating an unsafe environment.

5. The constant perceived rivalry between the U of I and BSU created a more pronounced "us vs. them" dynamic that did not play well with SBOE or Idaho legislators, who wanted state institutional collaboration, not competition.

"The U of I had lost its strong brand in the state," said Mary Kay McFadden, vice president for University Advancement. "Idaho had been the land-grant, research institution the people respected. But we started struggling to get our share of the students and improve fundraising. Neither were very healthy."

"The U of I was just adrift and seemed directionless," Scott commented. But he knew every president carefully selected by the SBOE did what they thought was best during their tenure. Sometimes those decisions yielded positive results, sometimes not so positive, but never malicious or nefarious behavior. And regardless of the safety steps the university put in place, some accidents happened, and the U of I had to face them and not shy away from them.

Thankfully, during those tough headline years, there were still impressive strides that kept the U of I highly ranked in *US News & World Report*'s Best Colleges and strong rankings in the Top 50 Best Value colleges (*US News & World Report* 2022). The U of I continued to be the State of Idaho's land-grant institution, with strides in research and turning out educated members of society, regardless of the negative spotlight that left an air of doubt and skepticism with some of the U of I's stakeholders.

Even after gathering all that intel, Scott had still been on the fence about whether to apply. However, one conversation tipped the scales for him. A call with William "Bill" Lee, his former boss and a co-managing partner at WilmerHale, gave Scott a chance to hear his take on the potential opportunity.

Bill knew how Scott's qualifications would weave intricately within a university setting. Bill had served on the Board of Overseers at Harvard University and the Visiting Committee at Cornell Law School. He was appointed fellow in the American College of Trial Lawyers and Harvard Corporation, where he became senior fellow. To say he knew something about university structure and culture would be an understatement. Bill's experience in both the corporate and the academic arena proved a perfect combination to lend Scott some perspective.

A brief discussion ensued, covering the U of I's financial condition, the challenges Scott could face, and his unconventional candidate status. They'd spent the lion's share of their time, however, discussing the students the university educated and the fact that they might not get educated elsewhere if that institution wasn't available to them.

The right words for Scott to hear at the exact right time flowed from Bill's mouth. "What you have to ask yourself is, when your career comes to an end, would you rather it be that you helped Hogan Lovells have another great year financially so the partners made more money, or would you rather be in a circumstance where you can say, 'I went into an academic institution that provides education to an important segment of Idaho and the national community, helped turn it around, and helped a substantial number of kids get educated?'"

Scott heard those words like a shout from a mountaintop. It had been a short phone call after Bill's profound words of advice.

Scott knew everything he needed to take the plunge. He would do whatever he could to heal and strengthen his alma mater financially and culturally. A strong urge grew within him to tell the whole world about the U of I—how it prepared its students to be competitive nationally and internationally, how it conducted world-class research and innovative practices, how it celebrated diversity and sustainable solutions that supported Idaho's citizens and industry. His desire to become a strategic part of how the story unfolded in the future overwhelmed him. His determination to be the right guy at the right moment to right the listing ship and strive to better his beloved university became his new life purpose.

Scott's Management Insight

Take the right job for all the right reasons. Others will see through you if you use the position as a steppingstone. Since I was born in Idaho and was an alumnus, some may have questioned my qualifications but not my motivation. Discuss what drives you to take the helm together with its responsibilities. Your transparency will help win hearts and minds. And just because you have a background in one career field doesn't mean your area of expertise doesn't apply to another field. You can contribute your insights and experience in a different, outside-the-box (or -institution) way. It is not whether you have the right degree; instead, do you have the right skill set to meet the institution's needs? In my case, my financial and managerial skill set working with accounting, investment banking, and law partners in global firms prepared me well for the challenges I would face at the U of I.

Smart Collaboration

501 Front Street, Boise, Idaho

"It's not very often when you need a Law School, there's a Law School for sale."

—Chandra Zenner Ford

From its beginnings in 1909, the University of Idaho College of Law would serve as the source of legal education in the state to assist in fulfilling the land-grant mission of the institution. For decades, the Administration Building served as its home, but in the 1960s, it outgrew the space, creating accreditation concerns and kicking off a years-long debate about where the Law School should reside—Moscow or Boise. The then-dean, Al Menard, stayed focused on Moscow, and a new building (named after the dean) completed in 1972–73 stood as a beacon of legal education on the Moscow campus for three decades.

In 1999–2000, the U of I and the College of Law convened a "blue ribbon panel" of three law deans from other law schools to explore possible future directions for Idaho legal education. The panel examined the merits of a "Moscow-plus" model, a move-to-Boise model, and a hybrid model involving both locations. Between 2006 and 2008, the College of Law conducted further strategic planning exercises, assembling a legal conclave to engage the law community to consider the options for legal education delivery in the state. During this process, Idaho's Attorney General received a legislative inquiry: Would the state constitution even permit the relocation of the College of Law? In an informal written opinion, the AG's office said it would violate the constitutional requirement that the U of I be located in Moscow; however, a branch campus would be permissible.

Don Burnett, dean of the College of Law from 2002 to 2013 and the U of I's interim president in 2013–14, knew it couldn't be ignored that Boise was growing, and the U of I had a responsibility to consider legal education extending beyond Moscow. This sparked a profoundly emotional reaction from faculty, alumni, and others—not just in Moscow—who worried the Law School would completely relocate to

(Continued)

(Continued)

Boise. There were also concerns about expanding to Boise being a costly proposition.

In 2008, the U of I and the College of Law proposed establishing a full three-year branch program in Boise. The SBOE declined to approve the full three-year program at that point but did confirm the university's statewide mission in legal education, authorized exploration of a third-year law program in Boise, and authorized exploration of developing an "Idaho Law Learning Center" (later named the "Idaho Law and Justice Learning Center") in the capitol city. The college prepared plans to enhance the Moscow program and establish a third-year option in Boise. U of I President Duane Nellis and Idaho Chief Justice Daniel Eismann agreed to join the College of Law in proposing to use the old Ada County Courthouse to house the law program, to serve as a new site of the Idaho State Law Library (administered by the college under an agreement with the Idaho Supreme Court), and to serve as a venue for law-related civic education and outreach.

In the summer of 2010, the third-year program received SBOE clearance for law students to complete their final year of Law School in either Moscow or Boise. The U of I housed the program in the U of I Boise Center (Water Center Building) until the old Ada County Courthouse renovations—funded by private donations and the Idaho Permanent Building Fund—were completed in 2014. Ultimately, the SBOE approved offering the second year and then the first year of law school in Boise, completing the full three-year branch concept.

Don stressed. "We were not uprooting the Law School by sending it to the state capitol. The imperative to expand arose out of the logical deduction about what it meant for the U of I to be the state university with the statewide mission to provide legal education and how we could fulfill that mission."

But the growth of the Treasure Valley population increased the demand for legal education. "It became clear that either the U of I was going to have to have more physical capacity for the Law School in Boise, or someone else was going to provide competition," Don pointed out.

And someone did. Concordia University School of Law arrived in Boise in August 2012 with a class of 75 eager law students in a new *building at 501 Front Street, only a stone's throw from the U of I Boise Center.*

* * *

Scott had appointed Johanna Kalb as the College of Law dean in February 2021. Before her official start date, Scott brought her into one of the monthly fiscal meetings with the current College of Law Dean Jerry Long, Special Advisor to the President Chandra Zenner Ford, and himself. Johanna was aware of the college's deficit and knew the meeting would outline her onboarding into that situation.

"The SBOE articulated that when I was hired, I needed to find out why the College of Law had accumulated a $3 million deficit and fix it," Scott explained. "When I looked into it, it was actually quite frustrating. The college was running about as efficiently as it could, so it became clear they were running a deficit because of space constraints in the Boise market. There was a demand that we weren't filling and losing potential revenue."

"We were running a three-year program but just couldn't grow beyond our entering class size of 65 in Boise," Johanna stated.

Enter Michael Ballantyne.

Michael Ballantyne was the managing partner of TOK Commercial and an old friend of Chandra's. TOK Commercial was the listing agent for the former Concordia building at 501 Front when it went on the market for sale in 2021. Concordia had filed for bankruptcy in February 2020.

"It was devastating when Concordia shut down. They got only days of notice," Johanna said. "Their faculty and students were scrambling. The U of I College of Law was able to hire several of their faculty and admit almost all students interested in transferring, which turned out to be over one hundred."

The old Ada County Courthouse was bursting at the seams.

It just happened by coincidence that Michael and Chandra had a meeting scheduled around the same time. "We get together about once a year to catch up," Chandra explained. "Towards the end of the meal, he brought up the Concordia building."

Chandra explained to Michael that the U of I couldn't afford to purchase the building. She was slightly surprised he would even ask,

(Continued)

(Continued)

considering he knew of the financial woes at the institution. But Michael posed to Chandra that if someone else purchased the building, maybe the U of I could lease it from that person.

As it turned out, Vandal alumnus Jeff Stoddard served on Michael's board of directors. Jeff was a fourth-generation Idahoan raised in Boise and had completed multiple degree programs at the U of I in 1975 and 1976 before earning his MBA at Harvard Business School in 1978. Jeff had several things in common with Scott, including serving on the U of I Foundation Board and establishing an endowment.

Michael broached the subject with Chandra about discussing the purchase with Jeff. Chandra also knew Jeff through their connections at CBE. When she talked to Scott about it, he immediately saw the potential and invited Chandra to continue with the plan. He also contacted Johanna to ask if she wanted the building and could she attract 100 additional law students. She said yes to both questions.

"Scott and I had a very brief conversation and agreed to proceed," Jeff outlined. "I've known all the university presidents from Hoover on, and although some of them tried to be bold, none of them have been like Scott."

"Another piece to this whole building acquisition process was the importance of talking with one of the College of Law's donors, Laura Bettis," Chandra continued. "Laura had made a $1 million gift through her family's charity, the Laura Moore Cunningham Foundation, to renovate the U of I's law library in Boise at its current location in the old courthouse." The Foundation supported the development of the Idaho Law and Justice Learning Center by renovating the old courthouse to accommodate the law program and serve as the new site of the Idaho State Law Library.

Chandra worried that if the U of I relocated the Law School to a new building, Laura would be disappointed they were leaving the space Laura's family helped renovate. Chandra discussed it with her and even took her on a tour of the Concordia building. Thankfully, Laura immediately saw the value of the new space and how it would position the law school for long-term success.

Chandra was also concerned that the state would not appreciate the law school moving out of the old courthouse building. But a conversation with Idaho Governor Brad Little revealed that the state needed the space because of its expanding needs.

"I still don't know all of the behind-the-scenes work that happened," Chandra said. "Jeff and Michael worked together to make sure Jeff put in a successful bid, and before we knew it, DONE DEAL."

Jeff Stoddard became the proud owner of the former Concordia University School of Law building, a 10-minute walk from the U of I Boise Center. "It's on the main thoroughfare through town," Jeff remarked. "The signage and visibility will be phenomenal for the university."

"Our advisory council, emeritus faculty, and alumni helped to get everyone on board," Johanna shared. "We moved during fall exams to be in the building by January 1, 2022."

Scott and Johanna had agreed that part of the financial model included addressing the $3 million deficit. "It effectively was a bookkeeping entry," Scott explained. "Once we knew that the model they were proposing was accretive, we moved the deficit from the books of the law school to the university, effectively wiping it out and not requiring the law school to repay the university."

"We made a fresh start with renovations and upgrades in Boise and Moscow," Johanna said. "I'm proud to be a part of an organization where nobody got left behind."

On February 14, 2022, large cranes placed an enormous Vandal "I" on the building at 501 Front Street, marking it the U of I's latest expansion into the Boise market.

The 501 Front Street location also serves as a portal for the U of I to assist the Treasure Valley community in more ways than legal education by offering space they can use. "They will have a chance to sort of experience what it feels like to be part of the Vandal community," Johanna smiled. "Scott was the right person in that moment because nobody's more Idaho than he is. He understands the value of bringing in new ideas and preserving our history."

(Continued)

(Continued)

501 Front Street, Boise, Idaho, houses the expansion of the University of Idaho's College of Law.

SOURCE: Reproduced with permission from University of Idaho.

Scott's Management Insight

When trusted colleagues think outside the box for unique solutions to problems or opportunities, you should, too. Our law school in Boise ran deficits and turned away students due to lack of space. We could not afford to buy the building but needed it. With the new building, we could grow enrollment and revenues and turn deficits into surpluses, even with the higher lease payments. It is a win for everyone. The university took possession of a built-for-purpose, modern law school, a more financially secure operating model, and a visible structure within walking distance from our other main Boise building. Jeff received a market rate of return on his investment and the sincere gratitude of Vandal alumni everywhere.

You must continually identify your strengths and opportunities to differentiate yourself in competing or new markets. We were the only law school in Idaho, but we hesitated to open, then grow in Boise. That allowed Concordia to successfully open in Boise. We got a second chance when Concordia's parent filed for bankruptcy. I was not going to let that happen twice. If you have a strength, you don't ever want to give that up; you want to continue to build on it. When an opportunity needs investment, calculate the ROI, and if it works, make the investment, and ensure you don't lose your edge.

When negotiating or asking for money, have the ground well prepared. Make sure you don't have to make the ask at the first meeting. Build a relationship with the decision-makers. Bring them along. There may be representations and strategic details only a president can provide, which is the point of a meeting so that the CEO or president can close the deal. Ensure your team has spoken to the parties involved before the ask so there are no surprises. A president should not be put into a position where he cannot ask or close because those involved haven't agreed upon a structure.

Chapter 3
The Nontraditional
June 25, 2019

"You're the only candidate who can wear that."

—*Kathy Barnard*

After logging 975 miles and spending a glorious, sleep-filled night in Madison, Wisconsin, Scott felt refreshed and ready to tackle the second day of the journey toward his new home. He settled his overnight bag and Joe Vandal in the car and took off.

As he navigated his way west through the Wisconsin dairy farms, his mind wandered again to his new job, although he didn't consider this just a job. Becoming president of the University of Idaho was more of a calling and one he welcomed. He knew it meant carrying the weight of the university on his shoulders like the cement football gargoyles held the weight of Memorial Gym on theirs. He also knew he wasn't alone in shouldering the monumental task of being the lead Vandal.

After concluding his extensive research and consulting, he'd enthusiastically thrown his name into the search for the new president. His gut told him he'd made the right decision, even though his head screamed that he was the long shot. Still, he'd quickly made it to the shortlist of contenders, along with four other highly qualified candidates.

When the SBOE named the finalists on February 27, 2019, a buzz of energy built up. Vandals started talking and sharing their thoughts about a nontraditional candidate, especially one named Scott Green. "We literally had alumni, friends, and boosters of the university contacting SBOE and pleading with us to find someone who was loyal," SBOE Executive Director

Matt Freeman shared. "The SBOE was looking for new leadership that was authentically collaborative and system minded."

Special Advisor Chandra Zenner Ford's network spanned the entire country but living in Boise among the highest concentration of Vandals, she witnessed an incredible sense of approval for Scott brewing. "One thing I did not foresee was the huge outpouring from the University of Idaho community of external leaders," she expressed. "Once they knew of his candidacy, they came out of the woodwork to support him. The response was insane, with letters to Governor Little and outreach to SBOE. It was an organic movement that took on a life of its own. There was a huge outpouring of support for Scott because many believed that the previous series of leaders were not the right fit, and given the financial situation, we needed something different."

Not all the feedback about Scott's candidacy was positive, however. "It was a mixed bag," Dr. Michael Parrella, dean of the College of Agricultural and Life Sciences (CALS), shared. "Some of the faculty were wary of appointing a nonacademic as the President. On the other hand, alumni and other stakeholders welcomed the outside perspective such a person would bring. The fact that Scott was an alumnus with close ties to U of I and Moscow made all the difference."

"There was a lot of excitement about Scott because of his credentials and background," Dr. Ginger Carney, dean of the College of Science, expressed. "But at the same time, there was some trepidation. Does he know how a university runs? Does he know how to work with the faculty?"

"Early on, I was somewhat skeptical," shared Dr. Philip Scruggs, interim dean of the College of Education, Health, and Human Sciences (CEHHS). "But it was less about President Green coming from a non-academic background as it was that it was another new person in the president position. Presidents before had set goals, but there weren't the foundational and follow-through pieces in meeting the goals."

Throughout the search process, Chandra communicated with Scott. She suggested to him what the U of I needed and what he could do to help the faculty see that he understood and would advocate for their perspective. "I already knew he would be passionate about the students, given his history, so that was a no-brainer," Chandra said, laughing.

The interviews commenced among the chatter about all the candidates—including Scott. As assistant vice president for Alumni Relations and Advancement Communications, Kathy Barnard was one of a handful of people representing the U of I on the search committee established by the SBOE. "I got asked to serve, which I was very happy to do. It was an honor," she shared. "When the committee interviewed Scott in March for his first interview, it was via videoconference because he was traveling on business. He was at Hogan Lovells's office in London, and we had to accommodate for the time difference. Keep in mind that videoconferencing wasn't all that common. It was unusual not to have an in-person interview, especially for the position of president. But again, his reputation preceded him, and he was on the committee's shortlist as a viable contender for the position. The interview went well."

Scott advanced to the next round of interviews and town hall sessions held in Boise and Moscow. During the interviews, Kathy recalled her experience as a search committee member *and* assistant vice president for Alumni Relations. "I didn't know Scott—had never met him," she stated. "The first time I ever met him in person was when he was in Boise, and I picked him up to take him to the interview. I took him an alumni pin, pinned it on his lapel, and said, 'You're the only candidate who can wear that.' He did a fabulous job at the interview. There was a faculty member on the search committee, and after Scott's interview, someone asked them, 'How do you think he'll do with faculty?' The faculty member said, 'Anybody who can work with that many lawyers will have no trouble at all working with faculty.'"

Scott remembers Kathy placing that pin on his lapel. "It was like she gave me a superpower. I was already a Vandal, I cared about the place, and no one else could care more. No one was better positioned to turn the university around. That kind act made me feel even more confident I was on the right path."

Scott held his enthusiasm, however. "After a couple of interviews with SBOE," he acknowledged, "I realized there were some strong academic credentials with the other candidates. I thought the Board probably wouldn't look at me."

The other candidates possessed substantial academic backgrounds compared to Scott. But many didn't see that as a problem.

"Looking at non-academics in a president search isn't bad," said Barbara Kirchmeier, who served on the U of I Faculty Senate from 2018 to 2021, including as chair from 2020 to 2021. "Many faculty are not specifically trained to do the work required of a university president."

Faculty Senate was the governing body ". . . empowered to act for the university faculty in all matters pertaining to the immediate government of the university. The Senate is responsible to and reports to the university faculty and, through the president, to the regents" (University of Idaho n.d.). As the primary voice for faculty, the Senate was a respected and influential body whose oversight consisted of an annually elected chair and vice chair, a secretary appointed by the president for a three-year term, and other positions and committees. When SBOE named Scott as one of the finalists for president, the opinions from faculty regarding his nontraditional status swung a wide swath from one extreme to the other.

Barbara continued. "Generally, there is discomfort in hiring someone from outside of academia to lead an academic institution. At first, I was skeptical. But after the interview process was completed, I felt like we made the right choice."

"There were always reservations when we brought on a new president no matter what path they took to get here," Dean of the College of Graduate Studies Dr. Jerry McMurtry said. "Scott grew up on this campus. None of the other candidates had that deep history. He also had a graduate degree, although not from Idaho, but nonetheless, he knew what both undergraduate and graduate students need and face in pursuing degrees, so he understood both sides of our campus, the undergraduate and graduate. He had been at the pinnacle of his career and wanted to come back home."

"One of the things that impressed me was that Scott genuinely was listening," Dr. Dennis Becker, dean of the College of Natural Resources, said. "He could go a long way if he just listened. I felt like maybe he would stumble in some areas, but he could recover. The one place that we couldn't afford to stumble was financially."

"When SBOE announced that Scott was a candidate, some people were very concerned," Shauna Corry, dean of the College of Art and Architecture, shared. "Academia was so traditional, and there were reasons why we were so traditional. There were reasons why we had the processes that we had that truly achieved the goals we needed to achieve. But that didn't mean they couldn't get worked out from a different point of view."

Terry Grieb, Faculty Senate Chair 2019–2020, shared his thoughts about Scott during the interviewing process. "He was in touch with real issues facing our university, and that came as a surprise to me. Of course, he was a sophisticated leader, and there were many positive indicators. On the research side, it was pretty clear he was less up to speed."

Smart Collaboration

Parma Research and Extension Center, Parma, Idaho

The Parma Research and Extension Center is a research hub for the U of I, where researchers conduct investigation and study involving entomology, nematology, plant pathology, plant science, pomology, and cropping systems. "U of I President Duane Nellis tried to close Parma down during his presidency because it was an aging facility, and there was a serious budget challenge at the time," Scott explained. "I wasn't at the U of I during that time, so I can't judge Nellis on what he was planning; the facility was old, but the research it housed was an invaluable part of the College of Agricultural and Life Sciences' (CALS) mission."

Some of the nation's best researchers were working out of decades-old facilities to conduct their work. The U of I houses one of the nation's leading nematode researchers there, Professor Saad Hafez. Nematodes are microscopic worms that can destroy a variety of plants, including potatoes, a crop near and dear to Idaho. Some are classified as invasive species, which magnifies their impact on producers.

"We also have a researcher there conducting work on growing almonds in Idaho," Scott continued. "There's research on stone fruits, apples, and grapes; you name it, the U of I is probably researching it there."

The discussion about shutting down the research station prompted stakeholders to donate private funds to keep the station functioning. "It still needed a refresh when I became president, though," Scott agreed.

Expecting funding from the state seemed futile, as Idaho Governor Brad Little initially took a hard line on appropriating any funds. But in March 2021, when he held his "Capital for a Day" event in Parma, nearly 100 stakeholders attended and emphatically explained the importance of the research station.

After misinformation swirled around the issue, Scott met with the governor and clarified the U of I's position. "The governor is a Vandal, and we supported him without reservation," he said. "We made that clear. The Parma Research and Extension Center was a priority and cornerstone of the land-grant institution's mission and needed help."

The governor agreed and added funding to the following year's budget.

"Much of the credit for the successful vision that led to the new center rests with the Parma Research and Extension Center's faculty, staff, and students," Dean of the College of Agricultural and Life Sciences Dr. Michael Parrella said. "Their hard work has kept Parma a relevant and valuable resource for growers state- and regionwide."

"Now that we have secured the state and private funding to complete the research lab facility, the future looks bright for the Parma Research and Extension Center," CEO SW Idaho and President's Office Special Advisor Chandra Zenner Ford shared. "The contributions from the station will continue to be an important benefactor to the ag community and keep farmland soil healthy."

(Continued)

(Continued)

Michael shared the collaboration of contributors to vitalize the research station. "We received $5 million from the Idaho State Legislature, $1 million from the College of Agricultural and Life Sciences (CALS), and $3 million from 12 commodity commissions that use the Center, including the Sugar Beet, Grape, and Hops Commissions, along with the J.A. and Kathryn Albertson Family Foundation."

"It was another win, but it wasn't easy," Scott commented. "We're grateful to the citizens, governor, and legislature on this one because that research would've gone elsewhere, which would've hurt the university and the state. The Treasure Valley is such a diverse growing area. Parma is an incredibly important research center for us."

The new lab facility, Idaho Center for Plant and Soil Health, will afford the U of I to continue research and extension programs related to the production and storage of vegetables, forages, cereals, fruit, field seed, and specialty crops produced in southwest Idaho. The Center also serves a critical function as it monitors the state for airborne pathogens so farmers can respond before they see damage to their crops.

A celebratory groundbreaking for the new Idaho Center for Plant and Soil Health took place on July 13, 2021, with Governor Brad Little in attendance. CALS plans to begin construction in 2022, with completed renovations slated for 2023.

Scott's Management Insight

The institution does not have to do it all by itself. Partnering with industry, the state, and federal government can accomplish what cannot be accomplished alone. I have found that the State of Idaho, in particular, is willing to make investments where private industry also has skin in the game. That collaborative support can be a game changer for your university.

During one of Scott's on-campus interviews with the Faculty Senate, Terry explained that a member asked about Scott's views supporting research—how money flowed through the system and how the U of I paid for the research. "It was the one question Scott whiffed," Terry said, smiling.

"He gave us a polite answer, but it was an uninformed answer, and word on the street was this was the weak spot."

Scott reflected upon that moment. He'd told the group, "I've had some practice dealing with a group of employees who were appropriately skeptical. Lawyers and faculty members aren't exactly the same, but they have that much in common. I invite you to look at my professional track record and how it shows there's a good chance I will do what I say I'll do, which is to right the proverbial university ship."

The Associated Students of the University of Idaho (ASUI) also had representation during the search. ASUI President (2018–19) Nicole Skinner recalled, "As the only student who got to serve on the search committee, I was incredibly excited and honored to be a part of the process. We were looking for someone who would lead the university into the future, prioritize the student experience, manage the university's financial problems, and embody values of equity and diversity. When the finalists from the search were made public, I remember heightened excitement across campus at the potential of an alumnus being the new university president." When asked about Scott's nonacademic background, she added, "I could see his professional experience transferring well to the role, especially paired with his background as a Vandal and former ASUI president."

CALS Dean Michael Parrella summed up his opinion on Scott's nonacademic ranking. "Faculty liked to see a president who came up through the ranks from an academic perspective. I don't believe that was necessary at all. In fact, I think that was maybe why we were in such trouble because we had people who couldn't really understand the fiscal aspects of the university. It was my job to deal with the academic excellence in the college. It was the president's job to handle the fiscal aspects of the university, to be a cheerleader for the campus, and to be on a good footing with all the stakeholders and legislators."

"Most of us became faculty because we love research and working with students," College of Science Dean Ginger Carney shared. "We didn't expect to worry about whether we have enough students enrolled in our classes. We didn't want the new president to throw everything aside that we'd been striving for as a university; we had a strategic plan in place."

"Academics are not trained or focused in their professional life on financial matters in a broader sense," U of I alumnus Jeff Stoddard pointed out. "They typically don't develop financial or management strategy skills, again in a broader sense. The U of I presidents since [Bob] Hoover struggled and failed, in my opinion, and the financial problem continued to grow. There was a lot of denial during that period. That set the stage for hiring somebody like Scott, who was a non-traditional and non-academic candidate. The need for somebody like Scott and what Scott could do had been a long time coming."

"What I loved about the whole situation was that if Scott had applied ten years before, I don't think he would have been as well received," Kathy said. "But even the faculty members on the search committee said, 'We have tried leaders from academia, and it hasn't been working.'"

Thinking about the process—the time he'd spent researching the underbelly of his university, talking with his family, alumni, friends, and colleagues about the job opening, applying, and interviewing—brought about a sense of peace for Scott. He'd done everything in his power to become part of the leadership at the U of I. It had become a waiting game at that point. He knew not everyone supported him and might condemn SBOE if they selected him as president. He was the nontraditional candidate, and even though he addressed it thoroughly in his interviews with the search committee, the regents and board, and the campus open forums, he still knew there were detractors because he hadn't gone through the ranks in academia. It might be risky for the board to name him president of a land-grant institution.

Scott refocused back on the road ahead. He exited the freeway in Mitchell, South Dakota. Joe Vandal needed to sack a palace—specifically a Corn Palace—and Scott needed to stretch and take photos to share with his Vandal family on social media.

Scott's Management Insight

Start with trusted friends, and treat the job interviews like a campaign, winning over converts along the way. Regents care what alumni and faculty think about candidates. Avoid discussing third-rail topics, such as which football division you should be in or the State Board of Education (Regents) structure. Focus on what you bring and your vision of what you can do to advance the institution. I had confidence that I had the financial chops to stabilize the university and put it on a more sustainable path. That vision sold well to the SBOE. That I was an alumnus and an Idaho native sold well to alumni and faculty who knew my family and me. I was returning home, not for promotion but to advance a struggling institution I cared about deeply, which helped form the person I am today.

Chapter 4
Lincoln's Vision

"Without it, there wouldn't be the University of Idaho or, at the very least, the powerful university it became in its 130+ years of existence."
—*Scott Green*

After stopping at the Mitchell Corn Palace and the famous Wall Drug in Wall, South Dakota, it seemed fitting to take the time to visit Mt. Rushmore. Scott made sure to click a few pictures and share his and Joe's adventures while there. Admiring the monument, Scott stole a moment to reflect on how Honest Abe Lincoln, the sixteenth president of the United States, made monumental strides and achievements for his country. Everyone knew the high points of the Civil War and the Emancipation Proclamation, but did they know about the Morrill Land Grant Act signed by Lincoln during the Civil War?

The Land-Grant College Act of 1862, or Morrill Act, provided grants of land to states to finance the establishment of "land-grant" colleges. Several books exist to discuss the long and tumultuous story of how the federal government acquired the land, but in the end, Lincoln's act catalyzed the creation of the U of I. The purpose of a land-grant college was to offer courses in agricultural studies, military tactics, mechanical arts (applied sciences and engineering), classical studies, and liberal arts. The Morrill Act also allowed Congress to assist with funding agriculture experiment stations to disseminate the knowledge gained through cooperative extensions (Smith-Lever Act of 1914). That equated to federal appropriations to the land-grant colleges to send agents to nearly every county in their state. And the military training required in the curriculum of all land-grant schools led to the establishment of the Reserve Officers' Training Corps, an educational program for future army, navy, and air force officers (Britannica n.d.).

Scott knew the impact of the Morrill Act. "Without it, there wouldn't be the University of Idaho or, at the very least, the powerful university it became in its 130+ years of existence," he reflected. He knew the rich history of his alma mater and was cognizant that when President Abraham Lincoln signed the Morrill Act on July 2, 1862, he unleashed a legacy establishing land-grant universities nationwide. Anyone even remotely involved with the University of Idaho knew it was *the* land-grant institution of Idaho.

During the 1880s, Moscow, Idaho, boasted several entrepreneurial and forward-thinking moguls in its population, including Willis Sweet and William J. McConnell, two of the brains behind planting the seed that their town needed a university. The seed grew into fruition with the help of Fred T. Dubois, one of Idaho's most powerful politicians at that time. Through sheer tenacity and will, Dubois maneuvered through Idaho's affairs of the state to get the university established in the farming community a year before Idaho became a state in 1890. Excavation for the new campus's first building site began in 1889 (Peterson 1987, pp. 16–17).

The world-famous Olmstead Brothers had designed the master plan for the university—the family of landscape architects was known for creating great places of beauty. The father of the brothers, Frederick Law Olmstead, designed New York's Central Park. The State of Idaho established the university as a stately, welcoming destination college, offering everything a student could wish for with an on-campus experience, although it started out on a patch of swampy, undeveloped ground dotted with a few bushes and not much else.

Because of Idaho's narrow-at-the-top and wide-at-the-bottom borders, the southern territory boasted the population base, setting the stage for a lifetime of an "us versus them" back and forth. The northern territory area took up a little over 21,000 square miles, or 25.4% of the state's total geography, versus the southern area encompassing approximately 62,500 square miles (Wikipedia n.d.). Dubois's execution of extending an "olive branch" from the southern territory to the northern territory to house the institution in Moscow seemed to put Idahoans on a course of collaboration as a state regardless of the unbalanced geography. Dubois and other legislators ensured the U of I's legacy by specifically entrenching it in the state constitution and naming it the land-grant institution. It would take a legislative act and a public vote to undo the significant status of the university (Peterson 1987, pp. 19–20).

The State Board of Education (SBOE) was established in the Idaho Constitution and Statute as the governing board as it had governance, oversight, and control over all public education in the state, from kindergarten through PhD. Idaho was one of only two states in the nation with that type of consolidated governance model. SBOE is the Board of Regents for the University of Idaho and the Board of Trustees for Boise State University, Idaho State University, and Lewis Clark State Colleges, so it wears many hats. It sets governing policies for the institutions simply for administration and management. But SBOE also approves many of the university's contracts, money for facilities, and several other functions (M. Freeman, personal communication).

Regent James H. Forney served as the first president, unpaid, with no students, classes, or faculty. He oversaw the construction of the administration building starting in 1891. The Regents chose Franklin B. Gault as the first paid president. Gault arrived in Moscow in the summer of 1892 with an inaugural class of 40 eager students and thirteen rooms completed in the new Administration Building to begin their education (the entire building wasn't completed until 1899). The first classes would fall under the "preparatory" category, with collegiate-level work coming a few years later. In 1896, the first graduating class boasted two men and two women (Peterson 1987, pp. 26–28).

The U of I evolved into the premier research institution in Idaho, growing onto 810 stately acres. The university survived many ups and downs, including the devastating loss of the beautiful and impressive Administration Building to an unstoppable fire on March 30, 1906. Following the tragic inferno, worries shrouded the town of Moscow that the main learning center of Idaho would most likely move away from their town, even though under the state constitution, the University of Idaho would remain as the land grant. Many believed the institution would become stagnant, small, and stunted in the aftermath of the fire.

But with a strong president, the U of I rose out of the ashes that day like a phoenix. Not even a blazing fire demolishing its linchpin facility would destroy the goals and dreams established for the academic gem. U of I President James A. MacLean stood resilient and commanded the construction of an even larger Administration Building. Its opening in 1907 symbolized that the University of Idaho would stay the primary institution of higher education in Idaho (Peterson 1987, pp. 44–46).

In its first attempts at recruiting, the U of I advertised many offerings in the early 1900s, including the College of Agriculture, the College of Letters and Sciences, the College of Engineering (civil, mining, electrical, and mechanical), the School of Law, the Preparatory School, and the Idaho Agricultural Experiment Station. Coursework in Domestic Economy, Music, Elocution, Physical Education, Literary Science, Military Science and Tactics and short courses in Dairying and Forestry rounded out the educational menu (Peterson 1987, pp. 43).

University of Idaho Administration Building.
SOURCE: Reproduced with permission from University of Idaho.

One hundred and twelve years later, the U of I comprised ten colleges with countless degree offerings, and another U of I president would stand resilient with the Vandal community to rebuild. This time it would involve numbers, not bricks and mortar, and set the university on a track to an infinite future of sustainability and excellence.

Colleges at the University of Idaho

Agricultural and Life Sciences (est. 1901)
Art and Architecture (est. 1981)
Business and Economics (est. 1925)
Education (est. 1920)
Engineering (est. 1907 in cooperation with the College of Mines, formally est. 1911)
Graduate Studies (est. 1925*)
Law (est. 1909, accredited by the American Bar Association in 1925)
Letters, Arts, and Social Sciences (est. 1901 as Letters and Sciences, 2002 changed to College of Letters, Arts, and Social Sciences)
Natural Resources (est. 1909)
Science (est. 2002)

*The U of I started awarding advanced degrees in 1897.

Standing before Mount Rushmore, Scott gave an imperceptible nod to the massive rock carving of Lincoln as if to say thank you.

Jumping back into the car, he and Joe cruised through the Black Hills to make it as far as they could before nightfall. They would hit Wyoming and Montana the next day, weather permitting. Again, the miles of the road lulled Scott back to his reflections. After the formal interviews, he'd put the whole affair out to fate to figure it out. But in March, his phone lit up with a 208–area code call that changed his life forever. After that momentous conversation, he called the person who started the whole thing in the first place.

"I got an offer."

Scott's words filtered through to Chandra's ears. It took her a beat, but she erupted over the phone when it clicked that SBOE offered Scott the job.

"She was pretty excited to hear those words after all our what-if conversations," Scott said while laughing. "We were all surprised. I didn't think I had a shot, and it was clear to me later that Chandra never thought I really had a shot at it, either."

"I was so happy I cried," Chandra said. "I could see a future for the Vandals that was better, stronger, and more optimistic. Scott did his research, and he over-prepared. It was a long shot, but he got this job on his own merit—with just a little help from a lot of passionate Vandals. This wasn't just some grand plan; fate made it happen."

But the offer wasn't Scott's official acceptance of the job; in other words, there were a few kinks to work out. Scott's contract at his current employer, Hogan Lovells, held the caveat that he would earn a bonus as a substantial part of his compensation. The bonus, however, hinged on timing.

"The timing of everything as outlined by SBOE meant I would have to forfeit my bonus, or at least a large portion of it, if I started when the board wanted me to start," Scott explained. "It was a substantial amount of money, so I had to really think through how it would all work out. Both the board and my employer took a hard line on what they expected of me."

Scott knew it wasn't about the money, but changing those numbers would have a ripple effect since he'd planned his life around receiving the bonus. He had financial commitments to his family's obligations, so it took some real negotiating to at least receive a partial bonus.

"I don't think many people realized Scott walked away from a seven-figure base salary to come to the U of I, plus some of his bonus," Chandra pointed out. "That should speak volumes about the commitment and passion he held for the university."

Several U of I constituents publicly voiced their opinions upon hearing the negotiations weren't going as smoothly as hoped, including Frances Ellsworth emailing the SBOE again. Her email dated March 18, 2019, showed how involved and concerned many Vandals were with the search and their dedication to Scott getting hired. She emphasized she'd heard through several channels and Vandals that the SBOE Regents might be making the priority of an arbitrary timeline more important than recruiting the best candidate for the U of I president. She shared that the Vandals communicating to her appreciated the search committee thinking outside the box, believed Scott was the best candidate, and wanted him for president. But they worried that his need for a little more time before an announcement would hinder his appointment. She also added in her email, "If one of the other candidates is selected to be the U of I President, there will be an extremely disappointed group of students, alumni, staff, and faculty. I say this because, like I said before, I have never seen so much interest in a presidential search or in a candidate, Scott Green. As you know, better than anyone, this is a very critical time for our great university, and it would be a shame if a few more weeks before an announcement would take away from this opportunity."

Thankfully, negotiations proved successful; Scott felt relieved when he and his firm reached an agreement for his exit. "In the end, Hogan Lovells did the right thing and stood by me, thanks to Steve Immelt and David Hudd," he shared. "I still took a hit as they also had a duty to their partners, but it wasn't as bad as it could have been."

And with that, on April 11, 2019, C. Scott Green officially became the University of Idaho's nineteenth president.

Scott's Management Insight

The period when you are first selected to be president or CEO will be your most visible moment. Use it to build your following. I utilized social media to build an audience as I crossed the country, allowing our alumni and students to track my progress, complete with pictures of the Corn Palace and Mount Rushmore with my stuffed, yet highly revered, Joe Vandal mascot. My contemporary, who had just been hired as the president of Boise State University, expertly used Twitter to build excitement leading up to her arrival. Years later, my new football coach used Twitter, Facebook, Instagram, and other platforms to build excitement about his arrival and recruiting travels throughout Idaho. Don't be afraid to share your story. Stakeholders want to take the journey with you.

Most long-standing public and private universities have a proud history of achievement, contributing graduates that help form their state and country. I was fortunate to know much of the history of the U of I, having lived much of it. Importantly, as a third-generation Vandal, I knew the fight song "Go Vandals Go!" and its companion, "Here We Have Idaho." Learn the institution's history to build trust; your alumni and faculty will know it cold, so you should, too. Along with that, and to the extent possible, align your goals and objectives to your mission and industry needs. That combination can be a powerful catalyst.

Smart Collaboration

Nancy M. Cummings Research, Extension, and Education Center Renovation, Carmen, Idaho

The Nancy M. Cummings Research, Extension, and Education Center is the U of I's primary cow-calf and forage research station. It provides land and facilities for cattle research at the scale of a working ranch. The center also provides continuing education for those involved in the livestock industry and learning opportunities for the U of I students (University of Idaho n.d.).

"The first time I went out there and visited that place, we literally had a double-wide trailer that served as the classroom and as a place for our faculty to live and house their offices and laboratories," College of Agricultural and Life Sciences (CALS) Dean Michael Parrella shared. "Cows, livestock, and dairy are extremely important in Idaho, and the facilities should reflect the size of the industry. So, we built a brand-new facility and opened it in July of 2021."

Along with private and industry donations, CALS funded the project for the $3.5 million facility on the 1000-acre ranch. "It's now more than just a cow-calf operation," Michael shared. "The facility has a 120-seat classroom for distance education, the offices for our faculty and staff, and a kitchen. The 4-H and FFA communities use the facility. This area has one of the poorest college go-on rates in Idaho. The fact that we have a beautiful facility now in Salmon, a spectacular but remote area of the state, is going to impact undergraduate enrollment growth in the future. This was an investment in the future."

(Continued)

(Continued)

Scott's Management Insight

The U of I is Idaho's land-grant institution and home to the state's agricultural college. Livestock—including but not exclusively beef, dairy, and lamb—is one of Idaho's largest industries. The work at the Cummings Center helps cattlemen identify which cattle put on weight most efficiently. This is important as you want to breed your most efficient producers rather than send them to market. The center also studies sheep, their DNA, and their food preferences. This work helps sheep ranchers determine where to place certain breeds depending on the food sources in a grazing area. These investments align with the university's land-grant mission and goals and strengthen our bond with important industry partners.

Chapter 5
Three Pillars
June 26, 2019

"I know no other fight songs."

—Scott Green

After a beautiful drive through Wyoming, Scott stopped in Bozeman, Montana, to take a stretch and a photo op with Joe. He was getting several comments on his social media posts. Vandals from all over shared their excitement, welcoming him home to Idaho. If all his planning worked out, along with some skillful driving, his head would hit the pillow in Moscow that night. He buckled Joe in, dead set on hitting the Idaho border within a few hours. He clipped along at a good—mostly legal—pace and again let his mind wander.

The entire search process was long and stressful, but a renewed sense of energy enveloped him when he was named president. Vandals worldwide espoused their excitement to have an alumnus in the driver's seat.

After serving on the search committee, Nicole Skinner, ASUI president (2018–19), agreed there was enthusiasm swirling around her university and its new president. "It was an exciting time. It felt like closure to a period of a lot of uncertainty and change."

"It was almost instantaneous," Kathy Barnard said. "As soon as alumni found out that a fellow Vandal was going to be in charge, the tone shifted from 'Goddamnit, we're going down hard by the bow,' to 'Wow, a Vandal's in charge; let's support him.' The alumni's biggest fear through all of the other presidents was that they didn't know or care about the place. Scott had instant street cred with alumni because, one, they knew that he knew the place and obviously loved it; two, he took a bajillion-dollar pay cut to come back; and three, the fact that he was a Greek helped. There were a lot of things that instantaneously put most alumni's fears to rest."

But not right away. When stakeholders pointedly asked Scott how long he would stay on as president or if he was just using the position as a stepingstone, the scars from several years of turnover revealed themselves. But Scott's answer was always the same, and one he hoped would bring a sense of trust from all Vandals. "I'll stay as long as you'll have me and as long as I'm providing value. What other institution would I go to if I left here? I'm a nontraditional candidate, and I only know one fight song."

"The revolving door of presidents just emphasized the need to have someone here who was investing in the institution, not in their personal career," Kathy stated. "And with Scott, there was no doubt. He showed on a daily basis that he knew the place and had deep roots here. He knew the state, and he cared."

Sometimes, Scott still couldn't believe his life was taking this unpredicted left-turn-at-Albuquerque twist. But he'd never felt more confident about a career decision. He knew there were unprecedented steps he'd have to take to right the ship and help his university heal. He also knew he was the right person for the job and could and would do it.

Scott accepted the job in person on the Moscow campus on April 11, 2019. He gave a passionate speech discussing his ties to the university from a young age and how he'd never ventured far from the U of I throughout his life. He signed a contract to begin that day in a voluntary capacity to get up to speed on what he would walk into on his official start date of July 1. "I worried things would get worse and not better, so I asked for a non-paid consultant contract to start April 11 through June 30, 2019," Scott explained. It wasn't unusual for someone at that level to start learning and participating before the official start date.

That particular day held many meetings introducing Scott, including the beginning conversations about the budget woes. "I was the vice-chair of Faculty Senate," Terry Grieb said. "Liz Brandt was Faculty Secretary, and Aaron Johnson was chair. Scott had asked to meet with us while he was on campus that day. He'd just come from a meeting with the finance folks, and there was a sincere look of surprise. That was when Faculty Senate leadership found out about the dire nature of the budgets. We knew Scott had been involved with the U of I on the Foundation Board and had access to the budget information, but that day it looked like a bit of a curveball the university threw at Scott."

After that day, President Staben assisted Scott with the transition. Staben encouraged the SBOE to include Scott in their meetings and processes as soon as possible so Scott could hit the ground running.

"It was a strategic decision between Chuck and Scott," shared Brenda Helbling, chief of staff to the president. "Chuck had to make some hard decisions and have hard conversations about the financial situation, so Scott didn't have to, including having a town hall with employees about the budgets and cuts coming."

"I started working immediately with then-Provost John Wiencek and the vice president for the Division of Finance and Administration, Brian Foisy, to gain a solid, more in-depth understanding of the budgets and financial situation," Scott said. "I also started working on various priorities like searching for a new athletic director. The SBOE also asked me to determine the feasibility of the ICCU [Idaho Central Credit Union] Arena construction, given our finances, and work with the board's executive director to make the final decision on that. I also started to put my team into place. I firmly believe in hiring talent and getting them into place quickly."

Scott was confident in his ability to build a cohesive team to put the university first. The right people would have some sort of tie or affinity to the area or university. Moscow was somewhat rural, with a population of over 50,000 when the U of I students were in town. For someone to work at the U of I, there had to be a draw, whether it involved their teaching or research program, the rolling hills of the Palouse, or the recreational activities around the city.

"If there wasn't a reason for them to stay, they could and probably would go someplace else," Scott explained. "That's how the steppingstone mentality worked. If there were no love or affinity for the place, it would be easy to leave to go to the next thing."

He requested President Staben hire Chandra Zenner Ford to report to Scott as special advisor and Toni Broyles to report to Chandra as special assistant, strategic initiatives. They would officially begin on July 1, 2019. Staben agreed.

"At the time, we did not exactly know how that would look," Chandra stated. "Scott only knew he needed a trusted advisor who had a history with the U of I, its processes, and culture. He knew his lack of academic experience would mean he had a learning curve, and he wanted to have people on his team who could help with questions, give honest feedback, and help move initiatives forward. I started as a special advisor."

Toni knew both Scott and Chandra through their shared connection to CBE. Toni worked with Chandra at the college, and Chandra knew she was highly competent to serve as special assistant, especially for any strategic initiatives that would inevitably pop up. Toni grew up in Moscow and had strong family ties there, especially with the iconic Corner Club, plus her mother had over 30 years of service to the institution.

Toni pointed out, "Chandra, Scott, and I are all the eldest children in our families, which is a fun anecdote, so we are always evaluating what are the needs and how can we meet them." First-born children tend to be trailblazers and leaders, gravitate to one another, and know how to nurture and protect.

Then came the search for a new athletic director. The university had fired the previous AD in August 2018 for allegedly mishandling sexual harassment complaints filed by female student-athletes. Scott spoke with the Big Sky Commissioner shortly after accepting the position as president, who suggested the U of I hire a search firm specializing in sports hires to find the next U of I AD.

"Scott talked with Daniel Parker on May 17, 2019, and sessions were held with athletics on June 6 to determine what they wanted and needed in a new director," Brenda explained. By June 21, the search committee's first meeting took place, and by August 7, Scott tapped Terry Gawlik as athletic director.

"Right out of the gate, the first three hires Scott approved were women, which included the first female AD in the history of the institution," Toni said.

"And although I didn't hire him, Torrey Lawrence had ties to the Pacific Northwest and had been at the U of I since 1998," Scott pointed out. "He taught classes in the School of Music, including the Vandal Marching Band, and moved his way up the academic ladder. He was vice provost for faculty when I started, and I eventually hired him as my provost."

Scott also hired Dr. Christopher "Chris" Nomura, the vice president for research and economic development, in 2020. "He didn't have any specific ties to the area, but he knew a few folks in Moscow and had small kids he wanted to raise in a great community. He was a great fit from the start," Scott said.

Thankfully, hundreds of existing employees demonstrated a willingness to work for the U of I. "I was determined to find a way to work with them," Scott emphasized.

Scott knew putting faculty, staff, and student fears to rest was vital to his success, but he also knew actions spoke louder than words. In addition to setting a foundation based on financial health, he would announce three strategic pillars to drive the university's course. Every early decision under his presidency would fall under at least one of the pillars:

1. Student success;
2. The path to R1 research classification; and
3. Controlling the narrative by telling the U of I's story.

Scott finally arrived on campus on June 26, 2019. The final Facebook post of his journey west, home to Idaho and his Vandal family, read:

> *Three days and two thousand miles later, we reached our Moscow campus. The trip back to Idaho, seen through more experienced eyes than my trip east over 30 years ago, helped me appreciate the beauty and diversity of our fine country. Joe usually sees cities to be sacked and bounty for the taking, but I think I saw his battle-hardened eyes moisten slightly when we crossed the Idaho border. He denies this, of course, and says Vandals don't cry or complain; they just "git 'er done." Hard to argue with that.*
>
> *And the campus just looks amazing. We are both glad to be back and excited to get started.*
>
> *Thank you to all that supported and encouraged us along the way. We could feel that Vandal spirit all the way from Long Island to University House. We are indeed a special tribe.*
>
> *Go Vandals!*

Scott's Management Insight

Set the tone early—your arrival is not a time for celebration but to get to work. Tell people what you plan to do, and then ensure there are plenty of visible signs that you are doing what you said you would. Set the agenda by discussing financial plans and emphasizing the strategic pillars.

Even if a strategic plan exists, setting three to five achievable goals will engage the campus. Communicate those goals over and over again. When there is good news, tie it back to those goals. There are certain drivers present in every successful university. Enrollment is a driver for every university and should be a primary focus. For the U of I, focusing on student success and recruitment would drive enrollments, a research focus would drive facility and administrative revenues, and telling our story would help better control the narrative and reputation of the university. There are others, but these levers fit our land-grant mission and culture.

Be sure to make it clear you want committed people and will help anyone who wants to get a job elsewhere land safely. It will make it easier to identify those who will self-select out and those who will be part of your team. I tend to give people the opportunity to be a part of the team. I don't come in and just start firing people and replace them with my own people, like what sometimes happens with a change in leadership or administration. My first three hires, Chandra, Toni, and Terry, were committed to the institution. We shared a vision of what the U of I could become. Over time, some would self-select out, including the provost, the VP of research, the CMO, and others. When the provost made it clear he would continue to interview, I publicly supported his move in a way that bolstered his chances of landing successfully elsewhere. We agreed to a deadline that cleared the way for succession planning. Those who leave are good people but just not in the right place. By going, they can land at a place that is a better fit, and I can recruit those that fit our strategy and desired culture.

You should focus on building your team with talented individuals who are smarter than you—recognized subject matter experts—and evidenced to work hard, are a bit humble, and don't know how good they are. Those who score high in these categories will be the best colleagues and contributors you will ever hire.

Chapter 6
Reunion

"Something in my gut told me to keep a chair and a couch."
—Brenda Helbling

The end of June on the University of Idaho campus offered massive swells of manicured green lawns, bright flower beds, and the famous Camperdown Elms lining the Administration Building. Hello Walk sat shaded by dozens of trees that had greeted thousands of students over the decades. Any Vandal who has enjoyed the slower pace of summer on campus knows those months are far different from the hustle-bustle of fall and spring semesters.

Scott arrived in Moscow a short three days after departing Long Island. He cruised campus, taking in the sights of his alma mater. As he rounded Rayburn Street, Memorial Gym greeted him like an old friend. A lump in his throat started to form, bringing a tremendous smile and a wash of nostalgia. He pulled to the curb and let his mind wander briefly to those summer days during his formative years. He'd started his Vandal journey in that very building with his grandpa Leon.

"Dad would drive my brother and me up to Moscow to stay with our grandparents in the summer," Scott shared. "I went to work with Grandpa at Memorial Gym. He hired me out of his own pocket to help an employee named Bill to wash towels and clean up the locker rooms."

His favorite time of day was when he and his grandfather walked to the Satellite Sub for an Orange Crush. Summer also brought Scott and his brother swimming lessons at Kirkland's pool. Eric Kirkland served as assistant professor of physical education at the time.

Scott remembered, "The Kirklands had this outdoor pool where my brother and I learned to swim. I was very young, but I remember going there, most likely because it was early in the morning and cold. I really did not want to do it at the time, but I became a strong swimmer because of it. Kirkland used to hold cookouts in the old Arboretum where the amphitheater was; they would put the whole pig underground to cook or hang huge king salmon on cedar lattices over an open fire, which I remember at the time were taller than I was. My grandfather and grandmother would bring me on those outings where we would eat and sing songs. I loved it. Good memories."

The U of I constructed a new Swim Center in 1970 alongside the Physical Education Building (PEB). "You know, Scott," his grandfather Leon would remind him, "I went to Washington to get the funds to build that pool and the women's gym." Scott knew his grandfather's legacy lived in those walls saturated with the smell of chlorine and competition. That pool was also where Scott received his lifeguard certification.

It was a foregone conclusion that Scott would attend the U of I after he graduated from Boise High School. "I don't remember where else I applied, but I do know that I couldn't afford anyplace else," he said, laughing. "I was looking forward to going back up to Moscow because my grandparents were there, but they moved out of Moscow just as I was moving there, which was disappointing. They moved down to McCammon, where my grandfather's family farmed and close to my grandmother's family in Bancroft and the surrounding Southeastern Idaho area."

Scott pulled himself out of his nostalgic reverie. He needed to get to his destination. He made his way up Rayburn Street, cornered onto Nez Perce Drive, and motored into the driveway of his new home perched on a hill on the campus he held so dearly. He got out of his car and took it all in. The Arboretum across the street flourished, and the familiar buzz of a lawnmower somewhere filled the sweet summer air with the scent of fresh-cut grass.

He was home.

* * *

He'd scheduled the moving truck to arrive in the next few days, which held the rest of his possessions, including his work wardrobe. He was ready to unpack the things he brought with him, along with his trusty copilot Joe Vandal, so he could hurry up and dive into work. However, walking into the newly constructed home, he faced a somewhat surprising scene: little furniture and no window shades.

He was aware of some issues regarding the University House project, but standing in the reality of it took him back a little. "I'd planned on living someplace else until project completion, but due to some unforeseen circumstances and my agreement with SBOE, I decided to stick it out in the new house even without furniture," he explained.

Brenda Helbling, his chief of staff, had wisely held back a few pieces of furniture from the old house. "Something in my gut told me to keep a chair and a couch," she said, smiling. "Scott needed a few pieces to be able to live in the house. It didn't match the house design or décor plan at all, but neither did the butcher paper I put on a few windows for privacy."

Ironically, Scott served on the Foundation Board when plans for University House were in full swing. Through a series of events, the Foundation didn't budget for furniture or the completion of the design features in the house. Ironically, Scott's wife, Gabriella, was an accomplished interior designer. With the approval of the Foundation and SBOE, she assisted a third-party company in completing the home's interior furnishings. It took several months for the UI Foundation to agree on the contract and budget to furnish the house, so Scott settled in, knowing he would be living a spartan lifestyle that first year.

"I am just glad it was me rather than a future president. I really don't care about my living space when I am in work mode, but anyone else might have been put off by that reception."

"Betsy Pascucci, the owner of Pascucci Design, worked with Gabriella with an eye toward utilizing Idaho materials and items," Brenda explained. "The Foundation expressed an interest in funding furnishings using Gabriella's expertise. Who better to coordinate the design than someone who was an expert in that area and would help manage those spaces because she lived there? But because of the extended design process, that furniture didn't arrive before Scott."

The name University House came out of discussions regarding the multipurpose use of the home. It belonged to the university to house the president and serve as an event space for various functions. Those functions required different furniture and setup options for consideration during the planning process.

"Gabriella had a lot of hard decisions to make to coordinate the design and the needs of the house," Scott said. "Downstairs was primarily a public space. We would use the downstairs but live upstairs in the private area."

Brenda also coordinated with Gabriella to select a bed for Scott. But the frame, headboard, and footboard had yet to be ordered, which left him sleeping for several months on a mattress on the floor—minimalist living at its finest. "I had a flashback to my college days on the very same campus at the Kappa Sigma fraternity with just a few pieces of furniture and a mattress," Scott said, laughing. "The irony was not lost on me. Everything moved so slowly."

Building University House started in 2017 with the demolition of the old "President's Residence" built in the 1960s. A refresh was long overdue. The design-build was awarded to Golis Construction out of Moscow and zimmerraystudios out of Seattle. Robert Zimmer, owner of zimmerraystudios and Vandal alumnus, deployed his exquisite talent and "merged the call for a gallery and entertainment space with the fundamental need for private living space, bringing them together in a visually stunning way" (University of Idaho n.d.).

Scott had an office at University House, and the official president's office sat only a 15-minute walk away in the Administration Building. The design team coordinated remnants from the old residence into the finished design, including the brick fireplace, garage, and repurposed carved front doors. Wood cut from a black locust tree in the backyard accented the gallery shelves in the main area. Larch trees cut by the U of I student logging crew out of the university's experimental forest were milled into flooring and installed upstairs for a warm and cozy feel. The home showcased all things Idaho—both the university and the state.

Unfortunately, the moving truck didn't arrive for days, leaving Scott with only business casual options to wear to his meetings the first several days in his new position. "I had no clothes and no furniture," he said, laughing. "But don't feel sorry for me. I loved being back on campus. I had a meeting with SBOE right out of the gate with no suit, just khakis and a polo shirt."

Everyone understood his predicament, including Assistant Vice President for Alumni Relations and Advancement Communications Kathy Barnard, who spoke to her husband, Tom (LaPointe), about Scott's living situation. Gabriella wouldn't be moving to Moscow immediately due to commitments with work and children on the East Coast. "We knew he was there by himself, so Tom and I invited him to our house for dinner," she shared. "Tom said to Scott, 'The dress code is shorts, t-shirt, tennis shoes.' And Scott showed up wearing shorts and an Eric Clapton t-shirt. Tom was like, 'It's my people, my people!' They sat in the basement and listened to Led Zeppelin. Full volume. The floor in my kitchen was like boom, boom, boom."

Scott felt welcomed to his new home in Moscow even though a punch list for University House loomed. "I just decided to roll with it," he said and smiled. Even when his new truck purchase didn't go according to plan, nor did it show up before he arrived, he took it in stride.

"I originally wanted to find an old truck, like a fixer-upper, to have wrapped with the university's colors. But living in New York made that unfeasible, so a Vandal alumnus, Bill Kerns, reached out to Dave Blewett, CEO at Kendall Automotive Group in Meridian, Idaho, to find me a new truck that I could have wrapped. They were very generous leasing me Dave's personal truck."

Scott coordinated with another Vandal, Ed Moore, owner of 116 & West, a Boise advertising firm. Ed and his creatives designed a full-blown wrap for the Ford F-150 pickup, complete with the U of I colors and logos no one could ignore. Bill Kearns generously donated the wrap.

"It was the best branding bang for our buck," Scott shared. "It definitely said, 'The President is in town.' I drove it to Fairfield, Idaho, for a meeting one time, and I saw some folks coming out of buildings to take photos of it. I found out later it was posted on social media and published in the local paper."

Scott paid for the lease out of his pocket and felt it was one of the most successful ways for him to reach out to anyone and everyone interested in the U of I. "It was a conversation starter, for sure," he said. "I've told the U of I's story to so many people simply because they came up to talk to me about the truck. I'll drive the truck anywhere I possibly can to share my stories about Idaho's premiere land-grant institution."

Scott in his Vandal truck.

Scott's Management Insight

Don't sweat the small stuff. Focus on what matters, what will move you toward your goal. The rest will fall into place. The lack of furniture and business clothes makes for a good story, and the Vandal truck was a conversation starter. Social media would blow up whenever someone would post a picture of the truck in some remote part of Idaho. It was a bit like "Where's Waldo." It was priceless exposure for the university and the beginning of taking back the U of I narrative. Find your differentiation, that unique thing that will be written about and followed. Tell your story.

Scott's Third Rail

Lawsuits

We are a country of laws, and the US legal system is constructed to administer justice in accordance with those laws. Having worked at a number of the nation's largest law firms, I have benefited by experiencing the business side of the justice system, and I am grateful for the exposure. One privilege of being a university president is that students, employees, and citizens on the political extremes, both right and left, will sue you. If your university is home to a College of Law, faculty and students eager to push the limits of their education will also sue you.

There are several kinds of lawsuits a president and their general counsel must manage, some mundane and some that put the entire campus at risk. Some of the more mundane include worker's compensation claims and denied tenure for faculty. As long as you have a fair process and strive for just outcomes, it is rare for a university to lose a tenure-denial lawsuit. And worker's compensation claims are usually insured, and the goal should always be a fair and just outcome for an injured employee.

Student claims are a bit tougher. There will be times when a student has been injured by an act that occurs on campus or off campus by another student or employee. When the facts are uncontested, a little empathy can go a long way. Often in such cases, specialist law firms with deep pockets will target the university. As distasteful as it is, it often pays to settle some of these claims early without admitting guilt before legal bills ramp up. The reputational damage is not worth the time and expense of a lengthy trial.

Then there are faculty claims made against the university for taking action to correct performance issues or claims they have been harmed due to their race or religion. It is critical in these circumstances that the university stays true to its processes and intently follows them. I have had to make hard decisions to fire faculty for performance and related behavioral issues, but if shared governance processes were closely followed and the decisions were made based on the facts, such actions can be well defended. While it is possible to negotiate an early settlement in such cases, the emotions of the claimants can often make reasonable discussions difficult. One also wants to be careful not to be known for being unwilling to go to court, thus incentivizing certain law firms to target your university.

The university has had employees on both the right and left of the political spectrum, within a religious and secular range of different races, and requiring accommodation who have all sued the university simultaneously. These suits carry financial risk and can tear at the fabric of the campus. The intersection of freedom of speech versus Title IX (harassment, discrimination) is not well defined yet by the courts, and, at least in our College of Law, there are politically and self-motivated students and faculty suing the university to prove their point of view. The university continues to intercede where necessary to maintain safe access to education for all our students, but we follow our processes closely, with empathy and patience, until the courts provide guidance. We often solicit outside experts to ensure we do the right things to manage our risks. I recommend soliciting second opinions, and where there is a complex Title IX investigation, bringing in outside experts to conduct those investigations. This will further protect the university from accusations of procedural missteps or bias.

Part II

Chapter 7
Broken

"It was a pretty sticky situation Scott was walking into, and there wasn't an easy answer."

—Brian Foisy

The University of Idaho was in a severe financial crisis. Scott had taken immense care to compile as much information as possible from the SBOE and university staff about the numbers during the search process and after he accepted the position. He started on April 11 to immediately root out the problems and prepare a game plan. His worry about the U of I's financial direction drove that decision more than anything; it was entirely possible things would get worse and not better, so why wait to dive in and strive for a solution? Even before he hit Moscow, he had a solid grasp of the extensive budgeting and spending picture.

Once Scott had gained access to all the data, he'd taken a deep dive into the financial black hole to get an accurate picture; he became intimately entrenched for the first time in the U of I's sea of budgets, spending, deficits, and financial models. He'd also discussed the numbers with then-Provost John Wiencek and Vice President, Division of Finance and Administration Brian Foisy. And what he saw raised a feeling of uneasiness in the pit of his stomach.

Scott recalled the day he was in his office in his Long Island home a few months before he left for Moscow. He'd leaned back from his computer, frustrated. He could shut his eyes against the glare of the computer screen but not against the glaring numbers on the spreadsheets. His alma mater was in trouble to the tune of $20 million in the current fiscal year alone.

Once the SBOE selected Scott and announced him as the incoming president, but well before his official start date of July 1, 2019, President Staben had agreed not to make long-lasting decisions without bringing Scott into the mix. Staben also decided to have some hard conversations with the campus community before Scott arrived.

Scott appreciated President Staben's position—he would be relinquishing his office. His willingness to assist Scott during the transition was impressive, especially under the circumstances. Most people on campus held Staben and some in his administration responsible for the budget woes.

"Nobody was making good decisions financially for the institution," he reflected. "Everyone was just kind of looking out for themselves, not just individually, but colleges and departments, as well."

It wasn't just the financial issues Scott investigated during his hiring process. He also inquired about the culture and morale of Vandals; his intuition told him they were somehow linked. His research revealed an institution populated with silos, each college and division working with their heads down, not looking beyond or outward. Without knowing it, that mentality exacerbated the financial issues.

"People needed to stop worrying about their patch and start worrying about the university as a whole," Scott stated. "That was hard to do, especially when they'd been fighting and attacking each other over resources, academics, and business issues for ten years. A lot of baggage existed that the campus had to get over."

Over the past several years, the revolving door with upper administration eroded trust on campus, thus creating a somewhat hostile and wary culture. Top that off with a new president named Scott Green—whom some saw as a wildcard due to his lack of academic background—and the culture on campus became a cauldron mixed with scrutiny, apprehension, and cynicism. Scott had a tough road ahead of him with some faculty, staff, and students.

"Not everyone, mainly faculty, was happy to have Scott as president due to his learning curve," Chief of Staff Brenda Helbling shared.

"It wasn't a universal opinion," Barrie Robison, director of Institute for Bioinformatics and Evolutionary Studies (IBEST) and professor of Biological Sciences, said, "but many of my colleagues had serious reservations about that situation, that he was not an academic."

"Faculty don't have to do what you tell them," Assistant Vice President Kathy Barnard pointed out. "They can tell you to go scratch, and there's not a thing you can do about it. So, it was all about building trust, building relationships, and showing leadership."

"Every president has his or her fans and haters; no president is immune," Brian expressed. "If you had to make those difficult top-level decisions, guaranteed there would be a subset of the population unhappy with you and a subset who loved you. When the Board hired Scott, I think most people thought time would tell. It was a pretty sticky situation Scott was walking into, and there wasn't an easy answer."

"The story to the community was that we were circling the drain and desperate for help," said Toni Broyles, special assistant, strategic initiatives. "Emotion controlled people, especially those who were here a long time. It was like going through the cycles of grief—sadness, shock, denial. People wanted someone to blame. Then there was a movement, thankfully, that we now had a businessperson running the university, which gave people hope. That didn't mean they started liking Scott immediately. The verdict was still out, but at least most people could acknowledge he had the skill set needed to get us up from rock bottom."

Scott knew he needed support from the entire university community because it would take everyone pitching in to fix the financial problems and restore a positive culture among Vandals. He wanted to start out on the right foot, especially with some of his biggest detractors—faculty—who adhered to a long-held tradition of decision-making through "shared governance," a very different environment than corporate America.

"Every university has a culture of shared governance," alumnus Jeff Stoddard shared. "The power with the faculty is to not necessarily move the institution forward but prevent change. All the presidents struggled with it. Presidents don't have a choice; it's built into the system. Resistant faculty could make Scott's life a living hell if they weren't on board with him. One has to commend Scott and his team for working within that culture because I'm sure many were appalled when SBOE hired a non-academic. Scott got them to come around and work to help solve these problems, which is truly remarkable."

"I could appreciate the shared governance convention with faculty at the U of I and higher education as a whole," Scott related. "I was hopeful the U of I's form wasn't where it was shared governance as long as they got their way; otherwise, it was tyranny. We were going to need consensus quickly to fix the finances."

"In times of true exigency, the concept of shared governance can sometimes delay needed action," voiced Brian. "Many of us have only ever known this governance model. We all felt a sense of ownership for the institution, and we all wanted a voice. But if you can't build consensus around the problem and/or the solution, how do you move forward?"

"There was a collaborative aspect to shared governance, a back and forth, and even an appeal process," Provost Torrey Lawrence explained. "Some people thought it slowed everything down. And sometimes it did. But we were better for it."

Torrey held a strong belief that shared governance helped build universities. "I always pointed out institutions across the country that had been around for a long time survived with shared governance. I suspect it also checked risk. As a leadership team, we were more open and accessible than some previous leadership teams. I believed in involving people in making decisions."

Making sure to include everyone at the table for discussion on the business and operations of the university—especially concerning budget cuts—could become complicated if everyone had a seat at the table. If the group was too large, the danger of accomplishing nothing was great, but the shared governance policy needed to remain in play. Everyone deserved a voice, but it wasn't feasible for everyone to attend meetings to vocalize their opinions. Faculty Senate and Staff Council existed to allow that function. Their representatives communicated with the administration, keeping with the shared governance goal.

"Faculty Senate is the branch of shared governance that gives faculty an opportunity to participate in conversations with other branches of shared governance," Barbara Kirchmeier, Faculty Senate chair (2020–21), explained. "It gives faculty an opportunity to understand what is happening across campus from the perspectives of the other branches. Faculty Senate advocates for faculty interests. Senators represent colleges on Senate, and faculty members are appointed to committees to ensure faculty voice in decision-making processes."

Scott felt the way to approach working with faculty and staff was to run the university like a business and higher education hybrid. He took the concept of the traditional President's Cabinet and immediately morphed it into a mixture of Cabinet and a corporate style—"Core"—operations group within his first days as president. The new Core Operations, or Core Ops, group met weekly to review the president's prior and current week activities. It shared operational status in each of the major divisions of the university (Finance and Administration, Advancement, Academics, Research, Marketing and Communications, Strategic Initiatives, Athletics, and Information Technology) for coordination across the divisions.

The Core Ops approach worked for Scott and fit the bill for rapid decision-making. He embraced the group's purpose and function and immediately charged them with communicating the university's activities to those needed to help execute management objectives.

Scott set up other groups as situations arose and reformulated existing groups for better strategizing. Groups established to collaborate with Core Ops as the need arose included (University of Idaho n.d.):

1. **Senior Leadership Council** was broadly representative and met monthly to share information, discuss initiatives, and offer feedback related to the institution's overall mission and vision. Led by the president and the provost, the council informed the strategic plans and decisions of the executive team based on input from the various divisions that made up the university.

2. **Academic Leadership Council** provided a venue for academic leaders university-wide, primarily deans and vice provosts, to discuss, coordinate, and communicate openly and transparently across the academic affairs division. The council developed recommendations and implemented actions to fulfill the university's mission and achieve the goals outlined in the strategic plan.

3. **The University Leadership Forum** convened two to three times per year and was composed of broad leadership representation. The meetings were typically topic-based for information sharing, feedback, and unification of messaging.

"In his first Leadership Forum, Scott talked about his key message that the U of I would start making decisions based on what was best for the university and not the individual," Toni recalled. "He was compassionate but stuck to the message that decisions had to be about the university; too many lives and families were at stake, which was hard for people to hear. There would need to be some sacrifices. Some people got that bucket of cold water in their faces. But everyone took a deep breath, and even though they might not have liked it, agreed that Scott was probably right, and they started working through things."

"People would come to the University Leadership Forums and ask questions cold, with no specific agenda," Special Advisor Chandra Zenner Ford shared. "Scott was so good at that. Those were some of his best days, listening to what people asked and thinking on his feet. He has this great ability to answer a question in just a couple of sentences. He was succinct. People were scared about the financial crisis because jobs could get eliminated, and Scott had to communicate how that would look."

The leadership groups allowed Scott to respect the shared governance tradition but also granted quick turnaround on urgent matters. His expectations for the leadership groups also established a clear communication path between the groups and their constituents (colleges, divisions, departments). He hoped this flow of information would start to address some of the campus cultural issues that had grown over the last several years.

It wasn't clear to Scott how long it took to evolve, but before his start at the U of I, the campus culture at the institution had gone from a reasonably positive environment, albeit nothing was perfect, to an unhealthy atmosphere hanging over the campus. It seemed like a freight train gaining speed, slowly starting with negative headline after headline and administration and leadership turnover, all the while, the financial situation amassing, little by little, until the problem headed toward a potentially disastrous end at an alarming pace.

Kathy Barnard worked for years in communications at the university but left in 2005 for a position eight miles west at Washington State University. Eleven years later, she accepted the position to return to the U of I as the assistant vice president for Alumni Relations and Advancement Communications. What she found was a completely changed atmosphere among Vandals.

"That revolving door with leadership made long-term employees back into their caves because that was the safest place," Kathy surmised. "I was surprised at how siloed everybody had gotten. During my first week back, I called Career Services, introduced myself, and suggested we start meeting to discuss what we do for alumni. The director of cooperative education, John Mangiantini, met with me and said, 'You're the first alumni director to call us in the last decade about how to collaborate.' Everyone had withdrawn. There wasn't any energy for integration or innovation or even just taking care of business *together*. That was kind of disturbing. There seemed to be such a disconnect between the tried-and-true folks who had been there forever. They would do anything for the institution and have over the years, both faculty and staff, but they felt helpless to intervene or help."

"When I became president, there were many people throwing others under the bus," Scott shared. "The culture was just broken, like in the TV series *Game of Thrones*. Everybody wanted to fire everybody else. In my first six months there, nobody on my Core Ops team escaped when one member would throw another member under the bus. And it wasn't always the same people throwing each other under the bus, which was disappointing. People told me to get rid of anybody who had anything to do with the previous administration. If I had listened, there would have been no one to do the work. It was insane. I had never seen anything that broken, even though I had brought several broken operations back from the brink."

The budgetary issues were like salt in a wound, causing already-frayed tempers to flare and fear to take hold. Many took the approach to save themselves first; they knew financial problems usually affected people because budgets were 80 percent people and only 20 percent operations.

"Even financially, the U of I was highly decentralized, which is not uncommon in higher education," Linda Campos, associate vice president for Finance, pointed out. "In some ways, we drove that decentralization by implementing financial systems that allowed colleges and units to process financial and personnel-related tasks."

"The university wanted to think we were a single entity and were all pulling in exactly the same direction with the same goals and vision," Brian said. "We were actually a loosely confederated group of individuals, departments, colleges, divisions, and units that had our own individual goals, desires, metrics, and visions."

Scott knew it would be a treacherous road to recovery if he didn't have cooperation from the entire U of I community to fix both the financial problems and cultural rifts. But for the U of I to move forward and continue achieving its strategic goals, he and his leadership groups had to find the cure to both problems and fast.

Scott's Management Insight

A good CEO sets the rules of the road and leads by example. Direct and open communication is needed to execute and adjust to the changing situation on the ground. The university always comes first. Set the tone from the top. Make sure the team knows that you expect no surprises. Hiding problems is not acceptable. We don't shoot the bearer of bad news; we help them attack the underlying problem by bringing university resources to address the issue.

Not everyone will want to take the journey with you. Take your time to assess the management team. You will get plenty of bad advice to fire individual cabinet members. Again, it's not my practice to walk into an organization, fire everyone at the top, and hire my own people. I believe that people deserve the opportunity to be a part of the team. They will self-select out if they are not on board with the direction or are not comfortable being held accountable to execute. The weekly updates and monthly financial meetings will bare any lack of progress in the light of day. No one likes that and will course-correct, either by seeking the team's help or leaving. Turnover is not always a bad thing.

Establish your Operating Committee as soon as possible; this is the key to quickly executing and working toward your success. It must consist of only those needed to accomplish short-term objectives and communicate present issues that require the help of university resources to address.

I included the provost, VP of Finance and Administration, chief information officer, chief marketing officer, VP for Advancement, VP of Research, athletic director, a senior advisor to the president and her strategic project manager, and the chief of staff/administrator of the President's Office.

While this group sounds like a lot, it does exclude the Office of General Counsel, Title IX, Compliance, ombudsperson, Audit, and the McClure Center for Public Policy, even though they all report to the president. I excluded them not because they aren't crucial to the health and operations of the university; rather, most of their work is confidential and long-term. I meet with all my reports a minimum of every other month and bring them into operational issues when needed.

Along with your team, use the traditional SWOT analysis model (strengths, weaknesses, opportunities, and threats) to identify your weaknesses and threats, but always make building upon your strengths a priority. Where are you strong? How do you differentiate from your competition or sister institutions? How can you cross silos to create opportunities? Answer these questions, communicate the objectives, and invest in those who can and will help you move the needle.

Chapter 8
The Holy Financial Trinity

"I walked into the U of I in the middle of a losing streak of $80 million over three years. . ."

—*Scott Green*

Like any good math problem—simple or complex—a solution existed for the U of I's financial woes. Scott knew he could provide the tools and environment to successfully help the campus community execute that solution.

After repeatedly inspecting and dissecting the spreadsheets for several months, his mind had raced with humble anticipation at tackling the spaghetti-like mass of overspending and underfunding. It might take a great deal of finagling, working, reworking, and sacrifice, but there was a way out of the financial hole. The university would find it because the Vandal tribe finally understood that this wasn't a "kick the can down the road" problem anymore. Too many people had already done that. It was a "we have to fix this now, and I mean right now" crisis.

"I walked into the U of I in the middle of a losing streak of $80 million over three years, $40 million of which were operating losses and $40 million of accounting adjustments, *and* a budget that, if executed as passed, would add to that number in a devastating way," Scott stated.

Faculty and staff sat poised for action, but that required everyone to have a working knowledge of just how the University of Idaho found itself in such a deep financial hole and how to fix it. The easy answer was that spending outpaced revenues, and the easy solution to remedy the deficits had always been the same—increase enrollment to increase tuition revenue to meet the budgets.

"At one point, after looking at the past several years of financial documentation," Scott said, "I sat back and thought, 'How's that strategy working for you? It isn't.' And there were so many layers to how the problems came about it was no wonder it was never an easy fix for any of the previous presidents who didn't possess the financial background I did."

There were dozens of details to finding and fixing the problem, but Scott identified four main issues to address:

1. Enrollment wasn't producing enough tuition revenue to cover the budgets, which the university historically based on unrealistic enrollment figures.
2. The U of I faced operational and unrestricted net position deficits that could not be fully addressed in one year.
3. The university was burning through its cash and using reserve funds and revenues from the sale of investments to cover deficits, which only provided a Band-Aid, but didn't address the core problem.
4. The University employee headcount (FTE, that is, full-time equivalent) was higher than it was during peak enrollment several years prior. Hiring continued while enrollments fell.

Scott knew there hadn't been a plan to immediately address the $20 million loss that he, then-Provost John Wiencek, and Vice President Brian Foisy identified for FY20, let alone a long-term solution to keep the U of I out of a budgetary crisis in the future. He dissected the problems to their core and generated a clear path for everyone to follow toward financial health. He just had to communicate that to leadership in a way to gain complete buy-in.

"Headcount was at a historic high," Scott stressed. "I couldn't find any other reason why expenses were going up other than the cost of people. The institution just lost complete control of the situation."

The university is a service-based organization with 80 percent of state appropriations and tuition revenue (also known as the General Education Fund, or Gen Ed) earmarked for salaries and benefits for personnel. "That expense was bigger than any of our other cost drivers combined," Brian shared. "And if headcount was going up, and your student enrollment, which was the main revenue driver, was going down, we were in trouble."

If student FTEs waned, why didn't employee FTEs on campus also decrease? Fewer students meant fewer employees needed to provide the college experience. See Figure 8.01.

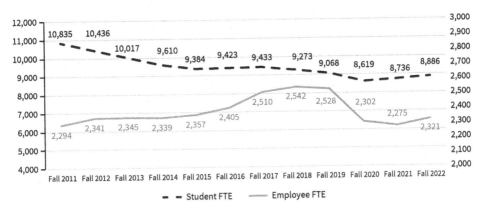

Figure 8.01   Student Full-time Equivalent (FTE) vs. Employee Full-time Equivalent (FTE). Between Fall 2011 and Fall 2019, student enrollment fell 16% while employee FTE grew by 10%.
SOURCE: University of Idaho Division of Finance and Administration. Reproduced with permission from the University of Idaho.

When the recession of 2008–09 hit, the Idaho State Legislature placed holdbacks on all Idaho education, which resulted in staffing cuts. The university started hiring again when the recession faded, and things began to look up.

"I think you saw rebuilding after those years, and I think we just rebuilt too far," Linda Campos, associate vice president for Finance, speculated.

"We couldn't just start cutting people due to contracts and tenure," CALS Dean Michael Parrella pointed out. "To me, it was a real balancing act on how the colleges determined where they would cut. If administration cut all the support staff for all the faculty, then what would be left was a skeletal college that had as many faculty as they had before, but with no support."

Scott discussed his initial findings with Brian, who brought in Linda, along with Kim Salisbury, associate vice president for Budget and Planning, and Trina Mahoney, assistant vice president of University Budget and Planning.

"I call Linda, Kim, and Trina my Holy Financial Trinity," Scott said, smiling.

Historically, the University of Idaho worked under an incremental budget model. The budget office would calculate each college and division's piece of the revenue pie by starting with the number allocated the previous fiscal year, accounting for annual salary increases and cuts from the legislature. Using the previous year's budgetary numbers as the foundation to build the next fiscal year's budget was the standard budgeting method.

"Using the incremental budget model allowed for consistent planning, but not *strategic* planning," Kim pointed out.

Michael shared his thoughts about the incremental budget model. "A couple of weeks after the university hired me in 2016 [as CALS dean], I had a meeting with Provost [John] Wiencek about budgets. I asked, 'Where did the $3 million figure out of the General Education Fund come from for our college?' And he replied, 'I have no idea; it's not based on anything you do. It's all historical.' As soon as he told me that, red flags went up like crazy. I thought, if that was how we were allocating resources, we were going to maintain the status quo and wouldn't be moving forward as a campus."

To generate those incremental allowances year after year, the budget office needed to know how much revenue the U of I would receive from the legislature and enrollment tuition for the upcoming fiscal year. Scott knew digging deep into those revenue sources could reveal the structural fault in the U of I's historical budgeting model. He vowed to locate and fix the problems once and for all.

Scott's Management Insight

You must collect all the data and then use the data to determine what to do. Empathy has a place, but you must calm the fear and hysteria with facts and data. I knew that we had to address the headcount. We had to determine the optimal ratio of students to faculty and utilize every possible opportunity to streamline the workforce to meet budgets. Some faculty argued that we were *not* overstaffed but rather understaffed. The data just did not support that argument. One professor tried to make that argument at a college town hall and provided peer data on a slide. In the end, he made my point for me when I pointed out using his data that the U of I's 14-to-1 student/faculty ratio was lower than the 16-to-1 at our most comparable peers. That does not sound like a big difference, but that is a multi-million-dollar delta.

Other confirming peer data, including the *US News & World Report* rankings, reveals the University of Idaho has one of the highest percentages of classes under 20 students in the country at 65 percent. Of the top-ranked 200 national universities, of which the U of I is one, just a bit over 20 have a higher percentage, primarily those in the Ivy League and similarly situated private universities, not public land-grant universities. The U of I also does better than many Ivy League schools, with only 7 percent of its classes having 50 or more students (*US News & World Report* 2022).

These are strengths to the extent you can afford to maintain them. So the data supported the notion that we were rich with faculty and staff. The real question is how we address this in a way that does not impair the quality of instruction and brings the faculty along with us. The answer was to do whatever we could to voluntarily reduce headcount before taking action to separate those who wanted to stay. So we began with voluntary retirements and separations.

Who can help you move the needle? Identify and elevate them. The Holy Financial Trinity helped create transparency by producing management reports and working with the Deans and VPs to help them understand their numbers. I really believe they were vital to financially saving our institution.

Chapter 9
Show Me the Money

"Know thy numbers."

—Scott Green

The U of I enjoyed several avenues of resources to execute its land-grant mission. In rough numbers, the Idaho State Legislature funded approximately 25 percent of the university's overall budget through appropriations, and student tuition and fee revenue filled in another 25 percent.

"We looked at financial needs, as well as goals around access and affordability and other factors to develop our annual tuition and fee rate proposal, which we sent to the SBOE each April," Trina Mahoney, assistant vice president for University Budget and Planning, explained.

Appropriations from the legislature and tuition revenue are combined to make up the General Education Fund. "Gen Ed includes the funding we receive from the state that in turn is funded by taxes," Trina continued. "We can receive less than what was appropriated due to holdbacks/rescissions/reversions (all mean 'budget cut'). We can receive more than what was appropriated due to additional state general funds passed to us by the State Board of Education. These are mainly related to the Higher Education Research Council (HERC), but also if the Board ends the year with a balance in their appropriation, they give that balance out to each of the institutions."

Those funds were mostly unrestricted, with the understanding that each college or division would use a portion to cover staff and faculty salary commitments. "Gen Ed funds for FY20 totaled $178.5 million, which included $73 million in tuition and $105.4 million in state funding," Trina shared.

"You can use unrestricted monies for anything," Scott lined out. "That was key because we could use that money if a downturn occurred. It could serve as a safety net. We could fill in the gaps with unrestricted funds."

Other sources of income that made up the remaining 50 percent of annual revenue included federal and state research grants, contracts, bonds, gifts, and Foundation endowments. Those dollars were restricted—only used for the specific purpose outlined with the receipt of funds. For example, the Foundation funded scholarships, contracts funded specific projects, and grants funded research. If the university didn't spend restricted funds on their intended use, it couldn't use them for anything else; the university would technically have to return those funds to the source. Scott knew that, given how the U of I managed its restricted funds, they weren't the problem. The General Education Funds would tell the story of how the university landed in the red for three years and sat poised to head there again.

"The complete annual budgeting cycle is more like eighteen months," Vice President Brian Foisy explained. "You see everything from building the budget in March and April for the next fiscal year, to completing the current fiscal year in June, to reporting the financial statements with the official accounting of all the revenues and expenses generated during the fiscal year by October of the following fiscal year. So even when a new FY began, we wouldn't finalize the previous FY for another two to three months."

Traditionally, the budget office accounted for all the possible revenue for any given fiscal year and then began building the budget. Again, the starting point was the previous fiscal year's allotment with salary increases or holdbacks from the legislature in the form of one-time or permanent cuts. Restricted funds went to their appropriate college or division for use on the specified initiative, leaving General Education Funds for consideration.

"We built the budget based on current year enrollments (including enrollment mix) and the tuition rates that had already been approved by the SBOE," Trina explained.

Once the U of I completed its budget, SBOE analyzed and eventually approved it.

"It's April when they pass our final budget. Then we know that on July 1, when our fiscal year starts, the legislature will allocate to us that specific amount of money," Kim Salisbury, associate vice president for Budget and Planning, explained. However, the tuition portion of the General Education budget wasn't an exact figure at the beginning of the fiscal year. "We didn't exactly know what we would get from the students until September after Tenth Day, which was the tenth day of class into the semester.

After the tenth day of classes, with few exceptions, students didn't get a full refund if they dropped a class."

"After Tenth Day, we'd see how net tuition revenue looked and made estimates for spring to arrive at an estimated total net tuition revenue in comparison with the budget," Trina outlined.

Once Tenth Day figures were calculated, the fiscal officers would share them with leadership to decide whether to cover any shortfalls using central reserve funds or via a university-wide budget cut. "This was a viable solution if we thought this was a one- or two-year issue," Trina added. "Why cut the permanent budget based on a short-term issue?"

Once leadership took all the numbers into account, the fiscal officers would lock in the fall budget four months into the current fiscal year, leaving approximately eight months in the fiscal year to meet the already-approved budgets.

"We would then make predictions for spring tuition revenue based on the fall numbers," Kim explained. "So by the time Tenth Day happened in January for the spring semester, we knew our exact tuition number. We then would 'true up' the budgets about the middle of the spring semester for the current fiscal year to know if we'd met our budget."

By that time, the fiscal year was well underway. There was no mechanism to adjust the budgets allocated to colleges and units to bring expenditures in line with revenue.

"The core of the problem occurred over many years," Associate Vice President Linda Campos asserted. "I wasn't here until 2016, but it seemed that, as an institution, the U of I didn't stop to address if they received less revenue because we didn't meet enrollment projections. It seemed like that wasn't acknowledged. The budgets were allocated, and everyone made spending plans. So unless someone explained to campus that we didn't get enough revenue to support the allocated budgets and was willing to adjust those budgets mid-year, we would end the fiscal year with a gap or deficit, which had to be covered by someone."

"There's a very strong and predictable ecology at universities, essentially a financial fingerprint," Brian pointed out. "The fingerprint reveals the trends and patterns that are unique to each institution—things like community interaction, student demographics, and politics. All of those variables factor into how students interact with the university." However, for the fingerprint to serve its purpose, the university had to acknowledge it, even if it didn't reveal a rosy picture or path.

"We usually assumed flat enrollment, which, while conservative in the eyes of many, didn't pan out for us as enrollments actually declined," Trina explained. "This was where I think we fell down time and time again. We weren't *wildly* optimistic; we didn't think we were suddenly going to go from shrinking to growing. We just believed each year that the next year we would stabilize, so if we budgeted flat, we would be okay, so we opted to use central reserves year after year."

For years, the university forecast more enrollment tuition than it received and then tried to curb spending at the last minute or cover the shortfalls with central reserve funds to slide in at the end of the fiscal year, barely meeting the budget. Those decisions based on optimism—albeit conservative optimism—rather than the reality of the fingerprint sent the U of I careening toward financial emergency and potential insolvency.

Scott's Management Insight

Know thy numbers. It is job #1 for any CEO or president. Enrollment is the lifeblood of all public institutions of higher learning. State legislatures subsidize public universities to make education more accessible and to turbo-charge their economies by providing an educated workforce. Any financial model must accommodate the ebbs and flows of enrollments and appropriations. An incremental approach to financing education does not flex if enrollments and appropriations both fall short. With state appropriations falling as a percentage of state budgets and an enrollment cliff looming, management needs uncommon discipline in such a system to respond quickly to reduce headcount because people costs are 80 percent of most institutions' costs base. Even with that discipline, there will likely be dislocations within each institution due to tenure and related job protections. You simply may not be able to cut where the cuts are needed. We recognized we needed a model that fit the U of I's unique financial fingerprint. The incremental model was not working. By intimately understanding our numbers, we were able to create a better financial model, one explicitly suited for our institution.

Understand your revenue drivers and focus like a laser on growing them. Enrollment, state appropriations, state, local, and private grants and aid, and gifts are the primary revenue streams for a land-grant university. Develop plans to grow them all sustainably. Cutting costs and investing in your revenue drivers are crucial even in difficult times. At the U of I, I explained why that is important, which may be true of many other campuses. The focus is usually only on the cost side of the equation, but increased revenues can help reduce the budget cuts needed. However, increased enrollments, additional scholarships, and more significant research revenues don't just appear; it takes investment in advancement (fundraisers), strategic enrollment management and marketing (enrollments), and grant writing (research).

Finally, ensure the revenue is in the door before you budget and spend it.

Chapter 10
Students Are Everything

"Our competitors were just trouncing on us."

—*Dr. Dean Kahler*

Enrollment drives everything at the U of I. In theory, if numbers went down, tuition revenue went down, and if employee headcount didn't also go down, enrollment became the budgeting problem. But when enrollment increased, tuition receipts increased (in theory), and enrollment became the budgeting solution. However, it wasn't that simple.

In 2016, President Staben had set in motion specific steps to focus on that arm of the university by centralizing enrollment management and naming it Strategic Enrollment Management (SEM). The division encompassed University Advising Services, Academic Support Programs, Admissions, Career Services, Financial Aid, International Programs, Military and Veteran Services, New Student Orientation, the Registrar, and ROTC.

Dr. Dean Kahler arrived at the U of I as the new vice provost for SEM in October 2016 with the directive to spearhead recruitment, enrollment, and retention, along with the marketing for all the functions under SEM to increase enrollment and tuition dollars.

One could argue that the president's office wasn't the only place at the U of I that had seen its share of steppingstone mentality. Enrollment had its own "churn at the top." That instability led to a fractured system to bring in new students and keep existing ones coming back.

"There had been six enrollment managers in the five years prior to me arriving," Dean pointed out. "The U of I had gone through a revolving door on enrollment managers. There was a lot of hard work here to try and bring everybody together onto one page. I just wanted to help students try to gain access to higher education. The focus on student success was very strong here, but enrollment had declined since 2012. I knew there were deeper problems than just declining enrollment."

"The SEM consolidation didn't turn the tide, unfortunately," Scott shared. Enrollments continued to stay flat. And the student mix wasn't optimal, either.

As much as the U of I loved its Vandals and saw them as unique individuals hungry to learn, the cold truth needed acknowledgment. When students registered to take classes at the U of I, they came in with a bill to pay for their education. The university assigned each student a dollar amount. Their student type or classification determined their amount due. There were several student classifications with a revenue value assigned to each, including in-state undergraduate, WUE (Western Undergraduate Exchange)/WICHE (Western Interstate Commission for Higher Education), out-of-state undergraduate (includes international undergraduate students), in-state graduate, out-of-state graduate (includes international graduate students), law, and dual credit (high school students taking classes for college credit). See Figure 10.1.

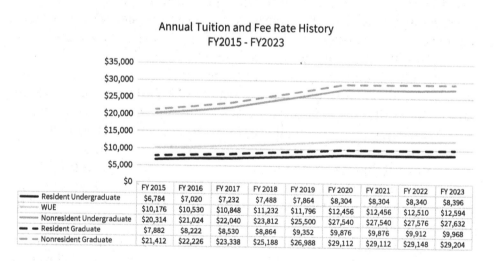

Annual Tuition and Fee Rate History
FY2015 - FY2023

	FY 2015	FY 2016	FY 2017	FY 2018	FY 2019	FY 2020	FY 2021	FY 2022	FY 2023
Resident Undergraduate	$6,784	$7,020	$7,232	$7,488	$7,864	$8,304	$8,304	$8,340	$8,396
WUE	$10,176	$10,530	$10,848	$11,232	$11,796	$12,456	$12,456	$12,510	$12,594
Nonresident Undergraduate	$20,314	$21,024	$22,040	$23,812	$25,500	$27,540	$27,540	$27,576	$27,632
Resident Graduate	$7,882	$8,222	$8,530	$8,864	$9,352	$9,876	$9,876	$9,912	$9,968
Nonresident Graduate	$21,412	$22,226	$23,338	$25,188	$26,988	$29,112	$29,112	$29,148	$29,204

Figure 10.01 Annual Tuition and Fee Rate History.

SOURCE: University of Idaho Division of Finance and Administration. Reproduced with permission of University of Idaho.

The key to successful budgeting was to not just look at the number of students enrolled but to drill it down to the type of student because the type of student made all the difference to the bottom line.

That certainly didn't mean the U of I didn't want a mix of all types of students; it just meant the U of I had to consider factors that impacted revenue and not just the enrollment number. For example, increasing high school dual credit students increased enrollment but did not add much to the revenue pot since they paid $75 per credit hour, a fraction of what full-time students paid. The uncertainty of the mix of students until after Tenth Day made creating a budget tricky.

"Dual credit high school students taking college-level courses were key to our long-term enrollment strategy," Vice President Brian Foisy pointed out. "The U of I reported increased enrollment because of more dual credit students, but the overall revenue wasn't affected. As much as we wanted them at the U of I, they added zero to tuition revenues from a budgeting standpoint. But we still welcomed them because we wanted them to go on to the U of I when they went to college."

Another classification of students involved the Western Interstate Commission for Higher Education, or WICHE. For years students took advantage of an offering called WUE (Western Undergraduate Exchange), a tuition reduction program administered by WICHE. WUE allowed out-of-state students to receive a significant tuition discount (paying 150% of the in-state tuition rate) compared to a regular out-of-state tuition rate. That value for the student could add up to tens of thousands of dollars over four years. Since it wasn't a need-based tuition program, many students took advantage of the more affordable education option (University of Idaho n.d.).

WUE awards were renewable for up to four years for first-year recipients with a minimum U of I GPA. The award was renewable for up to three additional years for transfer students depending on the number of transfer credits and with a minimum U of I GPA. WICHE states included Alaska, Arizona, California, Colorado, Guam, Hawaii, Idaho, Montana, Nevada, New Mexico, North Dakota, Oregon, South Dakota, Utah, Washington, Wyoming, and the Commonwealth of the Northern Mariana Islands.

To apply to WUE, a student residing in a participating state had to complete the application to attend the U of I. That was it; there was no additional paperwork. The U of I welcomed these students partly because they paid more than an in-state student.

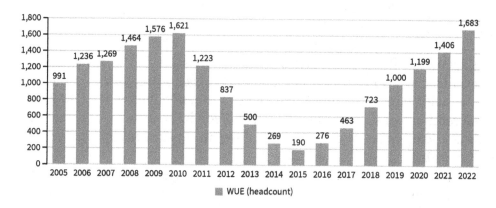

Figure 10.02   WUE Student Headcount 2005–2021.
SOURCE: University of Idaho Division of Finance and Administration. Reproduced with permission of University of Idaho.

"Around 2010, leadership decided to decrease the number of WUE students the U of I accepted," Dean explained. "That was before I came to the U of I, but I believe the thought process behind the decision was that WUE students decreased the U of I's revenue because of the reduced rates. If they weren't WUE students, the U of I would make more money because they wouldn't get the WUE discounted rate. But when the U of I didn't accept as many WUE students, the demand decreased because the price tag increased. By 2015, the U of I only had 190 WUE students. I was here four months when my boss asked me to explore opening WUE back up." See Figure 10.02.

The U of I reworked its plan and saw an immediate increase of WUE students in 2016 to 276, which remained a continuing trend. By 2021, the U of I's WUE student count had hit 1406.

Scott agreed the numbers showed the decision to reduce WUE did not result in more margin for the university as hoped; it resulted in fewer students and less revenue, as basic economic theory would predict.

On top of all those factors, the State of Idaho's "go-on," or matriculation, rate was also declining. The go-on rate was the number of high school graduates in Idaho who went on to get a postsecondary education. By 2015, it sat at around 47 percent (University of Idaho n.d.). That meant 47 percent (less than half) of Idaho high school graduates attended the U of I or another institution of higher learning. Many factors played into that number going down, but if the U of I couldn't attract more in-state high school graduates, how could they expect to draw them from other places?

"If the go-on rate was U of I's problem, the solution was to go explain to students why they should go on," Scott stated. "Before I became president, the U of I wasn't marketing to high school students in a way that they would want to engage with the university. The university was still doing old-line marketing, like sending out hard copies or emails. The world was now digital and mobile, so students wanted video, and they wanted it on their phones. Marketing was just so broken, from how they utilized purchased student lists to the tools they and the university used for direct marketing. Search engine optimization (SEO) was not even in the lexicon of either Marketing or SEM. I had a lot of CMOs work for me over the years. I knew what it was supposed to look like, and that wasn't what the U of I had."

"We overwhelmingly were missing students left and right," Dean expressed. "We did not have a robust enrollment marketing campaign. Our competitors were just trouncing on us. When I came on board, for probably the first couple of years, I heard over and over again from alumni and parents that we hadn't been communicating with their students. And that's probably very accurate."

Scott also recognized another hit to the university's overall success tied directly to Alaska Airlines cutting the direct flight between Boise, the U of I's largest market, and the Pullman-Moscow Regional Airport.

"So we had increased competition from in-state institutions, a declining in-state go-on rate, were turning away out-of-state students who did not pay full out-of-state tuition (despite high numbers), had a broken and outdated marketing function, and had lost air service to our largest market," Scott outlined. "Is it any wonder that enrollments declined? Students are everything to the health of a university."

Scott's Management Insight

When I arrived on campus, our entire marketing budget was spent on employees. We had no money to actually market to our students. I spent my first few months raising money from alumni to invest in marketing.

Who is your customer, and how can you best reach them? For 18-year-olds, it's a text, video, or gif on their phone. Email is so yesterday. Your marketing and communications departments should always stay current on the latest trends for your intended audience and employ staff capable of pivoting as those trends change. We found texts, videos, and gifs delivered on their phone and utilizing tools such as Instagram, Snapchat, and TikTok hit our target market at a low cost.

Participate in programs that benefit your customers, clients, or students. If they see value and come to you for service or education, your overall ROI will increase, even if they're coming in at a discount, because you'll attract more with a lower price tag. This was the case for our WUE students. The lower price tag still produces a greater margin than resident tuition, so these out-of-state students subsidize the in-state students.

Dig deeper than first-layer data. Again, know thy numbers. Just because your enrollment numbers are up doesn't mean the revenue tied to those numbers is up. Be knowledgeable if increases or decreases in your data truly mean increases in revenues (or expenses). Dual credit looks good from an enrollment perspective but does not immediately add to the institution's bottom line. It is a worthy investment for those students in your pipeline, but including the numbers in your enrollment reports may mask underlying issues. In our case, it looked like enrollment was meeting expectations when in reality, the number of students showing up on campus was decreasing.

Smart Collaboration

Alaska Air Service to Moscow, Idaho

The Moscow region lost air service to its most important market (Boise and the Treasure Valley) around 2010, and the U of I witnessed enrollments steadily decline. The road from Boise was long and dangerous, and the Idaho State Legislature continued to do little about it. Scott decided to see if he could bring the service back to the Pullman-Moscow Regional Airport.

Ann Nelson, a U of I alumna and retired KPMG audit partner for Alaska Airlines, arranged a meeting between Scott and the senior executives responsible for evaluating markets and flight routes. He then visited Alaska Airlines and negotiated an agreement to reestablish flight service between Boise and the airport, only a few miles from the U of I. The agreement guaranteed Alaska a 10 percent margin on the route up to $500,000 annually for up to three years. WSU agreed to take $100,000 of the risk because it would benefit from the opportunity for its students, too. "Worst-case scenario, I only needed an additional forty students to come to the U of I to break even on the

Joe Vandal celebrates the return of Alaska Air flights between Moscow and Boise.
SOURCE: Reproduced with permission of C. Scott Green (Book Author).

agreement," Scott analyzed. "I don't believe it was a coincidence that after we announced the flight, we had the largest incoming class in years. This endeavor gave potential and existing stakeholders better access to the Moscow and Pullman campuses."

"The Treasure Valley and Magic Valley areas in Idaho have exploded in growth," Don Burnett, former dean of the College of Law, pointed out. "We had to make ourselves relevant to all these areas moving faster, even if it included subsidizing an airline route directly between Moscow and Boise in order to facilitate movement back and forth. I was in favor of that. Scott and his team were on the right track with regard to emphasizing enrollment."

"That agreement equates to a $1.2 million central reserve funds commitment over three years," Vice President for Division of Finance and Administration Brian Foisy outlined. "But Scott made that commitment. Scott thought there would be a high ROI. We think it will

(Continued)

(Continued)

increase our enrollment, and the U of I will be better as a result of this decision."

"The cool part about the Alaska Airlines victory was that it took an accomplished U of I Vandal accounting graduate, Ann Nelson, to set the stage for Scott Green to meet face-to-face with the decision-makers at Alaska Air," said Chandra Zenner Ford, CEO SW Idaho and special advisor. "This direct flight makes it easier for parents and students to visit campus and travel home for holidays, not to mention it's so much easier for President Green and other UI employees to get to Boise more economically."

Scott's Management Insight

Enrollment is the lifeblood of a destination campus, and it is imperative that institutions have access to their largest markets. Identify the most important market and determine how to best take a share. Be bold and take calculated risks based on data if there is potential for solid ROI. Stay particularly aware of the in-state audience. If in-state enrollments are not meeting expectations, know the why behind that and adapt to attract them. In our case, our story was not reaching our target market, and we had geographic challenges. Refining our story, becoming more competitive financially, and addressing logistics would increase our market share. We had been bussing potential students to see the Moscow campus, and that program was reasonably successful with high yield rates. But without direct air service to and from our largest market in Southwest Idaho, we were losing students and their parents who wanted to easily visit their children on campus and have their student visit home, as well. In addition, our students in Eastern Idaho were much closer to Utah State University than the U of I, so we had to make getting to the Moscow campus easier. Negotiating the return of air service to and from Boise may be the most important move I made as president. After making that agreement, our freshman enrollment increased by over 30 percent in just two years.

Chapter 11
Aliens on Campus

"Growth covers all sins."

—Scott Green

Central Reserve Funds (or Central) serves as the revenue source for fixed costs at the university, including building maintenance, bond fund interest, utilities, and the benefits for all employees paid through the General Education Funds. Central also housed revenue for special initiatives that didn't fall under a specific college or unit. Central funds were a combination of tuition and other revenues to cover facility, administrative, and general costs, making it a cost center.

"Central was the 'folks on the hill,'" Linda Campos, associate vice president for Finance, indicated. "Whenever a shortfall arose, or a special project came up, it was common for the campus units or colleges to indicate that 'they' could help pay for it, meaning the administration would handle it using central reserve funds. The offices of the president and Division of Finance and Administration were located in the Administration Building, which was 'on the hill' near the center of campus."

"We kept the list of Central commitments at Finance and Administration," Brian Foisy, vice president for Division of Finance and Administration, shared. "It was always a long and disconcerting spreadsheet."

"We had to fund all the Central obligations, regardless of whether we had the money in Central to cover them," Linda said. "It was 2017 when I first heard Brian mention that we had a Central problem and needed a proposal to fix it. That was what started those conversations."

Ultimately, presidents determined Central money spending beyond existing commitments, and administration of the funds lived with the budget office. But Scott knew that after the administration finalized budgets and the accountants determined the final number to allocate to the colleges and units, the story involving the monies left over to fund Central was just beginning.

Upon receipt of their portion of the Gen Ed funds, each college and division then established their budget. They would allocate money for their annual salaries, operational expenses, and special projects specific to their area. Many of the colleges and divisions had a finance officer and staff who managed their funds with the dean's or VP's supervision. Finance and Administration oversaw the institution's planning, budgeting, and spending.

Scott had never been a micromanager and certainly wasn't going to start now with the various fiscal officers, but micromanaging and leading were two different exercises. "I had to give people some room to make decisions," Scott said. "I managed by objectives, an old concept. If people hit the objective, I would leave them alone. I also managed by talking to people to understand what was going on. Triangulation was important."

He had to walk the fine line of assisting in the overall deficit fix and showing all the colleges and divisions how to prevent it from happening again. He'd read the detailed reports dozens of times, taking in each spreadsheet, each number, and certain things struck him regarding Central.

Most importantly, no mechanism existed to hold back more than what was necessary for Central's commitments, nor did a revenue source exist that consistently allocated funds to Central to meet those obligations or any additions inevitably added to the list. Remember, Central was also where colleges and divisions turned if they ran a deficit they couldn't cover with their own allocated funds.

"I remember saying, 'Our institutional financing strategy for Central is luck,'" Brian said and shook his head. "That was our strategy. Luck. Please, let us have a warm winter so that our utility bills are low, and we have some money left over in Central."

There wasn't a policy stating that the colleges and divisions had to give back any leftover money at the end of the fiscal year to help cover any Central costs, either. Colleges and divisions would carry over those unused General Education Funds or reserve, which would make them unrestricted for the college or division to use however they wished. Over time, those reserve funds became like a savings account for the colleges and divisions; many used those reserve funds for special projects within their specific area or to cover overspending their original allocated funds. But this practice was considered cost-shifting rather than cost-cutting.

"Colleges and divisions had other fund sources for cost-shifting," Linda said. "Many had 'local service funds,' which were also unrestricted and often carried a fund balance from a prior year. But spending down these fund balances contributed to the unrestricted net position problem."

But that method of moving or "shifting" money from an unrestricted fund source never addressed the root of the problem—overspending. If a college or unit overspent one of its funds, it could use unrestricted funds to cover it rather than cutting the fund to align with the budget. And that overspending added to the university's overall expenditure list, even if unrestricted "saved" money covered it. That cost-shifting model would eventually land the U of I in hot water with SBOE when they inspected the university's unrestricted net position.

Another flaw with the financial model was that colleges and units received their next fiscal year's funds based on the previous FY allocation, not on the money they actually spent or "saved" as reserve funds. So those accounts grew in some colleges while Central funds diminished to cover overspending in others.

"I remember [then] Provost Wiencek saying once that there was $25 million out in the colleges," Dean Shauna Corry, College of Art and Architecture, said. "I certainly didn't have it in my college, but others did."

"So instead of a real budget cut, we were just spending a different color of money," said Dan Ewart, vice president of Information Technology (IT) and chief information officer. "We weren't addressing the root of the problem. Eventually, Central began to run short of money."

"At one point, the College of Education, Health, and Human Services (CEHHS) grew their reserve funds when the number of programs they were offering kept going down, along with their enrollment," Scott expressed. "Because the U of I strictly used the incremental budget model, the budget office was not authorized to change the amount CEHHS (or any other college) received each FY, regardless of the college's decreased enrollment. CEHHS just kept building their cash cushion. Meanwhile, the College of Engineering was growing but was cash-starved because they weren't getting more money at the beginning of each fiscal year to make up for their increased enrollment."

As long as tuition revenue stayed up, the flaws in the financial policy didn't reveal themselves. But when enrollment started to falter, and the money allocated to the colleges and divisions didn't materialize after Tenth Day, deficits ensued for some, and those colleges and units asked for central reserve funds to help balance their budget, even if they had carryover funds in some cases.

Scott grinned. "As long as the U of I grew, it could—and did—have the worst financial model in the world, and they were still doing okay."

Eventually, dipping into Central to make up shortfalls and not having any means to replenish the account caught up with the university. "And rather than correcting the deficits in colleges and units and keep Central funded, they chose to sell investments and burned through cash," Scott explained. "That could have been fine if enrollment tuition had stayed up, there were no cuts from the legislature, and there were unlimited investments to liquidate. But really, it wasn't fine. None of that was fine."

"It was like the aliens invaded and took over the institution and decided that we didn't need reserves; we would just spend them all down," Kathy Barnard, assistant vice president for Alumni Relations and Advancement Communications, commented. "Now, if I did that in my home finances, I'd be bankrupt, and the U of I almost was. We almost reached that point. And the credibility of the upper administration suffered so much because of that before Scott came."

"The whole issue with Central and covering deficits was gradual," Linda pointed out. "It wasn't anything drastic; it was just a little pinch here and there; pinch, pinch, *punch*. It added up."

"It was an unsustainable financial policy," Scott stated. "The U of I couldn't keep absorbing hits and spending cash and expect to stay solvent."

"No one acted in an intentionally malicious manner to harm the institution," Brian commented. "But we were circling the drain. In an effort to help people understand what was happening, we instituted a series of annual financial updates and other meetings for the larger leadership team at the university. But despite the information campaign, the financial full-court press just never seemed to materialize."

Scott's Management Insight

Don't keep doing what is not working. Insanity is doing the same thing over and over, expecting a different outcome. Pivot and create a new model. By some measures, we were 18 months away from running out of cash, and nobody seemed to have any idea how to fix it. Financial exigency became a real possibility. We knew the source of the problem and levers to correct our course. We now needed a mechanism to fix our short-term crisis and a vehicle to address a more sustainable long-term model to "stop the insanity." The first step is to stop the bleeding. In our case it was too many employees and too much discretionary spending. So we put in spending targets for each college and department to hit and began developing a program to reduce headcount.

Chapter 12
Right Size

"That was like throwing a hand grenade into the room. . ."
—*Dr. Torrey Lawrence*

Scott's Financial Holy Trinity—Linda Campos, Kim Salisbury, and Trina Mahoney—offered him a comprehensive look at how the U of I attempted to stave off the financial crisis before him becoming president. The massive hole didn't result because the university wasn't trying to cut budgets and curb spending. The lack of an administration willing to make the hard decisions to put all the pieces together literally cost the U of I.

"I felt pretty good about our data starting FY10 when I came to the Budget Office, but things started to get shaky going back further than that," Trina articulated. "We made a lot of changes to how we tracked budget changes when I came into my current role to improve tracking, but before that, it gets tough to verify."

"Before FY16, there wasn't a lot of reporting back after the budget allocations were made for a fiscal year unless a college or unit was in a deficit in their Gen Ed funding," Kim explained.

"We did monitor budgets and spending," Linda remembered. "I started working at the U of I in 2016, but it took a while for me to see some things weren't mapping out. I kept notes from meetings and noticed the first mention of a budget problem was in 2016 from [then] Provost Wiencek."

"During FY17, the academic side of the university started analyzing all monetary requests that came into the Provost's Office," Kim reported. "We identified funding sources, such as vacant positions, gift funding, and revenue generated funding that the college or unit could use to address their budgetary problems rather than granting additional funding from the Provost or Central."

The U of I also performed a round of Program Prioritization (PP) during the 2015–2016 academic year. SBOE mandated that all the state institutions perform PP every five years "to critically review their academic programs and non-academic support functions, building a culture of continuous improvement and internal reallocation to meet the institution's highest goals and objectives instead of reliance on new monies from the State of Idaho" (Idaho State Board of Education 2021). The U of I had implemented PP more than every five years to help cut budgets and spending.

Matt Freeman, SBOE executive director, explained the history behind using PP. "In 2013, during Governor [Butch] Otter's administration, he required and implemented the zero-based budgeting initiative for all state agencies and institutions. It wasn't a model that fit for higher education, however. So SBOE approved Program Prioritization. Once every five years, the universities would go through and review all their academic programs and rank them in quintiles based on several metrics, like degree production and number of students. That helped focus some of our institutions on the high demand, high ROI academic programs, and other programs that needed to be phased out. University of Idaho was not able to leverage this initiative as well as they could have, however, because of the turnover in administration."

Each state institution examined its programs based on criteria such as external demand, quality of outcomes, costs, and other expenses. The U of I established the Institutional Planning and Effectiveness Committee (IPEC) to oversee the PP process, ensuring the results enabled the U of I to meet SBOE's requirements and achieve its goals—including balancing the budget by cutting any low ROI programs or programs not meeting the U of I's mission.

"There were six metrics we used to measure each college," Kim explained. "We divided the departments into different types, like academic, centrally provided services, or student services, to ensure academic departments weren't compared to student service departments or facilities management departments. Every department had to prepare a narrative about how their strategic plan contributed to the university's strategic plan."

IPEC recommended budget reallocations among academic and non-academic units to help fill budget gaps or deficits. "The 2015–2016 PP marked the first time we used metrics to inform our budget reallocations or reductions rather than just giving out our usual across-the-board allocations," Kim recalled.

Because of the quintile system, programs could land anywhere in the rankings for continued investment, continued investment with improvements, or closure. No one wanted to land in the fifth quintile, which resulted in a struggling department in the spotlight to justify why it shouldn't close.

"One of the times we did PP, we published a ranked list of academic programs," Provost Torrey Lawrence recalled. "That was like throwing a hand grenade into the room because whoever was on top was excited, but everyone else hated them. We had enough competition in the university with resources and space; we didn't need to add this element. But PP can be a healthy process; it isn't just about finances. It really made us look at our programming."

"Everybody agreed to the process," former Provost John Wiencek stated. "They liked it because it tied to the strategic plan. But what I found was that whenever we ranked people and programs, the bottom half of the ranking were loud and complained. But a big surprise to me was that the top half said nothing. They weren't even in the room because they didn't want to be there and get beat up by the bottom half. There was sort of a bitterness lingering in the air."

"Cutting programs can really tear at the fabric of the place," Scott pointed out. "PP was emotional and hard for the institution to implement because they didn't get much bang for their buck."

Even with cost-cutting measures such as PP, the university still faced budget woes. In the Fall of 2017, Vice President Brian Foisy and then-President Staben decided to use the President's Leadership Breakfasts to communicate their growing concerns about the financial situation. Maybe if they raised the red flag, the colleges and units would consider that when spending during the current fiscal year and setting the FY18 budget.

The breakfast meetings included anyone with leadership responsibility, such as the president, provost, vice presidents, vice provosts, associate vice presidents, department chairs, deans, and associate deans. "We were in the room with one hundred twenty people, plus people from our Centers in Boise, Idaho Falls, and Coeur d'Alene participating remotely via video-conferencing," Brian shared.

"I set up a structure to those breakfast meetings to kick off each year with a sort of mini-retreat and talked about what we would focus on within the strategic plan," John shared. "The breakfasts weren't just finance meetings, but we'd heard a lot of grumbling about the finances, so we just decided to do it that way each year thereafter."

"Fall was a good time to do meetings with campus leadership because we knew the fall revenue number," Brian continued. "And because we understood the financial fingerprint of the university, and we knew fall tuition because it was after Tenth Day, we could forecast spring tuition and estimate the total tuition for the year." That allowed Brian and his team to share actual numbers for projected shortfalls.

Fall Semester 2011 10th Day – Fall Semester 2022 10th Day
Full-time Equivalent (FTE) Student Enrollment
Fall 2011 – 10,835
Fall 2012 – 10,436
Fall 2013 – 10,017
Fall 2014 – 9,610
Fall 2015 – 9,384
Fall 2016 – 9,423
Fall 2017 – 9,433
Fall 2018 – 9,273

Source: Adapted from University of Idaho Division of Finance and Administration.

"At the first breakfast, we asked everyone to look at what happened to our enrollment over the last decade," Brian shared. "By saying the last decade, we immediately clarified this wasn't simply the current president's fault because Staben hadn't been at the U of I for a decade. We identified that the U of I had a structural deficit issue. We didn't shift the focus to the Central reserve problem until the 2018 breakfast."

In other words, the structural problems with the financial model were not a secret—Scott wasn't the first person to point out the reasons behind the deficit difficulties. A committee was actively working on a new budget model that would place Central first in line to receive funding to cover institution-wide commitments (utilities, debt service, central computing, etc.) with a small reserve.

"People had a lot of time and effort invested in building a new financial model, but by that point, there was enough reputational damage done from myriad factors that trust was at an all-time low," Brian offered.

The breakfast presentations were succinct and to the point, but Brian and his team purposefully encouraged everyone to remain calm, that the sky was not falling.

"Brian explained that something needed to change, either with reduced spending or increasing revenue," Linda explained.

"People appreciated we made an effort to share information," John said. "But they were appropriately confused at times because it was a fluid situation. People were frustrated with the ever-changing story that we were getting about whether we were up or down in terms of various reserve balances and whatnot."

"We were coming through those broken processes that just weren't sustainable," College of Natural Resources Dean Dennis Becker remarked. "The degree to which it wasn't sustainable was not known, certainly not by me. I didn't believe other deans knew it, either. We had campus conversations, but they were conversations that we were living a little bit outside our means, and we needed to pull back a little bit."

Fall 2017 also ushered in two newly branded priorities by the University Budget and Finance Committee (UBFC). For the U of I to remain competitive, UBFC recommended increasing Teaching Assistant (TA) packages and investing more in faculty and staff salaries to improve that competitiveness, known as market-based compensation. PP identified $2 million in funding for priorities to couple with an additional $2 million in *anticipated* new tuition revenue to hit the $4 million target for the increased compensation (University of Idaho n.d.).

In theory, increasing the TA packages would increase graduate student enrollment starting the following fall semester, thus increasing enrollment tuition. Raising salaries would entice qualified jobseekers to look more closely at the U of I, improving the institution's quality of service.

"The U of I generally underpaid people; there was no question about it," Scott acknowledged. "People wanted to live in the Moscow area and raise their families, so they accepted the lower compensation as a pay-off for living in the Palouse area. But putting market-based compensation into place at the same time enrollments were falling just exacerbated the budget situation, particularly as state appropriations and tuition revenue were in decline."

Market-based compensation wasn't new to the U of I. Using market pay data to set pay levels was the established practice in Moscow and at the U of I because only eight miles away sat Washington State University. They offered higher salaries due to a larger student population and higher tuition revenues. The U of I always paid less than WSU due to countless differences between the two systems in different states. On several occasions, the U of I attempted to meet the market level of compensation for its employees.

"We based an employee's compensation on their percent of target and the position market, which drove how much of an increase they may have received or not received if they were already at 100 percent," clarified

Brandi Terwilliger, director of Human Resources. "We may have brought a person's pay up to a higher percentage, but that was because they were so much further behind where they should've been. Somebody may have gotten less of an increase because they didn't have as far to go to get closer to their market target."

But for market-based compensation to work and not drive the U of I further into its deficit pit, a revenue source had to exist to replace declining tuition revenue.

"When I realized that, I knew the U of I's problems regarding finances were structural," Scott stated. "What else would have been driving those numbers? Market-based compensation was the right thing to do, but the U of I had to turn around its revenue situation and headcount levels first. I wanted to see the university be more competitive with salaries, but there had to be a way to pay for it before implementation."

There were varied opinions on whether the market-based compensation played a part in the massive hole the university faced financially. "Everyone said the U of I's deficits were an enrollment problem; well, it *was* an enrollment problem because you can't raise compensation without the corresponding appropriation and tuition growth to pay for it," Scott explained.

In another twist, for the first time, the administration asked the colleges and units to give back some of their carryover funds. "We did something equivalent to gainsharing to shore up the Gen Ed revenue budget for FY18," Kim disclosed. "Each college and unit were 'billed' an amount based on their proportional share of the total Gen Ed carryforward."

The "gainsharing" process was not popular. "At one point at that year's Leadership Breakfast, I referred to 'passing the hat,'" Brian said, "which meant that if a division or college could operate profitably that fiscal year, some of those reserve funds had to go back to fund Central. I finally had convinced the administration that there had to be additional resources for Central, and the only way to get them was to have everybody take some of what they generated and put it in the hat. Some colleges and units hated it because they worked hard all year long and lived within their budgets to save or generate their own revenue but still had to pay a share back to Central."

"Units gave up one-time funding based on their prior year's unspent Gen Ed funding," Trina Mahoney explained. "We then allocated those funds out to a select list of areas based on recommendations from the University Budget and Finance Committee, plus some went to Central to offset tuition shortfalls. The total gain share amount was $1.8 million."

The U of I used the one-time carryover give-back to reinvest in faculty start-up, University Communications, the Graduate College recruiting efforts, and College of Art and Architecture technology updates.

Along with using PP, the university also implemented another cost-cutting strategy. "We used the Delaware Cost Study to look at what the average cost at a department or program across a number of institutions would look like if we built from the ground up," Kim explained. "After going through the data included in the Cost Study, the U of I used the findings to reallocate from colleges that seemed to be more highly resourced to those that were less well resourced."

There were detractors of using cost-cutting measures such as PP and Delaware. "Delaware didn't sit well with the colleges that looked to be more highly resourced," Kim explained. "Those were tough conversations because, unfortunately, we were also combining that exercise with budget reductions. It wasn't just that a college wasn't getting new money; they were getting a larger budget reduction than other colleges. It didn't feel fair to them."

"Believe it or not, things were actually looking pretty good from a financial statement perspective until 2018," Linda reflected. "But the increasing imbalance between unit reserves and Central reserves was problematic. We convened a reserve oversight committee with deans, associate deans, and others. That was the first conversation about a mechanism for colleges and units to contribute if we didn't hit tuition projections in the fall. It couldn't be Central eating it anymore."

"Colleges were where the teaching, research, and extension took place," CALS Dean Michael Parrella stated. "So how could administration not have deans at the table when making budgeting decisions? The big concern I had was, and there was no question this was going on, how would they balance the books if there were no deans in that upper group making decisions? The perception was that they were going to balance the books on the backs of the colleges and leave other units alone. We would do our share, but if they wanted to get deans on board to help balance the books, they had to tell the deans what the bigger plan was."

"People were starting to listen and get involved," Linda conveyed.

John instituted a control mechanism where the administration level managed faculty position turnover rather than the college or department level. The provost would then reallocate those funds where needed. That allowed for a bit more oversight on spending and managing headcount.

"President Staben created a process whereby out-of-cycle pay increases required president or designated approval," Brandi shared. "Before that, the individual units handled those approval processes. So there were strategies in place shortly before President Green came."

Those strategies may have been frustrating to many, but they provided some oversight and justification for adding a new position, increasing a salary, or even rehiring for vacant positions.

In January 2019, John sent an academic affairs budget update memo to faculty and staff outlining a $5 million reduction in the current FY's base budget due to the declining undergraduate enrollment revenue. In part, the memo read:

> As Executive Vice President and Provost, it is my responsibility to make difficult choices on things like budget reductions in the units that report to me, and I take it very seriously. In making this round of budget reductions, I took a strategic approach as opposed to across-the-board budget reductions for all units. A variety of factors influenced these final decisions, including program prioritization data as well as benchmarked cost data from the Delaware Cost Study. These data were used to help us better understand the relative funding levels of our academic units compared to our internal priorities as well as national benchmarks. I also reviewed the current resources available to meet the necessary budget cut targets in a way that would avoid employee layoffs.
>
> (University of Idaho 2019)

Of the $5 million reallocated from base funding, $3 million would address the ongoing tuition revenue shortfalls, with the remainder invested in UBFC priorities (TA package increases and market-based compensation) and a small strategic reserve (University of Idaho 2020). The annual budget and planning process for FY20 began shortly after John's memo.

When Scott officially accepted the position as president in April 2019, SBOE had already approved the FY20 budget. But Scott knew everyone still had their work cut out for them. Several conversations occurred between Scott, Brian, and John about making mandatory budget cuts to the spending plan. Another $20 million loss for FY20 and FY21 would generate itself in an ugly fashion if Scott left the numbers as-is.

Finally, he said, "Enough."

Scott's Management Insight

Rightsizing is always the right thing to do. Ensure revenues cover expenses and expenditures support increased revenues. This means making hard decisions and communicating them transparently. Employees will follow if they believe in the plan and you are straightforward. They will resist if they believe the plan is opaque or unfair. Several initiatives provided short-term fixes but not long-term solutions. Our administration took hard medicine, but we clearly articulated the goal.

Some initiatives will take so long to deliver results that they will not help you (and may hurt your ability) to achieve cost reductions. Program Prioritization, a process where you evaluate the relevance and contribution of certain programs, is important for the institution's long-term success. Taking resources from areas that no longer meet student needs and reallocating them to growing programs will help an institution thrive. These programs, however, take time to assess and implement, are politically unpopular, and can lead to lawsuits if we let go of tenured faculty. I did not find our process helpful toward moving the financial needle over the short term.

Even worse is combining colleges to meet cost-cutting objectives. Some will want larger colleges to absorb smaller colleges to save the cost of a dean's salary. But that is likely the only thing you will save, and the resulting larger entity will likely be less focused, less nimble, and harder to manage. Politically, your alumni will hate it. My view is that this lever is not worth the fight. Find those areas where you get the most bang for your buck and the least resistance. Prioritize them first. Avoid third-rail financial decisions (combining or eliminating colleges, program prioritization) as you will waste precious time debating the approach with little actual savings realized over the short run.

I recommend getting a cost study comparing the cost of your programs to your peers. Those programs that appear more expensive and less effective than their peers' are candidates for restructuring. Faculty will argue that "our program is different," and it will most likely be, but there will be a learning process with a light shining on the program in question. For the U of I, the Delaware Cost Study provided that light, helped us understand our programs better, and enabled us to push back on the "we are different" narrative. There is no doubt you can harvest some low-hanging fruit. That being said, this lever will take more time to properly implement than simply setting expense reallocation targets and is best suited for longer-term fine-tuning of a college's budget than responding to a financial crisis.

Chapter 13

Find Your Sense of Urgency

"One cannot slow-roll the fix when the ship is sinking."

—*Scott Green*

As if decreased enrollment with unrealistic projections used for budgeting, market-based compensation in a period of decreasing tuition revenue, and an unsustainable financial policy that relied on Central reserves to cover the self-inflicted deficits weren't enough, there was more.

Take the U of I's cash burn rate. For many years, the U of I enjoyed a "savings account," also called an investment account, with a sizable sum of money, $72 million in 2015. At some point in 2015, someone in a decision-making capacity suggested using that large sum to work for the university through investing. Before that, the U of I invested its "savings account" with the Foundation, but that changed, so the university needed to find an investment manager.

The U of I hired Wells Fargo and Clearwater Advisors to put their dollars to work. However, over time, the earnings and original balance began to whittle down, especially during FY19, when the university asked its investment managers to liquidate assets to cover losses and feed operations. At one point, the cash balance dropped from $78 million in 2018 to a low of $45 million at the end of FY19, a drawdown of almost $35 million. See Figure 13.01.

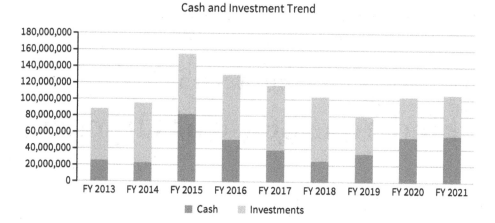

Figure 13.01   University of Idaho Cash and Investment Trend FY2013–FY2022.
SOURCE: University of Idaho Division of Finance and Administration. Reproduced with permission of University of Idaho.

Since there wasn't ever a set amount for the cash or investment funds, wiggle room remained for the "optimal" balance. "It's not like anyone ever said we needed X amount of cash in the bank because we ran some secret formula, and the number magically came up," Brian Foisy, vice president for Finance and Administration, said. "But what caused concern was the trend. We were spending more than we were bringing in. And every year, when that spending created losses, we would use those investment balances to fund our current year's operations. It was somewhat alarming because if we kept going, the $45 million in cash would be completely gone within a short period."

"After talking with Brian, what became clear was our burn rate was such that we were going to run out of cash within eighteen months," Scott agreed. "The cash was going down, down, down. If that happens, you're looking at possible financial exigency and losing control and your autonomy. And people were still spending money on things that weren't mandatory; they were optional. I wanted to ask, 'Do you see a problem? *Can you see a problem?*'"

"I remember them putting those numbers up at one of the Leadership Breakfasts, and I think there were a lot of people that were aghast," expressed Vice Provost for Strategic Enrollment Management Dean Kahler. "They were just like, we spent all our savings; we are down to only months' worth of operating budget."

"I made the comment once that we were spending money like a drunken sailor," recalled Dr. Larry Stauffer, College of Engineering dean. "Part of it was my college."

"I think we saw that we were still kind of trying to cover up some of the underlying issues that no one had dealt with and had come to a head," Dean of the College of Graduate Studies Jerry McMurtry shared. "We were running out of runway, and undergraduate enrollment had not turned around."

And how could Scott forget one of the other problems front and center, SBOE's requirement for the university to set aside 5 percent of expenses as a reserve for a safeguard? The U of I's financial situation starting about 2017 certainly warranted the use of safeguard funds, but the 5 percent wasn't there.

"The U of I didn't have an unrestricted net position [reserves]; they had a negative net position [reserves]," Scott pointed out. "There was a $10 million deficit in the unrestricted net balance, and the U of I was required to have a $20 million deposit balance, so it was a $30 million swing. The university was living off its liquidated investments, a finite resource. If you think about it, if the U of I had a negative unrestricted net position, they already had a call on those assets. I had to look at how the cash position stood with investments and everything else. How long could the U of I stay afloat, given how much cash they were burning? The answer to that, according to Brian, was eighteen months, maybe two years." See Figure 13.02.

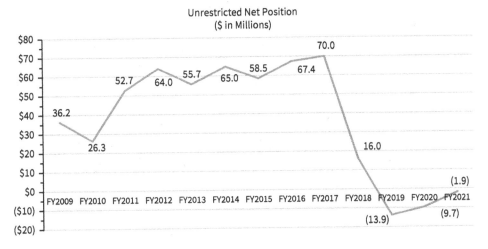

Figure 13.02 University of Idaho's Unrestricted Net Position FY2009–FY2022.
SOURCE: University of Idaho Division of Finance and Administration. Reproduced with permission of University of Idaho.

The structural deficiencies of the financial model had caught up with the U of I. Scott knew his alma mater was out of time. And in a state that had been reducing spending on higher education for years, he knew his options to fix the problem were limited.

Between 1989 and 2020, funding from the overall State of Idaho general fund for colleges and universities went from 15.5 percent to 7.8 percent of total state appropriations. The U of I's Gen Ed fund went from receiving 92.8 percent from the state in 1980 to 53.5 percent in 2020. See Figures 13.03, 13.04. But this number was overstated as the state counted tuition collected from students as state appropriations. It made some sense when they would fund compensation increases for faculty and staff supported by tuition, but the legislature stopped funding those increases during the 2010 financial crisis. After that, there was no other source but tuition to cover compensation increases tied to these dedicated funds. This became a source of tension as the legislature was critical of the university's increasing tuition, but so much time had passed that most were unaware that the university had no choice due to this structural issue.

FUNDING HISTORY
Percentage of overall general fund

Fiscal Year	Public Schools	College & Universities	Community Colleges	Health & Welfare	Adult & Juv Corrections	All Other Agencies
2020	48.5%	7.8%	1.2%	22.1%	7.5%	12.8%
2015	46.8%	8.6%	1.1%	21.7%	8.3%	13.5%
2010	49.1%	10.1%	1.1%	18.4%	7.5%	13.8%
2005	46.3%	10.7%	1.0%	19.6%	6.9%	15.5%
2000	49.0%	12.1%	.90%	16.2%	6.5%	15.4%
1995	49.1%	13.0%	.80%	17.9%	4.0%	15.1%
1990	51.0%	14.9%	.90%	13.1%	3.2%	16.9%
1989	52.2%	15.5%	.90%	12.1%	2.6%	16.7%

Figure 13.03   Idaho Higher Education Funding History 1980–2020, Percentages of General Fund. University of Idaho Office of the President.
SOURCE: Reproduced with permission of University of Idaho.

Those changes in state support were drastic; Scott couldn't go to the legislature and ask for more appropriations. Finding millions of dollars to balance the FY20 budget would boil down to cutting.

▌FUNDING HISTORY
Current College and University funding model

	State Support					Percentage of Total		
Fiscal Year	General Funds	Endowment Funds	Subtotal	Tuition	TOTAL	General Fund	State Support	Tuition
1980	58,600,000	3,165,200	62,765,200	4,873,000	67,638,200	88.1%	92.8%	7.2%
1990	115,500,000	6,342,100	121,842,100	18,374,800	140,216,900	83.2%	87.3%	12.7%
2000	201,960,100	12,340,000	214,300,100	55,108,400	269,408,500	75.0%	79.5%	20.5%
2010	253,278,100	9,616,400	262,894,500	131,587,500	394,482,400	58.3%	60.8%	39.2%
2020	306,026,000	17,290,000	323,316,000	289,979,400	604,295,400	50.6%	53.5%	46.5%

Figure 13.04 Idaho Four Year Institution Funding History 1980–2020, State vs. Tuition Percentage. University of Idaho Office of the President.

SOURCE: Reproduced with permission of University of Idaho.

Historically, no one wanted to be a "budget-cutting president." For years the university had enjoyed exceptional presidents who most likely didn't see the U of I as their final job location in their career; thus, a certain mindset existed. Sure, the presidents made hard decisions about various issues, and it wasn't like they *weren't* doing anything to try and keep the budgets in line. But did they want to make the tough calls that required potentially deep cuts to positions (people) or programs? Did they want a series of negative headlines? No, because if there was fallout from their decisions, a positive legacy with the university—which made it easier to get hired at another university—could be in jeopardy if the campus community was disgruntled or the books were in a shambles, or the press had a field day with their reputation.

"Spending down the reserves happened when our past presidents wanted to look good, so they funded things with reserve monies and left the U of I before they had to make painful cuts," speculated Director of the IBEST Barrie Robison.

Scott would have to become the "budget-cutting president."

Financial reporting was the final piece to the puzzle that still needed to fall into place. However, the U of I's system wasn't streamlined enough to know exact numbers throughout the institution. Cutting budgets using scalpel-like precision required reliable data.

"Our financial reporting system was complex," Associate Vice President Linda Campos said. "We didn't have any standardized budget reporting, so every college and unit reported their budgets and funds differently. Then-Provost John Wiencek regularly complained about the lack of clarity and comparability across colleges and units. That is what kicked off the chart of account redesign, which is the framework of how we gather and report data in our financial system, Banner. Our chart was outdated and wasn't optimal for standardized reporting."

"After seeing the various reports, I told Linda I couldn't imagine trying to get reports with the old system; it just wouldn't work," Scott shared.

"It was a two-year project," Linda added. "We kicked off the chart redesign in 2016, shortly after I arrived. Scott arrived in mid-2019, which was near the end of the first year with the new chart. The redesign created a strong foundation for the Budget Office to develop more meaningful reports that were standardized across all units. That set us up well for President Green to receive good and consistent financial information and use the same measuring stick for all the colleges and units. These reports were continually refined with his input. There should be no big surprises at the end of the fiscal year with good and regular reporting."

* * *

Scott knew taking the job as president of his alma mater was the right decision; he'd known it in his gut from the beginning. But running through the U of I's budget scenario over and over was almost mind-numbing.

The university's big financial picture was more like a complex George Seurat painting, made up of tiny dots, each representing its own problem, merging with the next to form the complete illustration.

Brenda Helbling, Office of the President chief of staff, made an astute observation summing up the situation. "Over the years, we had a lot of people from academia painting with the same brush and wondering why the color wasn't coming out different."

Scott's Management Insight

To create timely change, you must clearly communicate a well-supported sense of urgency. One cannot slow-roll the fix when the ship is sinking. By bluntly stating that the university was running out of cash, I provided that sense of urgency needed to get the institution back on track.

You also need real-time data to manage through a crisis. Identify those few key metrics that will drive your decisions short term. Get the reporting in place and ensure it becomes part of the culture through regular discussions of the trends. Headcount and cash are the metrics that can move the needle and, if properly managed, will lead to increased financial health—having detailed financial reports allowed us to have very productive monthly meetings to discuss our trends and techniques to turn the tide. With a sense of urgency and good management reporting, I could set objectives for our VPs and deans to hit and monitor progress every month.

When one of your main sources of revenue starts to decline, you must improvise and use different strategies to make up the difference, not just hope it'll get better. Minor cuts to budgets and tweaks to your financial model over time can add up to significant savings and leave you in a better position if the revenues keep decreasing. That had not happened, so we needed to operate at speed—as if our hair was on fire and our financial lives depended on it.

Chapter 14
Skeletons

"But it's never enough, right?"

—*Dr. Shauna Corry*

In May 2019, President Staben hosted his last Leadership Breakfast in a town hall format where faculty and staff could ask questions after a brief update. He used this opportunity to explain the U of I's financial position before Scott took the helm as president.

Brian Foisy, vice president for Division of Finance and Administration, took the reins to discuss how the U of I needed to live within its means (increase revenue and decrease spending) and address SBOE's concerns, including the U of I's net position. He emphasized that the U of I had reached a historical point and not in a good way. He plastered a slide on the big white screen. Yes, the expenses line headed north and crossed the revenues line heading south. See Figure 14.01.

"It was a classic example of what happens when a business loses customers," Brian shared. "In essence, the presentation painted the picture clearly that revenue was going down because enrollment was going down."

The expense line went up because, over several years, the U of I had not addressed budget deficits with cuts but instead allowed the cost-shifting practice, which never took the actual expense off the books. The U of I's lack of making impactful, permanent cuts to their base funding and not living within its means had snowballed, leaving them in the spotlight of SBOE.

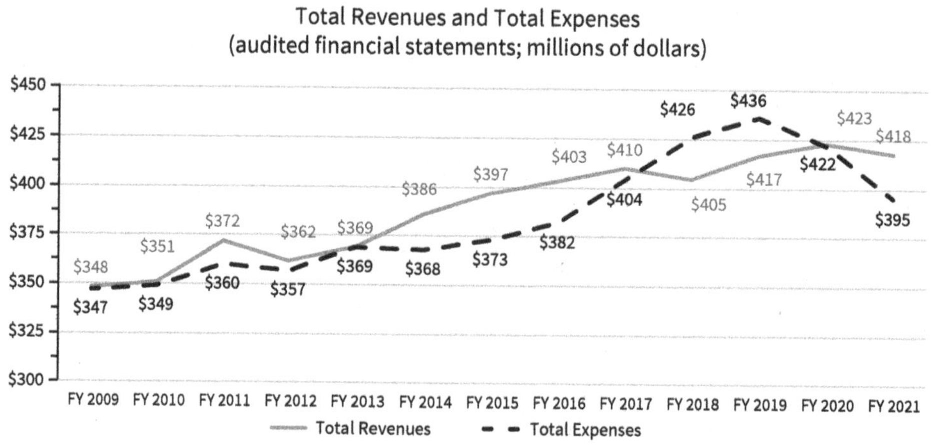

Total Revenues and Total Expenses
(audited financial statements; millions of dollars)

Figure 14.01   Total Revenues and Total Expenses, FY2009–FY2013.
SOURCE: University of Idaho Division of Finance and Administration. Reproduced with permission of University of Idaho.

Scott determined the U of I's net surplus/deficit (a private business would call it "net profit") by subtracting net expenses from its total general revenues. Obviously, the U of I wanted its net position as high as possible, but the unrestricted portion of the net position had plummeted to a negative balance by the end of FY19 and Scott's arrival as president. That amount alone made the SBOE uneasy, but in addition, a Governmental Accounting Standards Board (GASB) change in fiscal reporting known as GASB 75 handed the university another hit to its net position.

The U of I had promised decades before to provide specific employees health insurance for life, which was considered an Other Post Employment Benefit (OPEB). When the government implemented GASB 75, the U of I had to value all of those future benefits in current-year dollars, even though the U of I wouldn't have to pay the entire expense all at once. The difference between the current value of those benefits and the current funds set aside in a trust fund added a whopping $34 million liability, which plummeted the U of I's net position even further to a negative $55 million.

The hot mic set up for the audience at the breakfast allowed faculty and staff to put President Staben and Brian in the hot-seat. They asked pointed questions, voiced concerns, and tossed out a few backhanded critiques.

"It was a weird dynamic at that last breakfast," Brian voiced. "SBOE had made it clear that one of Scott's charges was to come in and turn around the finances of the institution. I think people were lining up to start pointing fingers before he arrived on campus."

"I was aware that we were approaching a very difficult situation," College of Art and Architecture Dean Shauna Corry shared. "But I truly was so focused on my college; I wasn't completely aware because I still saw spending. When Brian originally explained at a previous meeting that we had $70 million in reserve, a lot of people thought that was enough. But it's never enough, right? That's what I learned, how fast that can go."

After the breakfast, a certain unease settled over campus. Most people were now aware of a budget issue begging for immediate attention. Enrollment declines had led to tuition declines, and enrollment increases didn't necessarily lead to tuition increases. Administrations had used Central to cover deficits because, in many cases, the colleges didn't want to give any of their reserve funds back since they'd worked to save them. To top it off, the 5 percent the SBOE required the U of I to have available in case of a downturn didn't exist; the unrestricted net position (reserves) sat at a negative balance. Reporting was weak, so the numbers were convoluted, and the people raising the red flags experienced either a lack of concern ("The guys on 'the hill' will fix it"), deaf ears ("We had no idea there was a problem"), or silo mentality ("We're okay, so why worry about those who aren't?"). Whether past or current administrations had the will to fix the problem over the past decade, the desire to make the hard decisions hadn't existed.

Brian had implored the university not to kick the can down the road any longer, but some still lacked a sense of urgency. The U of I was a behemoth, and many believed it would take time to implement change, so there was time to turn the tide. Traditionally, it did take a while to right the ship in academia, most likely because the shared governance policy and responsibility to the SBOE added necessary levels of communication and debate. Many saw the situation as too complex to swiftly identify specific problems, let alone fix them by the end of the current or even next fiscal year.

But did it have to take years to fix? The U of I didn't have that luxury. The U of I's new president was about to put employees to the test by charging them with a seemingly impossible task, and failure to complete the job was not an option if the U of I was to remain solvent.

Scott's Management Insight

As a new president, ensure all skeletons are out of the closet. If the campus is not aware of them, they become *your* skeletons. By having the previous president, provost, and CFO hold a town hall and present the accurate financial picture to the campus, they laid the groundwork for employees to prepare for what was coming. By the time I arrived on campus, our employees knew more cuts were imminent. That cleared the way for my directive to cut $14 million from the recently approved budgets.

Part III

Chapter 15
Putting the Wheels in Motion

"I'm not sure he understood just how badly in debt we were when he got here."
—Dr. Michael Parrella

Scott's first order of business when he arrived on campus that warm summer day in June was to explain to the U of I community that they all had to pull together to cut $14 million from the current FY20 budget without touching headcounts due to contracts. He also had to communicate that the U of I would use different strategies to build the next fiscal year's budget that didn't leave the university on the precipice of a cliff with only 18 months of cash.

Scott decided to lead with that staggering reality to light the fire of inspiration with campus leadership. His second day on the job included a roundtable discussion with the ten college deans—without their fiscal officers.

University of Idaho Deans, July 2019

Dr. Michael Parrella, Agricultural and Life Sciences (CALS)
Dr. Shauna Corry, Art and Architecture (CAA)
Dr. Marc Chopin, Business and Economics (CBE)
Dr. Ali Carr-Chellman, Education, Health, and Human Sciences (CEHHS)*
Dr. Larry Stauffer, Engineering (ENGR)
Dr. Jerry McMurtry, Graduate Studies (COGS)
Dr. Jerrold Long, Law (LAW)**
Dr. Sean Quinlan, Letters, Arts, and Social Sciences (CLASS)
Dr. Ben Hunter, Library
Dr. Dennis Becker, Natural Resources (CNR)
Dr. Ginger Carney, Science (SCI)

*Dr. Philip Scruggs, Interim Dean CEHHS, June 2020–June 2022
**Johanna Kalb, new College of Law Dean, May 2021

Provost John Wiencek, Chandra Zenner Ford, Brian Foisy, and Toni Broyles were also in the room listening to Scott outline his directive to the deans.

Scott pointedly told the group, "Due to annual contracts, my hands are tied regarding people, so we can only reduce expenses by reducing non-personnel expenses and implementing a hiring freeze. The $14 million of the expected $20 million will have to come from operational expenses and not filling vacant positions. Any more cutting than that might do more long-term harm than good and impact the quality of the student experience."

Scott shared every detail about the financial crisis; he held nothing back. The deans responded, sharing specifics about their individual budget needs and woes.

"I remember the first time we met as a group with Scott," CALS Dean Michael Parrella said. "I'm not sure he understood just how badly in debt we were when he got here. We had to tell him the truth, so he knew what he would be dealing with. I sensed that it was a little bit of a surprise."

"I was so dismayed," Scott reflected. "I knew it was in bad shape, but when I got in, I saw just how bad it was. It turned out to be even worse than I'd originally thought."

Scott conveyed clear budget targets for the colleges and explained he would hold SEM and the other money-making arms of campus harmless to raise revenues (which didn't mean those areas wouldn't experience some cuts over the next few years).

"I think what Scott did at the beginning to get the finances under control was good," said Mary Kay McFadden, vice president for University Advancement. "But long-term budget-cutting doesn't help build or grow a university, so there had to be a mindset of making strategic investments, too, and university leadership had that in mind."

Scott did not mince words that day with the deans in his office. He emphatically spelled out that time was critical; the university could no longer wait. The cuts had to happen immediately. "If I didn't have a specific call to action and set clear expectations, how could I expect people to act?" he shared.

Scott left it to each dean to figure out how to find their portion of the cuts because they and their fiscal officers knew their college budgets better than anyone.

"I'm not a micromanager," Scott stated. "But I will dig down deep to figure out why something isn't working, analyze data, and get the right people involved to focus on the positives and what is working and turn the negatives around. I trusted people to develop their key performance indicators and programs to hit their budget targets."

Scott, John, and Brian had used the pro-rata allocation method to set the specific targets, meaning whatever percentage each division or college received out of the total Gen Ed budget each year was the same percentage they had to find for their share of the $14 million. For example, if a college received 10% of the Gen Ed budget that year, they would be responsible for cutting 10% of the $14 million total, or $1.4 million.

College of Natural Resources Dean Dennis Becker recalled meeting with Scott before the all-dean meeting because there was "starting to be the writing on the wall that we would have to make some dramatic financial changes." He did not mince words with Scott that day, either, announcing, "Scott, if we implement these changes, I will have to close down some programs and places that have a lot of visibility. I might even need to pull out of making our college's donation to the ICCU Arena. If you're going to implement this level of cuts, this is what I'm going to have to do."

John called Dennis later that day and asked if that was a threat.

"I don't do threats," Dennis had responded. "I just work in reality."

"There was some gamesmanship with some colleges," Scott admitted. "Colleges often put the most visible and loved programs up for cutting to prevent the cuts. CBE put up the Barker Trading Program, CNR put up the ICCU Arena, MOSS, and Taylor Ranch. I just said, 'No, you and I know you're not cutting your Crown Jewels; you will have to find other areas to cut.'"

"In the second day's meeting, however, Scott said we'd be out of cash in eighteen months," Dennis continued, "In any conversations I had up to that point, that was not a reality to me. The administration always presented that we needed to pull back, but not in the terms that we were running an operation financially built on an amount of enrollment we weren't reaching and creating structural deficits. I didn't know we were deficit spending as far back as 2014 and essentially hiding the money that we were spending out of our reserves to cover up those deficits. That was not known to me. That level of information would have absolutely changed how I viewed things. When I learned that, I was much more willing to concede those impacts; those cuts would have to be made rather than fighting them."

"We held a little bit of a roundtable as we all introduced ourselves to Scott," recalled Sean Quinlan, dean of the College of Letters, Arts, and Social Sciences (CLASS). "There had been a kind of progressive revelation about the depth of the fiscal crisis. We knew that we needed a deep dive to find the underlying cause of what we were facing and the scope of the crisis. President Green indicated that each of the sectors that reported up to him would be assigned a cut with the expectation we would internally manage how to work it out."

Scott didn't dance around it, didn't sugarcoat it, didn't paint with the same brush. "I'm charging you with a target of $14 million," he told the deans gathered around his office table. "By my reckoning, between not filling positions and non-personnel costs, we can probably, maybe, hopefully, save that much. I realize this is extremely aggressive. But let's just rip the Band-Aid off, handle the hurt, and get through it."

"Perhaps Scott was able to be a bit more direct because he was a nontraditional president with decades of experience in the private sector. In the end, he was the one who was finally willing to say [with respect to budget cuts], 'This is what we are doing, and if you don't like it, too freaking bad,'" Brian said, laughing.

"Scott could be a little abrupt and brutal for a guy with a huge heart and passion and Love—I use a capital L—for the university," said Brenda Helbling, chief of staff. "He could be a bit of a hard-ass, but everyone took the lumps because, you know what? He had the chops. He was the real deal."

"We had to have confidence in Scott to make those financial calls," Dennis shared. "We weren't trusting the previous administration, and even if they were saying it to us, we weren't listening to them. If Finance said they'd been telling us this for a couple of years, we weren't hearing it because we didn't trust it because we never had the full picture."

Dean Shauna Corry shared that her college, Art and Architecture, had been working with the Provost's Office on reducing their budgets. She voiced her opinion that day. "Scott, my problem is the college has already been in debt; we've already climbed out of it. We are cut to the bone."

The College of Art and Architecture had seen its share of turbulence over the past decade. "I became the interim dean after our dean accepted another position," Shauna continued. "We were in debt, and part of that reason was the decreased number of students brought about not only from demographics but because of the 2008 recession. Professional colleges were highly affected by the market and the economy. A popular news magazine highlighted architecture as one of the top 10 degrees not to get, and we lost over half our students. We had just come through paying off that debt. We were just barely going to start seeing the light and getting things back into shape. I was just at a loss for how we would run the college if we cut further. But when that call came from Scott at that meeting, we had to make some really hard decisions. They were very unpopular decisions. They weren't popular with the people of Moscow. They were unpopular on campus. We had to make those decisions because otherwise, we wouldn't have been doing our part. There wasn't anybody who could come and rescue us."

Scott further emphasized to the group that day, "It's imperative that you go through this process to understand how to avoid it happening again. Right now, your monthly financial reporting isn't as useful as it can be. Linda, Trina, Kim, and Brian have worked to clarify the budget reports because you need good financial information to be held accountable. And I *will* hold you accountable. Use the expertise of your college financial officers, but they will not be attending these budget meetings with you for now. It'll be you, me, and Brian every month until I understand your numbers, *you* understand your numbers, and *you* hit your target."

During that meeting, Chandra took notes. Listened. Watched. "Nobody knew what Scott's directive would be up to that point. I mean, this was his second day on the job. That table was packed. We did it in the president's office, and it was all the deans sitting in that little space. Everybody got up and walked out silently because they were processing."

"We were just trying to keep the dike plugged at that point," Dennis said. "We would talk about the future at some point. But that strategy served us well; it allowed the campus community to accept the situation. Until that point, I don't think we were really accepting the situation. Ultimately, we came to a middle ground where we ripped the Band-Aid off but allowed the colleges to take a scalpel approach to how we did things. That was a very early acknowledgment on Scott's part regarding the dean's role in this."

Deans at the table. A clear course. A specific directive. An offer to help with no micromanaging. Welcome to the new way of doing business at the University of Idaho *for* the University of Idaho.

Scott, along with John and Brian (and later Provost Torrey Lawrence), worked with deans directly for a time after that to understand their budget reports and their actual financial position, which made it easier to identify the cuts.

Shauna explained one of her first meetings with Scott, which also included Torrey, Brian, Chandra, and Toni. "When Scott had us come without our financial directors, I would prep for those meetings before and talk to my financial director. I knew our budgets in my version of the world. I would sketch pictures and squares with my financial director, and we would draw this plan so I could visualize what was happening with our numbers. But Scott would ask me a question, and it was kind of funny because I would have no idea what he was talking about. But he would always bring it back in a positive way at the end. It wasn't a rah-rah kind of way. It was more like, 'You can do this.' That was helpful, but I really liked it when I could bring in the financial director."

"The financial meetings were great," College of Science Dean Ginger Carney said. "I was forced to learn more about the finances in my college. I was thrilled that Scott wanted to meet with us regularly so I could also teach him about my college, especially the research collaborations involving faculty and students. I did not have a regular meeting with presidents prior to Scott."

"We developed new standardized reports, and Scott expected leaders to present, understand, and be accountable for the financial health of their area," Associate Vice President for Budget and Planning Kim Salisbury said. "Those reports significantly changed the financial mindset on campus. It encouraged knowledge by leadership. The tone changed, and people were much more cognizant of financial spending, planning, and learning how to best allocate resources to meet the intended mission."

"I didn't like the monthly meetings," Interim Dean Stauffer, College of Engineering, shared. "The first one, Scott asked me about a $67 charge. I told him I didn't know what it was for and that it was only $67. But he said we had to find out why our college spent that $67. I got together with my financial person and prepared slides to show Scott at the next meeting. I took charge and identified any little anomalies. I beat him to the punch. Some of the deans compared notes about the meetings, what worked and didn't. I understood; it made sense what Scott was doing. And we started chipping away at our debt."

Scott also conducted town hall meetings with employees to discuss the financial situation. He understood how uncomfortable and depressing it was to cut such a large amount of money from the existing FY budget. There was some pushback from some faculty who wanted a slower, more measured pace, but Scott always countered with, "We don't have time."

"Scott pushed our team in ways previous administrations had never pushed us," Associate Vice President Linda Campos said, laughing. "I thought it was awesome. This was the new pace—the speed of Scott."

"Scott stripped away all the reasons and excuses and explained we couldn't solve the problem by growing through enrollment; that would take too long. So, if we couldn't do that, we had to make some cuts," said Dan Ewart, vice president of Information Technology and chief information officer. "Scott knew those cuts were going to be difficult in their heart, and they were going to hurt people. None of us wanted to do that. But we had to because if we didn't right the ship and have that sound fiscal footing, how could we grow?"

"The budget cuts were extremely hard," Ginger shared. "We had to do a lot of tough things, like reorganizing our college. We merged several departments, including combining Geography and Geology, to create the Earth and Spatial Sciences department. It didn't make sense to me to do it until the financial pressures forced us. Luckily, we identified a leader outside the department but internal to the university to come in and serve as department chair. The faculty had to rethink their curriculum and student training."

"I lost out of my indirect overhead return account, which was the money I received from grants I wrote, about $70,000–75,000," College of Graduate Studies Dean Jerry McMurtry said. "I went from a staff of eleven down to six. But I didn't lose as much as others. And it was fine because, in the end, it was going to make the institution stronger. It forced us to rethink our processes; we became extraordinarily efficient."

Scott didn't just make decisions in a vacuum or act as a dictator. He, Brian, and the Holy Financial Trinity (Linda, Kim, and Trina) took the information to campus, maintaining the shared governance model but with the understanding that the cuts had to happen immediately within the fiscal year.

One professor told Scott at a Faculty Senate meeting, "I've come with a list of positions that you should eliminate." On that list was the CFO, Brian Foisy.

"I was sitting in the room, and this faculty member had no problem saying we needed to eliminate the CFO," Brian shared.

Scott looked back at the faculty member and said respectfully but directly, "You don't think we need a CFO?"

"We don't need *that* CFO," they replied.

Scott then pointedly asked the faculty member, "So, what you're really here to do is say that you have a personality conflict with one individual driving your decisions about what's best for the university and how we should make budget cuts?"

"Then that person kind of sucked down into their seat," Brian recalled.

There were bumps along the road. For instance, faculty and staff, along with various stakeholders—students, alumni, donors, and boosters—questioned why the U of I was building a new athletic arena during a significant budget crunch. Even people in the local area with no ties to the university wondered. The question swirled around the grocery store aisles and coffee shops. Why not continue to use the ASUI Kibbie Dome and Memorial Gym for athletic events and funnel the construction funds to cover the budget deficits?

Scott's Management Insight

Presidents have a fiduciary responsibility to do the right thing for the institution. Doing the right thing will also be right for your career if you are honest, communicate transparently, and bring your employees along. Presidents should not be afraid to make hard decisions. If you build trust and explain why the path you will take is the right one and be frank about the perils of each option, including the one contemplated, most hearts and minds will follow. We did that, and everyone did their part and more.

It's imperative to know the history and reasons behind the problems. But you must focus on the present challenges and future needs rather than dwell on the past. Placing blame or lamenting about the past is counter-productive. Focus on solutions. By supporting our finance team rather than allowing others to attack them for past problems, we built loyalty and trust among the team, and they responded in a big way. They worked days, nights, and weekends tirelessly.

A successful leader builds a strong team, sets clear expectations, and allows the talent to work. Set measurable targets, enable your management team the leeway to decide how to hit the target, and follow up as often as needed. Confirm the employees are executing plans and making progress to ensure they hit their targets. Your managers can find the best path to success if you let them manage the process (with some guardrails). That is what we did. We gave them the targets, the management reports, and the support to help them manage their cuts. Our deans and vice presidents decided how they could best hit their targets. We discussed their plans and were there to help, but they made the call on the actions they would take.

The successful team also communicates and is open to listening and collaborating. A good manager must reward that behavior. I was not accepting excuses, but I heard about barriers to improvement that would require collaboration to address. I could bring those needed resources to bear and encourage the desired outcome. Operating as a team builds confidence that no manager is on their own. They are part of a team, and that team can help them reach their targets.

Smart Collaboration

Moscow Police Department Renovation to Prichard Art Gallery, Moscow, Idaho

During the anguishing process of the first round of budget cuts in FY20, Shauna Corry, dean of the College of Art and Architecture, knew they faced a seemingly insurmountable task to meet their targeted cuts.

"Scott came in and had to make some major changes fast, and he did, and they hurt," she remembered. "We'd already cut so much out of our budget. I expressed that we had nothing left to cut. But I knew we had to do our share, which led to us cutting the Prichard Art Gallery. All our programs and research groups brought in revenue for students, with the exception of the gallery. Prichard brought in around $70,000 a year and cost the college $225,000 per year. That was just a complete loss of money draining out every year. And even though it was a wonderful gallery, and people spoke up that they thought highly of it and supported it, we didn't bring in donations. It just couldn't pay for itself. It was huge to cut that."

Since 1986, the gallery has sat in downtown Moscow as a beacon of art and social gatherings. Cutting the program and space wasn't just a hit to the college or the U of I; it hit the entire Moscow area art-loving community.

Scott didn't promise Shauna or the college he would bring back the Prichard Art Gallery after the big cut. "In fact, he didn't really say anything about it," Shauna shared. "I did get invited to tour a

(Continued)

(Continued)

building downtown and talked to Toni Broyles [U of I special assistant, strategic initiatives], who explained they were looking for a different building. I realized it wasn't that they didn't care; it was that the college had to be efficient. We had to be sustainable in terms of everything, especially finances."

"We decided to release the Prichard Art Gallery and purchase our own space," Brian Foisy, Division of Finance and Administration vice president, recalled. "We determined buying the old police station from the City of Moscow would be a viable option. There was a statute saying they could only sell assets at the appraised value. An appraiser said it was worth $975,000, and Scott ultimately agreed, but we didn't have $975,000 sitting around, so it got added to the Central Reserves list."

"At first, everyone was so upset; no one thought we'd close the gallery," Shauna shared. "People said, 'Oh, Scott wouldn't close the Prichard.' I just looked at them and said, 'It's done. But now we get it back. And that doesn't mean that we get it back for free. I still have to come up with the money to help support the renovation. And in the long run, the gallery needs to pay for itself, so we need to figure out how to do that. Our Prichard Art Gallery committee renewed its mission and, most importantly, looked at how the gallery could be sustainable. The way to do that was to have more revenue than we were bringing in before."

Some of the innovative thinking by the committee resulted in ideas to have a store for the college at the gallery. The Rhode Island School of Design and the Savannah College of Art and Design (located in Savannah, Georgia) were examples of how the college could sell student and faculty work to generate revenue.

Shauna explained, "Scott suggested that since we were a land-grant institution, to show and sell more than just contemporary art. The committee developed a vision that will be more inclusive and made suggestions on the design, how to fund the gallery's mission, and how to bring in revenue."

The vision for the Prichard Art Gallery in the new space and location will serve as a destination place downtown, a welcome center. The space will house the gallery, a satellite VandalStore, and possibly a small meeting space.

"The building sits at the core of Moscow, off Friendship Square," Shauna outlined. *"It sits on the one-way street going north on Hwy. 95, so it will be a place we can brand the U of I. It has some old façade elements; it's not a new building. We're on a budget and reusing, so it will be a sustainable project. It will be a different kind of gallery but still magical. It'll support student learning and the land-grant mission to provide art. Downtown Moscow has a historic designation on the National Register of Historic Places, and this building, if we bring back the original façade, could support that designation. It has meaning for people within the city."*

Shauna shared that she doesn't see Scott as someone who makes big pronouncements and promises. She sees him as realistic about what can be delivered in the required time frame. *"He expects people to do their job well and within a timeline,"* she expressed. *"But he provided help to do that, and I'm optimistic about our new gallery space."*

The U of I closed on purchasing the property on March 3, 2022. According to Ray Pankopf, director of U of I Architectural and Engineering Services, the next steps include a feasibility study for the desired renovations conducted by an architectural firm led by U of I alumni, Knit Studios. They are providing their services to the U of I pro-bono.

Scott's Management Insight

Invest in your community. Town-gown relationships are vital to the success of a destination campus. Some towns do not embrace their local university. The university must win their support. Small but visible support can be very impactful. The loss of the Prichard Gallery was a wake-up call that it was not business as usual at the U of I. I did not make the decision to close the gallery but did require Dean Corry to hit her budget targets. The gallery lost nearly $200k a year, a substantial sum for one of our smallest colleges. I believe she made the right decision.

We needed a new model, one that was sustainable. The old police station provided us with that opportunity. It has more space that can be used for retail sales—selling art alongside the exhibits. It also could

(Continued)

(Continued)

accommodate a VandalStore to sell Vandal gear. We did not have a store downtown and having a storefront on Highway 95 will ensure constant traffic. The old police station took some investment, but with the university's cost of capital less than 3 percent, the ongoing operating costs will be less than the previous private lease, and revenues will likely create a margin for those operations. Dean Corry made a hard decision, one not embraced by the community, but it was the right decision and positioned us to reimagine the Prichard and deliver an even better, more sustainable gallery to our community.

Chapter 16
A Project for the Ages

"The entire industry in Idaho came together in amazing ways. . ."
—*Dr. Dennis Becker*

A few specific issues gained attention during the budget crisis, most likely based on a lack of understanding and communication, but the optics created an air of negativity with some Vandals. The Idaho Central Credit Union (ICCU) Arena project was one of those attention-grabbers because some questioned why the U of I would invest millions on a capital project while requiring a $14 million permanent cut to the current fiscal year budget.

"Scott had to do some important messaging to all the communities involved," said Mary Kay McFadden, vice president for University Advancement. "Some people didn't understand that every dollar budgeted and spent on the ICCU Arena was restricted, meaning the U of I couldn't use it for any other purpose, even during a financial crisis. The optics of going back or stopping it would've been more damaging than moving forward."

The U of I's financial position was not especially strong, and the SBOE was undoubtedly aware of the impact of a $33 million GASB/OPEB commitment on the university's balance sheet and substantial negative net position. Those two factors played heavily into the SBOE's decision to make the approval for the ICCU construction contingent on Scott and Matt Freeman, SBOE executive director, hashing out the pros and cons.

"Once Scott was appointed president, but before he took office in July, he and I spoke and corresponded several times regarding the ICCU project," Matt shared. "On April 25, 2019, Scott sent me the financial summary for the Arena project. The most material aspects of the summary were that the U of I would finance the arena through the capital markets and still have $3 million to raise, which the VP of Advancement believed was very doable."

On April 27, 2019, Matt sent an email to Scott that confirmed what he, Scott, and Brian Foisy had discussed regarding a financing plan for the project. The email read in part (Freeman, M., personal communication):

> We discussed the value that the arena would bring to the University (recruitment, etc.) and the community and acknowledged that canceling the project would dramatically constrain future development efforts by the University. Delaying the project would likely drive up the total cost, assuming the construction bid environment remains competitive and would push project completion back at least 12 months. For these reasons, and based on your recommendations and assurances, I am writing to confirm that UI has full approval and authorization to proceed with the construction phase of the ICCU Arena at a total cost not to exceed $46M. Should bidding and guaranteed maximum price challenges cause the budget to exceed $46M, UI shall return to the Board to seek additional construction authorization.

When word got out that the Arena project was a go, the situation didn't sit well with some. And optics can play hell with morale, regardless of facts.

"There were two waves of backlash with the arena," shared Nicole Skinner, ASUI president (2018–19). "The first wave came from people who didn't believe the arena should be a funding priority for the university in the first place. The decision to pursue the arena felt like a slap in the face to students struggling to pay bills, staff scraping together funding for valuable programs, and faculty worried about losing their benefits. These very reasonable concerns were magnified by some misunderstandings around the university's finances, like thinking money already raised for the arena could be transferred to other funding areas instead."

The second, more intense wave of backlash with ASUI regarding the ICCU Arena came when the students thought the funding estimates for the arena project were wildly off. Nicole explained, "When it was announced that the cost to build the arena would be much higher than anticipated, there was a renewed wave of frustration. Even some people who initially supported the arena project felt the university didn't plan adequately."

ASUI certainly had an interest in the project due to the higher fee implemented on students to fund the arena. Assessments went from $30/year to $60/year. "The university administration approached the student government to request an increase in the student fee so they could complete the project," Nicole continued. "It put us in a difficult position because we didn't want to raise student fees unnecessarily, and we were already paying $30/year for the arena. However, abandoning the project and the funds already raised didn't feel like an option, either. To ensure that students benefited from the fee increase, ASUI negotiated an agreement to change the name of the Commons to the Idaho Student Union Building and secured a board of students that would help manage the building's future usage. Those wins made some feel better about the increased fee, but there was still frustration at the changes."

"The increase in student fees was committed to before I got to the U of I," Scott added. "The ICCU Arena project came in on time and on budget. The increases they referred to came from the project *estimates* made well before the U of I actually had approvals or began construction."

The ICCU Arena's celebratory groundbreaking occurred on June 6, 2019, just a few weeks before Scott trekked to Moscow from Long Island to take the helm as lead Vandal. Former President Staben's vision would become a reality with the help of friends.

"We're a residential campus of choice," Scott explained. "We're a destination campus, and you have to invest in your destination. ICCU Arena *is* Idaho, made with Idaho wood, manufactured by Idaho companies, and built by regional labor."

ICCU Arena with ASUI Kibbie Dome and Vandal Water Tower in the background.
SOURCE: Reproduced with permission from University of Idaho.

Scott's Management Insight

Send a strong signal that times will get better. Continuing a capital project that will benefit the entire community long-term can send that message, but you need to be clear that the money either has to build that project or be returned to donors to avoid criticism. Failure to over-communicate will build resentment. I knew we could have both a balanced operating budget and a successful project. My job was to explain how, several times over before it would take root.

Smart Collaboration

ICCU Arena Completion and Grand Opening (October 2021), Moscow, Idaho

Former President Chuck Staben made building a new events arena for the U of I one of his top priorities, formally announcing the project to the SBOE in February 2015. However, the talk of an arena wasn't new; university stakeholders kicked around the idea as far back as 1969.

The Kibbie Dome served as an excellent venue for Vandal sports, mainly football, but the cavernous space never quite clicked as a basketball venue. The Athletic Department did an incredible job making the massive football arena into an intimate basketball venue (Cowan Spectrum), but the desire for a designated court remained.

Staben knew support existed to build a new athletic facility dedicated to Vandal basketball. He hired Michael Perry, a seasoned fundraiser, in August 2015 to serve as his special assistant and coordinate with Vandal athletics to strategize support for the new building. The arena would be home to men's and women's Vandal basketball and the Idaho Alumni Club and offer a gathering place for various events.

"I give President Staben credit for conceptualizing, operationalizing, and getting the project going," Scott said.

After a tremendous outpouring of excitement for the project, funds to construct the arena came in from private and corporate donations, along with the SBOE agreeing to an ASUI-endorsed $30/year hike in student fees. ICCU became the namesake sponsor with a $10 million lead gift.

However, in July 2018, when the SBOE didn't renew Staben's contract, some wondered if the project would fizzle. But Staben stayed true to his goal and continued to raise funds and support through his final year as the U of I president, even though original cost estimates proved too low, and there were still millions of dollars to raise. The SBOE became concerned about whether the university could afford to build the arena. Nevertheless, on March 14, 2019, the SBOE unanimously approved the U of I's request to proceed with the bidding and construction phase of the project, contingent upon approval by the SBOE executive director in consultation with the new U of I president once named by the board (Idaho State Board of Education 2019).

When the SBOE tapped Scott as the incoming president, they asked him to determine the arena project's feasibility, given the U of I's financial situation. "The SBOE left it to their executive director, Matt [Freeman], and me to decide if we should move forward," Scott recalled. "We looked at it hard because there were a lot of sunk costs, and most of the financing was in place. I explained to the board that it was a capital project with restricted monies unavailable for operations, so it made more sense to continue rather than stop it and lose all the contributions made for its construction."

Scott remained concerned about the millions of dollars yet to raise, but Vice President for Advancement Mary Kay McFadden reassured him that they could raise enough to erect the arena at its final budget of $51 million.

"I told Mary Kay to tell me if she had any doubts," Scott emphasized. "If she did, I could be honest with the SBOE about whether we could raise the remaining funds or finance it without affecting operations during the financial troubles. I told the SBOE that our team was pretty confident they could hit the $51 million mark."

Scott received Matt's approval to proceed with the project, knowing that it would be a difficult decision to explain to the campus. "We would have to return those funds if we scuttled the project. The lead donor, ICCU, also made it clear that they would not continue with the project if we did not break ground that year, so delaying made no sense, either. There was some consternation on campus about moving forward with the project, but most seemed to understand the argument for continuing."

(Continued)

(Continued)

Scott knew that once completed, the arena would signal a new day. He believed that by then, the university would be in a better financial place, and the new building would provide pride and momentum.

July 2019 saw the official groundbreaking ceremonies with guests like US Forest Service Chief Vicki Christiansen and several heads of Idaho wood-product companies. The partnership between the U of I and Idaho's $2.4 billion wood industry was the lynchpin of the project. As the country's first engineered wood venue of its kind, the ICCU Arena's roots stemmed from trees grown in the Gem State. Idaho Forest Group harvested trees from the U of I's 10,000-acre experimental forest and surrounding areas in the state to produce lamstock (glued laminated timber or glulam) beams. Other than a few reinforcing pieces of steel, concrete flooring, tension rods, and some supplemental building parts, everything was made from wood to construct the state-of-the-art facility.

"Amid a financial disaster, we built that arena," Dean of the College of Natural Resources (CNR) Dennis Becker said. "And CNR played a major part."

In late spring 2020, one of the largest general contractors in the Pacific Northwest, Hoffman Construction, oversaw the first 35-foot-tall wood column placement, setting in motion the remarkable architectural design that harkened to the rolling hills of the Palouse and its sister athletic venue, the Kibbie Dome (University of Idaho 2020).

"We had an event in July 2020 out in the open with masks during construction, and it was the first gathering the university had since having to close for COVID-19," Dennis mentioned. "My college organized the event for donors and our industry partners to say, 'Come watch us put these beams up because it's really damn cool.' There was a feeling like we can get back to doing some things that we need to do in our business."

Idaho Forest Group processed timber to lam, Boise Cascade in Homedale, Idaho, and QB Quality Laminators in Salmon, Idaho, processed the glulam beams for the walls and roof structure, with PotlatchDeltic in St. Maries, Idaho, processing the finished veneer plyboard for the roof. Tri-Pro Cedar Products in Oldtown, Idaho, processed the finished cedar siding, creating a modern architectural design.

Inside, 442 tons of beautiful glulam beams towered over the first court dedicated to Vandal Basketball since Memorial Gym opened in

1928. More than 45,000 cubic feet of Idaho wood products created the foundation and atmosphere of the 67,000-square-foot arena. Compared to other conventional construction methods, the wood products also offered long-term carbon storage and a small carbon footprint.

"The entire industry in Idaho came together in amazing ways to complete this one-of-a-kind construction," said Dennis. "Showcasing Idaho's wood is great for the industry. The arena served as a living laboratory for our students as we train them to be the next wood-industry leaders."

The $51 million project came in on time and within budget. On October 8, 2021, the official ribbon cutting arrived in grand fashion. The "Brave. Bold. A Promise to Idaho's Students" campaign also kicked off with festivities inside the new 4000-seat arena. This facility will be a sustainable Idaho icon and a destination for generations.

Under Scott's leadership, the ICCU Arena's completion became a full-circle moment for him. His grandfather, Dr. Leon Green, served as head of the Department of Health, Physical Education, and Recreation beginning in 1951 and then as athletic director starting in 1973. He supervised the building and completion of the iconic Kibbie Dome, also at a time when the university was under some financial constraints. Dr. Green had to raise the money to complete the project and found William Kibbie, a contractor who contributed $300,000 (quite a sum at the time) to have the dome named after him.

Thanks to a gift from Clint and Kim Marshall, the university named the highly visible terrace at the front of the new ICCU Arena the Dr. Leon Green Vandal Terrace in honor of Scott's grandfather. The university announced the honor during a basketball game, much to Scott's surprise. Clint, Kim, and Scott's family had all managed to keep the naming a secret.

"The day the Vandal Terrace was to be named for my grandfather, strange things began to happen," Scott said, smiling. "I offered to have my good friends Clint and Kim Marshall stay with me and see a basketball game. They were receiving an honor for their very significant gift to the university and the arena. Clint was on our Foundation Board, so I did not think twice about having him visit the campus to be recognized. But when he showed up at University House, he had my youngest brother, Stephen, and his partner, Kirstin, in tow. I was

(Continued)

(Continued)

surprised that Stephen showed up, but he often joined Clint and me for golf outings, so I shrugged it off. But at halftime of the basketball game, Mary Kay and her Advancement team took Clint, Kim, my family, and me to one of the conference rooms. This was also odd. I thought we were going to the court to recognize Clint. It was then that I knew something was up. Clint told me that he and Kim were naming the terrace after my grandfather. It was admittedly an emotional moment for both of us. We then went up to the Idaho Alumni Club overlooking the terrace for the dedication. The room was packed. My grandfather and I had been very close while he was living, so this moment was very special to me. I was so choked up that I could not speak and had to go to the restroom to compose myself, but I returned for photos and the celebration. It is one of those life moments I will never forget."

Scott's Management Insight

Understand the difference between capital and operating budgets and manage them accordingly. Depending on how the institution finances capital projects, they can have a little or a lot of impact on operating budgets. If financed solely with debt, it can be an additional burden. If funded with donations and future student fees, there is little to no impact on the operating budget. The U of I had the capacity to build the arena given the funding sources, and once the operations and cash flow for the university were in balance, the university would be solvent and have a new arena to celebrate. The arena's opening was a proud moment for the campus. It was beautiful. It was built mainly with Idaho-sourced and -constructed wood products and labor. It came in on budget, proving we could accomplish big things if we utilized smart collaboration.

Chapter 17
The Values Wall

"Everybody on this campus should be a recruiter."

—*Terry Gawlik*

The ICCU Arena construction brought an air of hope and optimism to some, regardless of any controversy it created with others. Watching the massive wooden glulam beams go in one-by-one stirred excitement and started to shore up the eroded morale of Vandals near and far, especially within the Athletic Department.

Like many collegiate athletic programs, Idaho Athletics was, in some ways, its own entity. But they were undoubtedly an essential part of the institution and campus, highly invested in anything affecting student-athletes and constantly working to build a positive, safe, and compliant infrastructure around its beloved Vandals. For years, the department had been hit with compliance issues, budget deficits, and athletic director (AD) position changes.

Scott brought Terry Gawlik on board to fill the AD position because of her tremendous 25 years of contributions to a powerhouse athletic program at the University of Wisconsin and her expansive participation in the NCAA. She had the depth of knowledge and experience to morph Idaho Athletics into a stronger program and help build that infrastructure. Her love for fly fishing and her husband's ties to the area didn't hurt, either.

The department had experienced some rough years before Terry's arrival, including financial ups and downs.

"Most universities, including our own, don't have cash cows in athletics," Interim U of I President 2013–14 Don Burnett said. "Yet, if you're going to be competitive, you have to invest in it. When I served as interim president, I did have a connection with that and had to decide how much nonrestricted revenues would be allocated to athletics. That was a hard discussion. My predecessors and successors all have had similar problems. But we can't forget the most important aspect of athletics—the student-athletes. They come from a variety of geographical and diverse areas and are assets to the whole community. They aren't just wearing a uniform; they are members of the Moscow community."

Athletics had also weathered a storm of lawsuits filed by student-athletes involving student-athletes. In August 2018, the SBOE dismissed the AD because of how he managed the impacted students. The department, however, landed in good hands with interim AD, Pete Isakson, appointed in Spring 2018. Vandals around the nation knew Pete for his commitment to the U of I and the community of Moscow and his constant positive attitude and spirit. January 2020, however, cast a dark shadow over campus and in Vandal hearts when Pete suddenly passed away. To say U of I Athletics had been turned upside down with the loss, struggling in a constant state of flux, and compliance issues would be an understatement. But that didn't scare Terry from applying for the AD job.

Terry shared, "I asked a good friend of mine, who is a sitting AD, whether I should look at getting an AD job, and he said, 'Terry, honestly, there are no bad AD jobs; there are just bad presidents.' So I took that to heart, and it was true in so many ways. I did my recon on the U of I, and I'll be honest, the president was intriguing to me—his grandfather was a former athletic director. This one here, this guy, Scott, was a visionary. It quickly became apparent if you weren't getting on his rah-rah wagon, you were going to get left behind."

Terry's collegiate athletic experience gave her extensive knowledge about regulations, policies, and procedures within the athletic world and NCAA. Her vast insight included experience with Title IX, equity in athletics, and sexual assault and harassment training.

"I have high integrity," she said. "I'm a black-and-white rule follower, and when I arrived at the U of I, my goal was to establish policies and procedures, which were nonexistent in many ways. I also saw a disconnect between athletics and campus. We are not our own entity; we wouldn't exist without campus or students. I said we would do everything we could to be great partners. We were going to rebuild and do it brick by brick with honesty, integrity, and a focus on our student-athletes. Unfortunately, we found a lot of compliance violations embedded along the way, which honestly, I wasn't shocked given there were limited established policies, procedures, or monitoring."

"We had two NCAA level 2 violations to clean up that Terry and I inherited, which impacted our ability to compete until the summer of 2022," Scott shared. He wholeheartedly agreed with Terry's rebuilding attitude for Idaho Athletics. "We had to have winning programs, a strong system, and the compliance issues behind us. With Terry leading her team, we could."

The rebuilding also included settling into the Big Sky Conference. After President Staben announced in 2016 that Idaho Athletics would rejoin the Big Sky, a chasm formed between two camps of thought—one for and one against moving out of the FBS (Football Bowl Subdivision) and into the FCS (Football Championship Subdivision).

"It was a balancing act between investing in competition at the higher levels against the well-known teams and over-investing to the point it became a budget issue," Scott outlined. "I was personally opposed to the move to FCS on financial grounds, but the reality was that if Idaho Athletics was going to compete with those schools in an FBS conference, they had to have consistent funding, a consistent winning program, and a consistent culture of compliance that didn't create problems for the university. They didn't have any of those pillars."

It was a highly controversial decision, however, with alumni especially. Vandals fans from all over were voicing their dismay.

"We're not nearly as good as we used to be!"

"We're going backward!"

"We're a university in decline!"

As assistant vice president for Alumni Relations, Kathy Barnard heard it all. "That narrative got galvanized when we returned to the Big Sky among some. I found out there was a segment of the Vandal family that live, die, and breathe by athletics. When we moved back to the Big Sky, they were mad. It reinforced their dialogue about 'my university's going down hard by the bow.' That was the culture at the time Scott and Terry came."

Many hardline Vandals threatened to stop contributing to Vandal Athletics and the U of I. Returning to the Big Sky proved to be a flashpoint, and Scott understood that the boisterous boosters felt unheard by the previous administration. "But we're in a new day," he pointed out. "You're either onboard or not, and that's okay. But we're moving forward regardless for the betterment of the university and Vandal Athletics."

Terry also told alumni, "I'm not looking backward; I'm looking forward. We've got to build on what we have. We're in the Big Sky Conference, and that's the conference we need to be competitive in, and we need to work on that."

All that rebuilding also included facing a list of budget worries, but Terry realized the entire university needed to rebuild financially. "When I came to the U of I, I didn't realize campus was in the financial situation it was," she confessed. "In athletics, we always call it butts in seats. We wanted to have butts in seats at our games, so for us to survive as an institution, we had to get butts in seats on campus. Why wouldn't we want to help get students here? I don't see it as just our coaches or the admissions office recruiting. I think everybody on this campus should be a recruiter, faculty included. Students are our bread and butter."

Scott agreed with her thinking. "It's everyone's job to recruit on campus and to support Strategic Enrollment Management (SEM) in their job of recruiting and increasing enrollment, the go-on rate, and retention. We all rely on having those students because, without them, that's how we ended up in the mess we faced when I became president."

Scott's Management Insight

Tone from the top is a university's greatest strength or weakness. Compliance matters. To help set the tone in the right way, we borrowed a page from Villanova University's playbook and created a Values Wall that all the Idaho Athletic Department administrators, coaches, and student-athletes signed. It was a contract that we would *all* do our best to do the right things. I also signed the wall that first year and spoke to a cross-section of athletic leaders. I wanted them to know we were committed to compliance and working hard to repair our past mistakes.

A small handful of our alumni were acting up. They would publicly state that they would not give money to the university unless it went to the FBS football subdivision or fired certain athletic staff. Lamenting the past or how things used to be doesn't usually help current or future business affairs. You are better off rejecting any money tied to how the administration manages the university. The reality was that most big talkers always found a reason not to contribute. I was equally clear in public that real Vandals stick with their alma mater through thick and thin, and we know who the real Vandals are.

Terry cleared our NCAA infractions and began raising the competitive bar in athletics. We agreed that we didn't have much time to build a culture of compliance and competitiveness, so we are building a foundation that will last long after we are both gone. Some alumni would like to see us move faster, but we won't take shortcuts. We are building a quality and competitive program that will endure.

Scott's Third Rail

Athletics

Athletics is often called the front porch to a college or university. Its activities are visible to the greater community and bring alumni back to campus. We are all aware of the dollars associated with football and basketball, but there are Olympic sports that also bring students and pride to campus. Sporting events can be critical to the local economies of college towns. The Moscow Chamber of Commerce concluded that U of I Athletics annually brings in revenues of over $30 million to its hotels, restaurants, and shops (Moscow Idaho Chamber of Commerce 2021).

But Athletics also brings challenges. Student-athletes are on a stage, and when they do not behave well and get in trouble with the law, it can create issues for the university. Alumni can be deeply invested, and their disappointment with a team's win/loss record can create pressures for an administration and coaching staff. I often hear our alums say they will open their pocketbooks if we fire a particular coach, leave a certain athletic conference, or have a winning season. But I find those same alumni find different reasons not to provide financial support when a coach has been replaced, and the team is winning and playing big-money games. Coaches and alumni sometimes misbehave and put the president's job and the university at risk if the behavior is not addressed. As president, you should always make the decision that is right for the university, and the rest will follow.

Faculty can be the most critical of the Athletic Department. Athletics rarely makes money when looked at narrowly. Gate receipts, media rights, and donations will not pay for all the athletic scholarships, staff salaries, and facility operations. Some faculty will highlight these deficits and question why the university spends money on athletics instead of labs or advising. These are fair questions, and a president is wise to spend time understanding the total costs and benefits of the athletic program at their institution and patiently address queries raised.

In my experience, faculty analyses are often unintentionally biased and do not consider that the scholarships our student-athletes earn are revenue to the institution. Where athletics awards scholarships not fully funded by endowments, the department must come up with those

(Continued)

(Continued)

revenues. Athletes often have partial scholarships or are walk-ons paying full freight, including room and board. They may also have friends and siblings who also enroll at the university. And alumni not only give to athletic-related causes but often provide financial support for both athletics and university priorities. When well run, an athletic department can be a net contributor by increasing enrollment and gifts to the university. Even where there are deficits, the economic and social benefits to the community usually will dwarf any negative balances.

A winning athletic program can be the best advertising a university receives, driving enrollment, donations, and community spirit. On the other hand, student-athlete, coaching, and alumni behaviors can put an institution at risk, bringing NCAA sanctions and reputational damage. The president must ensure a compliance culture and fiscal responsibility in the athletic program because the NCAA holds them accountable. An athletic operation not properly run and managed can create discontent among faculty. Spend time ensuring your athletic program is well run, a strong university partner, and adds value to the community.

Part IV

Chapter 18
Priority Push

"Closing a program and letting tenured faculty go tears at the fabric of the university."

—Dr. John Crepeau

In addition to the monthly meetings with Scott, then-Provost John Wiencek and Kim Salisbury, associate vice president for Budget and Planning, regularly met with deans and vice provosts to hash out numbers.

"We now had a more uniform language to talk about finances than we did," College of Natural Resources Dean Dennis Becker said. "I didn't compare my finances to other colleges because we were different operations. But I think those monthly meetings with Scott, John, and the budget office allowed us to articulate that we were different from each other and appreciative that some colleges couldn't move salary around like I could. So their ability to deal with a budget cut was much more difficult than my ability to deal with it."

"We met every month until it got almost mind-numbing," Vice President Brian Foisy said and smiled. "But we kept doing it every month, every executive in charge of a budget. Everyone had their day in front of the president, provost, and me to show their previous month's balance and whether it was up or down. Everyone immediately started playing ball. They all wanted what was best for the institution. One of the things Scott did very well was to set expectations. He followed up and held people accountable. That was one of his superpowers."

"Scott knew a lot more about finance and accounting than I did," Dennis pointed out, "so it challenged me to learn. I knew the finances of this college, but after, I knew them even better. I sort of relished those meetings for the opportunity to show how we utilized our resources."

Throughout the process of finding $14 million in cuts, some of the hard-working individuals dissecting budgets unearthed a few nuggets of silver and gold. "We actually found some restricted funds we weren't using for their specific mission," Scott shared. "It helped the Gen Ed budget by not using unrestricted funds to pay for something restricted funds should have been paying."

The monthly reporting packages from the colleges and units fell into place as everyone hammered away at their respective targets. "Through the process, we realized we didn't have all the components in the past that we needed to paint the full financial picture during the course of the year," said Linda Campos, associate vice president.

"People's reports became a lot more standardized," Kim shared. "Scott met with everybody about what the budget office sent out; that process focused everybody's attention on one set of reports. That helped because everyone could go to those reports and determine if the figures they pulled up in a specific way matched the standardized reports."

"The Department of Finance and Administration needs to get a lot of credit for everything that's happened," expressed Chandra Zenner Ford, CEO SW Idaho and special advisor. "We couldn't have turned things around without the proper reports."

In the midst of working through the budgetary issues, in November 2019, Scott sent a request to the provost and the Institutional Planning and Effectiveness Committee (IPEC) asking them to offer their recommendations for a refresh to the Program Prioritization (PP) process. His intent was to use the refresh to also inform a finance and budget workgroup he was in the process of assembling. A committee of IPEC members with faculty and staff representatives and REAPP (Re-Envisioning Another Program Prioritization) focused on Scott's ask. After outlining their recommendations to him, REAPP would deploy the refreshed PP process and complete it by the end of the academic year in May 2020. A whitepaper tasked REAPP with respect to productivity measures and contributions to strategic goals. Metrics identified through the refresh process would outline themes relevant to establishing a new finance model and reward things such as enrollment, graduation, and tangible measures of research productivity.

Taking results from previous PP processes, REAPP met numerous times to evaluate programs, especially those identified in the lower quintiles. The task force compiled a list of recommendations regarding

(1) programs closed in the past but still in inventory for teaching out, (2) programs to be removed or merged, (3) programs to be discontinued voluntarily, (4) programs recommended for merger or restructuring by the task force, (5) programs recommended for adjustment for success, and (6) programs recommended for closure. The closure list resulted in eight programs voluntarily submitting closure by their deans (Stauffer, L., personal communication).

One program recommended for closure didn't fulfill the criteria outlined by the PP process but did not voluntarily submit for closure: Materials Science and Engineering in the College of Engineering. "Our college had to take about an 18 percent budget cut," Interim Dean John Crepeau recalled. "About 97 percent of our budget goes to salaries, so that meant we were going to lose people. Through our PP process and discussions with department chairs, along with weighing things like enrollment and grant funds, it seemed pretty clear to us that the Material Science program ranked the lowest on the PP scale. As a result, we phased out that program."

The closure would affect two programs and five faculty members on the tenured or tenure track list, so they wanted to make a final plea to reconsider terminating the program.

The university's final decision was to close the program and teach out the remaining students.

"It was a bummer because all branches of engineering need to have Material Science," John pointed out. "Things like aerospace and nuclear engineering use scientific materials to assist in designing a device. It was tough to see it go."

"I think PP was effective," Larry Stauffer, dean of the College of Engineering, acknowledged. "It made us take a step back and look at what we were doing. I had been through PP three or four times over the years, and we always cut things. This was the first time we actually cut something where we ended up laying off people. Material Sciences was a very valuable program. I didn't like getting rid of it. But we couldn't justify it due to low enrollments."

"Engineering was in a position where they had to make a more significant change," Provost Torrey Lawrence shared. "We terminated tenured faculty. There were only a few avenues where that could happen, and eliminating an entire program was one of them. We had to close the program because of its waning number of students. And we didn't just eliminate tenured faculty; there was staff in those departments."

"It was tough on the U of I when they closed that program," Scott said. "You don't just fire tenured faculty. It was a high-quality program; they were working with NASA. They'd been on the PP list before, but they waited until the final point to bring up solutions. That kind of upset me. Could I have kept it? Yes. Would that have been the right decision to keep it? No, not during a financial crisis. We made the hard call.

"U of I eliminated faculty and staff in material sciences, but there were also about seventeen students in that program," Scott pointed out. "The U of I had an obligation to teach those students, which took several years. Many of the students transferred because they didn't want to graduate from a program withering on the vine. So did the college actually save any money? I wasn't looking to eliminate programs to solve our financial problem. We would do better with voluntary headcount reduction programs and cost containment programs. In the end, it would take years for the closure of the Material Science program to add to the bottom line."

"Closing a program and letting tenured faculty go tears at the fabric of the university," John shared. "It can undermine trust because we're affecting human beings' lives and their families."

"The college had quite a bit of debt, too, due to hiring people associated with some grants," Larry explained. "So we had the debt and the budget cuts that amounted to losing about 25% of the college's Gen Ed funds over the course of a few years. But we were adding a new cybersecurity program at the same time."

On January 27, 2020, Scott and John hosted an All-Staff Town Hall Meeting to outline the process to address the current fiscal year's $14 million cut and future budget cuts.

Scott also established the first of several working groups to address the budget model at the university once and for all. The Financial Model group brought prominent alumni with strong business backgrounds together with faculty, staff, and student representatives. They would develop a new financial model using the work already accomplished by John, Brian, Linda Campos, Kim Salisbury, and Trina Mahoney.

"I learned about the depths of the financial scenario by listening at meetings and taking furious notes," Chandra said. She served as the President's Office executive sponsor for the Financial Model working group. "Everybody was making cuts, and at the same time, we started the working group to find a way to set budgets differently so that we wouldn't get in this situation again. Scott tasked us with putting in guardrails to make the model work. We focused on two primary financial goals: a balanced budget and a positive cash balance."

John and Brian made a presentation to the Financial Model Working Group at their first meeting. "We talked about various elements of the budget crisis," Brian recalled. "We took up most of the first meeting explaining what we'd already shared with the campus community."

The working group had their work cut out for them. There were so many details and layers to how the U of I got into the financial mess it faced. When Scott accepted the position as president, it loomed large, like a black cloud. People were nervous, untrusting, and scared. No one ever thought it would be easy. But with Scott's guidance and deans, vice presidents, vice provosts, and central executive officers meeting every month, hammering away at how to find $14 million, a sense of cautious optimism settled over the U of I.

Scott's Management Insight

Bring in outside subject-matter experts to work with faculty and staff to solve big problems. For the Financial Model working group, we brought in the retired CFOs of Simplot (think McDonald's french fries), Albertson's (the large grocery chain), and the retired chairperson of Deloitte & Touche. They brought business savvy and innovation to the models being discussed. We ended with a model uniquely suited to our institution.

Invest in quality, off-the-shelf analytical software and hire accounting, budgeting, and planning experts. Make sure your financial reports tell your entire fiscal story. If they don't, work with experts to fine-tune the data and how you're using it. Your reports should answer any and every revenue and expense question. Standardize reports so leadership, managers, and CFOs are all on the same page.

Scott's Third Rail

Accreditation

Anyone who climbs the academic career ladder understands the importance of accreditation. For nontraditional presidents, it is an enigma wrapped up in a conundrum. At the institutional level, it is required for its students to qualify for federal grants and aid. The process is all-consuming for administrators, college or department-level accreditations, and deans. The risks seem relatively low from a business perspective, as it is extremely rare for a university to lose accreditation. However, taking it for granted would be a mistake, as your faculty care deeply about the outcomes.

(Continued)

(Continued)

I have been through one department, one college, and one university-level accreditation process in my first three years at the institution. All were successful but with different outcomes. Each process was unique, but all requested a university response to certain questions. Faculty, staff, and administrators will sometimes take these opportunities to advance their agendas, so a president would be wise to review the answers to these questions before they are submitted.

For the university-level accreditation, the accreditors performed a helpful preliminary review identifying issues. The initial assessment allowed us to confirm or respond to some of the items the faculty interviews surfaced. One such item we received was a comment from some faculty that the working group constituted as a response to our financial problems was not as diverse or representative as in the past. This claim was simply untrue. The newly constituted working group was unpopular with some faculty, but the team we put together included faculty, students, staff, administrators, and outside financial experts. The group included the former chairwoman of accounting powerhouse Deloitte and Touche, former CFO of the national grocery chain Albertsons, and the retired CFO of Simplot, one of the nation's largest private companies known for supplying McDonald's with their frozen french fries. So the working group was *more* diverse and representative than a faculty committee, not less.

Additionally, we ran the resulting whitepaper through the Faculty Senate and the Staff Council and posted it on our website so all could comment. Finally, we made some adjustments based on the feedback received. The follow-up conducted by the accreditors determined that the process was inclusive and transparent, and their concerns were addressed.

For college- and program-level accreditation, the process usually ends with a presentation of the findings to the president, followed by a formal letter and a response from the institution regarding how they will address the findings. Institutional accreditation is even more formal and, at least for the University of Idaho, requires that the president travels to a hotel in Reno to present and respond to questions. In my case, I traveled alone but would recommend that a new president take their provost and primary academic liaison officer to ensure the team can answer questions at a detailed level.

The process requires that a president wait their turn in a lobby, enter a room to find all 20 commissioners (mostly presidents and chancellors of other institutions) and staff of the accreditation body standing, and remain standing until they tell you to sit. Once you are seated, the accreditation team lead presents an overview of their visit, commendations, and recommendations. The president then gets a chance to present. Specific questions from the commissioners then follow. It seemed to me that they let the president fully answer the question without interruption, giving as much time and rope as required. I would advise keeping your answers short and to the point. At the end of the question-and-answer period, all will again stand as the president leaves.

The committee followed up with a final letter a few weeks later. In our case, we had four commendations (citations for items they encourage we continue) and five recommendations with target dates they would like addressed, with the reaffirmation of accreditation. More importantly, we had a good review team that shared best practices gleaned from their experience at other institutions not included in the report that we found very helpful. While we have some work to do, our team considered this outcome a true success compared to previous reviews, where we had many more recommendations and no commendations.

Chapter 19
Magic

"There were a lot of things culturally at the university getting in the way of us doing our best and being our best."

—*Chandra Zenner Ford*

One of Scott's plans to help put the U of I on a course to financial and cultural success was to establish six university working groups. The working group model garnered input from internal and external experts regarding the institution's more significant challenges. Each group took a deep dive into all aspects of the strategic initiatives Scott selected and included:

Financial Model Working Group
R1-2026 Research Initiative Working Group
Comprehensive Campaign Working Group
Online Education Working Group
Sustainable Solutions Working Group
Magic Valley Working Group

The groups worked transparently to make informed decisions by offering a blueprint for action in each area of focus. Members of the groups represented all university stakeholders, establishing an all-encompassing process to set objectives and metrics to measure success. Each group presented recommendations to Core Ops, Faculty Senate, and Staff Council to ensure the shared governance approach for feedback.

Before Scott became president, four whitepapers existed regarding online education, but no implementation occurred, most likely due to a lack of funding or focus. "You can't just put the whitepapers out there and not execute," Scott pointed out. "This is an important management concept. Your working group needs a focus, a funding source, and a person responsible for managing its execution and completion."

CEO SW Idaho and Special Advisor Chandra Zenner Ford worked at the U of I before taking her position with the City of Boise (and then subsequently taking her position at the U of I when Scott arrived), and she recognized efforts similar to the working group concept. "My old boss at the College of Business and Economics, Jack Morris, ran a group that made several good recommendations about university finances. But they weren't called working groups. And only some of the group's suggestions were taken into consideration. There were other groups that would work together on a university problem by debating ideas, but they never assigned anybody to execute or be responsible for taking that next step. The turnover in presidents over the years at the U of I played into that, too. Even if somebody was working on execution for a university focus issue, sometimes a new president came in and decided it wasn't important. They focused somewhere else."

"I pulled together these working groups because that's how businesses execute," Scott said. "This was how to focus on an issue, to get good minds around it. Working groups can be almost magical. But universities weren't used to working like this; they were used to working internally. By bringing in industry experts, we took things to the next level and developed more innovative solutions."

Chandra explained that from the very beginning, Scott and his team spent considerable time building the group membership by taking nominations and considering who would be part of each working group. "One of the keys to making the working groups effective was bringing in representation from a lot of different backgrounds and areas so that we had diverse opinions at the table when it was time to debate. It wasn't just a slapdash thing. We took tremendous care thinking about who should be in the groups. At the same time, we knew they couldn't get so big they weren't manageable. In the end, there were probably people who would've been great to have in the working groups, but we had to have the right workable size."

As soon as the working groups completed and posted their whitepaper, an execution team met regularly to carry through on delivering results.

"Honestly, in the past, the university made some good faith efforts with larger issues, but they just didn't have the follow-through built into the process," Chandra said. "With Scott's working groups, the execution teams went through each issue and actually implemented the working group's recommendations."

Financial Model Working Group

Scott established his first working group, the Financial Model Working Group, in October 2019 to address the inner financial workings at the U of I. The institution's incremental fiscal model didn't serve the university's mission and ended up being unsustainable to the tune of $40 million in operating losses over three years. The Financial Model Working Group members built the Vandal Hybrid model using their combined decades of experience.

Scott announced the new Vandal Hybrid model on March 25, 2020. It established a more strategic perspective to budgeting and spending General Education dollars by providing funds to invest in programs that attracted students with an educational experience relevant to employers in an ever-evolving workplace. The model also addressed the need to regain fiscal strength, including aligning expenses with revenues, providing a permanent funding plan for operations and infrastructure, and reestablishing an adequate reserve position (University of Idaho 2021).

R1-2026 Research Initiative Working Group

From the beginning, Scott included research as one of his three strategic pillars. The path from R2 status to R1 status, where research and graduate education would be inextricably linked, kicked into full gear when Scott created the R1-2026 Research Initiative Working Group.

In January 2020, Scott established the group, and by April 2020, it finalized its whitepaper recommendation to move the university toward an R1 Carnegie Classification (very high research activity). R1 Carnegie Classification meant significantly larger amounts of funding in comparison to R2. The group encouraged a focus on new investments in postdoctoral scholar and doctoral research support and identified actions to improve research culture and incentivize greater research and doctoral degree productivity. P3 funds from the university's steam plant lease would fund the research strategy (University of Idaho 2020).

Comprehensive Campaign Working Group

Between January 2021 and August 2021, Scott, his advancement team, and the Comprehensive Campaign Working Group collaborated to set a $500 million goal to raise funds focusing on his three pillars of student success, research, and telling the U of I's story. Some saw the amount as aggressive, but Scott believed there was momentum going into the campaign. The U of I raised $54 million toward its goal in FY21 alone. The overall total raised going into FY23 was over $340 million. The "Brave. Bold. A Promise to Idaho Students" campaign launch took place on October 8, 2021, during the opening of the ICCU Arena. The campaign focused strictly on student scholarships, inviting alumni and donors to invest in scholarships, fellowships, experiential learning, and more to benefit students in Idaho for generations to come. The campaign closed the fiscal year raising $64 million, a new record.

The "Brave. Bold. A Promise to Idaho Students" campaign was the first phase in a two-pronged campaign designed to expand access to all of Idaho's capable students seeking a college education. Expanded scholarships would attract and retain qualified students by making a college education affordable. It also provided resources to further enrich the student experience in undergraduate research and study abroad opportunities, setting the U of I apart from its competitors and making its graduates highly sought-after in the workforce (University of Idaho 2021).

In October 2022, the U of I introduced its second phase named the "Brave. Bold. Unstoppable." campaign, which was more inclusive of university-wide priorities, in addition to continuing the student scholarship initiative.

"It's important to continue to improve and adopt best enrollment management practices to help students come to the U of I, even from out of state," Scott maintained. "Out-of-state students subsidize in-state students, helping replace the decades-long decline in state appropriations for higher education. We made tremendous strides in raising funds for scholarships during the campaign. The U of I raised more than $100 million for student scholarships in the first phase and, combined with previous endowments, awarded more than $50 million in scholarship tuition waivers and discounts in 2022."

Online Education Working Group

Scott established the Online Education Working Group in May 2020 with Dean Jerry McMurtry from the College of Graduate Studies as chair.

Through that workgroup and COVID-19 experiences, in November 2020, the group presented its whitepaper findings outlining the significance of online education even at the U of I residential campus (University of Idaho 2020).

"There were a lot of faculty who pushed back that online education wasn't as high quality and couldn't be done effectively or efficiently," Jerry stated. "Those questions and concerns got answered during COVID-19."

The group's recommendations led to Scott hiring Ken Udas in July 2021 as vice provost of Digital Learning to provide the leadership needed to implement the Online Education Working Group's whitepaper.

"Now more than ever, society expects a university to offer digital learning," Jerry pointed out. "The U of I was late to the game in that area, but we'll jump in now to identify the right programs for the state and Northwest. We already have some unique programs."

One example is the Theatre Arts MFA offered online. "A lot of people said it couldn't be done, but there were faculty in Theatre who just said they were putting it online. And they did," Jerry shared. "It takes a lot of video and time, but the Theatre MFA is now a niche program from Moscow, Idaho, that's gained national recognition."

Other colleges have turned the corner by offering even more online initiatives and in-person experiences. "The College of Business and Economics (CBE) faculty and staff built upon their experiences delivering distance education during the pandemic," CBE Dean Marc Chopin shared. "We now provide access to three existing degree programs through concurrent virtual delivery of courses—Operations Management and Human Resource Management through synchronous virtual delivery during the academic year and marketing courses online during the summer sessions."

"Another online program that has seen tremendous interest and growth is the Master's in Natural Resources (CNR)," Jerry said. "Dean Becker and the college saw a need in the industry. Federal employees receive a bump up in the salary scale with education. CNR built a natural resources–based degree that will help federal employees meet that educational component and move up the pay scale."

Sustainable Solutions Working Group

"When I started as president, I wanted to revive our research capability around sustainability," Scott shared. "When I looked at progress two years later within that focus area, we hadn't made much progress. To reach the goal of building the university's reputation as a leader in sustainable solutions, we needed degrees and certificates, something tangible, a product. I wanted every student who left the university to have some knowledge base in sustainability solutions and credentials to back it."

Scott admits he should've set up a working group right out of the gate to attain sustainability goals but didn't. "We made progress on everything that had a working group, so I should have done it with sustainability."

Again, Scott knew that when something wasn't working, he had to dig deeper to understand why. "It wasn't always about the people themselves," he clarified. "We had some of the best people working on this. They accomplished some great things, but they became frustrated when hit with campus cultural resistance."

"There were a lot of things culturally at the university getting in the way of us doing our best and being our best," Chandra articulated. "Since Scott got here, he's used all the tools he knows to remove cultural barriers on campus and collaborate to work across boundaries."

Scott was learning how to work in the shared governance model. "I used working groups in the private sector a lot," he explained. "I could just say, 'Go do this,' and they would go do it. It's different in academia, especially with the broken culture. I recognized not initially setting up a structure as a failure on my part. But I fixed it by establishing the Sustainable Solutions Working Group in November 2021."

The Sustainable Solutions Working Group finalized its whitepaper in September 2022 to establish an entity capable of executing the university's strategic desire to be known for sustainable solutions. The goal for a sustainability focus at the university offered three prongs (University of Idaho 2022):

1. Campus would embrace sustainable practices, such as recycling, and gain high LEED (Leadership in Energy and Environmental Design) ratings for green buildings.
2. Programming at the university would establish a cross-functional organization that could deliver degrees, certificates, and programs, along with incenting colleges to collaborate and create a sustainability curriculum that would appeal to incoming students at all levels.
3. The university would maintain a robust research program with sustainable solutions as a key focus.

Scott saw sustainable solutions as one of the most significant topics of focus for the U of I. He stated, "Literally every college at the University of Idaho will have a stake in this."

Magic Valley Working Group

Scott's most recent working group endeavor involves the Magic Valley. The Magic Valley includes Rupert, Jerome, and Twin Falls. Chandra explained the area is integral to the U of I's mission but was underserved. "We brought together a working group that included College of Southern Idaho (CSI), the local community college located in Twin Falls, to study the issue. We believe strong partnerships with CSI will be key to our future plans to better serve a growing part of Idaho."

Scott tasked the Magic Valley Working Group to finalize a whitepaper focused on options for Twin Falls and Jeorme. These locations will serve as companions to the research dairy (CAFE) and offer educational and tourism opportunities. The whitepaper is expected in late 2023.

Scott's Management Insight

Ignore macro trends at your peril. The share of destination campus education is declining and is at a cost disadvantage to online education. If you are behind in moving parts of your organization online, you need to make the required investment to catch up as quickly as possible. We invested in our online offerings because it would be mismanagement to not recognize the creative destruction hitting higher education and respond to it.

Identify the most significant strategic move the institution can make, given its current strengths. Megatrends such as sustainability can propel an organization to national prominence. We are known as national leaders in water research (quality, drought management, aquifer recharge, conservation, impact on infrastructure such as bridges, etc.). We have a world-class College of Natural Resources ranked at or near the top nationally for quality and best value. We also have strong soil, plant health, and plant breeding programs that play a vital role in sustainability. Even our policy arm, the McClure Center for Public Policy, published important work assessing the impact of rising temperatures on a broad section of the Idaho industry (University of Idaho 2022). So we have many of the parts needed to open a national center on sustainable solutions, a program that puts the U of I in a leadership position on the subject and positions us for generating future research important to Idaho and the country.

Smart Collaboration

Center for Agriculture, Food, and the Environment (CAFE), Magic Valley, Idaho

One of the most significant homeruns in Scott's first two years as president involved the Center for Agriculture, Food, and the Environment, or CAFE. Its evolution into a soon-to-be impressive research facility is a story that almost never was.

Agribusiness is a critical part of Idaho's diverse economy and a significant employer. Livestock, dairy, crop production, and food processing are growing sectors intersecting in challenging ways—in Idaho and beyond. CAFE will be a leader in addressing constraints on water usage and environmental quality while supporting the agricultural sectors of food processing, dairy, livestock, and cropland industries. This partnership between education, industry, and economic development stakeholders will result in dynamic research and education to solve complex problems. The university received a $10 million research contract with the USDA to help move the CAFE project forward, along with funds from the Idaho Dairymen's Association, the State of Idaho, and private donors.

CAFE will encompass three sites. The largest research dairy in the US will be located in Rupert, Idaho (Minidoka County), and execute research on a broad range of agricultural topics, including soil health, water, crop rotation, and sustainability. The dairy will house a herd of 2000 cattle in the heart of Idaho's dairy-producing region and make it uniquely positioned to address real-world issues facing the dairy and food processing industries (University of Idaho 2020).

It is proposed that CAFE Center be located in Jerome, Idaho (Jerome County), at the crossroads of Hwy. 93 and I-84 and will serve as a new center for partnership with CSI with classrooms, labs, dorms, offices, and a pavilion. The Magic Valley Working Group is currently assessing the feasibility of this proposal. The food processing site in Twin Falls, Idaho (Twin Falls County), will offer workforce training connected to the College of Southern Idaho (CSI).

"When I was looking at the job as president, I remember talking to President Staben," Scott recalled. "He wasn't sure CAFE was a viable

project because it was so big. He said I would need to decide on whether to proceed. I appreciated his comment because it was something I had to get my head around. When I left Idaho in 1984, the dairy industry was probably only in the middle of the pack out of all the states. It is now the third largest in the country, with companies such as Chobani and Glanbia making multi-million-dollar investments there. College of Agricultural and Life Sciences Dean Michael Parrella shifted our focus to Southern Idaho, where all the growth occurred. I saw the need, and there was even $10 million the state had previously appropriated, but no one knew where it was hiding."

One of the first tasks Scott assigned Toni Broyles when she started at the U of I in July 2019 as special assistant, strategic initiatives, Office of the President, was to find the $10 million. Upon her initial findings, she, Joe Stegner, state government relations director, and Kent Nelson, university general counsel, sat in disagreement about whether Scott could ask the governor directly to release it or if it needed to go through the legislature, which would mean it was dead on arrival.

Toni went to work and found the original documents of the legislative approval; the money was sitting with the State Division of Public Works. She set up a meeting with them to determine how the U of I could obtain the appropriated money. Toni then facilitated the strategy and drafted the letter sent to the State to get the $10 million in funds released and was successful. The CAFE project was on its way to becoming a reality.

"Remember, they'd never been visited before by a U of I president," Scott said, smiling. "It was great; we got a tour of the building and met with wonderful people. All we had to do to get the $10 million was to have matching funds. We'd just sold the Sandpoint Research Station and the first piece of our property in Caldwell, so we were close."

The U of I had two parcels of land in Caldwell, one with a large structure and a few acres, the other sitting in the Idaho Land Endowment controlled by the Idaho Land Board for the benefit of the University of Idaho (thank you, Morrill Act). After getting feedback about the two closed research properties' usefulness (or lack of), Scott engaged in one of his favorite management strategies of monetizing nonstrategic assets to redeploy them into productive assets. The two pieces combined sold for nearly $30 million.

(Continued)

(Continued)

When the first piece in Caldwell sold, the U of I wrote a memo to the state stating they would match the appropriated funds, and the $10 million was released. The CAFE design phase received the green light when the university received the SBOE's approval.

"The money had been appropriated years before and was just sitting there," Scott emphasized. "Nobody even knew it was there; it was like an urban legend. This will be the nation's largest dairy and research center that we're aware of, starting from scratch, ground zero. That allows us to study the effects of dairy on land, water, and air. I give Toni full credit. Our first big win came about two months into the presidency."

Scott understands the risk of constructing a large research dairy and experimental farm. "We've got a lot of good project management cost control around it," he assured. "Budgets are strict. Milk contracts are assured. We've learned from past mistakes, and we're being prudent every step of the way." Importantly, we leveraged that $10 million investment into roughly $80 million of federal grants to study solutions to dairy waste at the research dairy, study deep soil from around the state and nation at a world-class facility in Moscow, and implement climate-smart technologies on farms, ranches, and dairies throughout the state.

Scott's Management Insight

Take proceeds from the sale of outdated, nonstrategic assets and reinvest in those projects that will enhance the institution ROI. The Sandpoint and Caldwell research centers were outdated and useless due to a lack of investment. The U of I effectively mothballed them, but the land they sat on was valuable, particularly the Caldwell property outside Boise, now surrounded by housing developments. Selling them freed up capital to invest in productive research assets.

Smart Collaboration

Rinker Rock Creek Ranch, Hailey, Idaho

Rinker Rock Creek Ranch is a 10,400-acre facility doubling as a living laboratory for research, education, and outreach obtained by the U of I in 2019. It is unique as it covers an entire watershed (an area of land that sheds or drains water into a specific body of water) almost entirely protected from development, enabling research that is otherwise difficult to execute with reliable results from all variables in the habitat. The ranch offers hands-on experience with rangeland management and conservation, focusing on researching sustainable grazing practices and their impacts on wildlife. The facility provides programming for Central Idaho about plants, wildlife, stream restoration, and cattle management (University of Idaho n.d.).

"A lot of people live in this area that are interested in the natural environment and range practices," College of Agricultural and Life Sciences Dean Michael Parrella said. "There are cattle that forage on that range; there are endangered sage grouse; there are invasive weeds; there are fire issues; there are predation issues. We can conduct research that addresses critical areas in Idaho because we maintain the ecosystem services with respect to that rangeland. We can research basic questions, such as: How do cows move on the range? What do they feed on? What plants do they prefer? Will they feed on the willows that are there? We also maintain fish coming up Rock Creek and spawning from that reservoir, so we're restoring that entire system. It is one of the few places, if not the only place in the country, where you can perform controlled research on an entire watershed. The living research laboratory looks at issues not only in Idaho but in the West."

The Rinker Rock Creek Ranch conducts its research through the U of I's Rangeland Center, collaborating with The Nature Conservancy and Wood River Land Trust. That collaboration is, in itself, unique. It is rare when environmentalists, cattle ranchers, and researchers agree on anything, let alone all come to the table in the spirit of compromise. The land, ranching practices, and research will all benefit from the work conducted at this facility.

(Continued)

(Continued)

Scott's Management Insight

Collaborations are powerful but challenging work. Who would have thought you could bring ranchers, environmentalists, scientists, and government agencies together to agree on anything, let alone how to conduct research and conserve the environment in a sensitive ecosystem? But it did happen at Rinker Rock Creek Ranch. All the participants entered the negotiations for its formation, recognizing that they may only get 80 percent of what they wanted to achieve, but that is much better than zero. The result is essential research on sustainable ranching practices that protect the environment.

Chapter 20
Changing Levers

"You don't just dig yourself out of a $20 million hole by yourself or because someone is saying to do it."

—Dr. Blaine Eckles

So how did they do it? How did the U of I identify $14 million in current fiscal year cuts? The university put its financial house in order by facing reality and not shying away from the problem. They met the deficit by addressing headcount and operational budgets and taking new approaches to funding.

Headcount

The headcount issue was one of the main drivers of the deficit, so Scott implemented several programs that reduced a portion of the 80 percent of the General Education budget made up by people. "The FTE [full-time equivalent] ratio of faculty to students was too high," he said. "We had to achieve a reasonable ratio that our budgets could handle, not just for FY20 or FY21 but indefinitely. It's a difficult process because we deliver education programs, and people deliver that education."

Scott made it clear that there would no longer be willy-nilly hiring; if a college or division could make a solid case to the administration using data, they could fill a position. Otherwise, jobs were consolidated or shifted around to maximize efficiency and minimize salary expenditures.

"Sometimes departments would come to Human Resources and ask for opinions or thoughts," Director of Human Resources Brandi Terwilliger remarked. "They would brainstorm with their business partner or HR support person and figure out the best approach to use when eliminating positions or not rehiring. There was some confusion, though, that if a college or unit eliminated a position, that meant the person seated in that position was automatically let go, and that wasn't necessarily the case. We had to look at everybody in that group within a division, and the person with the least retention points in the division got laid off, even if it was in a different department. People were very conscientious about not negatively affecting another department and engaged HR in those conversations so we could help them see where the effect would actually happen."

None of the choices to bring the numbers in line were optimal. "Nobody thought this was easy," Brandi articulated.

The components put into action to reduce headcount weren't necessarily new to higher education or even the U of I. But Scott and his team felt the best solution to the problem was the tried-and-true one. "Separations made all the difference," Scott shared. "That got us back to equilibrium and financial health."

UNFILLED POSITIONS: Every position at the university that sat vacant when Scott implemented the significant budget cuts in July 2019 stayed vacant unless it was imperative to the institution's mission and goals. Each new position filled had to go through an extensive evaluation of whether the university could pay out that salary and continue the road to financial recovery because if a position sat vacant, the salary expenditure was zero.

"We lost a couple of positions, and that took a toll," Assistant Vice President Kathy Barnard shared regarding alumni relations. "We adjusted and stopped doing some things, so we could do other things."

Dean Dennis Becker, College of Natural Resources, pondered throughout the process, "How long could we go without a certain position? It was just a very delicate balancing act. FY22 would be the hardest because we would be living with the choices we made in FY20. There were difficult choices."

"We lost staffing positions in critical areas," CEHHS Interim Dean Philip Scruggs shared. "We didn't have anyone within our development area, so when you think about investment fundraising, we were without someone for a couple of years."

"Over the time period of 2017–2020, we lost roughly 20 percent of our faculty positions and just under 50 percent of College of Science staff positions that were paid from the General Education budget," College of Science Dean Ginger Carney recalled. "Most of those position losses occurred during the approximately $1.7 million cut that came just before/as Scott was starting as president, although we had lost a few each of the prior years due to smaller budget reductions. During that large cut, we had very little discretionary funding left in departmental budgets, so nearly all the cuts came from salaries. We consolidated from seven departments to five, which achieved some administrative and staffing salary savings, and we did not fill open staff or faculty positions. Those staffing losses affected every part of our work, from teaching to research to student recruitment and retention."

MARKET-BASED COMPENSATION RATE FREEZE: Scott immediately placed a freeze on market-based compensation and approved it for only the most severely underfunded positions.

"The Staff Council was anxious to get the program back," he pointed out. "They advocated for their people. I wanted to be able to pay hardworking people more. But I had to balance that and make sure we could pay for it first."

VOLUNTARY SEPARATION INCENTIVE PROGRAM (VSIP): Any employee who wanted to leave the U of I obviously could. The U of I offered 33% of their budgeted FY20 salary to employees who worked at the university for ten years or more without an already-approved resignation or retirement announcement if they chose to leave during the established period. According to Brandi, 36 employees took advantage of the VSIP program.

OPTIONAL RETIREMENT INCENTIVE PROGRAM (ORIP): Employees aged 55+ who worked a minimum of 20 consecutive years for the university or did not already have an approved retirement plan would receive 20% of their FY20 budgeted salary annually for three years. Payments would begin after the start of FY21.

"One of the downsides to both the VSIP and ORIP processes was that when people left, sometimes the ones we wanted to stay opted to leave; sometimes we had to take a hit," Scott shared.

Seventy-six employees chose ORIP.

"VSIP and ORIP created a lot of departures and the loss of institutional knowledge," Brandi pointed out. "But not all those positions were left vacant."

Overall, however, the cost savings to the university by offering ORIP and VSIP for a specified amount of time was significant and imperative to the campus hitting its financial targets.

VOLUNTARY FURLOUGH: The university put a voluntary furlough into play where people could elect to "give back" hours of pay but continue to work a regular week. According to Brandi, the university implemented the program for FY20 and yielded 9,559.53 hours, equating to $301,567.45 during the voluntary furlough period.

"Many people participated in the voluntary furlough," Brandi shared. "Even if they were feeling discouraged or morale was low, Vandals did anything they could to help. They took voluntary furloughs because they cared about the overall community. If we gave employees the option of taking a pay cut versus a colleague losing their job, we would see overwhelming support for taking a cut because they didn't want someone to lose their job."

The university even saw a handful of employees take a voluntary pay reduction to help their overall unit. They did it without the desire for anyone to know. It happened for more than one year, too.

"That's not an insignificant thing," Brandi stated. "Clearly, they were more concerned about the community in the Vandal family than themselves. That's pretty remarkable."

INVOLUNTARY SEPARATION and NONRENEWALS: Every position cut has a human component. Few people faced involuntary separation or nonrenewals, but some did.

"When you live in a small town, these people losing their jobs are your neighbors," Associate Vice President for Finance Linda Campos pointed out.

"There was only so much we could cut out of operations," Vice President of Information Technology and Chief Information Officer Dan Ewart shared. "I had to go to the personnel side to reduce IT's position count by approximately 20 percent, which meant sixteen positions eliminated, four of those filled at the time. Once I figured out the writing on the wall after trying every way to cut, I had to let those four individuals know. I gave them six months of notice, so they had as much time as possible to find another job or situation."

After the cuts, Dan knew it would be difficult for those remaining in IT. "I refused to ask them to do more with less," he shared. "I said we had to do different with less; we had to rethink how we would do things."

One day, well into the process of cutting people and positions, Linda saw Dan in the hallway at the Administration Building. "He looked pensive," Linda said.

"Hey, Dan, how are you doing?" she'd asked.

"I'm good, but I'm starting to have meetings with my team about delivering nonrenewal letters," he shared.

"The look on his face that day hit me," Linda confessed. "It was so real because I could see how it affected him. The cuts weren't performance-related; they were position cuts. He wanted to tell them months ahead so they could make plans."

"I took very seriously the responsibility that came with impacting people's careers," Dan said.

"There were a few separations that were not voluntary, although most were voluntary," Ginger shared. "My college [College of Science] was one of the few that laid off faculty who were on the tenure track. It was really tough—the hardest decision I've faced in my career. Those nonrenewals were made strategically, although the remaining faculty are not necessarily able to see that. They don't know the circumstances as they are confidential."

"Before I came to the U of I, I had never done a reduction in force [RIF] as a result of a budget cut," Vice Provost for Strategic Enrollment Management Dean Kahler pointed out. "I had to lay people off in SEM. That was not fun because I knew those decisions impacted people and families. I understood what we had to do as an institution, but it was tough."

"I chose to do cuts through vacated positions in Student Affairs," Vice Provost of Student Affairs and Dean of Students Blaine Eckles recalled. "I got through that whole budget cut by eliminating just one person. But that one person was still affected."

"I didn't have anything else to cut in terms of programs or faculty in the College of Art and Architecture," Dean Shauna Corry recalled. "We cut staff, and then we reorganized our staff. We cross-trained everyone; we created a centralized pool of staff. Some faculty didn't like the idea; they didn't have a program assistant of their own. Instead, we had a program assistant for *all* the programs. I was a faculty member while also serving as dean who had concerns about moving to this new model. It was a challenge, but I think we learned a lot. I think individual people grew in their positions; it was a professional development experience for many of our staff. It brought people closer together to try to solve problems."

A total of 56 involuntary separations or nonrenewals took place in 2021.

Operational Budgets

Out of the smaller component of the General Education budget—20 percent—came the most significant portion of cuts. Operational budgets included everything from travel to paper clips. "There were many complaints," Scott remembered. "Some professors told students they couldn't give out blue books anymore because they didn't have them, which was untrue. Others said they couldn't afford to make copies, so they couldn't give exams or quizzes. I wanted to go out and buy paper for people. But that's the kind of stuff some people did just to push back on the administration, putting themselves first instead of the university. But at the end of the day, they were an incredibly small handful of employees. The super majority put the institution first and made it work."

Faculty and staff left no stone unturned when looking for cuts within the operational budgets. Looking at university processes took time and may have cost some upfront funds, but in many cases, those exercises turned up potential long-term savings in operations through streamlining.

New Approaches to Funding

LEVERAGING PARTNERSHIPS: "We made a very conscious strategy in this college [Natural Resources]," Dean Dennis Becker shared. "Scott gave me the confidence during all this, and we said, 'Let's not just hunker down, hope the whole thing blows over, and then deal with it on the other side.' We decided to be very aggressive at telling our story and leveraging our partnerships. We encouraged more partners to invest in what we were doing because we had an amazing story to tell."

Dennis collaborated with partners for joint positions with agencies who heard CNR's story and felt they were doing important work for them and the industry. "We paid for half the positions, and our partners paid for half the positions," he explained. "It was through those kinds of arrangements we pulled out of that soft salary challenge that I had to endure when I became the dean. I think Scott had a similar perspective in that CNR and the U of I had these legacy programs and partnerships. Shame on us if we didn't leverage them for more than just good press. We started challenging our partners in many ways to put their money where their mouth was, and that was a Scott strategy."

PUBLIC-PRIVATE PARTNERSHIPS (P3): "Scott's breadth of knowledge was key to the budget-cutting process," Brenda Helbling, chief of staff, emphasized. "But he also used new approaches to address long-standing problems, which tied directly to his background, and why he was the right person for the job at the right time."

For example, the P3 the U of I struck up with the global finance and infrastructure consortium of Sacyr, Plenary, and McKinstry, a world-class utility operator.

A public-private partnership, or P3, involves a government agency collaborating with a private-sector company to help finance projects or initiatives. The U of I would procure the services of an industry partner to utilize their resources and expertise.

"I'd read about Purdue University doing a P3 for housing," Scott explained. "But we had a lot going on with budgets and cutting, so pursuing a P3 wasn't my highest priority. It was top of mind, though, because I recognized it could be used to raise revenue to fund our strategic initiatives. At some point, Mike Fery, an alum, said he had some people who knew how to do this, and I thought it was probably time to get the process underway. I asked Brian's team to research all our assets to determine which candidates would be good for a P3."

Brian Foisy's Division of Finance and Administration team returned with extensive data for Scott to consider. They decided to focus on the utility system because it would give the U of I the biggest bang for its buck and have the least impact on students. They could pull out the most money and not lose anything because it was a nonstrategic asset. It then went out to the RFP (request for proposal or bid) process. Scott knew working a P3 deal would fulfill a vital need; the U of I had an estimated $80 million of deferred maintenance on the utility system alone. At that time, the university wasn't receiving sufficient funds from the state to keep up with deferred maintenance.

"If we were going to do this, we needed to do it right to build trust on campus," Scott stated. "We had to take care of the employees of the Utility and Engineering Services team properly. We had to make sure to address their PERSI retirement funds. With McKinstry, our current U of I steam plant employees would work for an organization with a bounty of expertise and where they'd have a career path outside of the U of I steam plant. Our steam plant operators could end up going to Seattle or anywhere around the country if they wanted because McKinstry would help develop real skills. That's what they do. They're subject matter experts."

"One of the most amazing parts of this deal was that Scott and Brian were willing to spend money to retain these employees," said Lee Espey, division operations officer, Division of Finance and Administration. "Brian and I spent a few months pouring over these folks' retirement data to design 'transition packages' that essentially 'kept them whole.' This was one of my first meaningful contributions at the U of I. We were able to transition nineteen out of twenty-one Utility and Engineering Services team members to McKinstry."

"You should have seen people's eyes get big when Scott talked about monetizing assets, like the steam plant for P3 money," Brenda said, laughing. "Scott was taking us in different directions to reset the course of the university, both financially and culturally."

"It was a brutally complex transaction from finance, insurance, and legal standpoints," Brian shared. "It was one of those four-inch-thick-binder deals."

"I currently manage the P3 relationship, and I live and die by the four-inch binder that sits on my desk," Lee commented. "I would move it, but I'm scared I might need it."

And what a deal it was. For 50 years, Sacyr Plenary will lease the U of I's steam plant and utility system. The partnership provides a unique way for the U of I to invest in strategic initiatives. McKinstry handles the much-needed $80 million of deferred maintenance on the utility system, with the U of I paying that back over time as depreciated.

"The deal involves steam and condensate, compressed air, chilled water, domestic water, reclaimed water, and electricity," Lee explained. "It goes beyond the steam plant, but the general gist is that it covers production and distribution."

Sacyr Plenary provided the university an up-front payment of $225 million (finalized in Spring 2021). A portion went to defease outstanding bonds on the power plant and reimburse capital improvements paid for by the partnership. (Defeasance is a provision in a contract that voids a bond or loan on a balance sheet when the borrower sets aside cash or bonds sufficient enough to service the debt.) The university invested most of the upfront payment in a Strategic Initiatives Fund (quasi-endowment) to support revenue-generating programs aligned with student success, research, and telling the U of I's story objectives, such as:

1. Student scholarships;
2. Development of online offerings;
3. Hiring postdocs to supercharge the institution's march to R1 research status (and getting more federal grants in the process); and
4. Investing in digital marketing to increase enrollment.

The P3 investment in research could potentially increase competitiveness for research funding. In addition, the project provided an opportunity and incentive to maximize the efficiency and effectiveness of a key element of the university's infrastructure that had long suffered from a lack of funding and deferred maintenance.

"Scott walked in one day and said, 'We're doing this, Brian, and I want it done in nine months, and let me know when it's done,'" Brian said, laughing.

Enter once again the speed of Scott.

"I'd never done one of these deals before," Brian continued. "In fact, there were only two university CFOs in the entire nation who had at the time. We started from scratch. There were some tense moments when I was trying to figure out how to tell Scott that we couldn't do what he wanted within the time frame he gave us."

"I knew it would take longer," Scott said and smirked. "But I had a lot of experience both from the investment banks and the law firms I worked for to know that the longer these took to get to market, the more expenses would rack up, so I put an impossibly short deadline on it knowing it would go longer but keeping our foot on the gas so that we did not rack up needless costs."

"The P3 project was a game-changer," Brian stated. "There was no part of the university that wouldn't be transformed as a result of what we did."

"It makes total sense to monetize nonstrategic assets," Scott pointed out. "So we did. We're in a better place than we would have been having not done this. Not only do we get money from the fifty-year lease with a concession agreement that will ensure investment in strategic initiatives, but we brought in talent that can help improve the operations of that facility. We'll keep that plant operating in tip-top condition and continue to make capital investments in electricity generation there using the three newly installed Microsteam turbines."

When U of I finalized the deal in Spring 2021, one of the top corporate officers indicated to Brian one of the deciding factors of partnering with the institution. He told him, "We're doing this deal with the University of Idaho because it's a good investment opportunity. It's also because of the university's heart, soul, and commitment to its mission and students. That's why we picked you."

"The great part about this story was that in the first year, $6 million was generated by the new endowment," Scott shared. "That increased the number of scholarships available. We also invested in developing our online classes so we could reach students wherever they were. Some of the funds also went into research and telling our story. We made investments in marketing and digital outreach and signage around the state to reach new and returning students."

For FY23, the university has $7.3 million to distribute to those same focus areas and bring sustainability initiatives into the mix. "The campus immediately saw the benefits of this deal," Scott said.

INSOURCING VS. OUTSOURCING: Insourcing and outsourcing were other potential cost-cutting tools Scott investigated. "There's a place for both, but you have to do your research to ensure it saves you money and is the best move for the university. Sometimes, it will end up costing you more."

Scott asked Brian to investigate outsourcing the university's Facilities Management (FM) branch. However, after the process concluded, Scott held little confidence in the vendor that they would potentially select. They realized FM outsourcing would do more damage than good.

"FM addressed its management issues by bringing in outside experts to set objectives and a clear path to success without outsourcing," Scott shared. "The manager we had in place was reassigned to a different job where he excelled, and we hired a new manager to effect needed organizational change. Their efficiency and customer service metrics saw sustained improvement. Gone were the days of doing something because it was the way it was always done."

Scott and his team also recognized that the opportunity to outsource the textbook portion of the VandalStore to Texas Books was a viable solution and excellent ROI. The outsourcing allowed the U of I to keep control of the retail apparel side of the bookstore, avoid an annual $250,000 loss, and receive payment of $200,000 every year in franchise fees from Texas Books.

Scott's Management Insight

Use the lease or sale of non-strategic assets to fund strategic initiatives. Think outside the box for nontraditional funding sources. Identify company and industry partners and government opportunities that can become funding sources. Launching the public-private partnership to lease the steam plant was a transformational transaction for the campus.

Find where you are hemorrhaging financially, and stop the bleeding. Even smaller but easily achievable amounts add up and combine into significant savings. When investigating something like outsourcing as an option, ensure the vendor can win hearts and minds and save you money. If not, you are better off hiring strong people to create change. Fortunately, we had a strong VandalStore manager, but books were just not in our wheelhouse. Carving that piece out and handing it over to subject matter experts resulted in a $450,000 financial improvement.

Going through all the cost-cutting scenarios can reshape your university culture, both positively and negatively. When you reduce headcount through various options, realize you may lose some top-notch employees. Be prepared for those changes and hire new talent accordingly. We had to look at how to reassign duties. Some lower priority duties were distributed or discontinued, but there were times when we would have to replace the employee who voluntarily separated or retired, but we were usually able to do this at a lower cost. When implementing an RIF, don't ask employees to do more with less; ask them to do things differently and provide support to help them figure out how that looks.

Smart Collaboration

Hiring Process Evaluation

"I knew one of my major areas of focus and responsibility when the U of I hired me in 2015 was the hiring process," Brian Foisy, vice president for Finance and Administration, shared. "The classification and compensation system for employees was broken. And within three months of my starting, Brandi Terwilliger [director of Human Resources] and I convened a group to address the hiring process, which had become more cumbersome, complex, and lengthy than it needed to be."

That undertaking revealed that the group, a hiring streamlining committee composed of 30 employees from across campus, wasn't open to the fresh approaches Brian suggested. "At one point, I said that requiring people to go through a full-blown search process, including getting a search committee convened and on-campus interviews every time we hired the positions that were on continual hire, was ridiculous. For example, we hired custodians all the time, so did we need to perform full searches for every benefits-eligible position on campus? And almost every person pushed their chair away from the table and said how dare I suggest such a thing."

The group's reaction was so visceral to the idea that each position required or warranted a search committee, regardless of the constant hiring of the same position, Brian and Brandi dropped the subject.

The group's focus shifted from benefits-eligible hires to how the U of I could hire part-time positions on campus more quickly. Brian and Brandi worked to chip away at the number of hiring steps, or "stops," to make filling a position more efficient. Even removing one or two stops was a win in their book. But they knew there was still room to improve.

When Scott became president, he'd heard from Brian, a few deans, and direct reports about the concern over the cumbersome process of bringing on new employees. At one of their monthly financial meetings in 2020, College of Natural Resources Dean Dennis Becker and Scott talked about the process; Dennis pointed out that the university's hiring procedures were antiquated. He should know; he served on the

(Continued)

(Continued)

hiring streamlining committee and knew the history behind the efforts and tortoise-paced conversion to more up-to-date practices.

Dennis had explained to Scott, "The processes are hurting our ability to bring in good talent. And worse yet, they're causing enormous internal and institutional conflict."

When he shared that the current hiring procedures created unnecessary expenditures, Scott wanted to hear more. Dennis gave him the example that he would spend more on salaries to get a $5,000 change in somebody's administrative stipend than the $5,000. "I'll spend $20,000 in people's time trying to get that $5,000 change," he'd shared.

Scott replied, "I just can't believe that would be true. I'm not questioning you and saying that it isn't true, but that's hard to believe."

Scott discussed the tidbit with Brian, who agreed that an outdated and cumbersome hiring method most likely cost the university money. Brian explained to Scott his desire to update how the university hired people and Brandi's history in trying to do so since 2013. She'd suggested at previous meetings with Brian to hire an outside consultant. Brian knew the timing was right to present that idea to the president.

"Where it was costing the U of I the most money was having unfilled positions," Brandi remarked. "We were trying to recruit, but our process was taking so long, we'd lose candidates. That took away our competitiveness. Candidates didn't want to hang on from the time of the job posting to four months later when nobody was communicating with them, and it took so long to fill the position."

Pinpointing the problems and finding solutions would cost the U of I even more money, but in the long run, Scott agreed the university needed to get a handle on the situation to create efficiency and possibly save some expenditures. He gave Brian and Brandi the go-ahead to hire a consulting company. They tapped Segal as the consulting firm to examine the entire picture and offer their findings and suggestions.

"We asked Segal to look at the time to hire," Brandi explained. "Did it make sense to remove certain people or stops from the process? They found that there were one hundred thirty steps to complete in the standard hiring process. Generally, that included nineteen approval requirements with thirty-one handoffs between units, which included

the back-and-forth within the department and with HR to check for things like compliance."

"Our hiring processes were completely upside down," Dennis said. "It created an enormous amount of stress and cost a lot. My college was getting hit over the head for our inability to follow the process; we just didn't understand why it had to take so many steps."

"We wanted Segal to look at our workflow and who absolutely had to be involved with the stops," Brandi continued.

"They found that the U of I had about three times as many hiring steps as our peer institutions," Brian recalled.

"Another finding was that out of 1515 positions, the U of I had nine hundred thirty-one job titles," Brandi shared. "They suggested we quit creating unique titles because it created an additional burden. We had ten people across the institution doing the same job but had ten different titles. We had to streamline those."

Brian likened it to Dr. Frankenstein building the monster. "Over time, the university inadvertently created these weird processes. We'd take an 'arm' from over there, a 'head' from over there, and a 'leg' from back there. We'd pull it all together and put it in front of everybody. It was this horrible, unruly thing."

But the university could integrate and simplify those 931 titles while still adhering to compliance issues regarding laws and regulations to morph the "beast" into a manageable instrument to attract and hire qualified people to work at the U of I.

"We wanted to reduce this huge hiring burden for campus," Brandi shared. "In 2016, we made progress; we went from a flowchart going around my office five times to one that went around it twice. It was a win, but we had a lot more work to do. We had discussions with departments regarding their frustration, especially when people left the university and took their institutional knowledge with them."

"But through that process of losing the people with institutional knowledge, we also got rid of some roadblocks we found to be outdated," College of Graduate Studies Dean Jerry McMurtry pointed out. "We had some longtime employees who left, and we were able to create new ways of doing things."

Along with addressing Frankenstein's monster, Segal also helped to manage a conciliation agreement from the 1970s that required the

(Continued)

(Continued)

implementation of certain functions when hiring. Segal pointed out that the hiring environment had significantly changed between 1970 and 2021; they recommended revising the agreement with current practices using the university general counsel's expertise.

"Segal recommended the changes occur in three phases," Brandi outlined. "We were already working on things in phase three as of March 2022. We had the momentum and a supportive environment."

After the separations during the budget cuts, Scott knew hiring new people would be tough for a few reasons. "We told Human Resources to get out and hire good people even though we knew it would be challenging with things like lower wages," he clarified. "We knew if we didn't hire anyone, it would be good for our financial numbers, but it would also be horrible for operations and morale. Losing that many people—over two hundred and not all in the right places—would make some people feel overwhelmed."

Scott's Management Insight

Department management will generally hesitate to bring in outside consultants to evaluate their operations. How the CEO or president communicates such initiatives will be critical to its success. Leadership or administration should assure those managing the department that no one will be punished or fired for the results of an audit; rather, it is an opportunity to improve, and management will be credited and celebrated for implementing those improvements. If there is still resistance, it may be necessary to replace leadership to find that change agent. In this case, that was not necessary. The management team embraced the findings and adopted a road map to implement the recommendations.

Usually, over time, rules and steps are added to institutional policies and procedures, and often those executing the steps did not design them or even know why they were in place. Regularly evaluating core processes for efficiency and ROI and documenting the why behind the evolution of the policies and procedures (institutional memory) can help save time and money.

Chapter 21
Healthy, Wealthy, and Wise

"The way you move an organization is to build trust."

—*Dr. John Wiencek*

By December 2019, Scott was settling into his role and felt more comfortable as lead Vandal. "Scott was a quick study," Mary Kay McFadden, vice president for University Advancement, observed. "He was always strategic, friendly, and disciplined, and that made for a good fundraiser and president."

The colleges and deans were deeply rooted in budget-reduction mode. They left no stone unturned that could reveal a cut or source of revenue. Everyone pitched in, some willingly, some grudgingly. Regardless, the deans and division heads inspected and dissected every aspect of the university's fiscal body and set on a path toward fiscal health and rejuvenation.

"The way you move an organization is to build trust," then-Provost John Wiencek said. "Transparency was a key part in building that trust with Scott."

Scott and John talked about how to bring along the colleges that weren't entirely on board. "I suggested he meet with the college advisory boards as soon as possible and explain the budget cut situation," John said. "Many colleges made up their advisory boards with businesspeople; they all had the capacity to understand. Scott could sort of cut things off at the pass to not let things unravel at the dean or board level."

"Provost Wiencek, Brian, and I felt $14 million was the deepest we could cut at one time without hurting the institution or its mission," Scott shared. "The U of I reported losses in FY17 and FY18 of over $25 million, and FY19 reported a $19 million loss. We'd all worked together to squeeze out every non-personnel cost we could for FY20 since the state had already approved the budgets and spending was happening. Ultimately, the employee separations got us where we needed to be."

Scott was completely aware that losing people, either voluntary or involuntary, would play with the morale on campus. People might feel overworked to fill those holes or that their work dynamic changed because people they enjoyed collaborating with left. But again, he looked at the data. "The metrics told us that even after the separations, we were still properly staffed for our university size and type."

People were sometimes bitter and felt angst toward individuals they blamed for the budget crisis, but much of that hinged on the information they received. "As long as someone knows what they've got in front of them, they can work with that," John shared. "But if they're confused or lack trust, it's hard to focus on the problem and fix it. Despite that, everyone did their work."

The deans voiced a resounding consensus that the key to finding the $14 million for FY20 and reorganizing the fiscal model was the monthly meetings with Scott.

Those meetings showed Scott was watching and expected everyone to deliver. But along the way, they became forums for the deans to get to know their president better and form vital relationships built on trust and mutual professional respect. Those relationships would prove essential, especially in finding the next round of cuts for FY21.

"If we had not changed presidents, I'm not sure we would be here as a university," College of Agricultural and Life Sciences Dean Michael Parrella stated. "We have a campus that did come together to address the crisis, but not willingly. It took a crisis, and it took the leadership to make that happen. Scott deserves the credit for having the vision and the accounting chops to recognize the severity of the fiscal crisis that we faced. I'm very supportive of everything he did."

"We instituted the budget cuts, implemented new financial reports for managers to use to monitor their operations, and I met with deans and VPs monthly to review their financial reports," Scott recalled. "We were making great progress."

The fall semester had flown by, with Scott experiencing many firsts as the new president. He started his goal of visiting every College of Agricultural and Life Sciences extension office in 42 of Idaho's 44 counties. He attended his first football game and homecoming as president. University House slowly started taking shape. By the time his first Winter Commencement ceremonies were complete, Scott felt elated about the university community's successes in just six months.

Scott, his wife, Gabriella, and their two kids celebrated the holiday season together, anticipating the possibilities 2020 offered. Scott knew he had much to give to his alma mater, and the U of I community had so much potential. With the budget overhaul underway and so many wonderful things going on at the university, he felt a swell of pride, a rush of gratitude. Vandals had grit, gumption, and drive. Yes, they were unstoppable, and 2020 would be their year.

The academy was firing on all cylinders. It hadn't been easy; it was challenging, emotional, defeating, and polarizing at times to cut, scrimp, and change course. But the campus community rallied itself. A sense of pride and trust crept into a once timid, untrusting, fearful Vandal family. Scott had offered a sense of ability, confidence, and accomplishment, but the entire cast of faculty, staff, and students did the work. And the work paid off. Yes, they could do this; they could get on the other side of the $14 million hump they'd so desperately worked to conquer and then do it again for FY21 for $22 million. They were well on their way. They were Vandals, and no foe would subdue them.

And then COVID-19 hit.

Scott's Management Insight

It was amazing how fast we made progress in finding savings. The monthly meetings were a catalyst as they brought us closer as colleagues, and we could celebrate progress every month. It was a real morale booster as we closed the budget gap. It may not be a normal process at most universities, but I believe it critical that a president meets regularly with the deans, not just the provost. They are each CEOs for their college, content experts, and lead fundraisers for their units. Regular conversations build trust and inspire free-flow communications. It allows a president to evaluate each dean and play to their strengths. Those connections are essential in his role as chief fundraiser; a direct relationship with deans is critical, not to work around the provost, but to strengthen all elements of the connecting threads.

Smart Collaboration

Visiting College of Agriculture and Life Sciences Research and Extension Center Locations (July 2019–April 2022, Idaho)

Scott set a goal to visit every College of Agricultural and Life Sciences (CALS) Research and Extension Service Center in the state, including 70 stops. He drove his U of I branded truck whenever possible to let everyone know the president was in town. CALS Dean Michael Parrella saw Scott's unprecedented visits to every location as critical for morale. After personally visiting the sites, Scott understood the programs at the locations and connected with staff and faculty who didn't work on the Moscow campus. Employees at the Research and Extension Centers witnessed face-to-face Scott's interest, sincerity, and loyalty to the university. Scott gained a depth of knowledge by getting "boots on the ground" experience at the locations, which gave him credibility when sharing the U of I's story.

Michael said, "The wonderful thing was, he really got on board. He quickly recognized how important agriculture is in this state. We have two hundred fifty faculty, and one hundred thirty of those are off campus at the county offices and nine Research Extension Centers. We are embedded in the communities around the state; we have the legislative contacts. Scott listened to people and was passionate about the interaction. People said to me, 'He really cares about what I'm doing.' He's been a breath of fresh air."

Scott's Management Insight

I like to manage by walking (or driving) around. I find you learn so much more about an operation by seeing it. I frankly don't know how some managers are comfortable making decisions about their far-flung operations when they have never seen them or met the people working there. A visit will help you gain the support and trust of your employees. The pandemic would prove to slow me down, but we still managed to visit all 70 of our extension offices, research centers, and satellite campuses during my first three years. These visits enabled me to identify a site's capabilities, where investment was needed, and even where something was wrong. A few of our extension offices did not get the equipment upgrades we invested in during the pandemic. Others had no signage identifying them as a U of I extension office. I was able to help fix those things. I also met dedicated employees committed to our mission and supportive county and town officials. The Vandal truck became a favorite backdrop for pictures in many of these rural towns.

I encourage a president to visit every college department or outpost, no matter its size or location. The support you gain for this small investment of your time will pay huge dividends when you have to make an ask of your employees.

Part V

Chapter 22
From One Crisis to Another

"You never really know how strong a family is until it's been tested."
—*Scott Green*

Vandals worldwide toasted New Year's Eve, December 31, 2019, but that date also marked the moment governmental authorities in Wuhan, China, confirmed several cases of pneumonia with an unknown cause. Several days later, Chinese researchers identified a new virus that had already infected dozens of people in Asia. By January 11, Chinese media reported the first known death due to the virus. The first known case in the US arrived on January 19 when a man who traveled to Wuhan returned to his home in Seattle, Washington, and tested positive for the new virus. The contagion now had a name, the 2019 novel coronavirus, or COVID-19, and with ground zero in the US on the West Coast, only 300 miles away from Moscow and the University of Idaho, some Vandals watching the news started to take notice.

* * *

Scott prided himself on being a well-informed individual. He read anything he could to stay current, from politics and foreign affairs to health and education, and, especially now, topics that had or would have a direct effect on the University of Idaho and the State of Idaho. He constantly kept an eye on local, regional, national, and international news, diving deep into various issues that piqued his interest or affected the global markets.

He took note when he heard about a new virus coming from Wuhan, China; it seemed serious but an ocean away. Still, the world had become small, and something involving health was nothing to ignore. "I watched CNBC every morning," he explained. "The financial markets had always been pretty good at assessing risk. They initially were unsettled about COVID-19 but not panicked."

"I've always watched the news sporadically, but not daily," Provost Torrey Lawrence confided. "But after this started, I felt like I had a real responsibility to keep up with what was out there in the world as it evolved. I suddenly felt like part of my job was keeping current because if I stopped for a week or even a day, a lot had changed."

Scott would continue tracking COVID-19, but with the new year came meetings with the State of Idaho Legislature regarding appropriations, the continued cutting and monitoring of the current FY20 fiscal situation, and the task of setting the path to making cuts to the FY21 budget. Scott juggled a variety of issues morning, noon, and night but looked forward to the upcoming spring semester, filled with exciting events that showcased the U of I. One of those events was the U of I's annual, world-renowned Lionel Hampton Jazz Festival, held February 28–29, 2020.

For two days and two nights, the campus came alive with students from around the Northwest participating in performances, clinics, and workshops taught with the help of jazz greats. Evening concerts sizzled with some of the greatest jazz icons performing alongside the student winners. For 53 years, this tradition in music showcased exquisite musical talent and saluted its namesake, the great Lionel Hampton. However, for the first time in those 53 years, a foe cast a shadow on the weekend of music and tribute.

"There was a student from one of the high schools in Seattle who was not on the trip to Moscow for the Jazz Festival but was one of the early reports of getting COVID-19," Scott explained. "His exposure to the students who did attend the Jazz Festival was a concern. We called Idaho Public Health. They indicated they thought the risk was low that we had COVID-19 in our community given that the infected student was still in Seattle, but we implemented sanitizing protocols and finished the festival without incident."

"I became involved with our hospital's response to COVID-19 when we had the Jazz Festival in February 2020," Connie Osborn, a nurse at Gritman Medical Center in Moscow, shared. "Our admin team got the lowdown on potential exposures from students from King County, Washington. We started that last weekend of February and set up our incident command. We had it going full bore by March 1."

"In February, we began talking a bit about COVID-19 from a supply chain point of view," shared Kara Besst, Gritman Medical Center Hospital CEO. "Our materials directors started looking for additional personal protective equipment (PPE). We kept incident command mobilized after Jazz Festival, and when Seattle's cases increased, we started having more in-depth conversations about how to prepare."

"That scare during Jazz Festival, even though it was a third-generation exposure, was a pivotal moment," Torrey shared. "I remember saying to my staff that it would be interesting to watch what Seattle universities do. The University of Washington (UW) was only a few miles from the nursing home where COVID-19 really blew up. I said this could be the beginning of a domino effect in higher education because UW was a monstrous institution with one of the best medical schools in the country, and they do incredible research. When they went online so quickly on March 6, that was a big moment."

"We activated our Incident Command Center at Gritman because of the proximity that we were a border state with Washington and Moscow, and Pullman had two major universities that shared staff," Connie pointed out. "We started having incident command meetings twice a day and getting our staffing in order."

Seemingly, the university dodged a small bullet with the Jazz Festival incident because no one reported any cases of COVID-19 in the Moscow area within the weeks following. "We were making great progress on the financial front and other university initiatives," Scott shared. "But as I learned about the arrival of COVID-19, my concern turned to the safety of the campus regardless of the financial impact to the university."

"When COVID-19 first started, I was actually out of the country on vacation," Human Resources Director Brandi Terwilliger shared. "I was starting to hear things in other countries about COVID-19, and a week after I returned to the US, I started hearing these things about what was going on with COVID-19 locally. And then suddenly, it was like the tablecloth being pulled out with all these issues on the table we needed to navigate."

"I remember thinking it could be a rough semester because we were dealing with the FY21 budget cuts due in February," Torrey said. "Program Prioritization was going on at the same time, which was designed to inform some of those cuts. And it did. But I remember thinking that semester was going to be dark because we had to lay off people. The incentive programs took the sting out of some of that, but people leaving was anti-tactical because we didn't know who would take it. I was in the vice provost for faculty role, so I knew I would be dealing with faculty dismissals, which would get complicated. Then COVID-19 hit, and suddenly, it became a weird distraction from the financial crisis."

Scott was initially concerned about an overreaction, so he deployed one of his favorite management tools. He would use reliable data to determine the course of action and calm any fears with facts. "People were freaking out, and I was trying to keep my team calm," he recalled. "It made some initial meetings on the subject hard to work through all the emotion. You learn a lot about your team when it is under such stress. You learn whom you can lean on and whom you need to isolate. I decided early on to follow the scientific data and rely heavily on Idaho Public Health and Gritman Medical Center leadership for advice. That proved to be critical in making good, informed decisions on how to respond. It helped keep everyone feeling like we were managing the situation rather than just reacting to all the emotion."

"Scott has good emotional intelligence," College of Natural Resources Dean Dennis Becker pointed out. "Part of that was understanding when not to get worked up and not build a plan to all the hype because if he did that, as a leader, everybody around him would start acting the same way. Before long, our organization would be in a fire drill, and nobody would be able to focus on what they should be doing. Intentional or not, Scott had a calming effect."

Scott's concern also stretched 2600+ miles to his wife and kids on the East Coast. He could have very easily let emotions play with his thinking. Gabriella was still in Long Island; she wasn't in the ground-zero hotspot area of New York City with its first case reported on March 1, but she was too close for comfort. "Eventually, when schools closed, my daughter [attending George Washington University] and son [attending Villanova University] were back at our house on Long Island," Scott said. "I was happy they were there with my wife. It was a safe community where we had a lot of friends and support. While I would have liked to have them in Idaho, we still had minimal furniture in the University House. Gabriella and the kids needed their creature comforts; plus, I had to stay in Moscow to manage our response to the pandemic. I told some of our team that if they needed the University House for an infirmary, they could use it as it was basically empty."

Little did he know at that point, but his sparse furnishings would be the least of his issues. COVID-19 was shaping up to become one of the biggest, most challenging foes the University of Idaho had ever faced.

Scott's Management Insight

Manage using reliable data to determine the course of action and calm the fear. Employees will look to their leaders and how they respond to a crisis. I was in the first attack on the World Trade Center in February 1993 and, with our entire office, walked down 100 flights of stairs to get out of the building. In that stairwell, I saw the best and worst of leadership. It formed my response to future blackouts, floods, and, recently, the pandemic. It is critical a leader responds in a composed and thoughtful manner. If leadership is spooked, the response will be panicked and chaotic. A sense of calm and assessment will help settle your employees to focus on a thoughtful response. A measured, thoughtful response has a better chance of being well executed with a successful outcome.

Chapter 23
Many Hands Make Light Work

"In about two weeks, COVID-19 impacted every part of our operations."
—Dr. Torrey Lawrence

Not knowing exactly how serious the outbreak might get, the U of I started working on getting ahead of the COVID-19 situation by the end of January. The U of I hosted dozens of students on international exchange, and one of the priorities was to communicate with them whether to stay in Moscow or return to their home country. It was especially vital to reach out to the students from China. The U of I also had Vandals studying abroad and needed to communicate with them.

"At the time, no one saw just how significantly the whole world would change," Blaine Eckles said, who sat in the middle of the brewing storm as vice provost for Student Affairs and dean of students. "We had a meeting around the first or second week of the spring semester for all of our students from China to assist them and help them navigate the rapidly changing landscape."

Concerns revolved around whether international students could get home and whether Vandals abroad could return to the US. "Some students studying abroad got stuck because that's when airports were starting to get closed down in certain countries," Blaine continued. "We were very limited on what we could do, so we encouraged them to talk with the State Department and hunker down and not worry about classes. We assured them we'd help get them out if needed and if we could."

The International Programs Office (IPO) scheduled regular meetings to communicate with all the students on exchange. "IPO did a great job communicating regularly to let Student Affairs know what was going on and how the virus was impacting students," Blaine remarked. "We were also opening avenues to get students to engage with our Counseling Center." The stress of COVID-19 was just beginning for students and employees.

Toward the end of January and into February, many offices started playing the what-if game. They tried to determine how to handle programming and people if COVID-19 threatened business as usual for the university.

"About a month before the U of I closed, the alumni office started talking about virtual programming," Assistant Vice President for Alumni Relations Kathy Barnard shared. "COVID-19 made it very clear that we would not be able to keep doing what we've always done, which was meeting with alumni in person at events across the nation."

Everyone on campus in a leadership role saw communication as paramount. Students, employees, and the Moscow community deserved the most up-to-date information. Now was not the time to wait to reach out. The administration and university leadership worked with University Communications to establish several critical lines of messaging.

"University Communications kicked butt," Special Advisor Chandra Zenner Ford said. "They worked so hard. We were in crisis mode, and they pivoted. Every day they had to write messages and send things out. It's almost like they leaned into it and said, 'Here we go, we can do this.'"

On February 28, 2020, Blaine emailed students, faculty, and staff after the Jazz Festival regarding the low risk of COVID-19 and that the university was monitoring the situation locally and globally. Idaho reported no cases, but the university's Infectious Disease Response Team (IDRT) remained current on any new information from Idaho Public Health and other news sources. IDRT had started as a health crisis management team for one-time or short-term responses, not a global pandemic. They focused primarily on preparation and met once or twice a year, but they implemented the university's initial responses to COVID-19 issues.

The IDRT members consisted of the provost; vice provosts; associate dean of students; assistant VP for Auxiliaries; directors of Vandal Health Education, Recreation and Well-being, Communications, Housing and Residence Life, Fraternity/Sorority Life, Facilities, Human Resources, Campus Safety, and Administrative and Business Operations; general counsel; an Idaho Public Health representative; and eventually, the COVID-19 project manager.

Blaine's email also urged Vandals, especially those traveling for Spring Break in a few weeks, to take every precaution, including washing hands often, avoiding close contact with sick people, and employing cleaning protocols. He also reminded students to contact the IPO for any up-to-date questions regarding international travel, visit the Vandal Health Clinic with any health concerns, and file a VandalCARE report if they believed a campus community member was in distress. The VandalCARE team's mission was to provide care and concern for students, faculty, and staff in potential distress.

"The talk on campus became about the virus and how to protect our students, faculty, and staff, both mentally and physically," Scott explained. "There was no question that we were in reactionary mode at that point, and even though the virus was not in our community, we began having faculty prepare for conducting their classes online. My biggest concern beyond the safety of everyone was whether our IT infrastructure could hold up under a switch to full online instruction."

"We were predominantly an in-person lecture university, be it an in-person lecture in Moscow or at one of our Centers in Boise, Coeur d'Alene, or Idaho Falls," stated Dan Ewart, vice president of Information Technology and chief information officer. "We had some video classes where faculty in Moscow taught people in Coeur d'Alene or Boise, but it was fairly limited in number. Historically, video classes have not been our specialty; that's not our strength area as a residential campus."

"Professor Jaap Voss with the College of Natural Resources taught a popular class online at the U of I Boise Center in the mode of live broadcasts from a studio inside the Water Center," Scott pointed out. "But going fully online would break new ground for the U of I. Before COVID-19, there was a lot of faculty in opposition to online coursework. They felt that it was just not the same experience as attending college classes live."

"Online didn't mean long-distance courses; it meant through Zoom," Dean Shauna Corry pointed out. "I called that a virtual meeting. My colleagues in Art and Architecture had already been doing that because we had a campus in Boise."

On March 1, Matt Freeman, SBOE executive director, reached out to the presidents of the state's four major public institutions—the U of I, Boise State University (BSU), Idaho State University (ISU), and Lewis Clark State College (LCSC)—asking them to take a coordinated approach to COVID-19 preparedness and protocols. Scott immediately agreed to collaborate with Idaho's higher education institutions; he shared that Blaine would lead the response from the U of I.

"In those meetings, we talked about institutional responses, and I remember sitting at the first meeting in a room at the Stueckle Sky Center on BSU's campus as the representative from the U of I," Blaine shared.

"They spaced out the seats, but this was before face masks were a thing. I called it the statewide COVID-19 group, and it was a total collaboration."

Brandi and Senior Director of Communications Jodi Walker were also representatives for the U of I. After that initial meeting in Boise, the entire group met remotely every morning, including weekends, for almost two months due to the rapidly changing landscape.

"Early on, we knew we wanted to make sure all were aware of what was happening," Blaine emphasized. "We talked about things like how we were navigating students staying in the residence halls or how we were handling our international students. It was a good statewide collaboration and a good brainstorming session."

"It was a statewide university group, so people from all across the state came together," Brandi recalled. "We reviewed the impacts of COVID-19, the numbers, and what the health department was seeing. It was a roundtable for everyone involved to share what they were doing at their institution. We discussed how we should think about certain things, like graduation or student access to online classes. We'd expanded our institutional teams to a large group of professional individuals who think about things differently, especially as they related to the populations we were serving."

Thus, the start of dozens and dozens of emails utilizing the information gained from those state-level meetings began to keep all parties involved and up to speed on the virus that would take over the world.

"There were tons of other meetings," Brandi voiced. "COVID-19 consumed our lives for a long time. We often saw that what the University of Idaho was doing was happening much sooner than perhaps others; we weren't tooting our own horn. But it enabled us to collaborate and help others in our state."

Somebody had to be first to offer ideas and share experiences in unprecedented times. Why not the University of Idaho?

On March 6, then–Vice Provost Torrey Lawrence sent an email to faculty recommending that although no decision had been made to change campus operations, everyone must recognize that a move to electronic course delivery could be an option in some circumstances.

"In about two weeks, COVID-19 impacted every part of our operations," Torrey recalled. "From trash collection to the residence halls, everything changed at least a little."

* * *

Along with IT, faculty and students seriously contemplated the what-ifs. What if they had to switch to all online classes? What if faculty had to convey their unique in-person educational method using Zoom? What if that delivery method changed the students' path to success? What if faculty and students didn't have the right technology at home or in a dorm room to participate in online learning? The questions and roadblocks seemed immense and overwhelming.

But in one particular area, Vandals considered the biggest what-if of all. What if *they* could help?

As a residential land-grant institution of higher education and research, the U of I employed faculty and staff with extraordinary skills relating to virus testing. Barrie Robison, IBEST director (IBEST later changed to the Institute for Interdisciplinary Data Sciences), explained, "A bunch of evolution and genomics faculty over the course of many years built up IBEST. IBEST encouraged and fostered interdisciplinary collaborations that blended the expertise of several accomplished researchers to examine the underpinnings of evolutionary biology. Many components of the U of I's land-grant mission relied on understanding and applying the evolutionary process" (University of Idaho n.d.).

Understanding evolution is essential to improving human well-being because evolutionary processes drive critical health challenges such as antimicrobial resistance, the origin and treatment of diseases, such as cancer, mental illness, obesity, and emerging infectious diseases, such as COVID-19.

Barrie knew their lab had the talent and equipment to assist with virus testing like COVID-19. IBEST's core lab facility, the Genomic and Bioinformatics Resources Core (GBRC), was established through large grants from sources like the National Institutes of Health. GBRC provided U of I researchers access to technology, experience, and expertise in molecular biology methods, including equipment to work with DNA and RNA. The interdisciplinary focus of the university resulted in a wide range of fields that could benefit from the GBRC lab's work, including agricultural studies, forest management, and animal science, perfect for a land-grant institution.

GBRC researchers worked on projects such as bighorn sheep bacterial genomics, trout landscape genomics, tick surveillance, mouse genotyping, amplicon sequencing in soil microbes, and genome sequencing for several species, from snails to Killi fish, and dozens of other research projects. The lab was capable of performing high-throughput sequencing, also known as next-generation sequencing, which was the rapid and economical way to sequence DNA and RNA.[1]

The GBRC staff make-up included knowledgeable and experienced researchers capable of quickly pivoting to master COVID-19 testing techniques and understanding the constantly changing landscape of information. "GBRC staff talked early on about what it would take to deploy our infrastructure in service to the COVID-19 situation," Barrie recalled. "The staff were already thinking of testing by sequencing and other new approaches. We were pretty much the only place on campus that had the combination of the hardware and the people to be able to consider testing for COVID-19."

GBRC lab staff knew it had limitations to diving immediately or easily into COVID-19 sequencing and testing. The Food and Drug Administration (FDA) required labs dealing with clinical diagnostic testing to be certified under the Clinical Laboratory Improvements Amendments (CLIA). The GBRC lab did not perform clinical research; therefore, they didn't have CLIA certification. "That architecture didn't exist in our GBRC research lab," Barrie explained. "With clinical diagnostic testing, very real implications for people's health and privacy existed, thus the need for CLIA to protect both."

But roadblocks only meant slight detours for the innovative and clever GBRC staff. A pathway for them to help existed; they knew it would just take buy-in from various departments and organizations to set up a testing lab and a bit more time to hit on the *aha* moment that could propel the U of I into the realm of COVID-19 testing.

Scott's Management Insight

Many hands make light work. Break down the problem into manageable bits. Some tasks seem overwhelming, but breaking them down into their component parts and delegating those pieces of work to others makes the project manageable. Opening our own testing lab seemed impossible to some, but we successfully opened and operated our own lab by breaking down the steps and distributing tasks to empowered employees, faculty, and staff.

Note

1. Sequencing refers to the process of using molecular biology to essentially read the components of a target DNA molecule, ranging from a whole genome (of a virus, or a fish, or a snail) to smaller pieces of particular interest called amplicons (which might be a DNA fragment containing only one gene or part of a gene). The components of a DNA molecule are called nucleotides. DNA is made up of four nucleotides (adenine, guanine, cytosine, and thymine—often abbreviated A, G, C, T) and the order of these nucleotides determines the function of the genes they encode (Robison, B., personal communication).

Chapter 24
It's Official
Wednesday, March 11, 2020

"It was like watching a slow-moving train wreck."

—*Jacob Lockhart*

By March 11, the World Health Organization (WHO) reported 118,000 COVID-19 cases and just under 4300 deaths worldwide. This day also marked WHO's official labeling of COVID-19 as a pandemic. The world sat stunned at the speed COVID-19 spread and the harsh way it invaded bodies and took lives. Luckily, cases at the U of I and Moscow remained zero. WSU and the town of Pullman also reported zero cases. But that didn't mean the U of I, the City of Moscow, and the whole of Latah and Whitman Counties (including WSU and Pullman) weren't scrambling to develop a game plan to deal with the virus. No playbook existed for a pandemic of this potential magnitude. Yet, many leaders felt there was still time to craft a strategic method to handle COVID-19. It hadn't hit the Palouse—yet (World Health Organization 2020).

But within a matter of days, business as usual at the U of I went out the window. Each hour brought new questions, challenges, and fears, and March 11 was no different—it served as one of those "marker days" and started the clock ticking on an unprecedented time in the U of I's 130+ year history.

The SBOE hosted a Presidents Leadership Council meeting in their conference room on the morning of March 11. The eight presidents of Idaho's public higher education institutions attended to discuss the state's response to COVID-19. Leadership from the U of I (Scott and Special Assistant Toni Broyles), BSU, ISU, LCSC, College of Eastern Idaho, College of Southern Idaho, College of Western Idaho, and North Idaho College knew the entire state and nation were on a trajectory toward unparalleled times. The seriousness of the situation had reached critical mass with WHO's declaration of a pandemic that day. Idaho Governor Brad Little cleared his calendar to attend the meeting, armed with the best information he could obtain from Washington, DC.

"Governor Little emphasized that each institution needed a plan because the entire nation was entering into unchartered territory dealing with the pandemic," Toni explained. "He strongly urged the university presidents to take the virus seriously and emphasized that we needed to work together to make health and safety on our campuses a priority. He wanted us to make a plan for the remainder of the spring semester. His office was getting information hourly, and he committed to sharing it with us constantly. We all understood the seriousness of the situation and that we had to act quickly without knowing exactly how COVID-19 was going to roll out."

After that meeting, IDRT gathered to assist with disseminating information about how the U of I would cope with COVID-19. Everyone agreed that one of the crucial tasks for the university involved communicating with all parties. The massive lift to keep everyone informed would prove seemingly insurmountable due to the swift nature of the virus and the spaghetti-like web of information coming from myriad sources.

"After a few days of meetings, IDRT dramatically grew as they needed more input," Scott explained. IDRT became known as IDRT Core, and it focused on the actual response to COVID-19. It encompassed representatives taking the lead in their area and reporting back to IDRT Core. Those groups could tackle issues more quickly and ensure everyone communicated and listened to each other. The teams included: CARE, classroom, communications, cleaning, community, travel, and employment, and the representatives were from:

- Academic – Classroom Response
- Facilities – Cleaning buildings/classrooms
- Vandal Health Education – Signage, website, vaccine clinics
- Communications
- Dean of Students Office – Student Response/Care
- Auxiliary Unit Response – Targhee Hall Infirmary/Food delivery
- Human Resources – Employee Response

- Housing and Residence Life – Community Living Response (added later)
- Greek Life – Community Living Response (added later)
- Public Health
- General Counsel

"We also formed the 'small group,' the COVID-19 Executive Leadership Committee, for more tactical decisions that couldn't wait for the larger group," Scott continued. "We had some pushback that there were two groups, but IDRT Core and the subgroups that came out of that were more strategic. There were just too many in that larger group to make quick decisions. We needed both."

"The small group started coming to life to address more tactical issues," Vice Provost of Student Affairs and Dean of Students Blaine Eckles explained. "I was on the road but kept talking with the provost and the senior director of communications. The three of us consulted with the president regularly. What were we doing? What were we hearing? The small group actually started at that point in time because we saw issues and challenges needing immediate attention."

The small group members included: the president, provost, dean of students, senior director of communications, VP for auxiliary services, and the president's office COVID-19 manager and advisor.

"Even with the IDRT Core group and the small COVID-19 group, it became pretty apparent that we still needed to make sure we were communicating to the larger campus leadership," Blaine said. "We formed the COVID-19 Leadership Forum, or the 'large group,' to regularly communicate what was happening."

The larger COVID-19 Leadership Forum included all vice presidents, the vice provost, directors of branch campuses, chairs of Faculty Senate and Staff Affairs, general counsel, the athletic director, the chief diversity officer, the chief marking officer, and the directors from Human Resources, Health Promotion, Campus Safety, and Communications. The ASUI president and a representative from Idaho Public Health also joined this group.

"The Leadership Forum created a space where other voices could also come to the table," Blaine clarified. "It was more of a sharing and feedback group; it was not a decision-making group. And there was another group, the COVID-19 Advisory Committee, stemming from Faculty Senate to further the voices offering input. They came a bit later after we were well into planning that allowed for additional thoughts and insights to come forward to the IDRT Core and the large and small groups."

"All those meetings with all the groups were time-consuming," admitted Brandi Terwilliger, director of Human Resources. "But it helped everybody to hear the same message and then help distribute it out to the larger audience."

The group rosters showed Scott's acknowledgment of shared governance by giving a voice to all parties and keeping them involved and informed. "ASUI President [2019–2020] Jacob Lockhart was an important addition to the larger group because he helped us get the right tone in our communications with students," Scott articulated. "Having that many people from all these different backgrounds in the groups allowed us to attack the problem from all these angles that we probably wouldn't have thought about if it was just a president or provost making the call."

"I have no doubts that there were folks out there who wanted to be included in the groups," Blaine said. "To a certain extent, it was hard to argue against that. If I had to jump into my 'short-term-way-back machine' and go back in time, I likely would've advocated adding other folks to the teams to get some of that input."

One of the critical calls Scott and the COVID-19 groups made immediately was how to get the campus ready to go online, even if it might be for only a few days. After marathon calls, dozens of meetings, countless conversations, and the biggest what-if game in history, the dominos were falling at an alarming speed.

Scott finally determined that the best thing for the U of I family was for classes to go online for a two-day "practice" period the Monday and Tuesday after spring break, March 23–24. That would give the university the week of spring break (March 16–20) to set everything up for the transition. This experiment would show if the U of I was ready to deliver courses via Zoom and help set up the structure if online coursework delivery lasted longer than two days.

Scott and then-Provost John Wiencek emailed their plan to students, explaining that classes would go online the Monday and Tuesday after spring break. They also asked students to be mindful of their spring break activities and prioritize safety precautions.

Jacob shared what many of the students were thinking at the time. "There was a level of uncertainty about COVID-19 leading up to the switch to online classes," he explained. "At the beginning, most folks felt like they didn't know what would happen. And then, once they decided that we were going to be online for two days, at least in my sphere, we were all on the same page and felt it wasn't just going to be a couple of days. There was this outer expression that it would go a little bit longer than that. There was no way we could handle it in just a couple of days."

The administration also emailed detailing how faculty, staff, and students should prepare to go online. The email shared information on how faculty could participate in specialized training with CETL (Center for Excellence in Teaching and Learning) during the week of spring break to pivot to online teaching. They urged faculty not to cancel their classes on the Monday and Tuesday after spring break because IT needed to know if the systems could handle going entirely online.

"One of the most awesome things that came out of all this was IT's relationship with CETL," Vice President Dan Ewart shared. "IT ran all our communications through CETL because they already had that direct connection with faculty. We cross-listed their content with ours, so they were getting information regardless of how faculty tried to find the information. CETL had a heck of a lot of work to do to assist faculty who previously had never engaged in any technology-based teaching. But now, there was no choice; faculty had to do it. CETL was a very good partner."

Brian Smentkowski ran CETL with a small group; they had instructional designers and some technology people who supported the Blackboard course management system and related components. "They became kindred spirits with IT," Dan said, smiling. "They were techies like us."

"We had an amazing group at CETL," CLASS Dean Sean Quinlan said. "My colleague Brian and his team did an enormous amount of work trying to provide resources and help faculty navigate the technology."

"CETL enabled us to accommodate faculty to translate and deliver these courses online," Scott conveyed. "I found they are a high-quality support service that enabled us to go fully online."

The multiple layers of communication went far beyond emails. IDRT Core coordinated the production and installation of signage explaining the hygiene protocols in buildings around campus for when students returned on Wednesday, March 25, after the two days of online classes. Vandal Health Education, Creative Services, and a team of stakeholders developed the Healthy Vandals Tool Kit, a library of adaptable printable signs, digital displays, and graphics campus could download and use. See Figures 24.01 and 24.02.

Every department implemented measures to mitigate any spread and be ready when students returned to in-person instruction. The Registrar's Office dissected classrooms for social distancing. Facilities enhanced their cleaning protocols. If possible, the U of I would try to remain open but would have systems in place if they had to shut down for a few days or weeks.

"The idea was to test all of our systems because I was convinced at the time, having worked in private industry for a long time, that our infrastructure would struggle to deal with so much," Scott explained. "It seemed

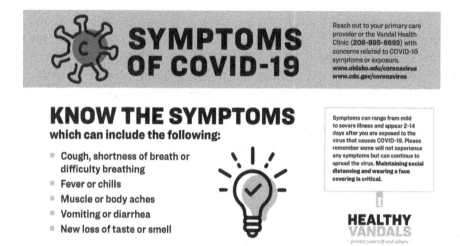

Figure 24.01   "Know the symptoms of COVID-19" graphic from the Healthy Vandals Tool Kit.

SOURCE: University Communications and Marketing. Reproduced with permission from University of Idaho.

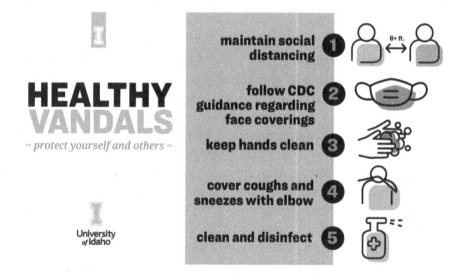

Figure 24.02   Healthy Vandals Tool Kit graphic with guidance for protection against COVID-19.

SOURCE: University Communications and Marketing. Reproduced with permission from University of Idaho.

imminent that we would go online for longer than a few days. You would've had to have your eyes closed not to think that the thing was spreading. We just didn't know enough about the virus to say that we could stay open for sure. All we knew was that it was highly infectious and presumed to be deadly, particularly in the elderly. It was helpful to the faculty to plan to go online early and go through the online test period without panicking."

"I remember sticking my neck out a little bit at the meeting that night [March 11], saying to the group that we had to discuss the game plan again of closing and going online for an indefinite period of time," Provost Torrey Lawrence said.

The group batted around ideas and agreed to resume discussions the next morning. In the meantime, the here-and-now stood squarely in the university's face. Blaine communicated to all the U of I students outlining timely answers to various questions. Yes, residence halls, the Library, ISUB, and Campus Rec would remain open during spring break if students didn't want to travel. Yes, IT prepared Chromebooks and iPads for students to take home to participate in the two days of online learning. No, no one had diagnosed anyone at the U of I or anyone affiliated with the university with the virus. Yes, if you traveled to a Level 3 or Level 4 country during spring break, you would have to self-isolate for 14 days before returning to classes. Yes, you would have to stay home if you felt sick.

Thursday, March 12, 2020

Conversations abounded the following day regarding what to do about COVID-19; the plan to have the two-day test period was good, but looking beyond, everyone started the what-if game once again, trying to foresee how to continue with online education beyond those two days or what it would look like even to close the U of I. Making the right—almost immediate—decision was critical.

"On Thursday morning, we met again, and I said we need to shut down after spring break," Torrey stated. "I just laid it out. Two days would not be enough. We didn't know how long COVID-19 would last, but the way things were going, it was clear that it was not going to be a two-day event where we're all back and happy by the third day."

Torrey pressed IDRT Core to decide because it was already the Thursday before spring break officially started. Students would begin leaving campus even as early as that day for their week recess. "If we can't tell them by Friday at 5 p.m., they've already left, which means they'll have to come back to get all their stuff," Torrey said. "This was a mess. I even suggested sending a Vandal Alert (the university's emergency alert system) to immediately inform them that we were shutting down."

Again, all the groups continued to meet in various combinations to acutely analyze the options while trying to stay abreast of the breakneck speed of ever-changing information.

By the end of the day, Scott made one of the most difficult decisions he would ever have to make as the U of I president. Even though there was no evidence of COVID-19 in the community, its arrival was imminent—no more waiting or what-if scenario debates. The university would immediately transition from face-to-face learning to online/remote instruction starting the Monday after spring break for an indefinite period.

"It was like watching a slow-moving train wreck," Jacob said. "We knew it was happening, and we knew it would hit us, and it wasn't going to be great. But we couldn't get out of its way. We couldn't help but watch what was going to happen."

After Scott's decision, Torrey felt reassured. They now had a pathway to follow with a defined course of action. "We could get communication out immediately with more details to follow," Torrey said. "But then I was told we couldn't do anything. We had to wait for the SBOE, and they weren't meeting until 3:00 p.m. on Friday, which was 4:00 p.m. in Boise, which gets us to right where I didn't want to be—telling students at 5:00 p.m. on Friday. I was frustrated. I didn't think it was in their purview to make that decision, and they later recognized that. They wanted to coordinate with all the schools. I appreciated their willingness to do that. But all the schools in Idaho weren't in the same place and spring breaks were not concurrent. The U of I was far ahead of some of the others making that kind of decision. So we had to sit on this huge decision. I couldn't tell you the messages and calls we received asking, 'What the hell are we doing?' All I could say was that we had a plan, but we were waiting for the SBOE. I wasn't blaming the SBOE. They were trying to be responsible. But we were ready to roll based on our situation in Moscow. Even WSU was moving in that direction; they ended up moving ahead of us regarding the decision timeline for going online and closing."

Friday, March 13, 2020

Friday the 13th (note the date) brought changes and significant decisions. First, Scott's Friday Letter went out early in the morning. It reiterated the previous day's email to faculty and staff that the U of I was not closing but heavily emphasized that online classes would most likely extend further than the Tuesday after spring break. The waiting game was on to see what the SBOE would decide for the state's education system later that day, so Scott's hands were tied to outline any alternate plan.

Scott had trekked to Boise for the Big Sky basketball tournament, and his day was jam-packed with meetings pertaining to COVID-19 taking center stage. He sat in on a meeting with other presidents from Big Sky Conference schools. "The presidents at that meeting were largely voting to continue the tournament since no cases were reported," Scott recalled. "But the presidents not in attendance at the meeting who participated by Zoom largely voted to cancel."

The desire to cancel prevailed in a split vote, and the women's basketball tournament currently underway in Boise came to a screeching halt.

The determination hit the Vandals hard as the women were the favorite to take the conference title and head to the Dance (the NCAA women's basketball tournament).

"Our men's team had been eliminated, but our women's team would play in the conference championship game on Saturday," Athletic Director Terry Gawlik explained. "We were in Boise when President Green called me to say the Big Sky presidents had decided to call off the remainder of the tournament. The student-athletes were out in the Boise community doing a reading at a school, and when they got back, we had to tell them the conference made the decision to cancel their game. The team we would've played, Montana State, was automatically going to the NCAA. Odds-makers picked Idaho to beat them, so we were probably going to the Dance. They knew what canceling meant. You can imagine how terrible that was for the players."

However, later that afternoon, NCAA President Mark Emmert and the board of governors canceled all Division I men's and women's 2020 basketball tournaments and all remaining winter and spring NCAA sports championships (Boone, K. 2020). Even people who weren't into sports knew shutting down collegiate athletics, including the beloved March Madness, was unprecedented. The Vandals weren't going to the Dance. No one was going to the Dance. Not one team. The decision sent the nation's sports fans into a tailspin.

"The U of I would host the first and second rounds of the NCAA tournament in Spokane," Chris Walsh, associate athletic director, explained. "That was a huge task that we'd been planning since the previous fall. I remember telling Terry that we'd probably have to have thermal scanning at the games due to COVID-19. I was on the sports medicine side of the house for the tournament, so I was receiving a lot of questions from the NCAA about how we'd make it work. I didn't even know where to begin; I'm not a public health guy or infectious disease expert. In the back of my mind, I had a feeling that the tournament wasn't going to happen. Ultimately, they canceled, and all those preparations went away."

The hits kept coming on Friday the 13th as Idaho reported its first confirmed case. COVID-19 became a menace; it was no longer a short-term inconvenience or something happening elsewhere.

The SBOE met late in the day, and by 6:21 p.m. PT, Scott's email to faculty, staff, and students outlining the online transition to indefinite status blasted the Vandal cyber-waves. The university called off events, including the UIdaho Bound recruiting event and alumni functions, setting COVID-19 up to take its first significant swing at the University of Idaho. Canceling the U of I's largest spring recruiting event at its destination campus would pummel potential enrollment and the already precarious financial situation. This virus could potentially derail everything the Vandal family had worked so hard to achieve.

Scott had faced crisis management situations before working in the corporate world, including dealing with blackouts in New York and being present in the first World Trade Center attack. He relied on his experience to remain safety-conscious, data-driven, and controlled. "When I worked in the corporate world, there were times that required us to fall back on our disaster recovery plans," Scott explained. "I worked for large global law firms and used to say, 'We're going to have a disaster somewhere in the world almost every year, maybe a flood, a blackout, loss of Internet, terrorist attacks, so we needed to be prepared.' And it did happen; we had flooding in Eastern Europe, blackouts in New York, a trawler that cut an Internet line between the UK and the European Continent, and a terrorist attack that killed one of our young attorneys in Paris. We always had something going on. From that perspective, my anxiety regarding COVID-19 was high, but this wasn't the first time I faced safety issues regarding our people. Panicking wouldn't do anybody any good."

Scott's Management Insight

Refer to your training, experience, and team members to lead using facts, not fear. During a crisis, getting your faculty ready to test systems and anticipate going online will help them feel prepared when you pull the trigger. We went online faster than expected, but the faculty had already thought through how to do it and assembled a couple of days' worth of classes, so the transition, while bumpy, was successful.

I also knew canceling our recruiting events would seriously impact future enrollments and related finances. We were a destination campus; we did not have a large local population that we could draw from. Applications and admission that spring were through the roof. But as soon as we closed, all that changed. Safety was our first priority, and we would just have to deal with the financial fallout.

Chapter 25
Uncertainty
Saturday, March 14 and Sunday, March 15, 2020

"It was the great uncertainty."

—*Dr. Blaine Eckles*

Vice Provost for Student Affairs and Dean of Students Blaine Eckles could not have been more spot-on when he said, "It was the great uncertainty." Literally, no one in the world knew what COVID-19 had up its sleeve. Saturday, March 14, and Sunday, March 15, IDRT Core, Executive Leadership, and Leadership Forum met for long days of strategizing and decision-making, attempting to wrap their heads around the foe they faced. Scott was cognizant of the university's shared governance tradition, so he made sure that all groups had an opportunity to be heard through their representatives on the various COVID-19 response teams.

Blaine's summary notes from the state-level daily meetings became talking points for leadership to use for communications and decision-making. University Communications worked tirelessly to craft messages and inform students, faculty, and staff of the fluid COVID-19 situation.

Everyone felt a bit dazed at the accelerated pace of trying to stay ahead of COVID-19 rather than in a catch-up reactionary state. It would take a meeting of all minds to hash out all the details, big or small.

Provost Torrey Lawrence (who was vice provost at the time) sent an email inviting a long list of key players to a three-hour meeting scheduled for the afternoon of Monday, March 16. His directive was for each person invited from Core Ops, the Provost's Council, and the full IDRT Core to prepare a two-minute briefing that listed challenges in their particular area. He asked them to touch on aspects such as navigating whether the university remained open or it went entirely online or how would canceling large events happen and impact the institution? The group would convene in person but also offer Zoom capabilities to acknowledge the somewhat uncomfortable new normal emerging on campus.

The meeting's discussions would also clarify the responsibility areas for each team and address whether leadership needed to develop additional teams. In addition, the meeting agenda outlined time for essential updates regarding communications and the sure-to-come financial impacts of COVID-19.

"A few times, I paused to have that heart-stopping moment from the pressure of all the things going on," Torrey shared. "But most of the time, we were just motoring, dealing with one thing at a time, and figuring out the next steps with so many unknowns. Our brains are not wired to deal with this many unknowns. It created decision fatigue. It was hard to figure out the right thing to do when there were so many options and opinions."

Scott's Management Insight

The more severe the threat, the more communications are needed to reassure your community. Just as you need to continually repeat your strategic plans before they will be believed and adopted, staff will default to fear in the absence of communication. Only truthful, transparent, and regular communication can calm that fear. Your institution needs to know you care about them, are constantly evaluating the situation, and will make decisions with their and the institution's best interests in mind. Bringing the team together to participate in those decisions helps assess risk and prepares the leadership team to regularly communicate with the broader community.

Chapter 26
Keep Calm and Vandal On
Monday, March 16–Friday, March 20, 2020

"We knew COVID-19 would alter our entire course as a university."
—*Toni Broyles*

Spring break 2020 went down as one of the most bizarre, tiresome, and pivotal weeks in the U of I's history.

On March 14, Dan Ewart, vice president for Information Technology (IT) and chief information officer, and his family had flown to Hawaii to enjoy spring break, but he spent the lion's share of his time on the phone trying to determine how IT could deal with the shift to online. "There was a lot of discussion about what preparations needed to happen since, at that point, we hadn't decided on exactly how we were going to offer courses. I was on a leadership call for seven hours on Monday, March 16. After I hung up, my wife said just go home. So I got on a plane and flew back to Moscow that night. I got back to work on Tuesday, March 17." He was determined to be a part of the unprecedented discussions and actions that followed.

The three-hour, massive COVID-19 discussion with all leadership held at the Pittman Center in the Vandal Ballroom on Monday, March 16, started the colossal undertaking of facing COVID-19. Critical questions with weighty, life-altering answers felt almost suffocating. How does the U of I send students home? What would it look like going online for the rest of the semester? How would an institution move its 130-plus-year-old residential campus to remote learning and working in a matter of days?

"We had conversations about everything in those meetings during spring break, including if we had to stay online," Provost Torrey Lawrence recalled. "We even talked about how the mail would get delivered, which seemed so inconsequential. But if we were going to be closed for weeks or months, what were the mail people going to do? We had to figure out how employees would work at home. What do we do about people with jobs they couldn't perform from home? What about people taking all this equipment home, which was not typically what we did with state equipment? Did everybody have a camera to do Zoom? Did everyone have a microphone? We had to revisit every part of the university's operations because every part of operations changed. It was a crazy time."

"As far as messaging, the university was sending student-wide emails to keep everyone informed of what was happening," recalled Jacob Lockhart, ASUI president (2019–2020). "I didn't necessarily get to form those messages, but ASUI leadership was fortunate to see them before they went out. We gave the communications people our take on how students would perceive the emails. There's a tendency in academia, really any large institution, to walk a fine line between being transparent and holding back everything. Deciding the middle line between those two extremes was difficult. Our role in ASUI government was to push the messages more toward the truthful and personable position. If they didn't have those things in the message, it would cause the administration to come off as cold and dismissive of what was happening. This was a time when they had to be open and honest about what we were facing and recognize that this was a challenge and very impactful for people. They would compile something and ask how it looked. I would determine if they understood what's going on and how it affected students."

Amidst the craziness, then-Provost John Wiencek accepted the executive vice president and provost position at the University of Akron. The process leading up to his getting the job had taken him out of town during those crucial weeks at the end of February and the first part of March.

"As the U of I president, I wanted direct reports who felt like they wanted to be part of our team," Scott outlined. "John had been through a lot, and I appreciated what he did. But it was in everyone's best interest that he accept this new opportunity back in his home state, and we all move forward from there. To his credit, he was very honorable throughout the whole thing. He understood the rules. A couple of others in leadership positions played out like that. I held no grudges if someone was trying to better themselves."

As vice provost for faculty, Torrey filled in for the provost when he was out of town. "I'm glad that I was covering for him," he shared. "When he left, I wasn't playing catchup. I was already there. That was so important with COVID-19."

The countless hours of trying to thread the needle to do what was best for students, faculty, staff, and the larger Moscow community created a somber cloud over campus. The pivotal week of spring break finally revealed the awful truth.

Online classes wouldn't be enough to ensure the safety of the U of I students and employees.

COVID-19 had managed to shove its way into every Vandal's face. Scott knew what he had to do: prepare for the worst. The university stood at the threshold of going entirely online and having to close all but essential services and business operations on campus. Would they take that step?

"One thing we all learned about COVID-19 when we were talking about making a shift, giving people advanced notice was always helpful," Torrey stated. "But if we decided something critical too early, we could be wrong, and we'd have to shift back and possibly create bigger problems. It was a challenge to decide the point at which to make a decision."

After a meeting with medical and public health professionals on the afternoon of March 20, Scott signed a Temporary Emergency Policy to swiftly address substantive changes in operations to protect the university community. This was one of the few times in the university's history it activated the Temporary Emergency Policy. Scott signing the policy sent a clear message of COVID-19's impact already and what the administration expected to come.

Pursuant to Faculty Staff Handbook (FSH) 1460 C-3, Scott adopted FSH 6990 COVID-19 Virus Emergency Response (University of Idaho 2020). The temporary emergency policy went into effect immediately for a term of 180 days (extendable) unless withdrawn by Scott before the end of the term. The meeting that spurred the decision left Scott with a sense that the university would have to go to "virtual operations as a campus, with exceptions for essential personnel, very soon." FSH 6995 outlined policies on face coverings, physical distancing, indoor and outdoor settings, and the enforcement of the policies (University of Idaho 2020).

Late that night, Scott hauled himself to University House to finally get some rest. "I just remember being so exhausted after that week," he shared. "I knew I needed to talk to Terry Grieb, our Faculty Senate chair at the time because we were hitting them cold with the Temporary Emergency Policy. I knew they might think it was a power grab. But it really wasn't. I was just bone-tired from that week because we'd spent hours talking about public health, dealing with student and faculty spring break petitions, and responding to related issues. It was late, and I had just hit a wall. I went to bed and woke up to an email from Terry, who was truly soul searching because he trusted me. This hit him out of nowhere. He represented the faculty, and here I was, taking emergency powers to respond to COVID-19 and didn't contact him. I immediately called him and said I understood and apologized. I assured him it wasn't a power grab. There were a lot of things that had to happen quickly, and I would consult him every step of the way."

"I wasn't stressed about Scott getting back to me or that a power grab was at hand," Faculty Senate Chair Terry Grieb clarified. "I knew that Scott and everyone else were working in full-on crisis mode, and the administration had been very responsive to my communications all year. And in fact, there had been a number of communications back and forth between the provost and me on this particular issue."

Terry and then-Provost John Wiencek would have to present FSH 6990 to the Faculty Senate and be prepared to defend it and answer all questions and concerns.

"Provost Wiencek and I knew each other's roles in discussing and creating university policy, and the roles were meant to be complementary, not adversarial," Terry emphasized. "This was similar in nature to conversations that John [Wiencek] and I had been having all year about the budget crisis and our approach to addressing that challenge. I genuinely liked working with John and grew to have a tremendous amount of respect for him as an administrator and as a mentor."

"The president has a lot of decision-making authority to override," Torrey said. "The question was, what happens after he does it? And I don't mean just for Scott. If a president comes in and ignores everyone, what buy-in do they have from everyone? It could set up the next discussion in a negative way. There was an element of power and authority versus the practical side of the long run. How would all that work?"

"Scott's affection and stewardship for the U of I were clear and strong," Terry expressed. "Here was someone who had served on the Advisory Board for my college [Business and Economics], had been a key leader for the U of I Foundation, and a whole host of other contributions to the U of I before becoming our president. I knew things like power grabs were not his style. The fact that he was concerned that this would be perceived as such just highlights the value he placed on shared governance."

Scott had always shown good faith in trying to understand how the structure of a university differed from the corporate space. But here was a new policy that provided him sweeping powers similar to exigency. In good faith, Terry believed it was his job to share with Scott precisely what that meant for the faculty and the university as an institution.

"FSH 6990 was lawful, but it also had the potential to challenge the very fabric of our university's structure," Terry stated. "I felt that it was my duty as Senate Chair to make sure that President Green fully understood the gravity and power of the policy he'd enacted."

Terry had two specific concerns about FSH 6990. The first concerned delegation of authority (i.e. whom would Scott delegate the responsibility to enact and enforce decisions). Providing for the delegation of this authority down to the VP level was too broad. Faculty could see that going beyond the executive administration level of delegation could be precarious and present a risk of abuse that outweighed expediency. These decisions had to come from the President's Office, but recognizing the role of the provost as chief academic officer seemed like a reasonable delegation in limited circumstances.

The second concern involved precedent. "The power to set aside the Faculty Staff Handbook for the purpose of managing the university's immediate needs was a dangerous thing in the bigger picture," Terry remarked. "It was critical to the success of FSH 6990 and the long-run success of the university that there be clear guiding principles highlighting the conditions where the president could use this policy and where he couldn't. It was also critical for everyone to understand that this was an extreme circumstance. We needed FSH 6990 to deal with the COVID-19 crisis. But to allow this policy to echo into the future would be a grave mistake and one that could jeopardize the institution."

If it was this easy to establish something like FSH 6990 for COVID-19, what would prevent it from becoming the go-to policy every time a serious issue faced the university?

"Note that we had negotiated a profound budget crisis that threatened the U of I's survival without a policy like FSH 6990," Terry pointed out. "So FSH 6990 needed a clear context that it was an extreme measure that needed application in a highly focused and nonrecurring fashion."

Scott and John both respected this point of view. Scott used FSH 6990 for several COVID-19 policies with consultation and transparency. Faculty Senate and Staff Council were part of the communication loop, and Torrey excelled with outreach to the faculty.

During this critical period, Scott didn't pass anything he didn't discuss with Faculty Senate leadership. Having the Temporary Emergency Policy in force made everyone stay focused on the same page and act quickly.

"The things I signed were executive orders my team needed or things that originated from the Faculty Senate," Scott said. "Some important items originated with our general counsel, but most came from the provost and Faculty Senate. For example, we had to suspend the need for SATs and ACTs because high school students couldn't sit for those exams. We had to determine whether to weight student evaluations for promotion and tenure. We had to make sure to change the catalog for the mode of class delivery. Those were just a few of the dozens of things that had to get addressed under university policies and procedures. Most of the items involved suspending technical rules so the university could continue operating in this emergency environment. This was important procedurally so we could respond quickly for both administrative issues and the university's academic needs."

March 22, 2020

Constant communications kept all Vandals abreast of the ever-fluid situation. On March 22, an email from the administration to faculty, staff, and students emphasized that reducing face-to-face interaction was the best mode of operation. The City of Moscow had restricted access to some local businesses, and the university limited some campus services in light of COVID-19.

The Moscow campus sat like an island surrounded by COVID-19. Things were literally hitting too close to home. Positive diagnoses of the virus, even in people under the age of 30, popped up in Whitman County to the west (Pullman) and Kootenai County to the north (Coeur d'Alene). The COVID-19 response teams proactively communicated the course for online learning, working at home, and only essential workers on campus.

Scott received an online petition from students listing their concerns over the financial implications of traveling to move out of residence halls or Greek houses, job loss, stresses of balancing moving while classes started after spring break and dealing with personal struggles over families being isolated or sick. The petition asked to delay the start of classes.

"But to do so could have resulted in students returning to campus when they should have been sheltering in place," Scott said, "so we didn't do that."

Remote classes would begin the following day (March 23), and having students stay at their permanent residence was one of the most impactful things they could do for community safety. To address the students' concerns and petition, a second email dated March 22 from the administration emphasized the importance of staying home and gave information on how students could retrieve personal items from their dorm rooms or Greek houses.

Amid extraordinary changes and related upheaval, a nugget of hope emerged. A five-word phrase at the end of that email became a vital and everlasting message. The email's valediction read: Keep Calm and Vandal

On. That catchphrase during the unprecedented times became a battle cry for Vandals to take on the challenge to help subdue this foe.

"That phrase came out of a meeting where a few folks were freaking out about COVID-19," Scott said. "Someone in the room said, 'Keep calm. Vandal on.' And it stuck."

The university could only do so much prepping, planning, and protocoling to keep its community safe. The U of I sat surrounded by the Moscow community and Latah and Whitman counties; an entire population existed outside the institution's purview. Scott and campus administrators shared their concerns publicly about people continuing to move freely through the community, risking the spread of the virus if they weren't feeling any symptoms. They also pointed out local testing limits, whether unavailable or delayed, that could impinge on stopping the spread. Messages from the university and City implored everyone to be flexible, patient, and, most importantly, safe.

Wednesday, March 25, 2020

By late afternoon on March 25, Idaho Governor Little officially declared a 21-day-statewide-stay-at-home order, closing all nonessential businesses. The state deemed educational systems as essential, but the governor reiterated that employees who could work at home do so. It wasn't mandatory but highly recommended. This day set another marker in its history when the University of Idaho closed its doors literally to everyone but essential workers and the few students who had nowhere else to go.

COVID-19 was real. COVID-19 was official. COVID-19 was unprecedented.

"Scott will say his saddest day as president was having to close the university," Assistant Vice President Kathy Barnard shared. "It hit him hard because everything he believed in was going to walk out the door, and we were going to have to do everything a new way."

"That was probably the hardest call I ever had to make because I knew financially what that would do to us," Scott said. "But I also knew the health and safety of our people came first, and the financial things came second. That became a theme throughout this ordeal."

"The only thing I could compare it to, not on the scale of severity, but similar feeling, was 9/11 when the FFA grounded the entire US airspace," Torrey shared. "That was monumental, something I don't think had ever happened before. COVID-19 impacted everything and everybody. We didn't have many things that, for a country our size, impacted every citizen. I remember thinking, 'Whoa, closing everywhere. . .this is big.'"

The university continued consulting Idaho Public Health officials for direction. They advised working remotely for those who were able as the best way to help stop the spread of the virus. Scott sent the directive to all employees at all locations of the U of I's interests around the state to work from home if possible. Human Resources required no paperwork to work remotely, one of the results of Scott signing the Temporary Emergency Policy. He understood that not everyone could work from home; he also recognized issues from working in the home, mainly caring for children and family members. He encouraged staff to work with supervisors to figure out how to balance the family and work life, now both suddenly taking place in homes.

The response from faculty and staff to the closure and work-at-home order was mainly relief. "Many were scared and glad we took this step," Scott shared. "They recognized that isolating people at home could help arrest the spread of the virus." Even Scott often worked from his University House office.

"One thing that helped our community stay safe in those early days was that both universities—the U of I and WSU—decided to move classes online after spring break," Gritman Medical Center CEO Kara Besst said. "The mask mandate that the City of Moscow put into effect was significant, too, and they enforced it effectively. Gritman worked to put protocols in place to continue to safely care for our patients in the clinics and the hospital."

In the haze of all things COVID-19 and trying to run the university remotely, Scott approached Torrey toward the end of March regarding the vacant provost position. "I think you need to be the interim provost," he'd stated. "There's no time to conduct an interim search. I need to appoint someone immediately."

There wasn't much discussion. "I accept," Torrey had answered, knowing he and Scott had a good working relationship, plus he'd been in the middle of the budget and COVID-19 crises since day one.

"I think he trusted the work I did," Torrey shared. "We were still dealing with fires in every direction. I wish I'd kept a journal. It would have been fascinating to reread everything because there were so many unknowns about the virus and how to deal with it. I'd been through crazy before, and this was twenty miles past crazy."

Scott's Management Insight

Make the hard decision, keep calm, and carry on. The health and safety of the campus and community are paramount. We used the little data we had and the advice and counsel of health-care professionals to guide our decisions, not the fear of certain faculty, staff, students, or the Moscow community. We isolated the fearmongers and leaned on those thinking clearly and leading. That approach served us well throughout the pandemic. The right decision was to close the university even though we knew it would exacerbate our financial woes. But our employees had already found ways to save even more money than we asked, generating savings well above our revised budgets. Those savings gave us some financial flexibility to respond to the pandemic. With that bit of good news, we started thinking about different options for the fall.

Part VI

Chapter 27

Meanwhile, Back at the Financial Crisis

"If we could resolve the financial challenges within two years, there's no telling what we could do."

—*Brian Foisy*

At the same time the U of I was furiously dealing with the "twenty miles past crazy" environment of COVID-19, the budget reconciliation issue fought to share the limelight with the onslaught of pandemic unknowns. But despite the unprecedented reality of closing down the U of I and through tremendous dedication, communication, and good old-fashioned blood, sweat, and tears, the university was going to survive the first round of budget cuts to squeak through FY20 without a deficit.

Scott was exceedingly proud of his Vandal family. "The majority of people did more than we asked them to do, knowing we were in financial trouble. It was amazing."

It was especially amazing since everyone was facing uncertainty with COVID-19 and another round of aggressive cuts for FY21 to the tune of $22 million. Scott had identified an additional $8 million and added it to the $14 million cut previously identified to avoid going into the red during FY21.

"That amount was clearly one of the largest—if not *the* largest—cuts in institutional history," Vice President Brian Foisy shared.

"I had a friend who once said, 'The great thing about metrics is if you pay enough attention to them, they start moving in the right direction,'" Scott said, laughing. "That's exactly what was happening at our university."

"If we could resolve the financial challenges within two years, there's no telling what we could do," Brian offered. "Scott was the one who was finally willing to say that we needed to reduce budgets by $22 million. We needed to make the cuts instead of waiting around for enrollment to turn the corner. People weren't going to like it, but it would be done once and for all. And imagine how much better we would be on the other side."

Chandra Zenner Ford, CEO SW Idaho and special advisor, voiced her thankfulness that things were looking up for the university because of the hard work, dedication, and sacrifice of every college, unit, department, and division. But she offered special accolades to the Department of Finance and Administration. "I'll tell you this, between the financial stuff, creating all the reporting we needed to track our finances properly, and the P3 deal, it was a miracle that Brian and his staff were all still working for the U of I. They knocked it out of the ballpark. We turned the corner from the cliff of burning cash, which was putting the whole institution at risk. Once the reserves are up to the level required by the SBOE, we can set the stage for a new era of prosperity for our students, our faculty, and our state."

"I always told folks, your budget is my budget, and my budget is the provost's budget, and so on," Vice Provost for Student Affairs and Dean of Students Blaine Eckles shared. "When we started collaborating and working together, we accomplished great things. A rising tide will lift all boats, and that's the approach everyone tried to take."

What came out of the Financial Model Working Group's time and diligence was a beautiful creation called the Vandal Hybrid Budget Model. "It primarily combined elements of incremental budgeting with movement to performance-based budgeting," Chandra explained. "It involved key components, including accountability incentives for growth, efficiency, entrepreneurial thinking, and improving financial strength. If enrollment within a certain college went up, that college would get more money as an incentive to deal with more students." See Figure 27.01.

FY22 would be the first fiscal year the university fully implemented the model, allocating money to colleges based on metrics. "It was simple," Scott pointed out. "If the colleges and units hit their metrics, they got more money. Attacking enrollment by providing incentives to colleges would deploy the theory that recruiting was everyone's responsibility. No one could blame SEM if their college didn't get more students; they could only blame themselves. It would become all our responsibility."

"The higher education industry was becoming increasingly competitive," Associate Vice President Kim Salisbury stated. "If we didn't rise to the top in our cost and budget allocation analysis, we were at risk of losing out to institutions that did."

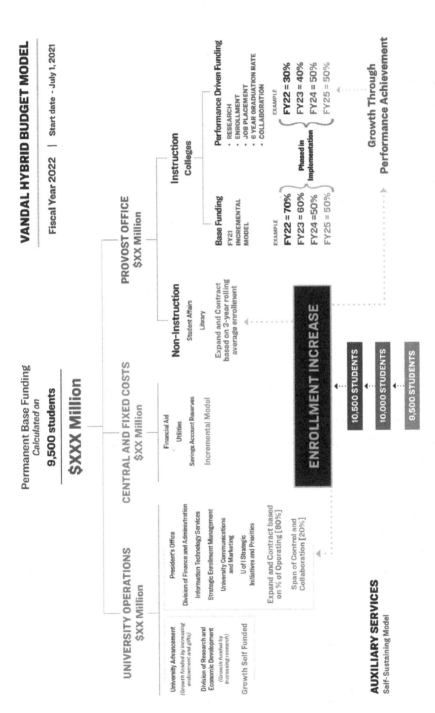

Figure 27.01   The Vandal Hybrid Budget Model aligns expenses with revenues, provides a permanent funding plan for operations and infrastructure, and reestablishes an adequate reserve position, along with incentivizing growth.

SOURCE: Karla Scharbach, University of Idaho. Reproduced with permission of University of Idaho.

"Before the creation of the Vandal Hybrid Budget Model, there was no great incentive to perform well other than just personal pride," commented Dean Dennis Becker. "We weren't rewarded financially. It was an exciting thing for me because I was getting to fix a lot of processes. But in doing so, we were still observing how broken the processes were. We couldn't afford to be that broken because of the political and financial pressures that existed. I didn't ever think there were any malicious attacks. But even though a lot of deans got along well, that family dynamic broke down because previous administrations weren't meeting our individual needs. That changed with Scott."

Enrollment continued to be the key to opening all the doors at the university. By freezing tuition temporarily and offering as much assistance as possible to people interested in attending the U of I through programs such as Enroll Idaho, the U of I placed students, both potential and existing, first. The silos still existed, but by making enrollment everyone's job as they performed the functions of their titled job, projections started to look promising.

"We were all a part of the enrollment process as far as student recruitment and retention," CEHHS Interim Dean Philip Scruggs stated. "And we all benefited from that through enrollment growth. We achieved enrollments by how we engaged with people and focused on the aspect of quality education. Every engagement prospective students had with staff and faculty, myself included, should have left them with a sense that we cared, they were important, and the engagement was meaningful."

"We came a long way toward growing enrollment that helped the budgets at Idaho," SEM Vice Provost Dean Kahler reflected. "I looked back at the road. There were a lot of potholes and a lot of stuff out there we got through. It was the team. It was the entire campus that righted the ship."

The Enroll Idaho program was just one of the ways the U of I showed its enthusiasm to have students enroll. Pre-COVID-19, U of I employees visited high schools to share their excitement and story. "We would explain how a college degree makes you healthier, wealthier, and wiser," Scott shared. "College graduates earn $1.2 million more over their lifetime, live nine years longer on average, and are more involved in their community."

University employees would also talk about how to finance an education and offer to enroll them in any of Idaho's public institutions of higher learning, not just the U of I.

"I led by example," Scott said. "I started visiting high schools to recruit before COVID-19 hit. I put over 25,000 miles on my truck to get to as many places as I could to share the U of I story and inspire students to join the Vandal family. Anyone who gave me the name of a potential student, I called personally. I took every opportunity to explain why students needed to go on to college. We were willing to help them do that. Even if they didn't want to attend the University of Idaho, we could help them."

The university also employed a new and effective enrollment marketing plan that engaged potential students via smartphone, social media, video, texts, emails—whatever it took to speak their language to interest them in the U of I.

The Strategic Enrollment Planning Fiscal/Financial Aid Workgroup also looked at ways to address the enrollment decline. "We noticed trends toward increased out-of-state students," Kim shared. "We identified top-producing high schools and recommended the U of I reach out more in those areas. We also recommended increasing financial aid to targeted populations."

Scott's Management Insight

Lead by example. It is an old saw, but if employees and alumni see that you believe something is important enough to do it yourself, they will believe it is important and follow suit. Hitting the road to help recruit students and calling individual students to sell the U of I sent a powerful message: recruiting is essential, and we are all accountable—especially the president.

Smart Collaboration

Education within Education

As the oldest public education institution in Idaho and the land-grant university, the University of Idaho takes its responsibility seriously to serve the people in the state through education, research, extension, and collaboration. Idaho had been faced with diminishing numbers of educators going on to become principals and superintendents within the state's school districts.

"It's been challenging to replace the K–12 administration professionals within the state," Interim Dean of the College of Education, Health, and Human Sciences (CEHHS) Philip Scruggs said.

What better way to remedy that situation than for the U of I and CEHHS to collaborate with school districts to offer an educational leadership program and help educators expand their career path

(Continued)

(Continued)

options? The Educational Leadership Program isn't new to CEHHS and the U of I; they began offering graduate degrees over 30 years ago. The original idea of Educational Leadership cohorts developed in the early 2000s but was dropped. The revival of the teamwork approach to growing the principal and superintendent cohort within the state came when CEHHS set up a new cohort with the West Ada School District, the largest in the state. The two-year curriculum for approximately 20 teachers within that district identified to become principals offers a laser-focused curriculum to provide credentials needed to become school leaders within K–12 education.

"We completed our first year of the West Ada Principalship Cohort in 2022," Philip said. "By the end of the program, the district will have approximately 24 new potential principals. They will be certified within the State of Idaho, so they can go anywhere in the state as educational leaders as principals. There was a great need for principals, and the U of I has worked to meet that need through collaboration."

Philip shared that it was a team effort in partnering with the West Ada School District, with the Educational Leadership faculty (Drs. Wargo, Tenuto, and Bauscher), the Leadership and Counseling Department Chair (Dr. Laura Holyoke) and Administrative Coordinator (Michelle Weitz), and the U of I Boise Center Executive Director (Chandra Zenner Ford) all taking hold of the reins. "The collaborative work was also made possible by the support of President Green and Provost [Torrey] Lawrence. We are all excited about the fruit that will be borne from this and future collaborative partnerships to meet the needs of Idaho."

"It's a powerful and novel way to provide a career ladder for K–12 educators," said Jerry McMurtry, dean of the College of Graduate Studies. "We've lost a lot of space in education in the state, but programs like this will help gain some of that back."

"The U of I Educational Leadership team is currently working with other districts in the State of Idaho to continue developing this cohort model where local learning and contexts are a key aspect of the curriculum," Philip said.

Scott's Management Insight

Peter Drucker, the management guru, famously said that "culture eats strategy for breakfast" (Drucker, P. n.d.). There is no question in my mind that this is true. Culture is a strong force. In short, you can have the best strategy in the world, but if you don't have the right culture, you will not succeed.

From the beginning, I wanted to set the tone from the top as being one that puts students first, supports the culture of the Vandal family, and that our team is brave, bold, and unstoppable. We can make great things happen by collaborating and working together.

The collaborating piece has come a long way but still has some challenges. We brought in Heidi Gardner from Harvard University, who wrote the book Smart Collaboration: How Professionals and Their Firms Succeed by Breaking Down Silos *(Gardner, H. 2017). Her work helped reshape how our management team looks at our challenges and addresses them. Getting our culture rebuilt enabled our strategy execution. There is now confidence on campus that we can achieve big things, and I am excited about where this will take us.*

Chapter 28
Turning Off the Lights

"What the hell else are you going to throw at us, Universe?"
—*Dr. Blaine Eckles*

The 21-day-statewide-stay-at-home order directive from Governor Little on March 25 left no wiggle room for the U of I's actions. The safety of the Vandal family was the priority. "That's where state politics really did come into play," Dean of Students Blaine Eckles pointed out. "Many states were moving in the same direction, shutting down schools. Those were hard decisions because how do you stay open in a safe way when you don't have a vaccine? It was clear for President Green to make that decision. He said more than once he liked being in the herd on this particular issue. I fully supported his decision."

Scott had been at the U of I long enough to build credibility with faculty, staff, and students, so when he decided to have everyone work at home who could, most Vandals agreed. No one said let's take the chance. Most felt their president absolutely made the right call at the right time, even though the impacts to all the communities on campus felt the sting of COVID-19's reach.

Associated Students of the University of Idaho (ASUI)

The impact on the student body created massive concern from the top down. The U of I was historically a residential campus, where most learning occurred among stately old and new buildings, rolling hills, luscious trees, and a brave and bold sense of belonging. Even education at the U of I Centers in Boise, Coeur d'Alene, and Idaho Falls took place in beautiful buildings with the latest technology and high levels of Vandal spirit.

It was springtime on the Palouse, with flowers starting to bloom, lawns showing new green sprigs of grass, and the disk golf course awaiting the "thunk, clink" of plastic frisbees hitting their mark. Once Scott declared campus closed, she sat like an end-of-the-world movie set, with the grounds sparse and once-vibrantly filled buildings empty, cold, and quiet. Instead of the whirlwind of spring events, classes, and commencement planning, COVID-19 stole the remainder of the spring semester, along with the thousands of Vandals who populated the beautiful campus. The fear of the virus canceled concerts and events, forced Greek houses to shut down, and the few students and essential workers who remained on campus lost any semblance of social activity or face-to-face contact.

"It was an eerie feeling," said Jacob Lockhart, ASUI president (2019–2020). "ASUI government was responsible for making sure that the administration prioritized students in their emergency response process. But personally, it felt hollow. Students weren't sure what was happening. It felt like the rug was pulled out from under us, and we were just kind of floating there. We didn't know what was going to happen. Campus was practically empty; people just didn't come back. Everything ended very abruptly. It's a weird feeling to experience when everything shifted so dramatically."

"I came on campus more than I stayed off," College of Art and Architecture Dean Shauna Corry admitted. As dean of the College of Art and Architecture, she felt a deep sense of responsibility for her students. "We had international students here, and they were alone, away from their families. The university tried to provide a safe home for them. Our college had a computer studio where students could log in and go around the world remotely. But I had students living on campus, and they couldn't go anywhere. They would come into my building every day and work in the computer lab. I was not going to have them sit up there by themselves. I could interact safely with them and did. . .a lot. I would open the door, say hi, and check to make sure everybody was wearing a mask. We had a protocol that they could only use every other computer. It was just walking on an empty campus and walking into an empty building that got me. We had three or four students at the lab every day for eight hours a day, if not longer. I just felt a responsibility to have someone there with them."

Anyone familiar with the U of I knew its educational and research tentacles reached statewide—north and south, east and west. But during

COVID-19, that geographical bragging point became magnified. With Vandals learning and researching everywhere, the administration had to ensure everyone was working in a safe environment, and it may not resemble what was happening in Moscow. The U of I campuses and extensions around the state took precautions specific to their areas.

"What was happening in Boise with COVID-19 was never quite the same as Moscow," CEO SW Idaho and Special Advisor Chandra Zenner Ford shared. "We did go fully online for the law school and other classes, but everybody had security cards for this building, so we left it accessible. We have so much space; if students wanted to use the facility, they could. College of Art and Architecture students had big projects, so I think some came here to work on them."

To the fullest extent possible, Blaine and his team at Student Affairs also worked tirelessly to meet the needs of every student. "We put some students on buses to get home," he shared. "We paid for it. We got some of them a few flights, but remember, this was when airlines were starting to shut down. It was difficult; people were nervous about being in an airport around other folks they didn't know. This was before masks were readily plentiful, and there was some mixed messaging from the government about whether we should wear a mask or if we were supposed to save the masks for our medical practitioners." For many students, it was a confusing time and a time that brought worry about their future.

Shutting down the campus also meant canceling Commencement 2020. There would be no pomp, no circumstance, no black gowns, or decorated mortarboards getting tossed with the gold tassel spreading out into the spirited air. The sense of completion, hope, and what's next was gone, never gaining momentum toward that one day in May when all the hard work and dedication were supposed to spectacularly merge. There would be no period at the end of that sentence or even any idea of how long the sentence would be. Commencement exercises existed to acknowledge the years of effort and study that led to a degree. Canceling was like lopping off the final cadence of a symphony.

"There were a lot of students who felt like COVID-19 robbed them of their graduation experience, and I get that," Blaine sympathized. "I tried to explain there have been times when students didn't get their commencement, like during World War II when people missed their graduation. At some point, we had to make personal sacrifices."

"It was hard on the senior class in particular," Jacob confessed. He was one of the 2020 graduates who lost the opportunity for a final public hurrah. "We felt like we lost so much in that process. The sense of finality wasn't there. There wasn't that level of celebration and communal drive.

Missing Commencement wasn't the most important thing in the grand scheme of things. I was mostly upset for folks who were first-generation students being the first ones in their families to graduate; that's a huge deal. And folks who had financed their entire time there or had been there for five or six years, it was finally time to graduate. Those were the stories that made me sadder than my personal story. The precautions were necessary; we were doing our part to keep the community safe. But it was sad, and it hurt for a lot of folks."

"I was hoping to find a way to do it in a way to keep everybody safe in a very controlled manner, but there were just too many moving parts," Scott shared. "We made the right decision; there was just so much we didn't know about the virus at that point."

Students became isolated either at home or on campus, learning in the Brady Bunch–like setting of Zoom. No study dates, no contemplating and debating, no Mom's Weekend, no spring sports, no tubs at the Club—suddenly, higher education boiled down to a screen on a digital device with hopefully a suitable Internet connection.

"I taught a class, and what struck me was the students struggling with mental issues," Shauna shared. "Some were harder hit than others. I had a student who was not doing well in my class, had not accomplished the things they needed to accomplish, and wasn't meeting deadlines. I zoomed with them to talk like I normally would, and the student was sitting in a basement room, wrapped up in blankets. They hadn't had a shower. Their hair wasn't done. They were so depressed. I tried to talk with them about how I could help and what they needed to do to pass the class. They started crying, and I started to cry with them because it was just so hard, and there was only so much I could do to help them. This student did manage to get their work done, pass the class, and graduate. But I'll never forget seeing that student in their own environment in a basement apartment with very little light, so depressed, sitting on a cell phone, trying to figure out what happened and what to do."

"As soon as we went online, some students struggled," remarked Interim Dean John Crepeau, College of Engineering. "I even had one student I was teaching tell me they were 'devastated' going to online classes. For the most part, students were disappointed but realized the constraints, and they made the best of a tough situation. On very short notice, the College of Engineering had to switch our biggest spring event, Engineering Expo, from live and in-person to some form of online format. Undergraduate students showed off their required senior design project at Expo. We invited school kids, community colleges, faculty, and industry leaders. The students spent their entire year getting ready for this event, and we had to figure out how to go from in-person to online."

A plethora of stories like that played out with students, faculty, and staff. The U of I employees worked to meet the needs of the students, especially those who remained on campus, focusing on their online learning experience and safety regarding food and housing. Targhee Hall (dormitory) became the on-campus infirmary for any student who remained on campus to receive COVID-19 care. The IDRT Core hired an isolation manager to oversee all operations at Targhee; the manager stayed at Targhee with the students, away from their families and homes, to meet all the student care needs.

The U of I also retained the services of a retiring professor and MD from WWAMI to serve as a medical advisor. The advisor served the critical role of informing Scott and the senior leadership in decision-making. He also offered expertise with the students in isolation. After the MD retired, the U of I brought on one of Gritman Medical Center's physician's assistants to continue caring for and supporting isolated students.

The Counseling and Testing Center worked to provide mental health care as best they could in the new environment. "You'd think that counselors working with students could just do it via Zoom," Provost Torrey Lawrence said. "But we actually ran into some challenges." Some counselors lived in Washington, which presented quandaries about practicing across state lines. "But we worked it out."

"We did a lot of things to support our students during that time frame," Blaine said. "We had to transition our entire counseling department online. I'm nothing but proud of how we responded during that time. It was incredibly challenging and difficult. And then, on top of that, we had a big earthquake."

The state's second-largest earthquake in history shook Idaho on March 31, 2020, reaching a rattling 6.5 magnitude. The Idaho Geological Survey couldn't initially perform a ground survey inspection of the impacted region due to heavy snowfall and a statewide travel ban that was in effect due to the COVID-19 pandemic. Two overflights, however, revealed avalanches and landslides across minor highways (US Geological Survey 2020).

"I was in a meeting with my exec team at the time it hit," Blaine shared. "We were talking about COVID-19, of course, and all of a sudden, we had an earthquake. We'd also had a late spring snowstorm. And we were all like, what the hell else are you going to throw at us, Universe?"

Enrollment and Recruitment

The financial crisis hung over campus like an ominous storm cloud. The U of I was still in the throes of fighting its way through the financial situation, but COVID-19 didn't care how the university would permanently cut $22 million out of its FY21 budget. The worry of how enrollment would pan out for the fall was on everyone's radar even before the world shut down. When COVID-19 hit, recruitment and retention efforts stopped; there was no in-person outreach, no contact with high school graduates, and no events showing off the U of I campus and all its offerings.

"I had recruiters all over the place, so we had to work with our teams to adjust," recalled Vice Provost Dean Kahler. "Everybody went remote. We had a huge tech lift that Dan [Ewart] helped with tremendously. Potential students didn't know how to stay in touch with us, so we had to figure out how we could stay in touch with students. Everything practically came to a grinding halt on the recruitment side. But we quickly adjusted, and, like everyone else, we went online with our events. We started getting attention in a good way, like, 'Look at the virtual tour the U of I is doing.' But I was still as nervous as a long-tailed cat."

Enrollment numbers dipped in the dual credit category because school districts closed in the spring around the state. Those students may not have impacted the financial side of enrollment, but they were vital to the overall enrollment picture because they most likely would come to the U of I upon high school graduation.

"The number-one form of retention was engagement on campus and how connected our students felt to campus," Blaine said. "We started to hemorrhage students because of COVID-19 and how limited we became in providing engagement opportunities."

Not having recruitment efforts and the unknown about enrollment tuition for FY21 weighed heavily on everyone. How would COVID-19 wreak havoc on the tuition fees and Gen Ed budget for FY21 or beyond? How could the U of I survive another hit from lost revenue?

There was one bright ray of light, however. Nationally, college applications were going down, but the U of I's applicant numbers had increased for students arriving in fall 2020, which could equate to higher tuition dollars if they held in the face of COVID-19. The U of I still sat on the precipice of an ever-fluid enrollment and financial situation. Most variables that could affect their situation were out of the U of I's control because of the nature of COVID-19.

"It was disappointing because our applications and acceptances for fall 2020 prior to COVID-19 were through the roof," Scott said. "They sat at 16 percent and 14 percent growth, respectively. But then COVID-19 hit, and everything just kind of came apart. But when we dissected the numbers in October 2020 after Tenth Day, they told an interesting story. If we took out the lower margin students, like high school students taking dual credit and non-degree-seeking students, like employees and part-time students, the enrollment figure only decreased by about 3 percent. The greater mix of out-of-state students mitigated the decrease by trading lower margin tuitions for higher margin tuitions. It could've been a lot worse."

Financial

"We had just cut $20 million and ended up with over 100 people taking voluntary separation and voluntary retirement," Scott recounted. "The financial picture wasn't complete because we still faced additional losses associated with COVID-19—lower housing, food, parking, and ticket revenues. We estimated we'd lose $30 million the next fiscal year by closing campus due to COVID-19. That weighed on me because additional cuts meant additional people needed to leave the university. We just couldn't lose the financial position we'd worked so hard to achieve if we didn't have to, so we began to weigh our options. For me, it was all about saving jobs and the hardship that layoffs have on families."

Campus Operations, Research, and Buildings

"In many cases, we couldn't just close down the buildings by flipping off the lights and locking the doors," Scott shared. "It had to be done in the right way. We had animals that needed care, and faculty didn't want to lose any research specimens. Some people had to remain on campus to address those things. We had to determine those who were essential and those who could work at home. Universities are complicated ecosystems. We couldn't just turn off the steam plant; we had to keep things warm and electricity flowing, especially to the labs and key areas, and we had to monitor our operating systems continually."

"The university always had a policy for flex time, flex place," Director of Human Resources Brandi Terwilliger clarified. "But it had been happening somewhat informally in the departments, which wasn't bad, but there was no record anywhere in a central location of who was on a specific flex work, flex place. HR became that funnel to help navigate requests regarding COVID-19 because it was important to centralize requests to properly navigate the available programs and offerings for employees. Working at home tied back to things such as benefits, taxes, pay, and where they lived because their flex place might not be in Idaho. Many employees lived in Washington. And we also had to pivot quickly to implement the federal funds allocated for COVID-19 sick time. FFCR (Family First Corona

Response Act) and EPSL (Emergency Paid Sick Leave) provided paid leave for various conditions or issues. The programs were great for employees, but we had to rapidly figure out how to incorporate them into our mechanisms for pay."

Those programs covered situations involving people who tested positive for the virus or were sick due to the virus and had to quarantine, lack of childcare while trying to work from home, and if they were caring for a COVID-19 patient at home. There were rules and caps related to receiving those federal funds, and HR had to ensure employees collected those benefits if they were eligible.

"It was great to have options for paid leave if someone needed it," Brandi acknowledged. "But managing that on the back end was something I don't think people realized was another challenge. It was a lot to learn and implement very quickly."

The integrity of the university's research projects also came into play. "There was probably $10 million worth of research throughout the College of Natural Resources that was on the line at the time," Dean Dennis Becker explained. "I was getting calls daily from research partners and agencies and faculty about what we were going to do if we had to shut it down. It was my choice to shut it down, but if I did, we would lose $10 million of work. That was going to be hard for us to recover financially and from a research standpoint. By coordinating with the president and university leadership, we worked through scenarios. We had the muscle memory from the budget cuts to quickly pivot and create common-sense approaches."

The technology expectations for IT were immense. Faculty had to deliver coursework in a useful way and manage student records (including grades) confidentially from home offices. Staff had to have access to the Banner database at home and be able to work with files, some confidential. Students needed the means to receive their lectures via Zoom and communicate with professors. Vandals interacted with the IT system in countless ways, and all those interactions came with the worries of delivery and security.

"We didn't have the same kind of monitoring, logging, tracking, and ability to prevent student records ending up on people's personal machines as they worked from home," Vice President Dan Ewart explained. "We had to avoid potential FERPA or HIPAA violations. And if people were conducting research at home, was their house as secure as our network? We had to worry about intellectual property being at risk. We only knew what we knew, so security was a constant concern. We put more things in place for prevention, and we educated people. We communicated reminders to everyone not to store information on their personal computers and to always use cloud-based mechanisms that IT supported."

Even though the University of Idaho essentially shut down due to COVID-19 starting mid-March, the institution was still trying to make a few key hires during the pandemic. "We were working with departments trying to help how to onboard people when they needed all those training pieces for their new job but were mainly working from home. How do we interact with them during their isolation or quarantine period? How do we process their paperwork in person? How do you make them feel a part of the community?"

Zoom replaced some in-person interviews, which made many people nervous. How did they know the person they hired was a good fit without that crucial interpersonal interaction?

"Originally, a lot of people delayed their start dates because of the complexity of onboarding at that time," Brandi shared. "But we couldn't just stop hiring."

The U of I managed to bring on several new hires while maintaining the strict COVID-19 protocols to ensure everyone's safety. Even though the pandemic demanded constant attention, the business as usual at the university crowded in sometimes, reminding employees that their work was vital to the institution's success, especially during the trying times of the virus.

The stress of COVID-19, piled on top of the existing financial woes, caused some to agonize and others to blossom.

"It was interesting to watch how fast some of these steadfast people unraveled in a completely different way than they handled the financial stress," Special Assistant Toni Broyles shared. "In meetings, some kept putting their head in their hands or running their fingers through their hair in anxiety. I wanted to tell them, 'This is go time. This is the time where if you've ever risen to the occasion, we need you to rise right now!' But some people crumbled. And it was not the people you would always expect. It was hard to see. But then there were people who just said, 'Well, we have to get this done.' Some of those folks were under the radar before, and then they came out and showed up with their best selves to get this done."

On top of those stressors stretching everyone's nerves so thin, April 1 (no fooling) brought the first positive COVID-19 cases to Latah County, with three U of I students and one Latah County resident testing positive. One student was in Canyon County in Southern Idaho but had been on campus as recently as March 29 when they moved out of their dorm room. A Boise-based student attended classes at the Water Center on March 19. The third student lived out of state and conducted his studies electronically. The Latah County resident's case appeared travel-related, with no known connection to the U of I. Those four cases created a sharp reminder that COVID-19 wasn't going away.

"I wasn't shocked," Scott recalled. "We knew it was coming."

The first cases for the Vandal family brought fresh questions and procedures regarding reporting positive cases and stats. "At that time, it was still embryonic; we weren't sure how to report or what we ought to report," Scott remarked. "We knew there would be interest in the data we could share without violating HIPAA and FERPA, and we were trying to be as transparent as possible. Eventually, once the system was up and running, we would email updates every Monday with numbers and nonconfidential information."

The entire Vandal family, nation, and world faced so many challenges, so many uncharted waters, and so many unknowns. But Scott fell back on his experience to lead by example, use data and facts to clearly communicate and calm fears, think outside the box, rely on his team of experts, and put the community's health first.

Scott's Management Insight

Once safety and business continuity are assured, adequately focus on supporting your employees and students (customers). They will remember how you respond long after the crisis passes. A little empathy when managing a crisis goes a long way; however, one can't let emotions prevent smart, clear-headed decision-making. Transparently providing data through memos (where color commentary added context) and on the website enabled the community to remain calm and carry on.

Chapter 29

Zoom!

"We had people trying new ways of teaching that they probably wouldn't have tried before."

—*Dr. Torrey Lawrence*

Before COVID-19, the U of I had limited online programming since, historically, the university was a residential campus. Once Scott decided to send everyone online and close campus, everyone had their marching orders. COVID-19 forced the university to establish two new methodologies for class delivery: the hybrid method (HyFlex), which included in-person lectures and learning via video, and the complete online pedagogy. To get everyone through the spring semester, IT focused on getting everyone strictly online. The HyFlex model would wait for the fall semester.

"People learned very quickly they didn't have good Internet at home," Provost Torrey Lawrence commented. "I was one of them. I live out of town and relied on a hotspot for our Internet."

Vice President for Information Technology and Chief Information Officer Dan Ewart explained, "It was a huge impact on the faculty to figure out how they were going to teach their classes fully online. Fortunately, IT had made good decisions in the years leading up to COVID-19, where we had an enterprise license for Zoom already in place, so we were able to just start creating more accounts."

"Going online with COVID-19 just drove home the point about how classes were so different across the campus," Torrey shared. "People's different pedagogical styles, the ways they teach, the discipline itself. We have around 1600 classes a semester, so to say, 'Just tell faculty to do X' didn't work for all of them. They had to finish online what they'd started in person."

"I won't say it was easy, but for the College of Engineering, it was pretty straightforward," Dean Larry Stauffer noted. "Our Engineering Outreach program had been using compressed video for years. There was a lot of faculty already in the mode of teaching online. The biggest challenge was going to be how to teach labs. It was one thing to lecture class via Zoom, but totally out of the ordinary to conduct labs, which were ordinarily hands-on."

"College of Education, Health, and Human Sciences (CEHHS) already had established online programming, so I think overall, as a college, we were prepared because a lot of our faculty had experience with teaching online," Interim Dean Philip Scruggs said. "But there were some programs and faculty that didn't have experience and expertise in online teaching, and some program content isn't delivered effectively online (e.g. dance performance, some Idaho Fitness courses, hands-on authentic learning experiences). It was a very challenging time for instructors; however, they continued to prioritize student engagement and learning."

Over 2000 faculty and staff would be working from home, many of whom had never experienced that before. Not only did the reality of working at home command flexibility, like maybe parents working nontraditional schedules to accommodate children at home needing assistance with schoolwork, but also the logistics of a massive increase in the need for reliable connectivity.

"One of Scott's biggest concerns through that first phase was whether our partners and vendors, like Zoom or Microsoft, would be able to handle the capacity," Dan shared.

"Okay, what happens if Zoom breaks, and it goes down, and we can't use it?" Scott had asked Dan early in the transition to online.

Dan assured him, "Scott, we also use Microsoft Teams. If Zoom breaks, we just have to do a transition where we help faculty and students get into a Team's Room instead of a Zoom Room."

"Okay," Scott had replied. "What happens if Blackboard, our learning management system, goes down?"

"Well, then we use spreadsheets," Dan replied. He understood Scott's worry. "We'd never tested that capacity before because there had never been a need to test it."

"We were breaking new ground; there's no question," Scott agreed. "Before COVID-19, there was a lot of opposition to online coursework. Many faculty felt, and I felt the same way, that online learning was not as rewarding or rich of a college experience as in-person learning. But in my view, even though we weren't in the classroom, Zoom was a good second best."

On average, the U of I students brought three devices with them while attending college that connected to the Internet, so those devices had to be able to connect remotely. Some students relied on any of the 700 lab stations IT hosted around the state. The U of I would provide access to the software needed for classes and services; students, faculty, and staff could use the Virtual Lab (V Lab) to log in and get the software on their devices with the backend still running on U of I equipment. But Dan's team had to ensure the appropriate equipment was available to accommodate students and faculty wherever they were learning or teaching.

"Hundreds and hundreds of students use our computer labs," Dan said. "But they were not going to be able to physically be in the labs. I put all these various permutations in front of the team, and the ideas just started flowing. We had tons of capacity to get people to VPN back into our systems, and ironically, we'd just bought some old equipment from a partner institution matching our equipment, and that increased our capacity. We also had the software licenses in place, so we just started knocking down the list."

Dan's team visited every computer lab on campus and said, "We're taking your laptops." Then they rebuilt them as quickly as possible and offered them for student checkout. "We accumulated over 250 laptops and, in about a week and a half, got them ready to be checked out for online learning."

Each laptop took approximately two hours to reconfigure, but Dan couldn't precisely calculate the hundreds of hours it took to get all the computers ready for online education. Normally, ITS worked hard to test solutions before rolling out the computer or product to a customer. "Nope, not this time," Dan laughed, "I had to look at my team and say, 'What's your idea? That sounds good. Put it into production. Do it.' Typically, we never want to test in production. We had to make so many production-level changes and just go, 'Boy, I hope this works.'"

Thankfully, things worked out well. Dan's team took the time to think out the lowest risk and highest reward options and implement them to work through various foreseeable issues, leaving the unknown bugs to work out as they arose. "Most of our problems were very individualized," Dan recalled. "For example, we had faculty members trying to work from home and not being able to get connected. We had very little resistance. And that shouldn't be glossed over. People truly realized that everybody was in completely uncharted territory. The grace that people provided each other during that time was a cool moment for the university. The general attitude was we're all in this together."

Dan's team worked exceptionally hard in a seemingly impossible turnaround time to get the campus through the initial switch to online education and working at home. Their focus was strictly on getting through the spring semester, knowing they had to be ready to do something very different in August.

"The reality was, we handled the online transition incredibly well," Scott recalled. "It was my biggest miscalculation in a good way. I didn't fully understand all the progress these cloud providers had made and that they could ramp up and scale so quickly. The fact that this whole country could move online over a period of a month was amazing, and it only took a week and a half for the U of I."

"All of a sudden, I'm on Zoom ten hours a day, trying to do that and audio via my hotspot at home; that was not working," Torrey laughed. "But the Internet where we were was being upgraded. I was the last person they let into a faster Internet connection. They couldn't come into the house to install it, but I strung my Internet wire through my window. It was just a funny thing about timing; I needed better Internet, and suddenly, it was available."

Once again, a glimmer of silver lining started to shine through the disruption. "I heard from faculty that the students didn't want to leave their online class. They would stay after and talk to the faculty member," Dean Shauna Corry said. "I had a faculty member come in and tell me she just met all the pets of her entire class. Faculty felt that they got to know their students personally, even though our college gets to know our students well because we spend so much time with them. But just to see a student's house and meet their pets and meet their mom or dad or grandpa, the faculty were delighted by how much the students wanted to hang out with them."

"One silver lining was that we had people trying new ways of teaching that they probably wouldn't have tried before," Torrey pointed out. "They learned Zoom could be a good tool. We also focused on learning outcomes. For example, before COVID-19, we focused on lab number seven, but we couldn't hold lab number seven, so what were we trying to learn from that lab, and how do we get to that now? Those were fascinating discussions."

"It was difficult because we weren't all necessarily in the classroom with students," CLASS Dean Sean Quinlan said. "We heard things second or third hand and tried to understand what was going on. From the dean's office's perspective, I tried to listen and respond to the challenges out there, the concerns about students, and how they were responding. Technology access, for example, was a huge challenge. It was unprecedented when the university went online, and we had shelter-in-place ordinances. We tried to support each other and understand what was going on. It was a huge lift."

Another huge lift was figuring out how employees who couldn't perform their job functions at home would continue to work without using all their annual leave. "For example, how would custodians keep working?" Director for Human Resources Brandi Terwilliger elaborated. They could clean at home, but that wouldn't get the university buildings cleaned. The service they provided was especially crucial during the pandemic. "We had to implement some of the federal leave policies, and we gave them PPE and as safe of an environment on campus as we could to conduct their work."

HR also offered ideas to fill work-at-home hours with jobs that might typically get put on the back burner, such as updating policy and procedure manuals, getting caught up on any training, or checking websites for broken links or needed updates. "We created a document of things people could work on at home if their jobs weren't conducive to being off campus."

After the initial rollout of the new online educational world for Vandals, Scott urged all faculty, staff, and students to immediately start preparing for the fall semester. His goal was to open a hybrid form of education—both in-person and online or HyFlex. He wanted as many of his Vandals back on campus by August 2020 as possible and vowed he would do whatever it took to keep them safe if they came.

"Sometime in March or April, it hit me that we needed to start thinking about fall," Torrey reflected. "It was one thing to drive home on the spare tire we blew out in March and had to get home to May. But saying we had to get the tire fixed for another road trip in the fall, that was a different situation completely."

Scott's Management Insight

As a leader facing a global crisis, you must gather as much big-picture information as possible, communicate direction, then rely on your management team to bring it down further to the local or relevant level to maneuver through the crisis effectively. Our deans, CETL, and IT worked with faculty to develop and deliver their classes. HR worked to identify and provide a safe work environment for essential staff. Facilities worked on housing and safely feeding students who remained on campus with nowhere to go. We prepared to fight the pandemic, organize PPE, and consider our next steps.

There is also the management concept of single points of failure to work through. Single points of failure are those critical systems or processes that if they go down, your institution (or critical areas of it) also go down. Zoom and Blackboard had that potential, but Dan thought through those issues.

During my time as president, we experienced a few other single points of failure that threatened the university. One was a chlorinator that went down, cutting off a critical water supply to the campus. Given COVID-19-related supply chain issues, there was a shortage of replacements. We had a similar problem during the heat of summer when our chiller went down. We did end up locating equipment and fixing these issues before having to close the university. But we did have to close the university due to a lack of replacement HVAC filters during fire season. Filters are expensive, so Facilities Management did not keep enough on hand. I pointed out that closing the university is more expensive than keeping inventory on hand. We plan to eliminate these single points of failure, but I suspect more are lurking. A president must make it a priority to seek out single-point failures and eliminate them. It will be cheaper and less disruptive than shutting down the institution.

Chapter 30
Talks with Torrey

"The spectrum of opinions was always wide."

—*Dr. Torrey Lawrence*

"From day one, Scott took steps to do whatever he needed to get us back on campus as soon as possible," Assistant Vice President Kathy Barnard stated. "If someone is a proactive person, it isn't just in one part of their life: they're proactive in everything. That was Scott. He knew that we couldn't just wait COVID-19 out. I also think he was the only president, maybe in the country, who understood that if we could get back in person before the others, it would be a huge business advantage."

"Scott was a well-read man in so many subjects," Special Assistant, Strategic Initiatives Toni Broyles shared. "He *knew* testing was going to be key to our survival. He didn't get bogged down with what the American media was spoon-feeding us; he dug into what other countries were doing and found that the testing was ultimately key to opening campus."

"There was a reasonable argument to be made that if we had quick testing, we could identify where the virus was and put it down," Scott reflected, "and, more importantly, identify those who were asymptomatic. So that's what I knew we needed to do if we were going to stay open in the fall. Also, our financial condition was such that we had a lot of incentive to do that."

But how could the U of I open campus safely when no vaccine existed or even testing protocols for universities were established yet? Phrases like "flatten the curve," "do your part," and "social distance" were barked out at every opportunity in the media and even between friends. The division between "stay open" and "close down the world" caused a rift that would last long past the spring months.

"The spectrum of opinions was always wide," Provost Torrey Lawrence shared.

But in Moscow, in the chaos of the great unknown and divisiveness, acts of kindness began to multiply in the face of the COVID-19 foe.

Daolin Fu, assistant professor in Plant Sciences, offered his lab's PPE equipment for Gritman Medical Center staff to use in the face of supply chain issues.

"Our campus community tried to pull together all the PPE we could when we first started getting cases in Latah County," Scott shared. "We sent everything to Gritman Medical Center early on because there was some concern whether there would be enough for health-care professionals. We had people stepping up, like Daolin Fu and one of our employees in Advancement, who made masks and gave them out to anyone who needed one. I wore one from her for most of the first wave of COVID-19; they were good masks. People were thoughtful and trying to do whatever they could to help."

Sunday, April 9 brought the welcome news from Matt Freeman, SBOE executive director, that he'd attended a briefing from Secretary of Education Nancy DeVos regarding the Coronavirus Aid, Relief, and Economic Security (CARES) Act fund for higher education institutions. The government allocated the first tranche of postsecondary funding for emergency financial aid grants for students to cover expenses related to the disruption of campus operations due to COVID-19. These funds would address the concerns voiced by Vandals to cover such things as food, housing, course materials, technology, health care, and childcare. There were regulations on how students could use the funds, but the relief was on the way. The government set up a simple application process with defined parameters, although they further clarified that process as more funds became available. Matt also confirmed his office would handle any reporting requirements on behalf of Idaho's education system to help alleviate the pressures of institutions reporting individually.

Less than a week later, on April 15, Matt again contacted state institution leaders regarding the Distance Learning and Telemedicine Grant, which provided financial assistance to enable and improve distance learning and telemedicine services in rural areas. The U of I received $1.8 million from the Department of Treasury to the State of Idaho, which allocated the funds. It was agreed by many in Scott's world that the government had never moved so fast.

Thursday, April 16 brought another swift and crucial action on the Palouse regarding COVID-19. That day, an email started one of the most course-altering processes involving the virus for the U of I and Moscow. Adina Bielenberg, from Schweitzer Engineering in Pullman, Washington, contacted Scott and Kara Besst, Gritman Medical Center CEO, via email on behalf of Ed Schweitzer, the company's president and owner (Green, S., personal communication). Adina shared a link to a *Wall Street Journal* article posing the question of whether government agencies including the FDA would coordinate with the country's academic labs to temporarily allow them to legally validate any number of approved COVID-19 tests. Temporarily "deputizing" a working, FDA-compliant academic research lab (CLIA) to screen tests could allow for an additional 500,000 to 1,000,000 test validations with a turnaround time of less than a week (Lipton and Sortwell 2020).

The idea that testing was key was gaining traction nationwide.

"Adina used to work at Gritman, and we were in communication as things developed," Kara said. "She shared a bit about what Purdue (University) was doing to help with COVID-19 testing. Our leadership team began discussing what this could look like from a hospital standpoint. We needed to determine the testing process and the necessary equipment, which we did not have."

"The medical practitioner from Gritman Medical Center at our Vandal Health Clinic on campus was on the original IDRT Core and part of our conversations," Dean of Students Blaine Eckles shared. "We had already been collaborating with Gritman Medical Center for years because they ran our health clinic on campus, so we engaged in COVID-19 conversations with them early on."

Scott knew Gritman Medical Center would be pivotal in how the Moscow campus would handle COVID-19. In the beginning stages, he didn't know if their relationship involving COVID-19 would involve testing, student care, or both, but collaborating with them as the only major hospital in Latah County seemed like a no-brainer.

The email from Adina sparked the conversation about Scott's idea to set up a testing lab on campus. He knew there were significant roadblocks. The U of I didn't have its own teaching hospital, but it did have a group of experts on pathogens and vector-borne diseases.

Scott reached out to Barrie Robison at IBEST, asking how their lab's infrastructure could relate to COVID-19 testing. As director of IBEST, Barrie welcomed the opportunity to share what the GBRC lab staff had been noodling around since February. "When Scott emailed us, we explained we had the equipment and the knowledge, but there were some big obstacles," Barrie shared. "One of the biggest was that we were not a CLIA-certified lab."

Not to be deterred, Scott gathered the information from Barrie, did a little digging on his own, and emailed Adina, Kara, and Ed (Schweitzer), explaining the U of I had the lab and experts, but the FDA would need to lift the CLIA restriction mentioned in the WSJ article. The article's author shared frustrations felt by many researchers throughout the county who could assist with COVID-19 testing and wanted to help but couldn't due to the CLIA restrictions. When the WSJ article came out, no one had heard anything regarding lifting CLIA requirements, but the University of California, Berkeley did manage to establish a pop-up state-of-the-art COVID-19 testing lab in March, which added fuel to the discussion that universities could play a key role in testing for COVID-19 (Sanders 2020).

Scott emailed the potential collaborators and mentioned that the U of I could set up the testing for about $70,000, but it was moot unless the FDA lifted the CLIA restriction and allowed the U of I to test in their lab. But none of them were giving up yet; Adina replied to Scott's email with information and a link regarding Purdue University conducting COVID-19 testing.

David A. Broecker, chief innovation and collaboration officer at Purdue Research Foundation, shared details with Adina about their progress on human COVID-19 testing in their Animal Disease and Diagnostic Lab. Purdue's animal testing was almost identical to testing for humans with minor enhancements to their Laboratory Information Management System (LIMS). The key to CLIA was getting an MD with the proper credentials—board certification in pathology and CLIA lab experience. Broecker had outlined to Adina the front-end logistics regarding patient information gathering and handling testing samples to ensure safety and HIPAA (privacy). He shared back-end logistics that included a secure reporting system to share results with the patient in a timely manner (Nickel 2020).

That critical email set the ball rolling at a fast pace and confirmed that institutions were ready and willing to share any information so the country could strive to get enough testing facilities up and running to help mitigate the spread. Everyone was in it together.

Scott reached out to Kara and, through a series of phone calls and emails, determined that both the hospital and the institution would be open to collaboration. "So we decided to open our own lab with Gritman Medical Center," Scott explained.

"It was very nice to have somebody who was decisive in that way," Barrie shared. "Let me just say in terms of contrast, say to, oh, I don't know, prior to Scott arriving at this university."

"The fear of the alternative catalyzed us to do something that was very, very different and risqué at the moment," Dean Dennis Becker said.

"The U of I is a great community partner," Kara stated. "We didn't know how big this was going to be, but we knew it was important. I said yes and then turned the project over to Kane Francetich. I had the easy job."

"I remember that call very well," said Gritman Medical Center Chief Information Officer Kane Francetich. "It was on May 12, at 5 p.m., Kara and I had a call with Toni [Broyles]. The day before, I had a meeting with Dr. Isaac Grindeland, who was our medical director for our CLIA laboratory. He said we could probably handle all the testing using partner laboratories, but he wasn't sure we needed to do anything independently. The next day, we talked with Toni, and as soon as that call ended, Kara called me back, and we started talking. We agreed we had to do this. That's when everything started moving."

"We had been trying to figure out where we could put a CLIA lab on campus and what it would take to get CLIA certified," Barrie recalled. "Audrey Harris, the director of compliance at the time, was the first person to put it all together and suggest we move our equipment over to Gritman Medical Center, which already had a CLIA-certified physician and lab."

Would this collaboration be the key to gaining the ability to test and receive results for an entire campus and area population promptly? At that point in time, Gritman sent their COVID-19 specimens to Boise, and they were resulted by a third party located in Arizona. Results were taking 3–5 days. If the U of I and Gritman could get a CLIA-certified lab up and running, they could cut those result times to 24 hours or less. Opening the U of I for fall classes could be a reality with that turnaround.

Bingo.

The GBRC researchers would start working under CLIA physician Dr. Isaac R. Grindeland, MD, to establish a CLIA-certified COVID-19 testing lab in Moscow.

An analysis of qPCR-based (quantitative polymerase chain reaction) testing done by the GBRC manager outlined the costs for that type of testing. It wouldn't be cheap, but it was feasible.

"I figured we would spend about $3 million to get campus COVID-19-ready and the testing lab up," Scott shared.

"The president invested a lot of money in setting up the testing," Torrey said. "It was a big unknown there, a big financial commitment. But when he decided and said, 'Let's go for this, we will be ahead of people,' we were out of the gates so far ahead of other places. That was critical."

Some argued the expense was too great considering the U of I's financial crisis. "But if we stayed closed in the fall, we would definitely lose at least $30 million in revenue," Scott pointed out. "I added up the costs of lost revenue with COVID-19 we experienced with the campus closure after spring break, including tuition, retail, and other revenue generated by an up-and-running campus. But then I put the numbers aside and looked at the bigger picture and the longer term. The U of I would be in a desperate situation if we didn't open in the fall. I opened the checkbook and said, 'Do what you need to do.' Our people didn't have to put everything out to bid. The administration had suspended the processes so Vandals could go out and get what we needed to run the university in the fall with HyFlex learning, COVID-19 testing, and all safety measures in place."

Scott's Management Insight

Identify the bottlenecks and threats to delivering your product. Control what you can control. If it is testing, build a testing facility. If it is the supply of hand sanitizer, make your own. For the U of I, we knew we needed to have fast, reliable testing if we would open successfully in the fall. We recognized that other institutions and companies were also evaluating a response that could put pressure on the supply chain. So we embarked on one of the most complex projects in our history, with little time to accomplish it.

We quickly secured the equipment and supplies needed to open the lab and protect our campus. The availability of hand sanitizer was an early issue, so one of our faculty, Samir Abd El-Fatah, started producing FDA-approved sanitizer that we had dispensed throughout campus. Toni Broyles bird-dogged the equipment, reagents, masks, thermal scanners, and other items needed to execute our campus safety plan. The effort was enormous and occurring while a small number of our faculty, staff, and students did their best to ensure we would *not* open in the fall. I cannot say enough about the efforts of Barrie Robison, Toni Broyles, Samir Abd El-Fatah, and our partners at Gritman Medical Center, who remained focused and helped us achieve our objective to open the campus in the fall of 2020.

Smart Collaboration

Talks with Torrey

During the unprecedented time of COVID-19, the U of I leadership tried to think of different ways to communicate all the necessary and ever-changing situation details. "Communication was hard," Provost Torrey Lawrence shared. "We sent out so many emails. But another thing we did that worked far better than I thought it would was 'Talks with Torrey.' It was a cheesy name, but I wanted it to be informal, so I didn't mind the casual sound. It was an opportunity to give regular informational updates about what was changing and where we were with things."

"Talks with Torrey" started during the summer of 2020, when COVID-19 was still running amok, and the U of I employees were hovering between the work-at-home and the work-in-the-office environment.

"It was literally for anyone from the university to come into the Zoom [Room] and ask me questions," Torrey explained. "We let people submit questions in advance if they wanted to do it anonymously. That was great because I downloaded this list of questions, and if a lot or all of them were the same questions, that was obviously an issue we needed to address. It was helpful for us to see what people were hearing or not understanding. We answered all the questions, and they could also ask questions live. I was totally in the hot-seat for an hour, but I didn't mind."

"Talks with Torrey" was an engaging way to communicate and talk with staff, faculty, and students. "If people understood why the university was doing what it was doing, they might not have agreed, but at least we could try to work together to figure it out," Torrey emphasized. "We successfully explained the why, which took a lot of effort. I was able to bear the brunt of some of that with the Faculty Senate meetings. They were not afraid to ask questions. For 'Talks with Torrey,' I tried to be as engaging and helpful as possible because if they understood the system, we would hopefully have more buy-in and more trust. I think that those talks were productive and worked."

Staff, faculty, and students appreciated having access to leadership willing to answer questions. During "Talks with Torrey" Zooms,

(Continued)

(Continued)

other leadership would attend, and if Torrey needed more detailed information, he would often defer to another university employee to answer the question if they might know more than he did.

"We tried to be as transparent and available as possible," Torrey said. "I saw being in the hot-seat as part of my job. I also felt that since I'd been at the U of I for 24 years, if I didn't know the answer, I at least had an idea where I could go to get it. I liked interacting with people, even on Zoom. Sometimes it took longer when we involved more people, but the outcome was better if we had a lot of smart people working on things versus a couple or one. That kind of ties into our shared governance policies."

Each bi-weekly Zoom-based session with Torrey lasted approximately an hour. Although the forum began as an added layer of communication during COVID-19, its success continues to be a tool for leadership to talk about campus issues.

Scott's Management Insight

Sometimes, all you need is an informal setting for communication that opens a conduit between different areas or divisions in your institution or business. Find your spokesman. It might be you or your provost but find someone with the faculty's trust to keep in regular communication. "Talks with Torrey" was a brilliant idea. Torrey has excellent credibility with the faculty—he speaks their language and understands how they see issues differently than the administration and staff. His regular meetings helped us communicate our initiatives and provided feedback that helped us get out in front of faculty issues before they were allowed to fester.

Part VII

Chapter 31
Testing 1, 2, 3, Testing

"The logistics were brutal."

—*Dr. Barrie Robison*

"The process of setting up the COVID-19 testing lab was frustrating and exciting and terrifying," Director of IBEST Barrie Robison shared. "And testing wasn't the only piece to work. Whom did we have trained to collect the samples? How were we going to keep people collecting the samples safe? How would test results be shared with the patient while being mindful of confidentiality with HIPAA and FERPA?"

Barrie and the GBRC manager reached out to different universities, such as Purdue and Maryland, along with powerhouse institutions on the West Coast, to collaborate and determine the answers to the mind-numbing list of questions. "The staff in our core facility has great relationships with the bigger core lab facilities on the West Coast, such as Berkeley, University of California, San Francisco, University of Oregon, and University of California, Davis," Barrie explained. "We were talking with them because Berkeley, for example, had already moved to high throughput testing for COVID-19. We asked how they were doing the testing and what we should watch to occur. Professor Forney also connected us with a colleague at the University of Maryland setting up high-throughput testing. I thought to myself, 'Which of these schools doesn't belong in terms of resources? The University of Maryland, Berkeley, UC Davis, Purdue, and the University of Idaho? That was the scale of institutions with whom we collaborated."

Meanwhile, Kara Besst and Kane Francetich had to determine where to locate the lab inside Gritman Medical Center. "We thought that the negative pressure was a bigger deal than it probably needed to be but still seemed like a good thing to consider," Kane shared. "Connie [Osborn] and I had been here for so long; we remembered when part of our medical training center was the old ICU and had a negative pressure room. We started looking at that room and brought in the GBRC manager and other U of I folks to look at the space. We all thought that everything would fit in the one little room, but as we set up the lab, we had to expand to half of one other room, and then the rest of that room, and then out at the old nurse's station, all the storage units, and then out into the hallway."

This was not your ordinary—or small—lab.

"We started getting equipment in at the beginning of May, and by June 1, we were setting everything up," Kane continued. "In addition to the machines from the U of I and what we had at Gritman, we also needed biosafety cabinets and big ventilation hoods. We ended up ordering two hoods and getting those shipped here. Just getting those hoods into the building and set up," Kane paused, eyes widening and head shaking. "They were huge. We ended up hiring North American Van Lines to help; it just seemed so monumental at the time, all these little things that just took so much energy and time. But we had tons of help."

Barrie and the GBRC manager, along with an exceptional group of researchers and staff at IBEST, determined they didn't have enough equipment for both redundancy and throughput testing. Many people emailed Barrie, asking how they could help—could they donate their equipment? The comradery the campus and surrounding communities displayed for this crucial endeavor overwhelmed him.

"A cool element to the whole process was having several researchers on campus offer their machines qualified to do qPCR testing," Barrie reflected. "For example, Lisette Waits, distinguished professor of Wildlife Resources and Department Head of Fish and Wildlife Sciences in the College of Natural Resources, lent us a machine that ended up as our backup machine. Redundancy for these kinds of things was so important. Our researchers had past experiences of how a single point of failure brought things down, costs went through the roof, and the turnaround time collapsed. It had been a nightmare for them. We didn't want that to happen at our COVID-19 lab, so we moved Lisette's machine to the Gritman lab. Matt Powell and Brian Small at the U of I's Aquaculture Research Institute in Hagerman, Idaho, over 400 miles away, also had machines for us. The GBRC manager dropped everything, drove all the way down there, picked them up, and drove them back." The machines were then recertified for CLIA and added to the massive equipment lineup.

Barrie and the GBRC manager aimed to set up an architecture in the lab to sustain what they knew was coming—an entire region's COVID-19 tests, maybe hundreds a day. "We needed things like centrifuges and the little pieces that were missing so that we could sustain the testing pace we would need to maintain the goals of even having the testing lab," Barrie said. "We also purchased some additional equipment that nobody on campus had."

However, anything COVID-19-related was in high demand. Swabs, inactivation reagents, isolation reagents, isolation hardware, master mix, and assay-reading hardware—components needed to run tests for the virus—were in short supply. Suppliers even told hospitals that items for testing were on backorder.

"The GBRC manager had to navigate the supply chain issues," Barrie remembered. "There was one machine in particular that became a big stress point because we wanted to get set up for August, and we just kept getting bumped down on the list with the company that had the machine. Toni [Broyles] was just pulling her hair out."

"As you can imagine, the supply chain for the testing equipment just constricted immediately," shared Toni. "We were on the list early and then ultimately got stuck at the upper-middle management level in the company with sales."

One day Toni called Barrie about the machine.

"Is the GBRC manager being enough of a pain in the ass with this company to get this done?" she'd asked Barrie. "Should we have Scott call the company?"

Barrie shared with the GBRC manager the conversation he had with Toni. "They're talking about having the president call the company," he'd shared.

And the GBRC manager just laughed and laughed. "That company gets governors calling them every day for the same machines," he'd snorted.

"It turned out they were bumping us down the list because they didn't realize we were already fully set up and had the reagents, which others were struggling to purchase," Toni said. "They were prioritizing entities according to their lab readiness."

"Because of Dr. Chris Ball at the Idaho Department of Health and Welfare, we obtained a substantial supply of reagents from a federal stockpile for free, well, paid for by tax dollars," Barrie pointed out. "Once the company learned that we were sitting on the stockpile of reagents, they said, 'Well, why didn't you say so? We'll send you the machine.'"

"It took eight weeks from when we placed our order to get the equipment," Toni reflected. "But it also took us constantly following up. That company had governors calling in chits and asking for priority. The U of I was just a higher-ed institution, which wasn't a typical customer for them. But our dedication paid off, and we got that machine."

Toni, Barrie, and the team coordinating the lab and testing had to also consider the gravity of safety for those performing the testing. "The other important angle was who would collect these tests?" Barrie continued. "Who was going to stick those things up people's noses? Whom did we have trained to do that? Certainly not my staff. They weren't medical professionals; they were researchers."

Gritman Medical Center handled that piece of the puzzle, offering their highly talented nursing staff for the crucial job. The only thing left to address was the location for the testing. "That in itself was an engineering feat just trying to figure out how we were going to process that many people and collect all those samples," Kane expressed.

To aid in coordinating the maze of setting up the lab and classrooms safely and a million other details, the U of I finalized hiring COVID-19 Project Manager Seth Vieux in June. Seth wasn't new to the U of I; he arrived on campus in the summer of 2017 to run the Army ROTC program. He had been part of the massive COVID-19 conversation from the beginning through his position at ROTC. As the COVID-19 project manager, he would coordinate and operationalize mitigation efforts across the administration, faculty, and staff and synchronize them with the local health-care community and the City of Moscow.

"Part of my role was a whole lot of trying to get the right folks together and help them to figure out the plan of what to accomplish and how to implement it," Seth explained. "I was the only person that COVID-19 was the entirety of my job; everybody else had their other jobs, so I helped coordinate to allow folks to get ready for class in the fall. I needed to have an amount of patience with everyone involved. Everyone's schedules were different, but I worked to make sure that we could hit the hard deadlines we had."

"By mid-July, we were at the point to figure out where we were going to do the testing," Kane continued. "Our initial thoughts were that we would have a location at Gritman Medical Center and multiple locations on campus."

The initial plan was to set up a drive-thru at the WWAMI location on campus and a walk-up on the lawn in front of the Student Recreation Center. "Pretty quickly, we decided to concentrate our efforts on just the Student Rec Center," Kane shared. "I remember it was sweltering hot,

80–100 degrees. We were trying to figure out how to have thousands of students get through these big tents set up on the lawn and keep everybody safe and cool and socially distanced."

The first COVID-19 test trial run happened on July 27. "We invited about a hundred people from the U of I to be part of that testing," Kane shared. "And while it went pretty good, we figured out early on that doing it outside had its challenges. When I met Brian Mahoney, associate director of Campus Recreation, we talked about options. There was a little reluctance to use the indoors because they were still using the gymnasiums, and there was concern about doing any of the testing and specimen collection indoors."

Kane and Brian dissected the air exchange rates inside the Student Rec Center and how to limit the number of people coming in for testing. Gritman ended up using both gyms with a large open area in the middle. "When we first started, we had teams with a nurse and a helper, other runners, greeters, and registration," Kane said. "We initially started with eight tables and collected about twelve specimens an hour. At our peak, with a lot of experience, we collected eighty to a hundred—sometimes over a hundred—specimens an hour with a single person. It just became much more efficient as time went on."

So just exactly what was the COVID-19 testing process? Barrie explained the steps from the lab's point of view.

THE COVID-19 TESTING PROCESS—the genomic side
(See Figure 31.01)

The process began with a patient who either required or wanted a test.

1. Nurses used a nasal pharyngeal swab—the brain tickler—because those swabs were the most sensitive and accurate. The nurse swirled the swab in the patient's nostrils to gain a sample.
2. The nurse placed the swab with the sample on it into a tube filled with media (liquid solution).
3. The nurse placed the sample tube labeled with the patient's name inside a plastic bag. The nurse sealed the bag and put it with other sample bags, usually in a big cooler. A courier picked up batches of samples throughout the day and took them to the lab at Gritman Medical Center.
4. A technician removed the sample tubes from their plastic bags, placed each tube in a rack in a specific order, and then scanned the tube to get the patient's information entered into the computer system.

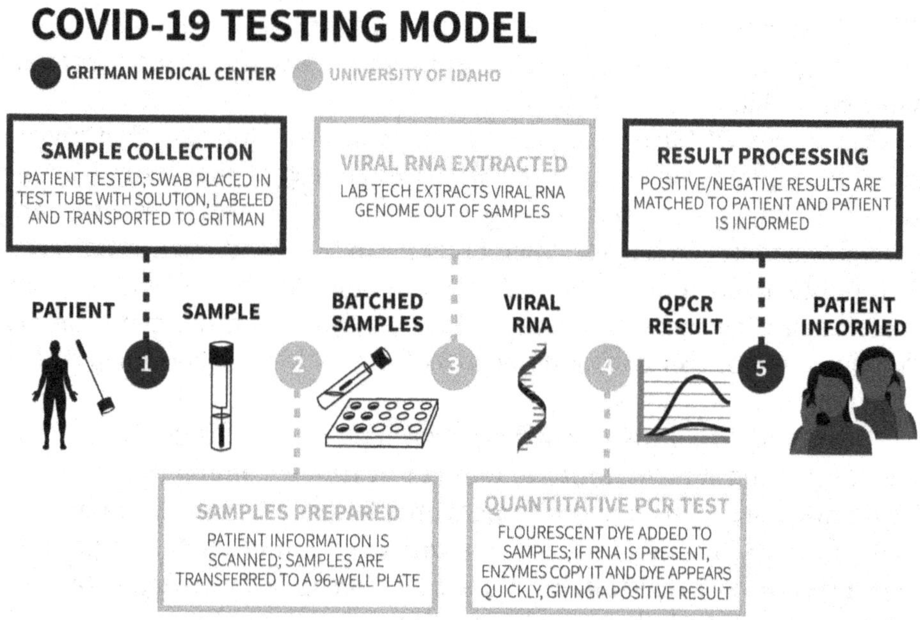

COVID-19 TESTING MODEL

● GRITMAN MEDICAL CENTER ● UNIVERSITY OF IDAHO

Figure 31.01 COVID-19 Testing process showing the genomic side to getting results.
SOURCE: Katy Lawler, Institute for Interdisciplinary Data Sciences. Reproduced with permission of Katy Lawler/University of Idaho.

5. With high-throughput genomics, the lab always worked in batches of 96—the key number because the rectangular plate for the samples had 96 wells, eight rows and 12 columns, which was the format all the machines could automatically process.

6. The tech arranged the tubes in cohorts of 96 (technically 94 because of controls) and placed everything into a biosafety cabinet. Even though they were wearing protective gear, the technician was further protected when the sample tubes were opened because the cabinet directed the airflow such that contaminants could not flow out toward the technician.

7. The lab tech used a pipettor to remove a small amount of the sample liquid from each tube and carefully loaded the samples into the 96-well plate.

8. The lab tech would then use a specific set of chemical reagents to extract the viral RNA genome out of each of the 96 samples.

9. The next phase involved quantitative PCR testing (qPCR). qPCR uses little chunks of DNA that contain a sequence complementary to (matching) specific targets in the viral genome (COVID-19).

10. The tests routinely used by most labs (including Gritman's) targeted three viral genes, each with a different fluorescent tag color. The complementary DNA probes for the three different genes were combined with the sample and other chemical reagents.

11. If there was viral RNA in the sample, a biological reaction occurred in which an enzyme made copies of the viral RNA. The more viral RNA, the more quickly the copies could be made (called amplification). As the enzymes kept making copies, the amplified targets accumulated the fluorescent-colored dye, which was detected by a laser in the qPCR machine.

12. The qPCR machines recorded and graphed the fluorescent signal as the enzyme amplified copies of the viral RNA. The amount of copies scaled with the concentration of the viral sample (that's what made it quantitative PCR).

13. If the viral RNA detected was low, the fluorescence took much longer to accumulate to detectable levels. If the concentration of viral RNA in the sample was high, the fluorescence reached detectable levels very quickly. The relative time, in this case, is measured in CT (cycle thresholds), which indicates the number of chemical reaction cycles before fluorescence is detected by the laser. High CT values indicated there was a low concentration of viral RNA in a sample or no reaction (providing a negative test result). Low CT values equated to a high concentration sample of the viral RNA (providing a positive test result).

14. The machine produced a result for each of the three genetic targets within each sample well of the 96-well plate, showing whether any samples exceeded the CT threshold that the test requirements specified as a positive test.

15. Once samples were classified as positive or negative, the lab tech would match the results to each patient and enter them into the Gritman Medical system.

16. And finally, to protect the patient under HIPAA and FERPA, a designated person with HIPAA training contacted patients who had tested positive for COVID-19.

"We established a workflow," Barrie continued. "We set up the sampling at the U of I Student Rec Center with armies of nurses sticking swabs up people's noses. When the samples showed up at the lab, they had to be batched and electronically added to the system and organized, which took a lot of manual labor. We recruited many qualified technicians from around the university. Several faculty let their people work in the COVID-19 lab at the expense of productivity in their own labs. We had everything from highly trained undergraduates to graduate students, to technicians, to PhD level, whoever knew how all this stuff worked. The GBRC manager trained them in the CLIA context, and then we plugged them into the workflow. We had a schedule of who was coming in and when. The logistics were brutal."

Logistics also entwined Toni's time. She asked Kane a crucial question among the chaos of equipment and personnel. "Kane, how are we going to manage the flow of students, staff, and faculty getting tested? It could end up being a feast or famine situation if not properly managed."

"I just got a new scheduling program called Schedule O that will be perfect for this application," Kane had answered her. "It was developed specifically for COVID-19 testing."

"I could kiss you," Toni had exclaimed, relieved that at least that piece of the puzzle might go in without much resistance.

Kane explained how the scheduling process for the resulting or administrative side worked from Gritman's point of view.

THE COVID-19 RESULTING PROCESS—the data-driven/administrative side (See Figure 31.02)

1. Gritman Medical Center set up appointment times.
2. A student, faculty, or staff member scheduled an appointment via the website or phone app.
3. Once they scheduled an appointment, the person getting tested received an email and text with appointment reminders.
4. Gritman Medical Center would take the schedule and, the evening before, download the identifying information for the people scheduled for testing, including their name, birthdate, and Vandal ID number.
5. Gritman Medical Center matched those people to those already in their electronic health record database or set up a new health record if they weren't in Gritman Medical Center's system. Gritman Medical Center's IT people created a custom script that ran on seven or eight computers to enter registrations.
6. Once the system registered all the people scheduled the next day for a test, it securely processed and printed barcode labels used for specimens and documents at the Student Rec Center.
7. The following morning, when people came in for their appointments, the registration staff at the Student Rec Center would find the person's labels, have them sign a form consenting for Gritman Medical Center to share the information with the U of I, and send the results back to

COVID-19 RESULTING MODEL

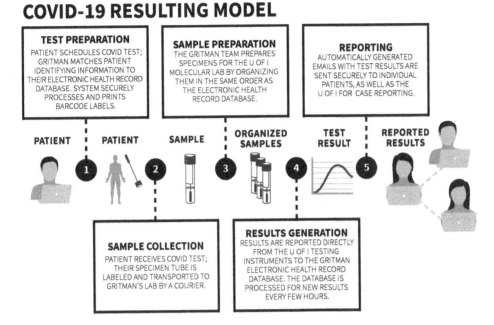

Figure 31.02   COVID-19 Resulting process showing the administrative side to testing.
SOURCE: Katy Lawler, Institute for Interdisciplinary Data Sciences. Reproduced with permission of Katy Lawler/University of Idaho.

the patient via email in a confidential way. The registration person would put the document labels on the signed consent forms.

8. The patient received the specimen tube. They would get swabbed and place the label on their specimen tube.

9. The nurse placed the specimen tube in a plastic bag and put it in a cooler.

10. A courier picked up a cooler full of specimens, sometimes as often as every hour at the busiest times, and took them back to the lab.

11. At the lab, Gritman Medical Center's team would match up the specimens in the same order as in the system and prep them so they were ready to be run by the U of I folks in the molecular lab.

12. An interface between the testing instruments and Gritman Medical Center's electronic health record systems allowed the results to get reported into Gritman Medical Center's health records system.

13. Gritman Medical Center set up a unique process to query its database every few hours, looking for any new results to automatically generate emails with the test results to send to the person.

14. Gritman Medical Center also created a file they sent securely to the U of I to use for reporting numbers and determining if someone could go to class or not. The file sent to the U of I only had their Vandal ID number, the test date, and whether COVID-19 was detected or not.

15. Gritman Medical Center also looked at any specific issues, such as if people didn't get their results, if they got registered with some weird name, or if there was just something odd with the registration. Kane at Gritman Medical Center and Seth at the U of I spent time dealing with those issues daily to correct them.

The whole process took about four hours. "Once the lab identified who was positive, that confidential information also went to Idaho Public Health," Scott shared. "It was used to notify people through contact tracing. Seth would work with people who received a positive result to help get them to the infirmary if they were on campus or give them guidance to shelter in place if they were off campus. We checked in with them to ensure they were okay along the way."

The U of I employees in the Dean of Students Office assisted Idaho Public Health as necessary with contact tracing. Caseloads in the region remained low enough that the Public Health professionals could quickly conduct the critical step.

"The theme of this whole enterprise was group effort," Barrie pointed out. "There were a whole bunch of individuals operating at completely maxed-out capacity to pull off the group effort. We almost killed the GBRC manager. He put in so much time; it was brutal. It took a huge toll on him. And the landscape and rules were changing constantly. It was a tough situation to adapt."

At the peak of COVID-19 testing, Gritman Medical Center staff could process over 1000 tests daily with a 12–48-hour turnaround time; they often produced the results the same day.

"For Toni and her team and the science folks, it was a huge lift to set up everything," Provost Torrey Lawrence conveyed. "It wasn't just a couple of things; it was a very complex system that ended up deciding if we continued as a university."

Scott's Management Insight

Again, many hands make light work. Get the right people involved, empower them, and let them get to it. Set up systems to stay current on the status of tasks on the critical path. Whether it is Gantt charts or regular meetings, the CEO or president needs to monitor progress and intervene when needed. Given that governors were calling, I might not have had an impact if I had called the test equipment provider, but my asking the question initiated a conversation with the supplier that revealed how they were making decisions and enabled us to get them the information they needed to move us up the list. Don't underestimate what your encouragement and focus can accomplish.

Chapter 32
Unethical?

"We had to be understanding of individuals."

—*Dr. Larry Stauffer*

With all the focus on setting up the testing and getting the campus ready to open as safely as possible for fall, there was a lot of "let's do this" energy swirling around Moscow. However, like most colleges and universities, the U of I's makeup was a diverse population with myriad opinions. Scott had always appreciated that part of campus culture; students existed in a safe environment to voice all sides of any number of topics, political or not. But COVID-19 morphed into a highly volatile matter fueled by the national (and international) conversation.

Scott's decision to lead the university toward opening in the face of COVID-19 brought negative backlash from a small but vocal group of faculty and grad students that raged on through the summer.

"Part of the resistance from some faculty stemmed from them successfully going completely online for half the spring," Dean Shauna Corry said of her College of Art and Architecture. "People kept focusing on, 'We were so successful in the spring; why can't we do it that way this time around for fall?' There were some cool things about being online. We were able to bring in people from around the world to critique, and we didn't have to pay them. We didn't have to fly them here. The students had such different opportunities than we ever had before, and people learned the technology fast. But there were some downsides to it. We wanted people here on campus."

"We have an intelligent workforce," Scott pointed out. "There will always be critics of the process, and that's fine as long as they're not working against the U of I. I want to hear differences and challenges, but once we decide, then help us achieve our objectives and don't fight every step of the way. Thankfully, the vast majority of faculty, staff, and students were with us."

"Our decisions weren't just about the university," Provost Torrey Lawrence pointed out. "What we were doing was disrupting a piece of everyone's lives. From classrooms to research projects, this whole thing disrupted most of them in some manner. Everyone's stress level raised because it was coming from all directions."

Even Washington State University (WSU), only eight miles west of the U of I, voiced their critique of the U of I's plans to open in the fall.

An online petition signed by 250 U of I faculty members arrived in Scott's email inbox on July 28, respectfully but firmly stating to him their position regarding in-person education during COVID-19. In part, it said that "an increasing number of UI employees find it both ethically troubling and pedagogically problematic to hold in-person, on-campus classes in a way that ensures safe and innovative conditions for teaching and learning" (Green, S., personal communication).

The idea that the U of I was taking considerable risks to open and remain financially solvent also sparked some commentary. Some even accused Scott and his team of trying to kill them all. "We had a small group of faculty who were beating the drum," Scott recalled. "Interestingly, most were from the liberal arts, not STEM faculty as one might guess, who suddenly were experts on everything from air quality of HVAC systems to the effectiveness of masking. Faculty and grad students started a few petitions. Then there was a Palouse area petition set up through Change.org, which was the funniest one because I learned, from looking at the signatures on that petition, the Palouse encompassed Malaysia, Korea, Texas, and Staten Island. People from all over the world signed it" (Kim 2020).

"I had a faculty member say we were only doing it for the money, but it was a matter of life or death," Shauna recalled. "I had another faculty member tell me, and this was truly his thought, that it was like Chernobyl—three or four people had to go into the nuclear facility and handle the core, and those people you knew were going to die eventually. So we had people equating it to that, and their perception was real to them. We had to be very careful about arming people with the reality of what we could do to keep everyone safe as possible. We knew that if we wore masks, were distanced, and followed the protocols, we could do it. But it was very difficult."

Scott understood the elevated stress level that came with COVID-19. He emailed a reply to the Change.org petition authors stating that he did take seriously the concerns of those who truly lived in the Moscow community and that the team would consider those concerns. He also pointed out that the claim regarding the number of ICU beds available at Gritman Medical Center was incorrect. The petition letter stated that Gritman Medical Center had three ICU beds and 25 accredited beds.

"Gritman Medical Center has five ICU rooms. We have four negative pressure rooms, two in ICU and two in the Med-Surg Unit," Gritman Medical Center Administrative Chief of Staff Danielle Breed said. "Being a critical access hospital, the government has licensed Gritman for twenty-five inpatient beds."

However, in March 2020, to prepare for a potential influx of COVID-19 cases, Gritman worked with community partners to increase that capacity. Additional rooms were identified or converted to give Gritman the ability to house up to 43 inpatients at one time.

"It wasn't just an issue of having enough ventilators," Danielle stated, "but it became an issue of whether we had enough staffing, personal protective equipment (PPE), or other resources available. But we developed creative solutions and remained flexible in order to provide the support and care that our community needed. For example, the Wallace Complex (a large dormitory on the university campus) had several floors with negative pressure rooms that they identified for Gritman to use in case of overflow or, for whatever reason, the hospital needed them. They also had a clean space where our health-care workers could stay after their shifts instead of going home, so they didn't expose their families."

Gritman never had to turn anyone away for care and provided consultation with other facilities if patients needed more intense medical services. Due to timely testing, masking, and social distancing practices deployed on campus and in the Moscow community, Gritman never hit the "crisis standard" of care threshold like many, if not most, of the hospitals around the country did during the pandemic.

Scott assured the petition sponsors that the U of I worked closely with Idaho Public Health and Gritman. The U of I would close if their guidance changed.

"We were receiving a lot of calls at Gritman regarding the university opening up, and I'm sure that the U of I and the City of Moscow were, too," Gritman CEO Kara Besst commented. "Early on, WSU had decided to go online early, but the U of I still wanted to have in-person classes. We started getting calls from concerned parents and community members. Less than two weeks before classes started, we had a parent in Hawaii call to ask if they should send their kids to school. We talked them through the many procedures we had in place to keep them safe, but ultimately, it was a personal decision."

"To some people, that's absolutely, genuinely how they felt; we were going to kill them all by opening," Seth Vieux, COVID-19 project manager, explained. "That's no exaggeration. There were PhD faculty members who held that view."

"We had to be understanding of individuals," College of Engineering Dean Larry Stauffer pointed out. "I had a professor who lost his uncle that spring due to COVID-19, so naturally, he was freaked out. I wasn't going to press him. He didn't want to do the hybrid teaching method in the fall, and I got that. People were good about contacting me and working with their department chairs, so we worked it out."

"I was surprised at some who lost their minds over the whole thing," Assistant Vice President Kathy Barnard remarked. "The negativity made a hard situation even more difficult until those few faculty and students got on board. When they were not on board, it was like, do you really think we haven't thought this through?"

A faculty member appeared on television, claiming that the COVID-19 testing lab was a fraud and would never open—it was a bridge too far. The same faculty member's personal opinion in a local newspaper article criticized the proposed HyFlex teaching model. The reporter wrote that the faculty member said they could deliver instruction to students in the fall if they weren't dead (Dennis 2020).

Another faculty member said actions to open the university in the fall were unethical. "It truly would have been unethical for us not to open the university," Scott stated. "By taking control, looking and testing for the virus, opening an infirmary, and taking care of our people, we *did* the ethically right thing. Bankrupting the university would have been unethical. People would have lost their jobs, and it would've affected families. If you were a distinguished professor with tenure, it was easy to say we shouldn't open the university. You have job security. To me, that was the pot calling the kettle black. Staying closed was clearly the most unethical route we could have taken, and that's the message I gave at the COVID-19 Town Hall on campus."

Scott and his team held a frank discussion with faculty, staff, and students about COVID-19 and the plans to open in the fall at the campus Town Hall. Scott had gained credibility as a transparent, no-nonsense leader through the budget-cutting process. He knew if he could clearly lay out the plan like he did with the finances, he would still have detractors, but at least they couldn't say no one informed them.

"I explained that if we didn't open, the financial impact would be severe. We already knew we lost at least $7 million in revenue just being closed for half a semester," Scott said. "We finally had a small surplus because everybody pulled together during the financial crisis. You don't have to be a math expert to understand we were probably looking at a $30 million deficit the next fiscal year if we *didn't* open. We'd lose housing revenues, food revenues, athletic revenues, printshop revenues; the list went on and on. Those were real cash losses that, at the time, we wouldn't have been able to cover. We were also looking at a dip in enrollments and state budget holdbacks. The U of I couldn't use the first round of federal COVID-19 relief funding for revenue shortfalls. So safely reopening the university was the only way to avoid those financial and related job losses.

"We had one of our data scientists stating that we were going to kill 176 people by opening the university," Scott continued. "We had our own modeling team, and they knew that was not true. I understood the modeling assumptions the data scientists used and their limitations. I also recognized how it was possible but improbable. Dr. Ben Ridenhour, [U of I] Department of Mathematics and Statistical Science, and Dr. Holly Wichman, [U of I] Department of Biological Sciences, helped us model and understand that if we did all the right things, the number of hospitalizations would actually be lower, not higher, than if we just closed campus and left it up to students coming to town to self-police masking and testing. By closing campus, we would abdicate our responsibility and ability to implement policies to manage the environment effectively."

Scott realized modeling was an important tool that relied on assumptions but that could help focus on hospitalization rates and what decisions the U of I could make to keep Gritman Medical Center open and operating under something less than a "crisis standard" of care.

Events around the U of I were happening quickly, and not everything was within the university's control. But there were various measures they could take to manage what they could. "That's why we went to such great lengths and did everything to assure Vandals that we wanted them safe but back home on campus," Scott stated. "And at the end of the day, that was the difference between being able to protect the community or not. We wanted to control our destiny and did."

"If you were to talk to the Staff Affairs people and the Faculty Senate people," Kathy shared, "they would say that by that point, most faculty and staff were comfortable and reassured by what was happening when they understood the science and that it was serious, testable reproducible science."

"I was totally impressed with the way Scott kept pressing us to be in person in the fall," Larry said. "In my mind, I was thinking this is never going to work. We had to count numbers of desks and people in classrooms and space everything out. It was going to be a monumental task. I already thought pretty highly of Scott before that, but I felt better about him because of his persistence. He didn't crack under all the pressure."

Seth outlined the massive list of measures the U of I took during the summer to make campus as safe as possible against COVID-19:

Mask mandate: Governor Little didn't mandate masks in Idaho; however, the City of Moscow imposed a mask mandate, and Scott imposed a mask mandate for campus. FSH 6995 approved the policy requiring face coverings inside buildings on campus, with limited exceptions. It also outlined face coverings for when social distancing wasn't possible. Most of the community was masked except for people protesting for political reasons (which made the national news) or who had medical or religious exemptions.

Providing masks for Vandals: "The director of purchasing services, Julia McIlroy, was the hero on this as she did all the leg work to procure thousands and thousands of disposable masks and branded cloth masks," Seth shared. "She and I worked together to build the distribution plan for the masks for departments and students. We distributed over 2300 Vandals-branded, reusable, cloth face masks for faculty and staff and more than 1200 reusable face shields for faculty."

Plexiglass: "We worked extensively with the colleges and other units to assess and meet their requests for plexiglass installation," Seth continued. "Samir Abd El-Fatah, executive director of Environmental Health and Safety (EHS), and his team conducted numerous room, building, and space assessments with me to determine the validity of the many requests. The EHS team conducted countless air movement assessments to maximize ventilation and track areas that might be more hazardous for stagnation and accumulation of particles. The Facilities Management (FM) team constructed wooden supports, cut the custom plexiglass, and installed the plexiglass for the units. FM also created an online request portal and worked with me and EHS to prioritize and arbitrate requests. That allowed the U of I to utilize the available materials as efficiently as possible across campus. The main areas of plexiglass installation were in units that conducted in-person point of sales, service, and counseling."

Food safety in dining areas: Dining services significantly increased grab-and-go options, call-ahead ordering, and social distancing measures for sit-down dining. "Cami McClure at Auxiliary Services worked with me to make UI-funded testing available to our food-service contract employees that weren't also U of I students," Seth shared. "We implemented walk-through thermal scanning in dining halls and the ISUB food court, where patrons wouldn't wear their masks to eat."

Making hand sanitizer and disinfectant spray: Dr. Samir Abd El-Fatah proposed that he possessed the technical knowledge, resources, and ability to make hand sanitizer and disinfectant spray. "He not only determined how to get the required materials through the U of I Chem Stores (the only entity with licensing to obtain the chemicals)," Seth explained, "but also how to get FDA approval." Vandals used over 350 gallons of the Healthy Vandals hand sanitizer (80% Alc.) by the end of the academic year.

Social distancing in classrooms: Classrooms were limited to 50% of their fire-code capacity, with seats taped off to create social distancing in classrooms, computer labs, and library spaces. Some higher-demand in-person classes split into two sections or used a weekly rotating in-person/virtual schedule (HyFlex), although this was not common due to some frustrations with that model.

Personal Protective Equipment (PPE) kits: Purchasing Services acquired and distributed PPE kits to over 200 departments and units on two occasions. The kits contained the Healthy Vandals hand sanitizer, disinfectant spray, a mask, disposable gloves, and paper towels (University of Idaho 2021). "All of the coordination was a full-court press that my mind has blocked out for the sake of my sanity," Seth said, laughing. "Facilities and Auxiliaries were absolutely instrumental with installing plexiglass, placing signage, and working directly with individual units. Outside vendors were not utilized beyond dining services and purchasing the needed resources."

Continuous emails regarding COVID-19 questions also kept Seth busy. "I'd get a couple of hundred emails per day; some days it genuinely felt like a thousand, from everything to questions about exposure to voicing their concerns." (Through fall 2020 and spring 2021, Seth viewed or responded to over 21,000 emails.) Those emails served as a lifeline to many. "I talked to students who'd just tested positive and were freaking out," he continued. "I'm no psychologist, but I'd worked with and trained people in that age group in the Army since I had been in that age group, so I knew they were away from home and scared of moving into isolation in Targhee Hall. I'd assure them they were young, healthy, and would feel better for getting through it and have antibodies in about ten days. Many times, parents called, and I assured them no one was abandoning their student."

Seth offered trusted information, assurance, and education, but always qualified to everyone that he was not a doctor or a lawyer. People ultimately had to make their own choices about what to do regarding the myriad questions he received due to the virus.

Through it all, Scott maintained that students always had a choice regarding how to attend classes, whether online or live. "We respected their personal independence and freedom to choose and kept the options intact as much as possible."

Scott's Management Insight

Don't overreact to a vocal minority. Rather, over-communicate what you are doing to keep the university and its people secure. Like children who don't get their way, those who don't agree with the plan will scream louder and begin stomping their feet. I made it clear to my leadership team that the noise about us reopening did not bother me, and it was likely to get worse. I was not ignoring it but managing it, responding calmly, and utilizing data and advice from our health-care professionals. I coached the team to stay focused on their tasks, and I would respond to the scaremongers at a place and time of our choosing. Our success would be our ultimate response to the alarmists and bullies.

Chapter 33
Test Case

"We charted our own course."

—*Chris Walsh*

"When we shut down campus for the rest of spring 2020, we knew we had to start thinking about football," Athletic Director Terry Gawlik shared. "Athletes always came back in the summer to start training and practicing. How would that look? No outside entity was telling U of I Athletics what to do. We didn't get a directive from the NCAA or conference, but Scott trusted us to determine what was best for athletics."

"We charted our own course and started bringing the football players back in June," explained Chris Walsh, associate athletic director.

During the spring shutdown, Terry and Chris strategized how Vandal football players could return to campus in the summer to train in a safe environment. Without knowing how COVID-19 would play out or even how the fall football season would look, they forged ahead with the goal for Vandal student-athletes to compete as usual.

"Normally, we bring the football players back to campus in the summer all at once, but we said we weren't doing that, Terry explained. "We brought them back during the summer months, but ten at a time to be in the weight room together. I don't want to say we were the pioneers; it was a hodgepodge. But we took control over what we thought we could control. They were coming ten at a time and wearing masks even while working out."

As each pod of ten football players arrived, Gritman and Moscow Family Medicine staff tested them at the lab using qPCR. Terry and Chris would add another pod of ten student-athletes when they deemed it safe. Coaches usually split up practices—offensive players trained earlier in the day, with defensive players following later in the day.

"We were bringing in players from all over the country," Chris related. "Obviously, the COVID-19 rates were different in every community, so that was a concern. When the athletes came back, it was well before anybody else was on campus. We screened and quarantined everybody, then tested them again after their quarantine period. We were as careful as we could be. There were some cases here and there, but we didn't have outbreaks in those summer months. We handled those positive cases extremely carefully and in coordination with campus and our local public health department. This was the first time bringing students back and having positive cases. It set the groundwork as sort of a test case for how everyone would handle things in the fall."

Meanwhile, the College of Education, Health, and Human Sciences (CEHHS) Athletic Training faculty, led by Dr. Matthew Smitely, spent the spring semester of 2020 moving quickly with much care and reflection to present their "test case" whitepaper. The whitepaper outlined why it was imperative the university should allow Master of Science in Athletic Training (MSAT) students to attend their intensive, summer-long, on-campus program in Moscow.

"It's face-to-face instruction component is critical for MSAT students' professional development and success," Interim CEHHS Dean Philip Scruggs said.

The question of how CEHHS would bring students onto campus for this crucial, in-depth piece of their degree in a safe manner loomed. "I was the department chair for Movement Sciences at the time," Philip said. "CEHHS MSAT was tasked with developing a whitepaper about the importance of bringing students to campus for in-person education. The faculty and program staff worked with Seth Vieux, Interim Provost Lawrence, President Green, and many others to develop the rationale and justification for these students to travel from all over the country during a pandemic to come to Moscow."

The whitepaper developed by faculty and staff outlined policies, procedures, and protocols in conjunction with the university's COVID-19 response plan to mitigate transmission within the CEHHS MSAT group of 52 students. "To some degree, I think we helped lead the way as far as the university's thinking about returning back in person in the fall," Philip shared.

The whitepaper explained the significance if students couldn't attend in-person instruction. Philip outlined highlights from the report:

In comparison to other MSAT programs nationwide, the format of UI's Athletic Training curriculum delivery in the summer semester is one of the key distinguishing factors that separates it from its competitors. The summer semester is the starting point for each incoming cohort. All participants learn important content during the semester and practice crucial skills under direct faculty mentorship and guidance. This face-to-face delivery format establishes and elevates professional and post-professional clinical practice standards in Athletic Training. This in-person curricular delivery format also allows program faculty to lay the foundation for subsequent semesters of distance learning in the absence of direct, physical interaction from UI professors in the fall and spring semesters.

These activities are necessary to provide students with instruction in and exposure to procedures/skills that are highly tactile, require specific equipment or manikins, and where in-person demonstration is critical to correct and safe performance of the skill.

Assessment of these skills is essential to the maintenance of program accreditation and is critical to the health, safety, and well-being of patients that will be under the students' care in the future (Scruggs, P., personal communication).

The MSAT coursework was already altered when the U of I shut down in March. CEHHS faculty and program staff worked to present several plans to implement education while maintaining the utmost safety for Vandals.

In the Athletic Department, Terry and Chris also developed protocols about what the student-athletes could or couldn't do based on the CDC and COVID-19 guidelines. "The NCAA did not come out with firm guidance and rules. Nobody did," Chris recalled. "The CDC said sports weren't their thing, and we should probably not be playing because the athletes couldn't socially distance and wear masks. At that point in the spring of 2020, the NCAA was just trying to cope with not having the basketball tournament and keep things afloat. It came down to people talking to people—other schools talking to other schools. For example, I reached out to my colleague at Oregon State University, and their team physician was the chair of the Pac 12 Medical Advisory Committee and NCAA committee. We all figured it out as we went and implemented what would work for us with the resources we had."

"Our MSAT students were still able to get a summer residential experience, even though it looked very different than it did before COVID-19," Philip shared. "The program was structured for safety and instruction while still addressing its accreditation needs. The Athletic Training faculty did an outstanding job delivering programming that summer."

Once the U of I/Gritman Medical Center lab was up, and testing began on campus in the fall of 2020, the Athletic Department coordinated a separate process with Gritman to test student-athletes since the department needed to test them more frequently than other students.

"Every Tuesday, most athletes were tested at least once," Gritman CIO Kane Francetich explained. "We did that at the Student Rec Center most of the time, early in the morning, before we'd start doing the other testing. Often, Shelly Nichols (MSU and CCU director at Gritman), who was operating and supervising all the specimen collection on campus, would go up to the Kibbie Dome and do the testing there."

"I could not have a higher opinion of anyone than Shelly," Seth shared. "Talk about Herculean efforts."

However, even with the testing facilities on the U of I campus available and all of Terry and Chris's specific protocols for the football players, the larger picture remained. Would the Big Sky Conference members be able to ensure all their football players were COVID-19-free during a game? Would their student-athlete "bubbles" and protocols hold up for external competition? No one could be sure.

Scott's Management Insight

Delegate to your subject matter experts. I did not have the time or training to properly design and implement a protocol to bring our athletics back to campus before we had our lab up and running. Our athletic teams worked with medical professionals from across the country to develop a plan that was effective in protecting our student-athletes and staff. It served as a pilot, and we used much of what we learned from athletics to develop our university protocols implemented in the fall.

Chapter 34
Do It!

"All 3900+ higher education institutions in the country that grant degrees were in the same boat and all in different stages of preparedness."
—Dan Ewart

The success of the hybrid model (HyFlex) teaching in-person and online to accommodate all situations hinged on the Office of Information and Technology (IT). "There was a lot of constant ongoing work with what we accomplished from March to May," explained Dan Ewart, vice president for IT and CIO. "But we were also planning, building, and preparing for August and a fall semester—we didn't even know how that would look. We did know that even if we came back in person, we were going to have sick students who would have to quarantine, and we would have sick faculty who would have to take their lectures fully online from HyFlex mode. I only had 80 classrooms technologically equipped, and I needed about 130. Scott's response was, 'Do it.'"

Dan and his team ran into supply chain problems with the entire nation and world ordering the same equipment needed for the shift to online learning. "Everybody was ordering webcams and monitors and projectors and screens and computers, and the whole supply chain fell apart," he shared. "There was a scramble, but we got what we needed. We were buying twenty things from here and ten from there, and just getting lucky on what was available when we were looking for it. All 3900+ higher education institutions in the country that grant degrees were in the same boat and all in different stages of preparedness."

Luck may not have been a sound financial strategy for the U of I, but it sure came in handy when ordering supplies during a pandemic.

Dan tasked his classroom technology team to design a solution that the U of I could afford, obtain the equipment, and get in place by August. "That team did the design, then had help from the rest of my team in ordering because that's a lot of little parts and a lot of logistics," he shared. "The Pitman Center offered the use of two large conference rooms where we had everything delivered and created an assembly line. I pulled people from across IT. We built podiums and racks for monitors and staged them in that area. Then we'd put them in the truck and deliver them around campus. That took all summer; it was a scramble. I won't lie; we went right up to the deadline of August 15."

The U of I started with 80 classrooms to offer online programming, and by the time the fall semester began, they were up to 209 across the state, with enhancements to the original 80. The team made it happen with an incalculable number of manhours, but not without a few bumps.

"We didn't have microphones through the ceilings in every classroom," Dan started. "We put in a mic for the instructor to use, which locked them to working behind the podium. Many hadn't done that style of instruction. I commend our faculty for their willingness to adapt because that was hard. We didn't have time to mount monitors to walls, so we rolled them in on carts. We had some initial problems with access to the rooms, ADA compliance, and fire code. We were able to get waivers on some of those things just because of the emergency nature of the pandemic. We didn't have a sufficient supply of batteries for the microphones. We ended up replacing all new cables in some places because the cables we had weren't long enough. Faculty members needed to be able to stand *and* sit to accommodate different teaching styles, and we needed to provide chairs. Nope, we didn't think of that until late in the game. There were all these details, but I would say that we hit 90 percent of the mark, which is great given the turnaround time we had."

IT performed all the classroom renovations and additions before the federal relief funds arrived. "The funding from the Higher Education Emergency Relief Fund (HEERF), the Coronavirus Relief Fund (CRF), and the Governor's Emergency Education Relief Fund (GEER) came afterward to backfill those expenditures," Dan explained. "Scott and the university decided to go ahead and do what we needed because we *were* going to be open."

Linda Campos, associate vice president for Finance, outlined the total amounts of COVID-19 relief funds the University of Idaho expended during FY2020–FY2022:

HEERF – Institutional $22,160,555.00
HEERF – Student Aid $17,407,451.00
CRF-CFAC $1,809,442.00
GEER $992,701.00
                    Source: Division of Finance and Administration.

IT received the GEER funds for faculty computers and software, computers for the new classrooms, and to build studios for better class content recording.

"We would get COVID-19 budget numbers from Linda to charge to with parameters of how we could spend the money," Dan said. "We spent in the negative to get things accomplished, and my finance person's eyes got like this big. It was Linda's job to backfill those, so they were positive at the end of the fiscal year. It wasn't a free-for-all; it was nerve-wracking for those of us who don't like red on our budgets and financial sheets. But I knew that we had supply chain problems, and if I didn't get things ordered, we wouldn't get them in time. I also knew that Scott and the rest of the university would figure this out; we'd already talked it through. So we made the orders."

"Every VP had an account for COVID-19 expenses," Linda explained. "Once we received the relief funds, we had to determine which expenditures qualified under the grants. We didn't have much guidance from the federal agencies initially, but it evolved over the course of several months. If expenses qualified under the guidelines, which most of them did, we would apply the appropriate grant funds and backfill what the college or unit had already spent to zero everything out."

The university kept meticulous records of all the COVID-19 expenditures for future mandatory federal audits.

"The appropriation was in two components, split 50/50 between students and the institution," Scott explained. "The first wave couldn't be used for lost revenues for institutional expenses. At first, it was a bit frustrating because the rules on distribution seemed to keep changing from the federal government, but we devised a good plan to take care of students who were most at risk."

"Our Financial Aid Director, Randi Croyle, provided the most significant boots-on-the-ground leadership for distribution of CARES Act funds to students," Vice Provost Dean Kahler said. "That included the cost of attendance, like tuition fees, food, housing, health care, and childcare. How students could use the funds was very narrowly defined. We had to identify and justify every dollar of why we gave it to a student. That was harder for us to do because some of them were already receiving full financial aid. But we were able to justify things like the cost of a computer or laptop, or maybe they had to get stronger broadband access because they were streaming courses. The funds going to students ranged from $300 to $1,000 based on class load, part-time or full-time status, and family finances. Every full-time student received some government money."

"We spent millions getting the campus opened and operating," Scott pointed out. "Fortunately, we could use the Higher Education Emergency Relief Fund II (HEERF II) as authorized by the Coronavirus Response and Relief Supplemental Appropriations Act of 2021 for lost institutional revenue. Even with the relief packages, it didn't cover all our COVID-19 expenses, but the funds from the federal government were key to getting us open and staying financially solvent."

On top of the COVID-19 expenses and keeping the university on track to stay within the set budgets for FY21 (which were $22 million lighter after all the cuts), Idaho Governor Brad Little announced a preemptive 5 percent cut ($200 million) from state budgets in the face of falling revenue due to COVID-19. The U of I's portion was $2 million (Dawson 2020). Upon hearing the news of even more budget cuts, morale on campus waivered; however, Scott's resolve to keep his alma mater heading in the right direction didn't. But what Scott had hoped he could avoid was no longer possible. Mandatory furloughs were the only way to reach Governor Little's ask, making opening in the fall much more critical to the university's future.

Scott's Management Insight

When things are most dangerous, travel as part of a herd. The presidents of Idaho's four-year institutions coordinated their actions, taking the same approach at the same time to help blunt criticism. Furloughs were understandably unpopular, but when all of the four-year institutions announced the mandatory furloughs simultaneously, it blunted the criticism. Approximately 80% of our expenses are people costs, and our employees knew that it must be needed if all institutions responded similarly. Clearly, we needed to open to keep solvent and protect our jobs. The furloughs raised the stakes even more.

Chapter 35
R1-2026

"You want to create an atmosphere for your university where it is spinning off all these different benefits."

—Dr. Christopher Nomura

Amid the chaos created by COVID-19 and the U of I taking painstaking measures to open in the fall, Scott took a crucial step toward achieving one of his pillars of success involving R1 research status. He opened the search to hire a new vice president for research and economic development.

Research plays a vital role in the U of I's success, from the actual research it produces to fulfilling its mission to educate students to become innovative thinkers and experts in their field of study. The U of I brought in over $113 million in total research expenditures in FY19, and Scott knew gaining R1 Carnegie Classification would put Idaho in the national and international research conversation (University of Idaho 2020).

"The goal to achieve R1 Carnegie Classification was on the back burner when I became president," Scott said. "It was a fantasy. There was no critical evaluation or program in place that detailed how to get there. We didn't have enough PhD candidates existing in our pipeline to meet the requirements or post-doctorate capacity to support additional research."

"Because of COVID-19, it was a weird time to transition to a new job," shared Dr. Chris Nomura, vice president for research and economic development. "I recognized there were some financial problems at the university. But there also seemed to be an excellent opportunity and a strong research base. Some longstanding community members in Moscow, who were friends with my family, and I spoke, and they talked about how great an area it was and the versatility. I applied for the position and was fortunate to get into the position. Taking the job was, on both a personal front and from a job perspective, a great opportunity."

Before Scott hired Chris, Bradley Ritts, senior associate vice president for Research and Development, served as interim vice president starting in December 2019. He said, "When we hired Chris, he did a great job stepping into the role and executing on the R1 mission by clarifying what had been just a concept before he arrived."

Gaining R1 Carnegie Classification had been a goal in the U of I's strategic plan for a while. "But it was clear that there was no understanding of how to get there or what the U of I would need to do to get there," Bradley shared.

That began to change when Scott came in with his three pillars: student success, research, and telling the U of I's story. Right from the get-go, he made it clear that research was part of his plan. The fact that he stated those three crucial things was a big part of his acceptance among much of the Vandal tribe.

When Scott started the R1-2026 Working Group, it brought a collaboration of stakeholders representing the entire university and external experts in their fields to produce a roadmap for R1 status. Bradley chaired the working group.

"It was a good combination of getting work done while maintaining the shared governance piece," Bradley pointed out. "By controlling the process, we could get an executable, realistic plan."

The R1-2026 Working Group produced a whitepaper that represented the insights of the committee experts while aligning with what would be realistic from the university's standpoint. Scott had earmarked some P3 money for the quest to R1 Research status but not unlimited funds. He needed the working group to be fiscally efficient and effective with their recommendations.

"We determined the best way to deploy the available $3 million a year investment," Bradley said. "Scott was clear that was our aim. We didn't need a strategy that was going to cost $20 million a year. Two months after Chris got here, we talked about what to do when the P3 money came and what steps would turn our plan from action into reality. Chris was the one who brought in the idea that the money would go to reward success."

The Carnegie Foundation for the Advancement of Teaching and the American Council on Education ranked the U of I as an R2 Carnegie institution, which meant "high research activity."

"There was absolutely nothing wrong with that," Chris stated. "But R1 meant 'very high research activity' and was significant. There are thousands of universities across the US, and only the top 275 or so are ranked as 'very high research activity.' R1 generally says that you are excellent in a well-rounded research portfolio for a university; you're performing at the country's highest levels of higher education institutions. This would put us in a national conversation, in addition to being the top dog in Idaho. People understand what R1 means within higher education circles."

The U of I obtaining the highest level of research capabilities would translate into another of Scott's pillars, student success. Chris continued, "Within those experiences with researchers, undergraduates would also benefit because they would learn from all these people who are experts in their research field. These people are making national and global impacts. As an undergraduate student who may not even know what they want to do after they graduate, to have the ability to be exposed to someone who's dedicated to a particular topic and be able to partake in that—that's a rare experience for students in general. If we have a higher research ranking, that affords more opportunities for that interaction to happen."

R1 also affects national and global status, like with *US News & World Report, Princeton Review,* and *Forbes* rankings. "Parents look at those things, too, if they're serious about where their son or daughter goes for their education," Chris remarked. "The stronger our research institution is within the state, the more outsized the economic effects are for the state itself. The graduates from a university that's performing at a high level are capable of contributing to the economy, both locally and regionally, in various ways. You want to create an atmosphere for your university where it is spinning off all these different benefits."

"We should be an R1," College of Graduate Studies Dean Jerry McMurtry stated. "We're doing everything we can to get and graduate more PhD students as well as recruit and support more postdocs."

January 2021, Scott allocated $3 million of P3 funds to motivate faculty toward robust research programs and building a sustainable and lasting R1 classification program. The U of I's total research expenditures for FY2020 came in at $112.8 million and $105.8 million for FY2021, down slightly from FY2019 but understandable in the face of COVID-19 (University of Idaho 2020). Those numbers reflect the global impacts of the pandemic, from travel bans to closures to illness. But the U of I research enterprise continues to thrive and move forward with some of the most diverse and innovative projects to date.

"The key metric we were watching at the time was the amount of awards won," Scott shared. "That metric was up 40 percent over a two-year period. COVID-19 prevented expenditures, and these awards built up like a coiled spring that would be unleashed and expended once the pandemic subsided."

Scott's Management Insight

You cannot hope a goal into existence; you must fund it and track it to make headway. Like many of the online whitepapers previously written, the goal to reach R1 status was a part of the strategic plan for years but did not move forward. The U of I didn't properly fund the initiatives and had no road maps prepared to achieve the goals. Simply stating them was not enough; they would not just magically appear. We raised funds by entering a public-private partnership that leased our steam plant. We placed the funds into an endowment and used the proceeds to fund our strategic projects. The university is already seeing the benefits of funding the R1 initiative. Our grant awards are soaring, and the pipeline of graduate students is full.

Deep Soil Ecotron Research Facility artist rendering.
SOURCE: Reprinted with permission from Deep Soil Ecotron/University of Idaho.

Sustainability may be a catchphrase now, but the U of I's history as a land-grant research institution has always revolved around assisting the stewards of the planet, including farmers and ranchers—the world's producers of food and products. Learning about the planet's soil at deep levels may not seem flashy and headline news, but the implications of "going deep" into the earth to study what's there are paramount in learning about life within the planet's underbelly. Deep Soil Ecotron research does just that. College of Agricultural and Life Sciences (CALS) Dean Michael Parrella shared the incredible journey of how the National Science Foundation (NSF) selected the University of Idaho to house the most advanced of the 13 Deep Soil Ecotron facilities on the planet.

"I have an affinity with Virginia Tech University (VTU); I graduated from there," Michael stated. "CALS was looking to hire a soil ecologist, and I saw Michael Strickland's file. He was an associate professor at VTU and setting the world on fire. His sister lived in Salmon, Idaho, so I felt we needed to take advantage of that connection and bring him to Idaho. The U of I's Nancy M. Cummings Research, Extension, and Education Center was also near Salmon, so I told him there would be an office there for him if he came to the U of I, as well as an office in Moscow. We were able to hire him."

Shortly after coming to the U of I, Dr. Michael Strickland received a prestigious NSF career award. "We have very few people on this campus who have that level of expertise," the dean continued. "He wrote a grant with another faculty member in the Department of Soil and Water Systems regarding the Deep Soil Ecotron project. NSF received 150 proposals, and they were only going to fund ten at $20 million apiece. Mike's proposal was selected and put on a shortlist with 30 other proposals for funding. When I heard he'd gotten that far, I knew it would be a major game-changer if he received the grant. It would be transformational for the campus and tie into the university's vision for sustainability." It would also assist in the U of I obtaining that R1 Carnegie Classification."

The grant awards committee looks at the total buy-in from a university; it would take collaboration from more than just CALS for NSF to award the grant to Strickland.

(Continued)

(Continued)

"Historically, the answer was absolutely not; we won't collaborate between colleges or units," Michael shared. "Nonetheless, Scott and Toni Broyles got involved, and the grant proposal became a presidential priority, which aligned the provost, vice provosts, vice presidents, Office of Research and Economic Development, and Office of Sponsored Programs with CALS. There's no question that we would not have that proposal if it weren't for Scott. The bottom line is that it all came together, and we got the proposal funded for $18.9 million. We're talking about a major infrastructure proposal to build a center for deep soil research" (University of Idaho 2021).

The facility, slated for renovation that began in 2022, will house 24 deep soil "eco-units," or towers, used to obtain core samples up to three meters (approximately 10 feet) deep into the soil. None of the world's other Ecotron facilities, mainly located in Europe, will go to those depths. "The towers will bring up the soil sample, and we can do replicated studies about the role of deep soil in terms of things like carbon sequestration and climate change," Michael shared.

"Researchers from around the world will come to our Moscow campus to study deep soil carbon capture, water quality, and variables impacting plant health," Scott said. "The results will help industry adjust to warmer temperatures in a sustainable manner."

After negotiating with the College of Engineering to use the space, the U of I will house the world's most advanced Deep Soil Ecotron facility in the J.W. Martin Laboratory on Moscow's U of I campus. Dr. Zachary Kayler, assistant professor of biogeochemistry, will serve as co-lead investigator with Dr. Strickland.

"From an urban perspective, an environmental perspective, and an agricultural perspective, understanding what's happening with deep soils can become a signature program," Michael stated. "There's a core of excellent soil scientists at the U of I. They should be able to bring in more extramural dollars to hire more graduate students and bring more undergraduates into a lab to do research. Then everything takes care of itself."

The Deep Soil Ecotron project will be an excellent example of self-sustainability while learning about and researching how to maintain soil sustainability.

Scott's Management Insight

A president or CEO must set goals and fund them and also be prepared to spend time and energy leading the organization down the chosen path. Look for opportunities to signal your commitment to advancing your goals. Spending your own time and resources will communicate to your institution that you are serious about your goals and generate energy and enthusiasm. Everyone wants to be a part of a "win." I personally put time into supporting the road map to R1 status and my other two pillars, student success and telling the U of I's story. I invested time and resources to help our faculty write successful grants and to invest in our nascent social media initiatives. I also dedicated time reaching out to high school students to recruit them to the U of I. Each action demonstrated to campus that I did not expect only our employees to do the heavy lifting; I also walked the talk and built momentum for these programs.

Smart Collaboration

Falcon Computer

The speed of technology can play a vital role in research. Obtaining timely results is the essence of research; once you receive the research output, you will know your next step in the research process. Technological speed can also benefit one's mental state; take Google, for example. People doing an Internet search want results as fast as they can think. No one wants to wait for the dreaded blue loading data line; we want answers, and we want them now. University of Idaho researchers are no different, especially when it comes to modeling and simulation.

"In January [2022], the U of I signed and executed a Memo of Understanding (MOU) with the other universities in Idaho and an

(Continued)

(Continued)

Scott with the Falcon Computer.
SOURCE: Reprinted with permission from University of Idaho.

acknowledgment agreement with Idaho National Laboratory (INL) to transfer INL's decommissioned Falcon supercomputer to the management of the University of Idaho," said Vice President for Research and Economic Development Chris Nomura (East Idaho News 2022).

INL "retired" the Falcon to make way for newer, faster systems, but the Falcon's massive capabilities in computing will still benefit the entirety of Idaho's higher education and research by giving the U of I and its sister institutions—Boise State University (BSU) and Idaho State University (ISU)—and Battelle Energy Alliance (which runs INL and operates Falcon) access to this powerful computing environment.

The collaboration didn't come without a little fuss; BSU thought the U of I was doing too much in the state by taking management of the supercomputer. "But both BSU and ISU said they couldn't take on the commitment, especially during the pandemic," Scott elaborated. "I told Chris to go into INL, speak to Marianne Walck, the deputy laboratory director for science and technology, and explain that we want to do this and that we're in the best position to do this. He assured her the other institutions would have access."

Scott wasn't trying to go around anyone; however, he wasn't one to sit back and see what would happen. Plus, the U of I had always been research heavy. "It made a hell of a lot of sense," he pointed out. "It was a hugely important game-changer."

The collaboration culminated in INL's Collaborative Computing Center (C3), a facility that brings the supercomputer and people together in a collective work environment, which is the key to success for all parties involved. Falcon is the 12th fastest supercomputer in the nation to join the ranks in higher education and can process huge mathematical models in a very limited time. Typical desk computers have eight processing cores, while Falcon has 35,000.

"Falcon is an incredible asset," Chris stated. "We're talking about a state with less than two and a half million people with the twelfth fastest supercomputer in the world. So as we recruit new people to the U of I, they can take advantage of this instrumentation. The level of research that our faculty will be able to produce is going to be competitive with anybody in the nation, essentially. We hired an associate physics professor in 2021, Dr. Zachariah Etienne, who does research on black holes and is involved with these multinational scientific projects involving scientists worldwide. They work on this program called LIGO, looking at gravitational waves. These guys visualized the first black hole ever in humanity, which was a theoretical construct until then. But Zach and his group and students here are working on several different computational methods to look at these types of things. The fact that we were getting this computer was a big reason we were able to recruit this young scientist to the University of Idaho. Falcon will be a powerful asset for recruiting others. The potential is just really quite amazing."

(Continued)

(Continued)

Scott saw the ROI with the U of I managing the supercomputer. It costs $300,000 annually to operate, but it will set the university to become an R1 institution by enhancing research capacity and competitiveness when applying for grants.

Scott's Management Insight

Opportunities do not always come at opportune times. Yes, the U of I was working our way out of financial distress, and yes, our sister institutions could not afford to take on the leadership and maintenance of the Falcon. But it was in all our best interests to make it happen. So we made a six-figure commitment to take possession and connect Falcon and signed an MOU with our sister institutions guaranteeing access (in return for sharing operational expenses based on use). It aligned with our R1 initiative, would speed up the research we were already doing, help us recruit faculty of the highest quality, and increase our visibility and partnership with the Idaho National Lab. It would also raise the amount and quality of research across the state while benefiting all public research universities in Idaho because of the collaborative framework created.

Smart Collaboration

Seed Potato Germplasm Laboratory

Since before Marilyn Monroe donned an Idaho potato sack as a dress in 1951, Idaho has been known on a national scale for its potatoes. Idaho is the nation's top potato-producing state and has a global reputation for producing quality spuds. The U of I's seed potato germplasm program through the College of Agricultural and Life Sciences maintains germplasm, or startup material, for Idaho's number-one crop—potatoes and seed potatoes. The laboratory ensures that the tissue culture used to grow potatoes is disease-free and high quality.

Idaho's potato industry uses the U of I's potato germplasm to produce about 90% of the potatoes grown in Idaho. About 60% of the spuds grown in the United States also can trace their roots back to the facility.

The new facility opened in March 2022 using the public/private collaboration model. Thanks to funding from the Idaho State Legislature ($3 million), the Idaho Potato Commission ($1.25 million), CALS ($1 million) and contributions from industry and individual growers, the new facility houses about 300 different potato varieties and ensures that contamination of Idaho's most precious commodity is a nonissue (PotatoPro 2022).

Scott's Management Insight

Don't run from your strengths; invest in them. It is easier to build on something already working than to start a new initiative from scratch. People identify Idaho as potatoes and vice versa. The university's germplasm facility will protect the health of the iconic Idaho potato. The facility will also produce the raw material for every potato product, from the well-known Idaho bakers to the beloved McDonald's french fries.

Part VIII

Chapter 36
The Grim Reaper

"We started working probably like we never had before as a community."
—Scott Green

After a summer of peaceful local protests, violent national protests, and no end in sight for COVID-19, August ushered in fall semester and brought a modified Greek rush, dorm room move-in, and an abundance of cautious optimism from Vandals. Thousands of students showed up, wanting their residential campus experience, and most faculty and staff wanted to deliver on the U of I's mission to educate students while keeping them safe.

Scott and the COVID-19 response teams had worked tremendous hours to ready the campus, as well as build a specific set of rules:

1. The university required all Moscow-based students to get tested for COVID-19 to attend in-person classes or live in the residence halls.
2. The U of I recommended that Moscow-based employees also get tested.
3. Testing was free and available by appointment via a website.
4. The campus would conduct random (surveillance) testing (participation was not mandatory but highly encouraged).
5. Students could attend classes depending on their comfort level, either online or HyFlex.
6. The university expected professors to teach in a HyFlex fashion with a rotation of in-classroom teaching days and online learning unless they had an exemption only to teach online.

This protocol was considered the gold standard for all the nation's universities that stayed open during COVID-19. The U of I continued constant contact with Idaho Public Health and followed CDC guidelines where applicable.

Communication continued between faculty, staff, and students, with the most up-to-date information and expectations regularly shared through emails and the university website. Students signed the Vandal Healthy Pledge (Vandals taking care of Vandals), agreeing to daily symptom monitoring, hand washing and disinfecting, and reporting any concerns and questions.

Facilities Management staff conducted constant deep cleaning and sanitization of buildings, especially in high-traffic areas. The Healthy Vandals hand sanitizer was available throughout campus. The mask mandate was in place in the City of Moscow and on campus.

"We really didn't have a problem with the mask mandate on campus," Scott recalled. "I know there were issues in the town of Moscow, but there was close to zero pushback to the masks here. People on campus just did it."

Faculty, staff, and students were working as a team. "There's just no question about that," Scott shared. "Morale wasn't necessarily high yet because we faced those mandatory furloughs with Governor Little's 5 percent cut as a holdback."

"The furloughs were tough," shared Director of Campus Visits and Events Angela Helmke. "It was like you had days off, but you didn't really, because you still had to get your work done. But the general feeling was that we'd much rather take prescribed time off and not get paid than have the person working next to us lose their job. That affects their home life, plus it adds more work for everyone still working at the U of I."

"People love the university, and they got it done with little micromanaging," Scott commented. "We started working probably like we never had before as a community. COVID-19 tore at our social fabric initially, but once we were up and running, it brought us closer together. We felt like we were accomplishing something, keeping our mission going."

"In my teaching, I asked myself what the students were supposed to get out of this," CLASS Dean Sean Quinlan confided. "What was it that really mattered? How was I spending this time with students, and what did I want them to get out of it? It reinforced one of the most important things we could do as a university, and that was to provide people with a nurturing environment. That was our business. Were we scaling our expectations and adjusting so students got what they needed out of their education even if it wasn't what we had normally come to expect."

However, there were still strong detractors to Scott moving the campus to its open-safely status. "We knew we were as prepared as possible with our meticulous planning and execution," Scott said. "The criticism seemed massive, but it was a small minority of very loud people using every tool they had to pressure us not to open."

"We're a smart bunch of people here, but some students were really offended," College of Graduate Studies Dean Jerry McMurtry said. "They thought it was unsafe to open, and we were putting their health at risk. We responded that we'd listen to the CDC, and we had very smart scientists at the U of I studying Corona viruses who had a good understanding of immunology and virology. We made the right decision."

During orientation events before the first day of class, a few students accused the university of putting profits over lives. They conducted a "die-in" by laying down on the pavement to represent dead bodies. The same group of about four or five grad students also exercised their right to peacefully protest, with one member always dressed as the Grim Reaper. They decided to protest at University House one afternoon.

"They just stood by the driveway," Scott shared. "When I drove into my driveway after work, I saw the Grim Reaper and two or three others, parked the car in the garage, and went into the house. They left. End of protest."

University of Idaho students conduct protest "die-in" during Fall Semester orientation.
SOURCE: Reprinted with permission from Kimlye Stagner.

A small number of faculty members were also actively working to undermine the university's reopening efforts. They contacted a U of I employee, telling him he was complicit in a conspiracy because he was helping the administration open their testing lab. "It was unbelievable," Scott uttered. "I had never seen anything like that in my entire career. These employees were badgering him about not being a 'pure' faculty member because he was working toward our mission. I was horrified that we had faculty bullying their peers, but I told the team to remain focused. We'd show our commitment to the U of I through our successes. Fortunately, the faculty member opening our lab believed, quite rightly, that if we were successful, he would be saving lives. He persevered, was successful, and is truly a hero. But to this day, he doesn't like us to talk about his role in our success."

Even the U of I student newspaper had a lot to say about the university opening. "By reading the *Argonaut*, one would think everything was just a mess, and everything was going wrong," Scott observed. "Interestingly, they never found a student to interview who got their test results back quickly or was happy with the way things were running. They never called the President's Office to ask any questions; they just made assumptions—often wrong."

But Scott could see both sides of the situation. "They're students, and they heard different things from people not aligned with what we were trying to do. I get it. I learned a ton about the press when I was a student on campus, and I believe those students will look back on this time as a great learning experience. When I was a young man on campus, there were periods when students and the *Argonaut* were critical of me and some of the decisions I made as ASUI president, and, at times, they were 100 percent right in their criticism. There is nothing better than cutting your teeth at a university. You can make mistakes in a campus environment and learn from them without a huge downside. That enables you to go out into the real world and not repeat those mistakes. I deeply value that experience as it helped me become a better manager of people."

"Whenever you have a campus our size, you'll have a diverse set of voices in perceptions and experiences," Dean of Students Blaine Eckles detailed. "We saw some very conservative approaches to COVID-19 like it was a big hoax; the media and government were just trying to scare everyone. Then we saw the other extreme, with people thinking there would be people falling over dead if they walked outside and breathed in air. The hard part was figuring out how to deliver on our mission and safely educate our students amidst all the uncertainty."

It was also frustrating that many detractors kept saying that the COVID-19 response groups, including the administration, were not communicating or being transparent. "The regular emails, 'Talks with Torrey,' town halls, dedicated website with all the virus statistics, and previous communications—the amount of time we spent communicating was epic," Scott said. "What we finally figured out was that the detractors were not saying we were not communicating; they just did not like what we were saying. We listened to the feedback, discussed it, then after much consideration, went in a different direction. That is very different from not communicating or not listening. Once we figured that out, things got easier; we quit trying to beat ourselves up over something that was impossible to deliver."

Positive feedback far outweighed the few negative pushbacks, however. "Many people called the President's Office with positive comments, which was nice," Scott shared. Letters, emails, and texts commended the U of I for their attention to safety and decision to be brave and bold.

"The tone of some of the most hardened naysayers started to change," COVID-19 Project Manager Seth Vieux recalled. "People called and emailed to admit they thought Scott was crazy but shared that they were glad we did it."

"A few people were not very kind in the way they pushed back, actually sending comments to a couple of public forums saying it wouldn't work," Provost Torrey Lawrence recalled. "But six months in, they acknowledged that it had worked. With COVID-19, there were no best practices yet. We were just trying to do the best with what we had."

One wildcard, other than COVID-19 itself, remained. What would students do outside of class? Would they use the same guidelines as they did on campus? "The semester started rough with a big party at the White Apartments [a large apartment complex just off campus that got its name from being painted all white] that I had to respond to and remind people that we were serious and that we did not want anyone at the university who did not care for their fellow students," Scott shared. "And we were prepared to act on that."

That wildcard extended to employees, as well. With the policy in place that exposure to COVID-19 meant a 14-day quarantine, schedules became a quagmire of coming to work, then quarantining due to exposure (usually not on campus), then coming back to work, then facing isolation again due to another exposure. "We could only do so much in helping people," Director of Human Resources Brandi Terwilliger pointed out. "We all had to do our part to avoid getting exposed."

Scott's Management Insight

COVID-19 was a common foe, but not everyone agreed on how to address the threat. Some faculty just wanted to teach remotely, most students wanted to return to campus, and the administration needed to safely open the campus if they were going to avoid more job losses. We stayed focused on the goal and did not let the bad behavior of a few distract us from achieving our objectives. We did open the testing facility for fall semester. We did test every student when they arrived on campus. We did deliver a mask to every student. We did teach live classes. We did manage social distancing throughout the classrooms, labs, and public spaces. We did make our own hand sanitizer and had it available at every entrance. We did test wastewater to identify virus concentrations and trends. We did open our own infirmary. We did communicate weekly that we were all in this together against this unseeable enemy. And we were.

Confidence in our handling of the pandemic had built momentum over time, and the campus could Stay Calm and Vandal On. Public Health never contact-traced a single case of COVID-19 back to a U of I classroom or a lab. We safely opened the campus and stayed open for the academic year. Nothing else mattered—not the bad behavior of a few faculty bullying their peers, not the Grim Reaper, not the *Argonaut* stories. We did not respond to the taunts nor crow about our capabilities. Our response was quiet success.

Chapter 37

Open!

"It was exciting to see people take their expertise and apply it to solving new problems."

—Dr. Ginger Carney

The week before classes started for the fall semester may have been one of Scott's most stressful in his quest to keep the university open, not only because of the pressures associated with that and receiving negative pushback but also because there was a slight delay in getting the COVID-19 lab open.

"It was frustrating because we met all the CLIA requirements and still could not get clearance for our lab," Scott relayed. "The FDA representative in Spokane made us jump through more hoops than were required, plus we were aware the lab in Spokane responsible for giving us regional CLIA approval was also a CLIA-approved lab and, therefore, a competitor. Gritman Medical Center had contracted with them to do their work before getting our lab up. That week before school started, we had students showing up, and we were still sending our samples out to be tested elsewhere, which took days rather than hours to get back."

Like many new operations, getting up and running took longer than the team thought. "I was concerned that politically, the Spokane lab didn't have any intention to certify us," Scott confided. "I was concerned enough that I started asking if we needed to find someone else to certify us. I'll never fully know what they were thinking. All I know is I was thrilled that we eventually achieved approval."

Thankfully, and to the relief of an entire region, the collaboration between Gritman Medical Center and the U of I produced a lab that was almost fully functional by the start of the fall semester, with the first two batches of COVID-19 test results arriving on August 18, 2020, with results reported by the GBRC manager:

> *2020.08.18: BATCH 01*
> *First clinical sample (94 total samples)*
> *Fully processed @ ~ 17:00, 0 positives*
> *2020.08.18: BATCH 02*
> *First clinical positive (94 total samples)*
> *Fully processed @ ~ 19:00, 1 positive*

According to the GBRC manager, "Initially, we were doing the entire workflow, end-to-end, with one person, but we soon transitioned to an assembly-line approach where we could do around thirteen batches per day via tag-teaming and floating positions."

The floating positions consisted of one person in the cleanroom setting up the qPCR reactions by combining extracted RNA with the testing reagents, two people in the dirty room extracting, one person in the dirty room batching to make up for Gritman Medical Center's occasional staffing issues, one person in the qPCR room for results and delivery, and sometimes an individual solely focused on handling results and putting out fires.

Not long after the lab was in full swing, it cut the time for people receiving test results from a few days to less than 24 hours. "That was where the 96-well format came into play," IBEST Director Barrie Robison shared.

"The turnaround time was the key in preventing the spread," said Kane Francetich, Gritman CIO.

Scott and his Core Ops team were leading by example. They were regulars at the testing site. "I was on the front page of the Moscow newspaper with that swab stuck up my nose," Scott said, laughing. "I had to get tested anytime I traveled; we still had legislative and U of I work to conduct in Boise. I got tested a lot, and I finally got used to it. I appreciate all the nurses."

"We did have some challenges in Boise," CEO SW Idaho Chandra Zenner Ford recalled. "The U of I Boise Center employees were annoyed that Moscow students, faculty, and staff had access to all that testing. We couldn't do that at the U of I Boise because we didn't have a lab. I had three or four meetings with the CEOs at St. Alphonsus Hospital, trying to figure out if they could staff a mobile testing unit. They looked into it, but they didn't have the ability or the staff. After that, I tried to figure out all kinds of crazy ways to do it. But as it turned out, there was drive-through testing just across the street from this building. We made everybody aware of that. It was free, and people could just drive up and get tested."

The U of I and Gritman Medical Center collaborated to test students off-campus in some specific cases. "The MOSS students down in McCall were being supervised and had interactions with K-12 students," Kane explained.

"It was risky, taking students from all over the country and putting them on a research site to live together for a summer," shared Dean Dennis Becker, College of Natural Resources. "They quarantined for fourteen days individually; then they quarantined for fourteen days together; we created a family."

"We tested them weekly," Kane shared. "We had a courier that made a weekly trip to McCall. We would place the orders online and print off the labels for those people. The courier would take those down for the following week's samples and pick up the new samples for the week and bring them back for processing. We had that going through most of the school year."

Weekly email updates to faculty, staff, and students included any new information regarding testing or COVID-19 protocols. Every Monday, the U of I shared the numbers of the weekly tests performed and positive result rates. This charted the ups and downs of the positive cases and showed the need to follow all protocols to keep the spread as slow and low as possible. The university also posted this information on a website for easy access.

Innovating thinking and ideas regarding COVID-19 continued to swirl around campus. Dr. Erik Coats, a professor in Civil and Environmental Engineering, began wastewater testing as an opportunity to monitor population-level infection.

"Not every community was doing that," Kane related. "Dr. Coats's team knew which area would see a spike, so if it was in the residence halls or Greek houses, our lab could then concentrate our testing for the following week in those areas. Once we identified those positive hot spots, the U of I also performed contact tracing."

"Later analysis by the team that performed the work indicated that they believed the largest spikes were predictive seven days in advance of increased illness," Scott shared. "It was helpful determining which blocks and houses the virus was coming from."

After a spike several weeks into the semester, the university asked Greek houses that had more than 10 percent of their students testing positive to go into quarantine and then test those who didn't feel sick. Once the lab identified students with COVID-19 and they isolated at Targhee Hall, the university lifted the house quarantine. The university also asked the Greek houses to rethink their sleeping porches to accommodate distancing.

"I'm really proud of the faculty and staff from our college for spearheading things like the wastewater monitoring and COVID-19 testing lab," said Ginger Carney, College of Science dean. "It was exciting to see people take their expertise and apply it to solving new problems."

September brought a few historical moments, including a campus with no football until the spring semester. The leaves changed, and the cozy and familiar fall feeling started to envelop campus, along with a thick fog of smoke. That smoke, coming from house and forest fires in California, did something that COVID-19 hadn't done that fall. It closed the university for a few days in mid-September to address air quality issues.

"If anything, it was almost a bigger deal to close because of the smoke," Vice Provost of Student Affairs and Dean of Students Blaine Eckles pointed out. "We knew that would drive people indoors or into confined spaces where the COVID-19 risk for spread was higher."

"People would ask me, 'How has it been going this past year?'" Scott recounted. "I would say, 'Well, you know, other than the pandemic and financial crisis and the earthquake and the drought and the smoke that shut down our university, and the fires that came after that, and the pestilence. . .it's been great.'"

September also brought the first COVID-19 inpatient to Gritman Medical Center. They'd worked diligently treating people through their area clinics and the ER, but there would inevitably be patients needing further care. "We worked hard to put messaging out to our community that it was safe to come to the clinics. We didn't want patients to delay their care," Gritman CEO Kara Besst shared. "Unfortunately, we saw people delay their care throughout the COVID-19 crisis." That delay sometimes resulted in patients needing more extensive care.

Amid the worst crisis the university faced maybe in its entire history, Scott and his COVID-19 response teams remained self-effacing. "We didn't brag about our successes purposely," Scott explained. "We had a lot of folks who wanted to write about it, but we weren't comfortable. We weren't even sure we were going to remain open. We had discussions as a team with our communications and media relations folks. What if we crow and then have to shut down later in the semester? We just weren't comfortable with that."

Scott and his teams *did* crow about the thinking-outside-the-box ways to deliver education that began cropping up all over campus.

"How people navigated made for some amazing stories," CLASS Dean Quinlan shared. "One of our colleagues, Gustavo Castro-Ramirez, a vocalist coach and collaborative pianist with the Lionel Hampton School of Music, was in his office with the window open and vocal coaching with the students outside. Christopher Pfund, associate professor of music, taught outside using his electronic keyboard, socially distanced. Dawn Sweet, assistant professor in psychology, figured out ingenious ways of structuring her laboratory so she could conduct lab work with students socially distanced and safe. And then the Theatre Department navigated with Zoom performances with incredible and innovative aplomb. These were stunning experiences."

CEHHS faculty Dr. Ann Brown, Dr. Anne Kern, and Dr. Liz Margo established the IDEAS Student Research Symposium for spring 2021, featuring undergraduate and graduate students sharing in the scholarly work they conducted that academic year during COVID-19. Interim CEHHS Dean Philip Scruggs explained, "The first spring it was delivered via Zoom, but it worked well as far as students sharing their work and participation from the faculty. We used gift money for awards."

"Much of our curriculum was amenable to being delivered virtually," Ginger outlined. "But one of the key things geology students had to do to earn their degrees was participate in a field camp, which they couldn't do during COVID-19. Two of our faculty collaborated with a colleague in the College of Education, Health, and Human Sciences to offer a virtual field camp based on the game *Minecraft*. Earth and Spatial Sciences Assistant Professors Erika Rader and Renee Love developed a meaningful, elegant, creative solution for something the students needed to graduate."

"It was amazing when students from the School of Music practiced social-distance style outside my office on the Administration Building lawn," Scott said, beaming. "How do you bring people together in a safe environment where they were blowing horns and reed instruments—which is inherently unsafe? Well, they found a way. The School of Music kept asking, 'Are we bothering you?' I emphatically told them no. I loved it. *That* was the sound of us showing how to be flexible. *That* was the sound of us succeeding. *That* was the sound of us being open. The Vandal Marching Band developed its own unique response, moving away from horns to all percussion. All of the innovative responses were inspiring."

Scott's Management Insight

Remain humble and stay focused on the mission even when you start seeing success. Don't declare victory too early. We possibly let a great promotional moment pass by us. I am still okay with that. The last thing you want is to promote your success and then have COVID-19 lay you low. We remained focused on the campus and quietly helped other universities that reached out to us. Our priorities were the health of our community first and the financial stability of our university second. That never wavered. Promoting our successes was not the right thing to do at that time.

Trust your colleagues. Do your best not to micromanage. Our faculty found innovative and fun ways to continue to engage and teach students.

No one person could have imagined all these different approaches. I remain proud of how our faculty responded. They were energetic and innovative despite having their own battles with a pandemic. Not to be cliché, but most persevered—often at great personal cost—with our students in mind.

Smart Collaboration

McCall Field Campus Overhaul (Home of MOSS— McCall Outdoor Science School), McCall, Idaho

Idaho Governor Brad Little visits University of Idaho MOSS.
SOURCE: Reprint with permission from C. Scott Green (Author).

The McCall Outdoor Science School (MOSS) is the U of I's K–12 program that utilizes the outdoor environment as an integrated context for learning through its Adventure Day Camps and School Residential Programs. MOSS encourages a hands-on approach to scientific discovery highlighting the relationships between biological, physical, and social systems. Students develop a sense of place, build scientific literacy, and learn effective collaboration and communication skills (University of Idaho n.d.).

MOSS's goal is to help students develop a science identity and science processing skills, along with social and critical thinking skills that are necessary to prepare them to be global citizens capable of addressing complex problems. Students practice science through hands-on exploration and experimentation, student-directed inquiries, and the opportunity to apply these skills and knowledge to real problems and situations. Socialization, teamwork, and group living skills are also an important part of this program.

For nearly two decades, MOSS has operated through the College of Natural Resources (CNR), bringing outdoor-based learning to over 2100 K–12 students and educators annually in Idaho. Director for U of I Institutional Research Wesley McClintick compiled data from an SBOE study and found that the college go-on rate was 20 percent higher for students who had participated in MOSS, a hugely influential presence for K–12 students (McClintick, personal communication).

During the pandemic, MOSS pivoted from hosting children from across the state at their outdoor science school to successfully teaching outdoor research to the McCall-Donnelly K–5 students for two days a week. That "thinking outside the box" method of handling COVID-19 provided financial stability for families (parents could go to work while their kids were at school and MOSS) and helped the local school stay open. Starting in September 2020, students attended MOSS during their typical school day, allowing a hybrid indoor/outdoor learning model in conjunction with their regular classes. CNR grad students taught a science-based curriculum to small pods of students in the outdoor setting of Central Idaho pines. The synergistic model focused on keeping everyone safe using COVID-19 protocols while ensuring students were bussed and fed.

MOSS will work to raise $14 million as part of the "Brave. Bold." campaign to improve facilities in McCall. CNR Dean Dennis Becker's goal is to offer MOSS education to every sixth grader in Idaho to encourage a hands-on approach to scientific discovery highlighting the relationships between biological, physical, and social systems.

(Continued)

(Continued)

Scott's Management Insight

To the extent possible, pivot to leverage your assets to aid the community through hard times. It will be remembered and benefit the institution long after the threat has diminished. School districts canceled their trips to MOSS due to COVID-19. But we had staff there and a great facility that could help the town of McCall continue to educate their children in a safe, fun environment. It cost us little to provide that support, and the town provided some funding to cover our costs. It was a true win/win partnership.

Chapter 38

A Tale of Two Cities

"Every state and institution faced unique factors and challenges in dealing with COVID-19 and its implications."

—*Scott Green*

Almost eight miles west, a different story unfolded at Washington State University (WSU). Washington State Governor Jay Inslee continued to keep the State of Washington on lockdown, but COVID-19 cases continued to grow statewide, including in Pullman and Whitman County, particularly among those aged between 20 and 39. WSU announced on July 23, 2020, it would remain online with coursework and campus closed other than for essential workers (Sokol 2020).

Unfortunately, 12,000+ students still arrived in Pullman for fall semester despite WSU being closed and wholly online. Many had already rented housing for the year. Even without in-person instruction, they wanted to be in Pullman with their fellow WSU Cougars. Pullman police announced at the end of August that they would begin issuing infractions and fines for large gatherings due to complaints about noise and a lack of social distancing. That wasn't necessarily a deterrent but rather an opportunity to collect donations at the functions to pay any fines incurred. August 24, 2020, was the first day of (online) classes, and 211 Whitman County residents had tested positive by that time. That number, of course, wasn't all WSU students (Zavala 2020).

Governor Inslee sent Washington State National Guard troops on September 8, 2020, to assist with testing at the Pullman campus. However, results took days rather than hours to arrive. And sadly, because of the smoke from the region's catastrophic forest fires blazing that summer and fall, WSU moved testing indoors because of poor air quality. WSU employees worked to get medical tents set up on campus for testing by mid-September, and the WSU administration asked their students to get tested by the end of September (Wolcott 2020).

A debate of sorts started brewing. Which method on how to handle COVID-19 was more effective? One side of the border ushered in the National Guard to assist with testing due to a large number of students returning to the City of Pullman even though the state required WSU to educate fully online. Eight miles away on the east side of the border, the U of I deployed the HyFlex model, offering in-person and online options while maintaining a stringent testing regimen to mitigate the spread of the virus.

Comparing positive cases on September 14, 2020, Whitman County Public Health reported 1054 cases, more than three and a half times the 288 positive cases in Latah County reported by Public Health Idaho North Central District (Kolpitcke 2020).

The U of I's "let's open for fall semester" approach began to give even the harshest critics pause. On one side, things looked good for the U of I and Latah County but could quickly take a turn for the worse, considering the contagious nature of COVID-19. On the other side, WSU's cases could begin to decline because of the fully online environment that could help mitigate the spread. Only time would tell the effectiveness of the alternative approaches to face the unprecedented foe.

The National Guard was initially slated to leave the WSU campus by November 20, but opted to stay until the end of the semester (December 17) at the university's request. The Guardsmen worked tirelessly, sometimes swabbing up to 400 people in a single day. Ultimately, they stayed until mid-January.

"The U of I did an excellent job working with the students and talking about the importance of the protocols they put in place," Gritman CEO Kara Besst shared. "I commend Scott and his team for enforcing those protocols. For Gritman, the partnership with the U of I was very helpful, especially in the early days of COVID-19. They were concerned for the well-being of the hospital, helped us prepare for the students' return, and provided us with additional PPE."

"We'd worked with WSU to be a mass community on both sides of the border regarding COVID-19," Scott pointed out. "We'd taken some funds out of a grant that we use for building that community between the two universities to promote things like masking. Unfortunately, the posters kept getting defaced by extremists for political reasons."

Scott publicly stated that he understood and could appreciate the factors that led to WSU's remaining closed. But he always stayed true to his commitment to open the U of I in Fall 2020 with robust safety measures to mitigate the spread of COVID-19 on campus. His and everyone's goal was to provide the safest learning, teaching, and working environment possible by following the science and data from Idaho public health officials and the CDC.

"Every state and institution faced unique factors and challenges in dealing with COVID-19 and its implications," Scott said. "While WSU is close in proximity to our institution, its decisions are based on an entirely different set of circumstances."

"We opened with a comprehensive plan," Special Advisor Chandra Zenner Ford stated. "Scott did crisis management before, and his past experiences helped the situation. He owned COVID-19 as our problem and came up with a plan to address it. We weren't going to hem and haw around; we were just going to do it."

As COVID-19 became more of a marathon than a sprint, the longer story included WSU requiring all students to show proof of vaccination for the 2021–22 school year unless exempted for religious or medical reasons (KIRO 2021). This included students living in university-owned housing. Other exemptions included if their class load was fully online or they weren't physically present on campus. If the university received no proof of vaccination, WSU students weren't allowed to register for classes in the spring. The requirement to have proof of the COVID-19 (and measles, too) vaccination or an approved exemption was made permanent in spring 2022 (Ellis 2022).

WSU also required employees and volunteers to show proof of COVID-19 vaccination or an approved exemption when Governor Inslee made it mandatory for all state employees by October 18, 2021 (Washington State n.d.). WSU did not make the vaccination requirement *permanent* for employees and volunteers. Regardless, the prerequisite forced WSU to fire 50 employees for not showing proof of vaccination, including the head football coach and four assistant football coaches.

Right, wrong, or otherwise, there were key differences in how each university, community, and state approached COVID-19. "It wasn't just Washington State," Scott pointed out. "There were other states taking the same approach. They clamped down harder and closed businesses, but Idaho's Governor Brad Little kept us open and operating."

Scott maintained communication with WSU President Kirk Schulz during the pandemic because so many people in that area crossed the state borders to live, work, shop, and socialize. Both appreciated the differences between the two states, political and otherwise, and how that equated to the different approaches to operating an institution of higher education during a pandemic. But communicating with each other to acknowledge the area's population mixing and merging daily was more about keeping the entire region safe than politics.

"You have to give Governor Little credit," Scott expressed. "The State of Idaho has been cutting taxes and still has record revenues because we were open during the pandemic. He threaded that needle, and the U of I saw demand because we were open and operating."

Scott's Management Insight

Embrace and own your differences. The approach taken by the U of I and WSU could not have been more different. It would have been easier for the U of I to just go online, but for the reasons already articulated, we did not believe that was the best path, and if the direction we were going did not pan out, the online path would still be available to us. We refrained from criticizing WSU's approach because there was not a guarantee that, despite our best efforts, we could remain open the entire academic year. Another, more contagious variant could (and did) make our testing less effective.

Chapter 39
We're Closer Than You Think

"It had to be a journey we took them through."

—*John Barnhart*

D r. Torrey Lawrence had served the university for many years, including as vice provost for faculty and the interim provost. But Scott still felt a national search was necessary to finalize hiring a provost for the U of I in the fall of 2020.

"Scott really wanted to have in-person interviews," Torrey explained. "He felt very uncomfortable hiring people off Zoom, especially in a leadership role where he would rely on that person a lot. That was one of the first job searches where we brought candidates to campus, and, of course, that got some attention. They brought five people to campus in late October and November, one of which was me. They wanted to get the search process finished before Thanksgiving [2020]."

"There was strong competition for that position," Scott pointed out. "At least one nationally renowned person was in that pool, but Torrey rose above the other candidates by far. Hiring Torrey as our provost was the absolute right decision. He has respect on campus and has been an incredible partner, not just when he became the provost but before. He was a team player and made some tough decisions as interim that weren't always popular among faculty, especially with the financial situation. He did an incredible job with the virus; he balanced all the competing interests and people freaking out. He was a calm voice. He led by example."

In September, Scott had hired Teresa Koeppel as the U of I's chief marketing officer and executive director of University Communications and Marketing. Teresa arrived at the U of I from her previous position as global director for communication, marketing, and engagement for Compass Group at Google. She joined an improving team of marketing and communication experts but brought with her detailed knowledge and processes that leveraged the U of I's social media platforms. One of the university's most successful marketing campaigns targeting enrollment was in the hard-core planning stage when Teresa started in her role.

John Barnhart, senior director of Marketing and Creative Services, shared the secret sauce of how his marketing team helped execute the delivery of a message many potential students needed to hear during the new normal of COVID-19.

"It was in the summer of 2020, and we had come through the beginning stages of the pandemic," John outlined. "The schools in California, the Cal State system, and the UC system had announced only months away from their fall semester that they were going remote. Scott sent us a note that said, 'I think there's an opportunity. I'd like you to shift some of our marketing focus to California.' And that was it. That was all he said. He didn't ask us how we'd do it or make sure that there were newspaper ads or a plane that wrote in the sky. He didn't talk tactics; he just said what he wanted us to focus on."

John pulled the marketing team together and explained they were going after California. "We did it in a very strategic way. We couldn't afford to market to the entire state of California. It was far too big," he explained. "We used data to influence our top five geographic regions."

The more geography they went after would equate to a higher cost, from TV ads to digital marketing. The team zeroed in on those top five regions with a combination of data:

1. From previous marketing conducted by the U of I in California showing the highest engaged geographic region;
2. From traffic to the U of I's website using Google Analytics showing where it was coming from in California; and
3. From enrollment data showing where current U of I students came from in California.

"We used concentric circles and selected the five geographic regions that had the highest likelihood that we could talk to somebody there and convince them that the University of Idaho was worth considering," John explained. "Our design team looked at the map to think how the creative [package] would look. They came up with, 'We're closer than you think.'

And from there, the rest fell into place. It was a beautiful decision on their part; that became our foundational campaign positioning statement."

For decades, maybe even for its entire existence, the U of I fought the stigma of being remote. In certain ways, it was. "The geography and demography of Idaho were not easy for the University of Idaho," Don Burnett, former College of Law dean, pointed out. "I credit Scott and the marketing team for developing awareness of the U of I and many of its distinctive characteristics."

Even though the U of I and the City of Moscow offered dozens of activities on and off campus, the area was a somewhat remote place to live, especially for a college student. Finally, a creative team took on that so-called flaw like gangbusters.

"We said let's address that one negative issue that people would bring up, 'Oh, you're so far away for me to go to school there,'" John recalled. "We backed it up with those unique value propositions, like the University of Idaho was ranked in the top eight percent of higher education by the *Princeton Review,* was the best public value in the West according to *US News & World Report* and had a spectacular campus in a beautiful town. We had those unique value propositions as part of our marketing package already, so we sprinkled those in." Plus, the U of I was safely open for business amid COVID-19.

The next step was to develop a robust marketing approach, unlike the traditional techniques that hadn't necessarily served the university in increasing enrollment or tuition over the years. "Email was fine, but it couldn't be email alone," John pointed out. "We had to back it up; we had to give them the opportunity to learn more. And as they learned more, they found that maybe there was something here. Then we asked them to apply. We couldn't just send an email, 'Hey, apply to the University of Idaho.' It had to be a journey we took them through. One thing the U of I didn't have when I first got here was a data-centric marketing team. So we started measuring engagement across all tactics, whether digital ads, Google Display, Pay per Click ads, or emails. When we started measuring, that allowed us to know where engagement was falling short and make the necessary adjustments."

The data revealed that if they sent digital marketing pieces out, and the engagement to the ad was good, but the bounce rate *off* the U of I web landing page was high, they had to make some adjustments in the students' landing page experience to keep them there and engaged. "We started to focus on that complete journey from the ad through the landing page through the application process," John emphasized. "It was hard work, but the team embraced the process, and we worked and worked and measured and adjusted. My motto is to get a little smarter every day."

The marketing team put together videos displayed on the California landing page to address prospective students' questions regarding a move from there to Idaho. The videos featured enrolled students from California—experts in the field of knowing all about that move. The peer-to-peer messages were authentic and included other key points, including that the U of I wasn't wait-listing students (like California schools), and it wasn't too late to apply to become a Vandal.

Scott identified the opportunity and asked marketing to focus on it, and during that time, he also took the opportunity to realize that Creative Services and Marketing needed to be connected. The previous marketing manager left the university during the financial cutbacks; Special Advisor Chandra Zenner Ford filled in the position for Scott until he decided to have John manage both Marketing and Creative Services on an interim basis.

The decision to have John serve in both capacities closed a gap in the process. The Marketing team would execute the plan and strategy, and the Creative Services team would make it come to fruition.

"In the 'We're Closer Than You Think' campaign, we showed where California was and where we were," Assistant Vice President Kathy Barnard pointed out. "You could come here; we were open. That understanding, that market advantage, worked. Just a handful of institutions nationwide pulled off what we pulled off during COVID-19 in terms of enrollment." See Figure 39.01.

The campaign also tied in nicely with the WUE (Western Undergraduate Exchange) program, which offered a discount to students from California attending the U of I.

Figure 39.01   We're Closer Than You Think marketing campaign graphic.
SOURCE: University of Idaho Communications and Marketing. Reproduced with permission of University of Idaho.

The U of I didn't see the bounty of those efforts pay off immediately. "COVID-19 caused the fall 2020 enrollment to dip by around 9 percent, which wasn't surprising. Much of the decline was in high school dual enrollment classes, so the incoming mix was actually pretty good," Scott said. "Core enrollment was down only 3 percent. Everyone was relieved it didn't drop more dramatically" (Green, personal communication).

However, by fall 2021, the messaging to students in a way they could relate brought a glimmer of hope with an increased enrollment of 4.8 percent, almost back to pre-pandemic levels, with the new entering class up 14 percent, the largest class since 2016 (University of Idaho n.d.). Student enrollment from California increased a whopping 44 percent over the previous five years.

"When the enrollment numbers came in for fall 2021, we had increased our enrollment from the state of California by almost 50 percent," John shared. "So yes, it absolutely worked. We caught their eye, we provided a message that resonated, we had an opportunity during a pandemic where the schools in California were going to close, we were going to be open, we shared that message with the students, we shared our value statement and the rest of those unique value propositions, and some of those students in California listened and ultimately enrolled."

The final successful piece to the "We're Closer Than You Think" campaign included messaging focused on beautiful fall and cozy winter seasons. Again, the Marketing team took a potentially negative aspect and converted it into a positive, reminding those students who trekked from California to Idaho that the Moscow campus would offer not only a world-class education but dazzling colors, falling leaves, and just enough snowfall to enjoy outdoor activities (or snuggle in with friends to drink cocoa and watch movies while the white stuff slowly fell outside).

* * *

Scott, Torrey, and the COVID-19 response teams continued regularly communicating with students, faculty, and staff. They encouraged students to seriously think about their activities and travels during Thanksgiving break and uphold the Healthy Vandal Pledge. The email also reminded them that the incubation period from COVID-19 exposure was six days.

After Thanksgiving break, the Moscow campus transitioned to remote course delivery for the remainder of the semester, including online finals. Scott and Torrey believed it made no sense to COVID-19 test all students returning to campus only to have them leave two weeks later for winter break. Scott and Torrey urged students to remain at their permanent residence and not travel back to campus. They advised faculty to schedule their office hours online. Staff statewide were put on a work-from-home status until January 8 with offices open but with a rotating schedule and other strategies to keep exposure to a minimum. The U of I required all Moscow-based students to get COVID-19 tested again before participating in in-person classes starting in January.

At the monthly Staff Council meeting held on December 9, results from their most recent COVID-19 survey asking staff about their environment during the "work from home" directive were telling. Three main takeaways negatively affected staff work productivity: (1) having dependents at home, (2) being overworked due to voluntary separations leaving many unfilled positions, and (3) helping dependents with online learning. Staff requested more flexibility with their work location and access to more and different counseling services. Human Resources began to work on addressing both requests (University of Idaho 2020).

The first virtual Winter Commencement via Zoom seemed somewhat of a letdown, but the president's teams tried to make it as special as possible under the circumstances. Graduates received at their home a Commencement box with a diploma holder in recognition of the graduate's achievements, but Scott was determined to have an actual ceremony for them in spring 2021.

It wasn't easy, but the U of I had prevailed. COVID-19 remained a powerful force on campus and in the community, but through cooperation and collaboration on a scale maybe never seen before in the Moscow community, the campus had remained open for most of the semester. The transition after Thanksgiving to online was more of a precaution than a necessity. It also didn't unnecessarily force the students through an additional round of COVID-19 testing. Adherence to the U of I's protocols and the Healthy Vandal Pledge resulted in Idaho Public Health reporting no transmissions of COVID-19 traced back to U of I classrooms or labs in the fall of 2020. They also reported significantly lower rates of serious health issues in Latah County relative to the state, region, and national averages (University of Idaho 2021).

"Spencer Martin, U of I director of athletic bands, was a real model on how to deal with COVID-19," Torrey observed. "I often think about how something he said hit me. He said, 'We cannot mourn what we can't do; let's just figure out what we *can* do.' That actually summed up the U of I's approach to COVID-19. We didn't spend our time focusing on or mourning the things we couldn't do. We always focused on what we *could* do."

The Vandal tribe from the north, brave and bold, tried and true, had subdued their foe to some degree, and as long as everyone continued the team approach to handling COVID-19, that foe would eventually falter.

Scott's Management Insight

Leverage the competitive advantage gained from doing things differently. California schools were closed to live instruction. We offered a different experience. The "We're Closer Than You Think" campaign was incredibly successful. As a destination campus, COVID-19 did affect our enrollments, but we saw significant increases in higher-margin California students coming to campus, which helped our bottom line. It provided the momentum we needed to eventually exit the pandemic stronger than we entered it.

Chapter 40
A Shot in the Arm

"We would do what we had to do for our graduates."

—Dr. Torrey Lawrence

S pring semester 2021 began with continued COVID-19 protocols, including the mandatory testing for all Moscow-based students (whether they lived on or off campus) by January 6 for the January 13 semester start date. The university expected registered students to attend in person or HyFlex unless they made arrangements with their professors to stay strictly online.

The university provided instructors with daily ineligibility lists for students who may have been ineligible to attend in-person classes. Not receiving test results back in enough time for class or not getting the mandatory COVID-19 test were just a few factors determining whether a student could physically attend class. The university encouraged instructors to work with students, but instructors were not required to provide long-term COVID-19 instructional accommodations outside the assigned course format. The administration asked students and employees to acknowledge an updated Healthy Vandal Pledge to agree to the expectations of keeping Vandals safe. The university scheduled a mid-semester re-test of all Moscow students (except those exempted by a prior positive test) after spring break.

As an incentive to get their COVID-19 tests, 50 students on the Moscow campus would receive a $100 VandalStore gift card if they met a specified deadline for getting the test. Those checking the testing lists would enter anyone who received a test before the deadline into a drawing.

This testing incentive program would foreshadow the vaccine incentive program offered in the fall.

The hype about vaccines started filtering through campus and everywhere else. Scott clearly stated the administration would not require vaccines to attend or work at the U of I. The university would not track who was vaccinated and advised supervisors not to ask employees about their vaccination status for any reason. It was a personal decision; however, the administration encouraged vaccinations. Scott received his vaccine and booster as soon as he was eligible. The university would remove students who received the vaccine from the random surveillance testing and required mid-semester re-test upon voluntary presentation of vaccination documentation.

The country's health-care providers and other priority responders were the first to receive the vaccine, but hope started to energize Vandals that the vaccine would become available soon for everyone. Again, communication was key to ensure every Vandal knew what the administration expected of them. Vice Provost for Student Affairs and Dean of Students Blaine Eckles hosted a vaccination question-and-answer session via Zoom with health-care professionals from Gritman Medical Center and Idaho Public Health so all students and employees were in the know.

Another energizing force on campus was, for the first time in Vandal football history, spring football. The road from a closed campus in March 2020 to playing football in spring 2021 presented an opportunity for Idaho Athletics to write its own playbook for navigating the unprecedented time.

"Terry [Gawlik] and the rest of the athletic department did a great job bringing the football players back during summer 2020, but they struggled with some COVID-19 cases among athletes in the fall," Scott remarked. "[Some students] couldn't help themselves when they attended parties or visited friends at WSU where everybody was sick, so we had some instances of a few spikes with the athletes that fall. But we learned a lot from the Athletic Department because they were the first to set up their own little bubble on campus."

Five months earlier, in August 2020, the Big Sky Conference's President's Council had voted to postpone the fall 2020 season to spring 2021 in the interest of student-athlete health and safety. "I'll admit, I was unhappy when the Big Sky voted to delay football to spring," Scott shared. "When they did that, I felt convinced that we probably wouldn't have a season at all."

But by November 2020, the conference had coordinated protocols with the schools who wanted to play a spring football season and announced the trimmed-down schedule. The U of I would play six spring games.

"Most teams stuck with the plan to safely play spring ball," Scott said. "I'm glad some did because I thought it was important for the student-athletes to get out there and play and compete."

"Eventually, the NCAA came up with an opt-out policy for student-athletes, but the majority of our football players came back," Athletic Director Terry Gawlik said. "They wanted to play."

Friday, January 29, 2021, brought on the pads and first official practice in the Kibbie Dome. Saturday, February 27, the season opened at the Dome against Eastern Washington University. A total of three home games in the Dome and three away games rounded out the spring 2021 season.

"It felt terrific to get out and play," Scott related. "It felt good for the students and to beat EWU. The excitement in the air was palpable. It was pretty emotional because it was another sign that things might get back to normal."

Vandal Football finished the spring with a 2–4 record. The other spring sports also took place with recognized COVID-19 protocols Vandal athletics put into place for the safety of their athletes. Again, testing was key.

But even with all the talk about how vital testing was to keep the university open, a small number of students enrolled in in-person classes remained untested. The administration informed them that they might restrict access to U of I online systems until the student provided proof of testing or unless an agreed-upon exemption existed. By February 1, an email from the president and provost informed students that the university would turn off access to education and service systems, including BbLearn, VandalWeb, Zoom, and Teams, by February 4 without proof of testing. This wasn't a threat; it was the follow-through necessary to respect all the other students, staff, and faculty who adhered to the safety measures. Still, a few students remained untested, regardless of the countless attempts by the university to communicate with them.

"How do you get people's attention today? You shut off their Internet," Provost Torrey Lawrence stated. "Those students couldn't log on to a campus system. In the end, there were some students who, frankly, had just left the building. They had checked out. They weren't hurting anybody; they just weren't doing any coursework. But we were spending all this time trying to track them down and help them, and unfortunately, they just disengaged from the university. It wasn't many but a few."

The U of I worked extensively with Idaho Public Health and Gritman Medical Center to provide large vaccination clinics to service the entire community, its students, and its employees. "One of the major collaborations between Gritman Medical Center and the U of I involved the ultracold refrigerator the U of I lent us to put in our pharmacy for the vaccine," shared Connie Osborn, Gritman nurse.

The Pfizer vaccine required an ultra-low temperature freezer for storage, so Gritman needed one to get the vaccines. "The U of I stepped up again and found ultracold freezers, not one but two," Connie smiled. "We put them in, and we got the vaccine. We started vaccinating on December 18, 2020, for first-line workers. We tried to do as much as we could within the hospital, but it started to overflow as the government opened more vaccination groups. It was one thing to vaccinate our frontline workers, employees, and medical staff, but as this was getting rolled out to the public, we knew we needed a bigger area to vaccinate, so we moved to the U of I's Rec Center."

Gritman CEO Kara Besst and Connie discussed whom they needed in a venue to vaccinate the masses. "It took Gritman Medical Center about twenty-four people to staff the clinics at the Rec Center," Connie continued. "We had six people to register and get consent forms signed, pharmacy techs drawing up and ordering the medication, twelve stations with nurses giving the vaccine, and then we had to monitor people who were vaccinated."

Vaccines first rolled out to the public for those 65 and over on February 18, 2021, with the Student Rec Center serving as Moscow's primary testing and vaccination site.

"The U of I was great because they used golf carts to help the people who had walkers and canes to get to the door," Connie observed. "It was the middle of winter; there was snow and ice. It was quite a production. We vaccinated on dates and times that were not the same as the COVID-19 swabbing. We gave over 13,000 vaccines. It was like clockwork from when we first got set up to where we gave our last clinic. We could have people in, consented, registered, and vaccinated in twenty to thirty minutes, and fifteen minutes of that was watching them for any reaction to the vaccine."

However, there was some confusion about the age restriction on the vaccine rollout. Several people under the age of 65 showed up for vaccination.

Scott explained, "Someone passed on a partial document, which made it look like vaccinations were fully open when the full document made it clear it was for a subset of the most vulnerable. This occurred possibly to create issues at the Rec Center. A few U of I employees showed up who got aggressive with Gritman Medical Center staff. One allegedly lifted her shirt to show her scars, apparently as evidence she was eligible for the vaccine. It really spoke to a lack of character, and I have incredible respect for the medical staff who stood up to them."

The week of March 1, the positivity rate lurched up a concerning 7.61 percent. Using contact tracing and wastewater sampling, the university identified incidents that seemed isolated to a few Greek chapters and, in partnership with public health, immediately put those houses into quarantine.

When the vaccine became available to everyone 16 years old and over in Idaho on April 5, 2021, a little over a year had passed since the U of I started down the extraordinary COVID-19 path. There was an encouraging vaccination rate among students. Notably, 400 U of I students traveled to Lewiston in April to get the one-dose Johnson and Johnson vaccine, even though the university didn't mandate vaccines. Special Assistant Toni Broyles helped organize the energized student group, taking another step toward keeping Vandals safe.

In an email dated April 5, 2021, just five weeks away from the end of the semester, Scott commended students, faculty, and staff for their exceptional response to the pandemic, "Thank you for continuing to keep your health and the health of those around you at the forefront of your decision-making."

At that point, the positive results rate stood at 1.16 percent, and the mandatory mid-semester re-test of in-person Moscow-based students produced only a 0.52 percent positive results rate. These numbers fell far below the national average of 5.1 percent of positive results as of April 1, 2021 (*New York Times* 2021).

Campus began making plans for the summer semester, including protocols for events and field camps that would take place; however, the U of I decided it would not perform mandatory COVID-19 testing on students for the summer session. Employees would return to their campus workspace as of July 1, unless they had an ongoing approved flexplace agreement or ADA accommodation. Things were starting to get back to normal, albeit a new normal.

Before the end of the spring semester, Scott also shared with campus the positive news about the finalization of the P3 deal with Plenary Americas USA Ltd., Sacyr Infrastructure USA LLC, and McKinstry, the three companies serving together as the concessionaire/operator in the 50-year lease of the U of I's steam plant. The $225 million up-front payment was the single largest financial transaction in the university's history. The monies resulted in the $6 million endowment to provide the university the dollars needed to invest in strategic growth.

The first initiative for P3 monies involved research. "We had about six or seven faculty in the first round of accessing P3 money because they successfully received federal grants," CALS Dean Michael Parrella said.

"If you don't have a federal grant, you don't have access to the [endowment] money. The U of I would invest a portion of the money where federal money was coming in. It would move us closer to becoming an R1 Research institution."

In May, the U of I family hosted six in-person—socially distanced and masked—Spring Commencements in Moscow, one at U of I Boise Center, and one at U of I Idaho Falls Center. U of I Coeur d'Alene Center graduates attended in Moscow due to the COVID-19 restrictions in Kootenai County.

The university invited the graduates from 2020 to the Spring Commencement ceremony since they couldn't have their commencement the year prior due to COVID-19. The additional ceremonies on campus required additional staffing and coordination, but the excitement of hosting in-person ceremonies brought volunteers together to make it happen for the classes of '21 and '20.

"I'm glad we did it and did it well," Torrey smiled. "I said I would do twenty ceremonies if we had to. I didn't care; we would do what we had to do for our graduates."

"We had a lot of students come back for Spring Commencement, which was great," Vice President for the Division of Finance and Administration Brian Foisy shared. "I felt very privileged because I had the opportunity to speak. Being a commencement speaker was one of the highlights of my professional career, especially with those two classes who survived COVID-19 to get there."

Scott smiled as he reflected. "May 15, 16, 18, and 19, 2021, were my best days since I became president. We had no idea what we were in for fourteen months prior when COVID-19 swept the world with a once-in-a-lifetime health crisis. Swift and comprehensive action allowed us to open in person in August, house students on campus, and provide the best experience possible in these circumstances."

Not only was it Spring Commencement, but it was also when Scott awarded the newly redesigned President's Medallion to the "heroes that helped us keep our community safe." The Pandemic Response Teams from the U of I and Gritman Medical Center received the medallions and celebrated at each of the commencement ceremonies (University of Idaho 2021).

"In a testament to an unshakable community spirit, dedicated employees of both organizations often put themselves in harm's way to allow U of I students access to a transformational in-person educational experience throughout the 2020–21 academic year," Scott stated during his presentation at commencement. "The U of I and Gritman Medical Center lab set the standard for others across the state, leading modeling efforts for Idaho

Scott conferred the President's Medallion upon five individuals during Spring Commencement 2021 for their efforts and sacrifice during the pandemic. Over 120 individuals also received a Commemorative President's Medallion for their collaborative and courageous leadership during the pandemic. U of I student Megan Biggs with support from U of I student Riley Merithew and their advisor, U of I Professor Delphine Keim, redesigned the medallion in the Spring of 2021.

SOURCE: Reprinted with permission from University of Idaho.

while allowing testing of every student ahead of in-person classes. The two institutions proved cooperation leads to successful results for the community as a whole."

The honor symbolized the dedication of more than 130 employees working within the COVID-19 response teams from the U of I and Gritman, who demonstrated commitment to putting people's well-being and their organization's mission first.

The U of I had also faced its financial situation, but, like dealing with COVID-19, they still had to remain vigilant. They'd far exceeded Scott's ask of cutting $14 million from the FY20 budget. The shutdown and hybrid teaching environments the previous spring brought fewer expenditures, which contributed to the university reaching its FY21 financial goals *despite* COVID-19.

"We were definitely spending less money due to COVID-19," College of Engineering Dean Larry Stauffer reflected. "We weren't traveling to conferences or alumni events. Our fundraising continued, and our engineering outreach enrollments held fairly well because those students weren't on campus anyway."

By late spring, Brian and Scott determined that there would be a surplus of about $17.5 million because of the incredible efforts of faculty and staff.

There was still the net reserve issue on the balance sheet, but Scott recognized his Vandals needed a morale booster. Taking care of his Vandal tribe and family was his focus. The U of I would address the SBOE-required 5 percent net reserve balance issue, just not yet. Scott wrote a letter to the SBOE requesting that the university use a portion of the surplus to return the mandatory furlough payments to each faculty and staff member in the form of an incentive payment.

"Employees who were still on the books as of a certain date received incentive payments equal to the salary lost via the mandatory furlough," said Trina Mahoney, assistant vice president, University Budget and Planning.

"It was the right thing to do," Scott stated. "Morale started to turn on campus because we got our financial house in order, returned the furlough amounts as an incentive payment, and made it through the pandemic pretty much unscathed. All that was hard on everybody, but people started feeling optimistic. They saw we could do incredible things."

Just about the time everyone thought the U of I was actually righting the financial ship under leadership keeping the numbers in the black, during the spring 2021 legislative session, state lawmakers cut an additional $500,000 out of the U of I's FY22 budget to address alleged indoctrination programs at the U of I. The accusation by a group named Idaho Freedom Foundation (IFF) set in motion a series of moves that would culminate in a showdown at the Joint-Finance-Appropriations Committee (JFAC) hearings during the next legislative session.

Scott summarized, "IFF did us a favor. They didn't just accuse us of indoctrinating students; they published a 'research report' documenting the allegations. Any educated person reading the report could see the research was deeply flawed and incredibly biased. They picked and chose facts to construct a narrative, ignoring facts that did not support their point of view. It was a political hack job, and they just handed us the proof."

Regardless, the U of I faced yet another hit to the budget to the tune of $500,000.

Scott's Management Insight

Celebrate progress against your goals whenever the chance arises. Returning furlough and taking the time to recognize all the campus did to keep COVID-19 at bay made all students and employees feel like part of a winning team. Awarding the President's Medallion to over 130 people was unprecedented, but it really meant something to the team that stood up to the naysayers and delivered us safely across the finish line.

Be patient and avoid responding emotionally to provocations. Generally, we ignored the IFF and other provocateurs, but their false narratives started gaining traction in the legislature. Fortunately, they had given us the work performed that was the basis for their accusations, and it was terrible work. They had given us all we needed to respond at a place and time of our choosing. That would be at the JFAC meeting at the next legislative session.

Chapter 41
Conflict Entrepreneurs

"They have their sights set on dismantling public education at all levels. . ."
—*Scott Green*

It was going to be tough. It was going to be tight. The already-razor-thin line between positive and negative hung in the balance with JFAC's $500,000 budget cut for FY22. Scott decided to cover the one-time loss out of general funds rather than going back to the colleges.

"Thankfully, we have a lot of friends in the legislature, so the cut could've been worse," Scott reflected.

The Idaho House of Representatives voted down the first FY22 proposed budgets for Idaho higher education institutions, including the U of I, sending a loud and clear message to purge "social justice" and "indoctrination" programs from their campuses. That move extended the regular session in the spring of 2021. The debate ended with the legislature passing the final budgets with $500,000 cuts to the U of I and Idaho State University (ISU) and $1.5 million to Boise State University (BSU). Lewis Clark State College (LCSC) received an additional $400,000 for its budget. (After the cut, the FY22 Gen Ed budget for the U of I totaled $176.7 million, including state funding and tuition.) Some—including Scott—argued the cuts were a direct consequence of the Idaho Freedom Foundation's (IFF) drive to eliminate any points of view in Idaho's schools with which they did not agree. They alleged the U of I, BSU, and ISU, had an "indoctrination program" on "critical race theory" (Idaho Freedom Foundation 2022; Green, personal communication).

Ironically, at that point in time, the Idaho Legislature had not officially defined the terms "social justice," "indoctrination," and "critical race theory" (Freeman, personal communication).

IFF is a 501(c)(3) group established as a self-described "state-focused, free-market think tank dedicated to Idaho issues." It defines itself as a "watchdog against government waste and marketplace intervention" and exists to advance Libertarian principles—limited government, free markets, and self-reliance. Many would argue that IFF created a rift within the Idaho Republican Party between more traditional Republicans and far-right Libertarians running as Republicans.

"Some said IFF started out doing good work," Scott elaborated. "But somewhere along the way, they got drunk on their own power, and it became solely about fundraising. They broke the rules of their ideology when it was to their benefit, such as taking government handouts. They also spun tales so outrageous that they worked their base into a frenzy. The more outrageous the tale, the more fear they could manufacture and the more money they would raise.

"IFF members are 'conflict entrepreneurs,'" Scott continued. "They create conflict and raise money around those consequences. They survived and enriched themselves; they didn't care about the truth. They wouldn't let the facts get in the way of a good narrative. They freely admitted they didn't believe that any public money should go into higher education. They didn't believe in government support, yet they took one of the forgivable loans from the CARES Act during COVID-19, which seemed contradictory to their preaching. Clearly, they didn't adhere to Libertarian principles; they didn't believe what they were saying. They were extremists who only cared about raising money and personal gain, regardless of the cost to the citizens of Idaho."

When Scott first moved back to Idaho in June 2019, he heard about IFF and that it was a conservative group. That didn't matter to him. He could work with both sides of the aisle. Scott researched the group and saw how they had been helping seed the Republican Party's central committees with like-minded people. The Republican Party in Idaho has a closed primary, and many Republican voters traditionally didn't turn out for the primaries. The low voter turnout allowed people on the extreme right to get on the ticket for the fall elections because groups like IFF made sure their members turned out to vote during the primary for the extremist candidates who aligned with their extremist agenda.

Scott agreed to meet with one of the founders of IFF, Wayne Hoffman, because Wayne's son attended the U of I. "I really didn't want to talk politics, but as a parent," Scott shared, "I'm always happy to meet to talk about someone's son's or daughter's experience at the U of I. But then Wayne launched into all this equity and diversity stuff once he was there. He also railed against the Confucius Institute. I did my best to listen because I didn't have much to say regarding politics."

The U of I was getting rid of its Confucius Institute, but Scott didn't mention that to Wayne because it was premature to announce the change. Scott was getting rid of the Institute for a lot of different reasons. "I was concerned about relying on a foreign country to fund a continuing program and thought we could do better with a larger Asian Studies program," Scott pointed out.

During that conversation, it became clear that the IFF was only interested in the information that suited their narrative and beliefs but not necessarily the entire story. They claimed to perform research, but it was more about marketing the information they chose to share rather than presenting facts. Some of the marketing materials aimed explicitly at the U of I, BSU, and ISU stated the institutions were indoctrination camps for the left.

"Any reasonable person, if they just stopped and thought about it for two seconds, would realize that 71 percent of the U of I's students were from Idaho," Scott pointed out. "If people considered Idaho's population, they would realize there was no way for the U of I to lean radical left. We had one of the most moderate campuses in the country, and if anything, we were more conservative than most campuses. Moscow is diverse, representing the entire political spectrum. It elected Republicans and Democrats to represent their legislative district. The community is great at respectfully debating issues."

Scott knew IFF was a 501(c)(3) and lobbied under the guise of helping Idaho. They put incredible pressure on legislators, yet they were a tax-exempt organization. "You're not allowed to maintain substantial lobby activities as a 501(c)(3), but the IRS seemed to have no interest in following up on IFF's lobbying activities whatsoever," he said. "IFF continues to be a danger to our society. They don't want to get involved in actually improving higher education; rather, they want to see higher education destroyed and lobby against anything they disagree with in the system. That really showed me the kind of people they were. They have their sights set on dismantling public education at all levels and are very clever and not shy at all about that objective. One only has to look at what IFF-backed board members did to harm North Idaho College by putting their accreditation at risk."

Scott continued, "They put out a lot of half-truths and then built stories around them. We're not Oral Roberts University, but we're not New College of Florida, either. The U of I has been a fairly balanced institution since its inception. Even the *Princeton Review*, a completely independent source, ranked the U of I Law School as one of the most conservative in the nation."

When a right-leaning U of I student recorded a Common Read at the U of I College of Law on anti-racism and shared the audio, the IFF promoted it as evidence of indoctrination but failed to report that the Federal Society also gave a presentation with the other point of view regarding the problems with critical race theory (CRT). That did not fit IFF's narrative.

"Some people said they didn't agree with that choice for a Common Read," Scott said. "But in a university and educational setting, you don't have to agree with everything taught. I've often told legislators that the U of I taught me about Karl Marx and communist economics, but they also taught me about John Maynard Keynes, Milton Friedman, and Adam Smith. As a college student, I developed my own opinion coming out of that. I learned to debate the pros and cons of each of those systems. I could have an intelligent conversation about it and, importantly, conduct business around the world, regardless of the economic system present in the market.

"Furthermore, and to the point of the College of Law's choice for the Common Read," Scott continued, "wouldn't you want your lawyer—if they're going to defend you properly—to understand and prepare for what the other side would argue on any issue? I know I would, and I worked in the legal profession a long time."

The primary goal of the U of I is to quell ignorance, show all sides, and allow freedom of thought in its student body. The university is in business to promote a well-rounded education and afford students the opportunity to hear both sides of every argument, and if the faculty member, staff member, or student inappropriately shamed another's point of view, follow a process to deal with it. "There was a lot of tolerance on campus," Scott pointed out. "People understood that everyone had a right to free speech whether they agreed with it or not."

The lies by omission or fabrication prompted Scott to send a memo to U of I stakeholders about IFF promoting half-truths to directly impact higher education funding by the Idaho Legislature. "I sent a communication to our alumni and advisory boards calling out the false narratives presented by IFF and the impact on the legislative budget process," Scott said. "It's fair to say that it not only opened the eyes of our alumni to what was happening, but because the media picked up the memo, it also awakened many citizens of Idaho. It was a warning shot intended to send a message that the U of I was not like our sister institutions; we were not afraid to speak the truth in the public square. But IFF was too arrogant to get the message. Their response was predictable. They bullied legislators who did not comply and painted me as some left-wing radical, yet another falsehood, one of a continual stream that was starting to chip away at their credibility" (Green, personal communication).

"Republicans used to be so great with education," Scott reflected. "The U of I exists because President Lincoln, a Republican, signed the Morrill Act. The Republican Party in Idaho has lost its way due to the libertarian extremists. Half-truths aren't truths. It's scary; it's like the Salem Witch Trials. You've got conflict entrepreneurs feeding legislators' fear based on highly inaccurate claims."

Scott laid it out to the Idaho State Legislature in a highly strategic move during his annual budget presentation to lawmakers in January 2022. He didn't mince words.

"In short, the entire social justice narrative on which the University of Idaho was penalized $500,000 for FY22 was a false narrative created by conflict entrepreneurs who make their living sowing fear and doubt with legislators and voters," he stated.

When Rep. Ron Nate, R-Rexburg, asked about the previous fiscal year's reduction with the intent that the U of I would eliminate spending on diversity, equity, and social justice programming and what steps the university had taken, Scott responded with solid answers. The U of I had hired Hawley Troxell, one of Idaho's powerhouse law firms, to conduct an independent review of House Bill (HB) 377 (2021) and HB 387 (2021). HB 377 prohibited indoctrination of students in Idaho's public education system; HB 387 specifically stated the $500,000 FY21 holdback was for the state to remove funding for social justice programming at the U of I, along with sister institutions BSU and ISU (Russell 2022).

Scott respectfully pointed out that HB 377 protected academic freedom and freedom of speech, thus protecting "Idaho's colleges and universities from government making decisions about what can and cannot be taught." He also pointed out that no one can "require students to affirm, adopt, or adhere to any specific belief." In short, HB377 takes away the tool of indoctrination.

He then shared that was why, in keeping with Idaho law, the U of I hired the law firm Hawley Troxell for the independent investigation into the allegations that surfaced in part from a document written by

IFF titled "Social Justice in Idaho Higher Education," by Scott Yenor and Anna Miller.

"In other words, the university asked Hawley Troxell to conduct an independent investigation under the professional code of conduct and make recommendations on how we can become most compliant," Scott told JFAC. "I quote the conclusions of the investigation verbatim here: 'After conducting our investigation, we were unable to substantiate the conclusions contained within the IFF report, including the allegations of the University of Idaho having a systemic commitment to forcing social justice ideology upon its students.'"

Conversation and debate went on for a while between lawmakers and Scott, but in the end, Scott was thoroughly prepared and shot down any claims of the U of I wrongdoing. Ultimately, Scott made a public record of shooting down every point IFF tried to make regarding the U of I and a nonexistent indoctrination program. He even made Hawley Troxell's report public for anyone to read.

Many supporters of higher education in Idaho also see IFF as a threat to education in the state. "This is the issue of our day," Scott stated. "It really is. Groups like IFF are a threat to higher education in Idaho, and that's because of the politics. My advice to the Republicans in the state is to take back your party; you have an extremist problem."

Scott believes the U of I must keep putting its message out and restating the facts. "Look up the studies," Scott challenged. "A college education helps you become healthier, wealthier, and wiser. If someone earns a college degree, they will make $1.2 million more in their lifetime, live nine years longer on average, be more involved in their community, and be happier."

Scott's Management Insight

Don't underestimate or fail to find time to address the new threats emerging while you are down. Be prepared to take them on, even if the threat has not fully developed. Those that will do or say anything to enrich themselves, advance their political agenda, or both, are dangerous. A college president must stay out of politics, but if a false narrative gains momentum, threatening the institution, a president must challenge narratives about their institution. You can let others take on the conflict entrepreneurs directly, such as businesses, the media, and political rivals. Your job is to tell the truth, protect your institution, and continue the mission of educating the next generation.

Scott's Third Rail

Politics

In the book *Lessons Learned: Reflections of a University President*, former Princeton University President William G. Bowen cautions that a university should avoid getting involved in politics and counsel neutrality. For Princeton, that meant staying neutral during the Vietnam War. Purdue University President Mitch Daniels, the former Governor of the State of Indiana, also pledged to keep politically neutral during his tenure. Wise words, but if you are a public institution, there are times when you will be dragged into someone else's political fight (Bowen, 2010).

During the pandemic, masking became political, with the far right wanting to outlaw mandatory masking, despite its proven effectiveness. On the left, you had those calling for the complete closure of the economy, despite the financial damage that would do to the nation's households. During this period, the U of I made decisions based on advice from our health-care partners at Gritman Medical Center and our public health officials. These experts green-lighted our plans to open, and we made masking mandatory to keep the virus in check. The other public four-year institutions in the state also followed suit by remaining safely open and masked. So we were open and masked, angering both the left and the right on the political spectrum but doing what was right for our institution while traveling with like-minded peers and fulfilling our mission to educate people.

During this period, based on a report prepared by the Idaho Freedom Foundation (IFF), a relatively effective group of conflict entrepreneurs accused the University of Idaho of indoctrinating its students as part of a leftist agenda. In the absence of a response, many representatives in the legislature believed the false narratives contained in the document. The IFF was effective at getting the legislature to cut our budget by $500,000, a relatively small amount given the Governor's holdback and the budget cuts we had undertaken at the university to close our budget deficits, but nevertheless unwelcome. The legislature also turned back $18 million in badly needed federal aid for early preschool programs under an intentional deception from the

(Continued)

(Continued)

very same group. They claimed that the money was tied to teaching these very young children critical race theory. It would have been funny if not for some of our legislators believing it.

We risked the fabrications about the U of I indoctrinating students becoming a fact in the minds of our legislature if we did not respond with the truth. Therefore, we hired a highly regarded Idaho law firm to independently investigate the claims. Their investigation completely exonerated the university and turned the tide on IFF's baseless accusations.

We also had to wade into politics when a memo providing guidance to a new, highly restrictive abortion law that went into effect in Idaho was posted on Reddit and quickly became an Internet sensation. Our General Counsel's office, at the request of numerous employees, issued some guidance on the new law, and under the rubric of "no good deed goes unpunished," they shot the messenger. Some faculty saw the guidance as a mandate or policy change impacting their academic freedom. That was not true, but that erroneous depiction spread like a virus, with even the president of the United States politicizing and repeating the false information, even after the record had been corrected. Our PR team pitched an interview with our provost to a respected Associated Press journalist, no strings attached, just to present the truth. That interview began to turn the tide, particularly with the revelation that we were not the only Idaho university struggling to provide similar guidance to its employees. We followed it with an internal memo correcting the record. One week later, the issue had passed, and we were back to business as usual, but not before one more salvo from inside the university.

Rolling Stone magazine interviewed a few faculty and students for a well-written and balanced article. At one point, however, the interviewer asked a question about our clarifying memo. One faculty member said it was helpful and welcome; the other, rather than recognizing that we were validating feelings around the subject and trying to correct the record, somehow determined that we had called her and others "a bunch of hysterical feminists." While in my opinion, a reader must use kaleidoscope glasses and employ deep magical thinking to twist our words into an insult directed at our faculty, the reality is that there are those in every organization who own those glasses and capabilities and will not be open to seeing your actions as you intended them. Just like those few individuals who claimed we were trying to kill them by opening the university during the COVID-19 pandemic, your time and university resources are better spent focusing on those faculty and employees who are respected by and carry great weight with their peers and are moving your institution forward rather than engaging the rock throwers. We never have enough time for our brightest and good-intentioned employees, and they are the ones who are the true fabric of your university and will carry the day.

The age-old adage to avoid politics is still good advice. But if you are dragged into someone else's fight, first, find allies to travel as part of a herd. Then, if necessary, find credible third parties to make the argument for you. Once the independent law firm released its report and the truth was revealed, the vast majority of legislators discounted what they heard from IFF. IFF's credibility began to wane. Once an AP journalist reported that the legal guidance in question was asked for by our faculty so they could protect themselves, that it was only guidance, not a mandate, and that we were not the only Idaho institution offering similar guidance, the tide began to turn and the vitriol dissipated.

Chapter 42

Every Challenge Has a Silver Lining

"Strangely enough, COVID-19 helped us in ways that you might find odd."
—Terry Gawlik

From the moment Scott heard about COVID-19 and determined it might become a threat to the U of I, he knew there had to be a way for his alma mater to get through it—not get around it, not ignore it, not hide from it, but get through it. He knew they would because they'd already started to make incredible strides in cutting budgets in an unprecedented way. Those actions showed that the faculty, staff, and students still believed in themselves and the U of I's mission. But it took COVID-19 for everyone to pull together and put that belief into action.

It took tremendous courage to pull off what the Vandal family did during COVID-19. Throughout the process—overcoming the shellshock, pivoting to online learning in a matter of days, setting up the testing centers and labs, and opening the campus safely for face-to-face learning—the culture and morale saw a positive uptick. Faculty, staff, students, and stakeholders were more comfortable and reassured with Scott because of his bold actions and positive outcomes.

"The COVID-19 job was great," Seth Vieux shared. "It was difficult and frustrating and stressful and maddening at times. When I took the job, I had just retired from the Army after twenty-one years. I took off my uniform on a Friday and showed up Monday in Vandal gear. It wasn't like my previous life, but I stepped into a great team with an important mission to fulfill. We had strong leadership that had a vision. Before I took the job,

I needed to know that Scott had a plan and that the plan aligned with keeping the university afloat. The most important thing for me taking the job was believing that was Scott's goal, pulling the U of I through everything."

"There was an element of making choices that we would survive through this," Provost Torrey Lawrence said. "Survive as people but also as an institution. We had discussions about what would happen if only half the students came back when we reopened. That was not a discussion anybody wanted to have. The provost's area had seen massive financial cuts like we had never experienced, and all of a sudden, we had to look at COVID-19. People's lives were more important than money, and that was a challenge to focus on both. Some critics only focused on one or the other. I was trying to keep 2400 people employed and 10,000+ students still going to school."

In its entire history, the university had rarely asked Vandals to isolate themselves from each other (they did during the Spanish Flu outbreak in 1918). "We opened in the fall of 2020, but we didn't have our traditional Week of Welcome events or many ways to connect students," Dean of Students Blaine Eckles shared. "So when we opened in the fall, we increased our engagement programs to try to connect students while also still navigating a pandemic."

For example, Megan Kingsley, a freshman from Nampa, hit campus in the fall of 2020 knowing no one. But she took a chance on a video gaming event hosted by the Office of Student Engagement—which put incredible thought into how to connect students amid the pandemic. By the night's end, Megan found a cohort. The next night this new group of friends walked together to the Screen on the Green movie and hung out together—fast friends and forever touched by the Vandal family (University of Idaho 2021).

Blaine's staff at Student Affairs created other unique events, like Vandal Airlines, which hosted students at a paper airplane contest in the Kibbie Dome and a glow-stick dance party. Students started to feel more engaged and connected in as safe an environment as possible. There was the worry of hosting a "super-spreader" event, but with masking and the other protocols, the U of I could create these relationship-building opportunities without seeing spikes in positive COVID-19 cases.

Torrey expressed one big silver lining: COVID-19 mobilized the nation's university and college networks and organizations. "We all took advantage of Zoom," he said. "I attended Zooms with different organizations, like the Association of American Public and Land-grant Universities, to discuss what we were doing with research and classes. We shared a lot and tried to stay connected to see if we could learn from what others were doing."

Many silver linings to COVID-19 revealed themselves, including:

- The U of I was a national leader in establishing a CLIA-certified lab to process COVID-19 testing in 12–48 hours. This fast turnaround time gave the U of I and the community an edge over the spread of COVID-19. Gritman and the U of I administered over 42,000 free tests to students and employees, and a robust surveillance testing program ensured the identification of asymptomatic Vandals to stave off the spread of the virus.

- The success of being able to open for the fall semester saved the U of I from a potential financial disaster, but more than that, the U of I and Gritman Medical Center went to extreme lengths to provide a safe environment for the entire Vandal family and Moscow-area community. "Having that testing lab was our biggest differentiator," Special Assistant, Strategic Initiatives Toni Broyles stated. "That was because Scott got out months ahead of everybody. Because we started in April, we were able to be up and operational and ready to go for the fall semester. We were the only school anywhere in Idaho that required testing for all in-person students. Not only did it help the U of I, but the testing was also used by the Moscow community and helped local commerce stay open, as well."

- The U of I was better positioned to offer hybrid learning, doubled the number of technology classrooms, upgraded all those classrooms, and got faculty, staff, and students set up to securely work from home. Vice President for IT and CIO Dan Ewart shared, "In a matter of days, my team figured out how to get this institution online and have Vandals work from home. And they came up with the most creative solutions. They reached out to other institutions and leveraged what they knew, and those institutions leveraged what we knew. And we got it done."

- The university cut an unprecedented amount out of its budget, including an additional $500,000 for FY22. COVID-19 allowed all the colleges and units to save money on travel and other operational costs, which helped during the budget-cutting process. "I set aggressive targets for financial cuts," Scott stated. "I never sugar-coated it. It was hard, but the campus community exceeded expectations despite the pandemic."

- The university saw its best fundraising year in history, with $54 million donated to the "Brave. Bold. A Promise to Idaho Students" campaign. People had time to consider how to help their alma mater through the tough times, but they also believed in leadership. "Scott Green's presidency helped every aspect of fundraising and moved the university forward," Mary Kay McFadden, vice president for University Advancement, pointed out. "[FY20–21] was our most successful fundraising year, even amidst COVID-19." That effort was followed by another record fundraising year in FY21–22 of $64 million.

- The number of research grant submissions increased dramatically, leading to some significant awards coming out of COVID-19, including a $50 million USDA grant for climate-smart agriculture; it was the largest grant in the U of I's history.

- Gritman Medical Center continued to offer COVID-19 testing through a new shipping-container-turned-drive-through site to provide a quick turnaround for results. "We started using that location to test the public after we dismantled the COVID-19 lab in the hospital," Gritman CEO Kara Besst shared. "Instead of patients coming to the clinics and hospital with COVID-19 symptoms, we have this location to test them and then direct them to the best care if they are positive."

- The budget office continued to meet bi-weekly with the academic fiscal officers to maintain the rigors of monitoring budgets. Scott continued to meet with deans and unit leaders regularly (but less frequently as the process took hold) regarding budgets since the reporting and monitoring systems had become more routine rather than cumbersome.

- New online programming from Alumni Relations continued. "It's such a great way to engage alumni worldwide," Assistant Vice President Kathy Barnard shared. "Cup of Joe focuses on cool alumni. People were home more, so we came up with trivia and the cooking classes to give the family something to do. It seemed to work once we started it and got in the groove."

- The College of Education, Health, and Human Sciences (CEHHS) Student Research Symposium that sprang out of COVID-19 as a way for students to showcase their scholarly projects expanded to include high school students sharing their senior projects. The college increased the prize money by adding scholarships to the mix and had four incoming students in fall 2022 who received awards because of their presentations at the symposium.

- Drawing from his field of Movement Sciences within CEHHS, Interim Dean Philip Scruggs created a document addressing workplace well-being and wellness. He introduced it to his college and then shared the concepts with others, including the provost and president. He encouraged faculty and staff to reflect upon their workplace environment and how they could engage in wellness and well-being during their workday. "When someone is well, they're more productive and a better colleague," he said. "Job retention and sustainability are also better. It's individualized and not required. I consider it part of the workday if you need to take time to refocus or reset." He suggested that type of self-care should be an accepted practice in the workplace. "There's a physical component to wellness, but also social, emotional, and mental pieces." The document was well received by CEHHS faculty and staff.

- "One of the real successes that the College of Engineering had was with the Engineering Expo," Dean John Crepeau expressed. "We'd had to cancel our live, in-person Engineering Expo and take it online. Our tech team helped set up Zoom sessions where students would make a formal presentation about their project and receive feedback from faculty and industry partners." John pointed out that when Engineering Expo happened in person, the student would make a presentation to around four or five people and a few judges. "There'd maybe be a girlfriend or boyfriend or mom," he shared, "but that's about it. We found when we did the Expo via Zoom, we had 40 to 50 people participating in the groups. We learned a lot from that; we give presentations live now, but also have an online forum so more people can participate."

- Idaho Athletics started rebuilding a new way of doing business to enhance their relationship with campus, boosters, and other stakeholders. "I was trying to figure out how to organize the athletic department so that I could start to focus more on my duties as Athletic Director," Terry Gawlik shared. "Strangely enough, COVID-19 helped us in ways you might find odd. Having all these Zoom calls made our staff closer. We could write a whole book about that. But one of the big things was getting people to trust me. Many people, especially coaches, didn't like change, didn't embrace it, and a lot of people, particularly coaches, didn't like being told what to do. So for the first time, these coaches were being guided differently by incentivizing them. We have made progress, but I'm never satisfied, and we will continue to build on our solid base."

- The College of Business and Economics (CBE) worked to expand access to the U of I and CBE education by leveraging lessons learned during COVID-19. They worked to develop a fully online bachelor of business administration program (approved by the SBOE in 2022). "After delivering courses both in-person and via Zoom during the pandemic, faculty in those disciplines chose to continue to offer their courses through a delivery mode that made them available to students and prospective students outside of Moscow," CBE Dean Marc Chopin expressed. "Those efforts will result in synergies across our degrees. Coordinating and developing courses for online delivery will be an ongoing effort in our college."

University leadership dedicated significant resources to encourage students to get vaccinated throughout the 2021–22 academic year. The President's Office, Provost's Office, and Dean of Students Office pledged funds to create a vaccine incentive program that provided $50 gift cards to the VandalStore or Idaho Eats to any student who submitted voluntary proof of completed vaccination. All enrolled students, full- or part-time, undergraduate, or graduate, were eligible for a gift card. In addition, throughout the fall 2021 semester, full-time students who submitted proof of vaccination were entered into weekly drawings of $1,000 in tuition credits and two drawings of $5,000, one to kick off and one to end the semester. The vaccine incentive program continued during spring 2022, with seven additional $1,000 weekly tuition credit drawings.

After the completion of the spring semester, the university decided not to require COVID-19 testing for in-person Moscow students unless there was an uptick in positive cases; the costs associated with that would've been prohibitive unless non-federal funds came into play. Home test kits and the Gritman Medical Center testing facility were readily available by then. The summer ended with no mask mandates in place. Thankfully, students were adaptive, and the new normal still offered a robust residential campus experience at the U of I, with myriad social activities amid the rigors of getting an education.

Regarding the controversy about opening the university in the fall of 2020 amid the pandemic, there were (and will always be) two camps, but one started getting smaller. "In the beginning, the faculty were like, 'Oh, my gosh, no, we can't do this. This is dangerous,'" Kathy shared. "There were a lot of them saying, 'You're trying to kill us all.' By this point, I would bet 99 percent of the faculty would say, 'Wow, we did that.' And we did, successfully."

"The student experience was impacted much more significantly by COVID-19 than through the budgetary cuts," Dean of Students Blaine Eckles said. "Quite frankly, I'm proud of our decisions; we didn't make every perfect decision by any stretch. Hindsight is 20/20. It will take a long time to see how COVID-19 affects alumni involvement, donor response from the 'COVID-19 Class' of students, student recruitment and retention, and most importantly, student mental health."

Unfortunately, the University of Idaho wasn't the only institution of higher education seeing spikes in student mental health issues during COVID. In a study by Shubham Goswami, Saujanya Chakraborty, and Sudip Pal in January 2022, relatively high rates of anxiety, depression, post-traumatic stress disorder, and stress were reported among the students during the COVID-19 pandemic in the US, along with several other countries. Although student mental health issues have been on the rise since 2013, the pandemic created difficult situations for students due to lockdowns, social distancing, masking mandates, and even the ability to provide mental health services (Goswami, Chakraborty, and Pal 2022).

"We saw vestiges of challenges with students having been reclusive," Blaine shared. "While the numbers in our counseling center didn't go up significantly, the acuity level spiked. It was hard to directly tie that right to COVID-19—it was more ancillary. But the isolation, the despondency, was exacerbated. We don't know what this will look like in the long run. There is no simple fix for mental health."

At the end of the spring 2022 semester, the U of I celebrated by holding in-person commencements. The main campus came through the pandemic open to live instruction without a single case of COVID-19 traced to a classroom or lab, financially solvent, and well-positioned for a future free of COVID-19. Finally, things seemed to be settling in with a new definition of normal that gave hope to a university on the rise.

And then darkness struck.

Scott's Management Insight

There is a silver lining to every challenge. Allow colleagues to think through solutions and empower and encourage them to act on them. Thanks to the entire Vandal family's hard work and innovative energy, we emerged stronger as an institution than how we entered the pandemic. We now view ourselves as not just a survivor but a "university on the rise."

Be prepared to let go of the sunk cost of previous investments to go where the data takes you. If a variant is more contagious, making testing ineffective (and being replaced by rapid tests), pivot and focus on where the investment can still pay dividends—vaccines. We did not require vaccines but provided incentives that resulted in a high vaccine rate and put COVID-19 on its back foot.

Smart Collaboration

COVID-19 Research

"We have a large grant on our campus run by Distinguished Professor Dr. Carolyn Hovde Bohach through INBRE (IDeA Network of Biomedical Research Excellence)," explained Barrie Robison, IBEST director. "We worked with Carolyn to get a $737,000 one-year supplement to that grant from the National Institutes of Health to sequence the genomes of all the samples we tested in our COVID-19 lab."

(Continued)

(Continued)

The research will examine the dynamics of a town and a transient student population and the university's mandatory testing of that student population. What strains of COVID-19 did they bring into the community? How did the strains spread to the community or not, and vice versa? Gritman processed almost 45,000 COVID-19 tests, with 36,000 of those through the U of I lab (they sent other tests to third-party labs until the U of I could get the joint lab going). Gritman kept 4000 positive results in their freezers for research opportunities.

"The university will look at the significance of collecting specimens from some of the same population at different times, like all students at the beginning of each semester when they returned from breaks," Gritman CIO Kane Francetich explained. "It's a unique population in that sense." Scientific Reports published the paper describing the sequencing on May 16, 2023 (Andrews, K.R., New, D.D., Gour, D.S., et al. 2023).

Another research study showing COVID-19-infected mothers' breast milk provides infants with antibodies. Dr. Michelle K. "Shelley" McGuire, professor and director of the Margaret Ritchie School of Family and Consumer Sciences, led the study along with University of Rochester Medical Center colleague Dr. Antti E. Seppo. The report expanded earlier findings that showed the milk of breastfeeding women infected with COVID-19 did not contain the virus (University of Idaho 2021). The team included researchers from the U of I, Washington State University, and other institutions. The journal Frontiers in Immunology *published its report in December 2021.*

The study was important because those antibodies remained elevated in most of the women for up to two months, which added confidence that mothers should continue to breastfeed even if they have COVID-19.

Scott's Management Insight

Well-researched, brave, and bold moves can produce their intended results and spur unintended benefits. Evidence again of the virtuous circle. By opening a lab, opportunities for grant money surfaced. The U of I's lab captured data that helped us manage the virus, keep it at bay, and learn what defenses worked and what did not as the virus mutated and spread. At the right time, we pivoted to administering and incenting vaccines.

Chapter 43
When Evil Visits Your Campus

"It was one of the most powerful moments I've witnessed. It was like a warm hug for the families."

—*Brenda Helbling*

Scott's Note: I debated with myself and others in my administration how to deal with the horrendous crisis that hit the University of Idaho, Moscow, the surrounding area, and the Vandal family on November 13, 2022. It certainly was something no one saw coming. After many careful and thoughtful discussions, I knew it fell to me to share the university's response to one of the darkest events in the institution's history. I also knew including a chapter in this book would be difficult; the situation was recent and still felt raw. It will for a long time. But this book is about telling the U of I's story and how to deal with situations, good, bad, or otherwise. Temple and I included this chapter to speak to the greater good of helping others manage through a similar situation with the hope no one ever has to refer to this part of U of I's story. We've outlined many critical lessons the institution learned when responding to the needs of students, staff, and faculty in the aftermath while remaining empathetic to the families of Xana, Ethan, Maddie, and Kaylee. We dedicate this chapter to them. There is not a day that goes by that I don't think about those four incredible Vandals.

—*Scott*

* * *

Sunday, November 13, 2022, started like any other Sunday, a day of rest for Scott. Weather-wise, it was a strange weekend, with the temperatures fluctuating widely on the Palouse for that time of year.

Scott had settled in at University House with a game of football on TV and thoughts of the upcoming fall recess and Thanksgiving only a week away. But as he watched the competition unfold on the screen before him, something just felt off—not with the game but in general. He wasn't sure what it was, but something was nagging at him.

Lee Espey's day started as a relaxing Sunday at home across town. Lee was the division operations officer for Finance and Administration at the U of I. "I woke up, spent time doing chores around the house, went on a run, and after cleaning up, had settled in to watch a basketball game."

Shortly after noon, Lee's phone rang. "I received a call from Jake Nichols, U of I executive director of Public Safety and Security. The only words that came out of his mouth were, 'Have you heard what's going on?' When I told him I hadn't, he informed me that there had been an incident on King Road. 'A quadruple homicide, likely students.' Jake informed me that he was out of town but heading this way, and I suggested that I go and start setting up a command center at the U of I Administration Building until he and others could arrive."

Lee knew it fell to him to inform and gather the Vandal tribe immediately. He called Scott. No answer. He quickly sent a text which prompted Scott to instantly call—a phone call all presidents fear. That fateful Sunday, just before 1:00 p.m., Scott learned of the tragic and brutal murders of four people in Moscow at a home on King Road near the U of I campus.

"The call was short," Lee said. "I let him know the plan to set up the command post, and he agreed to head to the Administration Building."

Vice Provost of Student Affairs and Dean of Students Blaine Eckles was preparing to go to Costco with his wife. Just before noon, he received an alert on his phone about an unconscious individual at a residence on King Road. "My protocol for stuff like that is that I don't do anything proactive because police or security is responding. They know to call me when and if it's an emergency."

That call came when Blaine was in the parking lot at Costco. Campus Captain Tyson Berrett from the Moscow Police Department (MPD) informed Blaine that four individuals were found dead and believed to be college-aged, most likely murdered. "I just couldn't wrap my head around what was going on," Blaine recalled.

He immediately contacted Provost Torrey Lawrence and Scott, while his phone buzzed and chimed with dozens of notifications. His wife drove them back to Moscow as he handled the onslaught of calls and texts. Once back in Moscow, he headed to incident command on campus.

The news that the victims were most likely killed only hours before and found dead in a house just off campus in an area where students frequently rented apartments would go viral in a matter of minutes, blowing up social media. The news and speculation sowed fear into the community and, despite the emotional toll, thrust the university into high gear to be at the top of its game and stay there.

Lee contacted the U of I's Safety and Security Team and Jodi Walker, co-chief marketing officer. "I also called and texted the leadership team asking them to meet at the Administration Building. Some had heard of the incident; others had not. All mobilized immediately."

The command center comprised the right people with the right expertise and decision-making authority, all focused on how to manage communications, to the extent possible, mitigate further risks stemming from the incident, and coordinate with law enforcement partners.

Thankfully, they weren't starting at ground zero. The U of I's Emergency Response Framework outlines the initial steps the Executive Policy Group (EPG) must take regarding a threat of this nature. The EPG consisted of Scott, Torrey, Blaine, Lee (to oversee security), Jodi (to oversee public relations), Acting General Counsel Kent Nelson, and Vice President of Finance and Administration Brian Foisy. They, along with Jake Nichols and other Public Safety and Security team members, immediately gathered in the President's Office at the Administration Building to invoke the university's crisis management policies.

First, the group quickly crafted and sent a Vandal Alert to the campus, informing that MPD was conducting a homicide investigation and instructing employees and students to stay away from the King Road area and shelter in place.

"At this point, we had no idea if there was an ongoing threat or if this was an isolated incident," Lee shared. "I remember pivoting between the Office of Public Safety and Security team and the EPG team sharing information. Once President Green and Provost Lawrence made it to the command center, President Green asked me what we knew. I remember the hair standing up on the back of my neck, looking into his eyes, and telling him that four people were dead, presumedly students. He let out a sound of disbelief, pain, and sorrow all at the same time and rubbed his eyes and then immediately began to look weary with the painful thought that four young lives had been cut short."

"Even though there was not much information, the mood was somber as we knew the victims were likely students," Scott recalled. "The team's immediate concern was for the safety of the students and employees sheltering in place. No one knew if there was still an active threat. At a minimum, the team knew there were U of I employees and students sheltering on campus at the University Library, the Pitman Center, the Hartung

Theatre, and the College of Law. I'm certain everyone was scared and wanted to go home."

MPD Captain Berrett reached out to Blaine to help coordinate getting the friends at the King Road residence away from the crime scene. Blaine immediately contacted Cari Fealy, associate dean of students, along with a U of I counselor and a U of I case manager to go to MPD and offer support, comfort, and resources to those individuals ushered away from the scene.

Blaine also contacted Director of Fraternity and Sorority Life Nick O'Neil to be prepared when MPD released the names of the victims. "We had a strong suspicion Greek students were involved because of reports we'd heard," Blaine explained. "But our protocol is whenever a student dies, we help track down contact information and give that to the police. We don't reach out directly to families initially; we give the police as much information as we can in a legal sense so they can do their jobs of notifying the families."

Details were few, but MPD informed campus Safety and Security later that afternoon that the attack appeared targeted from what they observed. They did not believe there was an active threat, but the community should remain vigilant. The EPG and Safety and Security teams sent another Vandal Alert:

> Investigation continues. Suspect unknown. MPD does not believe there is an active threat. Shelter in place lifted. Remain vigilant. If you have any information about the incident, please call Moscow Police. . .

This effectively gave those sheltering the green light to exit those buildings and travel home.

Throughout the afternoon, the EPG and Safety and Security teams coordinated an increased safety plan for campus. "With the security team's advice, they decided to double our security numbers and patrols on campus and reached out to third-party security partners to provide more visibility, vehicles, and additional bodies," Lee outlined. "Our internal team worked additional shifts, and we hired more guards. Our team set aside discussions of budgets and financial implications, empowering the security team to move and build the right structure to keep our students, staff, and faculty safe."

The teams collaborated with MPD to determine whether the victims were U of I students. MPD provided the names to Blaine, who confirmed that the four victims were all Vandals, victims of a senseless crime:

Ethan Chapin, a freshman from Mount Vernon, Washington, and a member of the Sigma Chi fraternity majoring in recreation, sport, and tourism management in the College of Education, Health, and Human Sciences;

Kaylee Goncalves, a senior from Rathdrum, Idaho, majoring in general studies in the College of Letters, Arts, and Social Sciences and a member of Alpha Phi sorority;
Xana Kernodle, a junior from Post Falls, Idaho, majoring in marketing in the College of Business and Economics and a member of the Pi Beta Phi sorority; and
Madison "Maddie" Mogen, a senior from Coeur d'Alene, Idaho, majoring in marketing in the College of Business and Economics and a member of Pi Beta Phi sorority.

Ethan, Kaylee, Xana, and Maddie were popular and active Vandals who kept up with the rigors of classwork and enjoyed the destination campus atmosphere at the U of I. The EPG members compiled student bios and campus ID photos of the four students to distribute once MPD assured they had contacted the families. At that moment, the reality printed on paper caused the full realization of the crime and its impact on the university to hit the team.

"Seeing President Green grapple with his first knowledge of the extent of this terrible crime was when I was first pulled out of the initial state of shock and felt the normal feelings that I think most people go through when confronted by something this tragic so close to home," Lee shared.

Blaine suggested to Scott and Torrey that, considering Thanksgiving break would begin at the end of that week, maybe they should cancel classes for the entire week. Scott agreed the tragedy would land hard on students and employees, especially those who knew the victims. He made the early decision to cancel classes the following day, Monday, November 14, and take the remainder of the pre-Thanksgiving week one day at a time.

Late that afternoon into early evening, Blaine, four counselors, and two case managers from the U of I Counseling and Testing Center began visiting the Greek houses directly impacted. "We went to Pi Beta Phi first, then Alpha Phi," he shared. "Then I drove up to Sigma Chi. By the time I visited each house, they'd reached out to their chapter advisors and some alumni, and they were there with the members of the fraternity and sororities."

The team began setting up drop-in counseling services to start the following morning to serve those needing help processing the vicious crime. Jodi prepared a more comprehensive communication to campus. At 5:17 p.m., the teams sent an updated Vandal Alert:

Moscow Police continues to investigate the death of four people near campus. They indicate there is no ongoing threat. More information available soon via email.

At approximately 9:00 p.m., Scott sent a memo titled "Classes Cancelled to Honor Student Victims" to the campus community. "MPD asked us to hold off naming the victims until they could ensure they had notified all appropriate next of kin, so we did not include that information in the first memo," he explained.

The entire area—Moscow, Pullman, and all the communities surrounding the two college towns—sat stunned, shocked, and scared. Doors that had never been locked before suddenly were; the hardware stores would see a marked uptick in the sale of deadbolts. Families sat at the dinner table having discussions they may never have had before—stay vigilant, don't go anywhere alone, and say something if you see something. Whoever committed the atrocity was still at large.

Around noon the next day, Scott issued another memo to campus identifying the victims. It was tremendously important to him that he also convey his empathy and share his own grief with the Vandal family. His message reiterated that drop-in counseling services were in place, described how to ask for help for a friend in need, detailed the presence of increased campus security, and gave the green light to students who wanted to leave campus and participate in classes remotely. Faculty would excuse student absences and display or record their courses for access via Zoom to accommodate students.

Understandably, the administration received pressure from a small number of parents and students who wanted the campus closed, but they also heard from many students who wanted to be on campus, together with their friends, during the emotional time. The university incorporated flexibility to serve both cohorts of students.

"We were getting a massive amount of calls and emails from parents saying we should cancel classes, and they were going to bring their daughter or son home," Blaine shared. "Students were scared. They were asking, 'Can I go home?' and 'What about my classes?' I just kept saying you do what you need to do. We'll help and support you in whatever way you need to figure this out. There's no rulebook for how to navigate through this. I'm nothing but proud of how our institution responded during such a horrific time frame."

Blaine and his staff also coordinated to send U of I counselors to classrooms when classes resumed the next day to encourage engagement and discuss available services; they also helped reach out to faculty and staff. "I didn't want anyone to learn about a significant death in their life through an email," he said.

Moscow, Idaho, suddenly became known internationally as media from all over the world converged on the small town, which was unprepared for the ways and tactics of big-city reporters, most ethical, some not. The teams worked to get MPD the information needed to conduct the investigation, prepared talking points for press conferences, and responded to media requests for information and interviews with university personnel in limited cases. They also worked aggressively to address student and employee safety concerns and the need for counseling and flexible learning methods.

Meetings to update the university's senior leadership team and provide them with talking points and gatherings with the victims' fraternity and sororities filled the following days. Hundreds of messages of shock and condolences poured in, and responding to the hordes of reporters that descended on Moscow took over all regular business.

"Frankly, the town was ill-prepared for a crime of this magnitude," Scott said. "Moscow had always been deemed a safe community, and the U of I campus, year after year, appeared on lists as one of the safest campuses in the country. After the incident, the town was ripe for a clash of cultures—the straight-shooting, trusting westerners and the big-city, take-no-prisoners national press. Combine that with the Internet sleuths who began investigating and calling out their own suspects, and we had a media circus unfolding."

At the U of I, the team remained empathic but circumspect. They were careful to whom they gave interviews and stayed on message, forgoing speculation but getting the word out on how they were beefing up security on campus and taking care of their students and employees. They did not want to add to the frenzy or the speculation and handled themselves accordingly.

"Scott expressed empathy in public and in private," Lee shared. "He expressed empathy for the students and those of us who served alongside him during this incident. He also expressed appreciation. At every turn, he thanked me, talked about how we all needed to find ways to take care of ourselves, and voiced confidence in our team."

Three hundred miles away, the "us vs. them" in-state rivalry morphed into an "us *and* them" show of support and solidarity when Boise State University held a candlelight vigil on November 17 to honor the four U of I students.

As Dean of Students, Blaine and his team began planning an on-campus vigil. Given that some students were leaving (at that point, it was estimated 25% left based on parking) due to fear and Thanksgiving break, they decided to hold the vigil when the student population was back from holiday. Blaine sent out a memo to students regarding the updated plan and reiterated the services available to help students process the emotional impact of the crime.

"Initially, I wanted the vigil outside," Blaine explained. "I wanted to create a space because we knew this was going to be impactful for the entire community. If we had it inside, we wouldn't be able to have candles. But the decision to move it inside was the absolute right call to make. One reason was because of the weather. The second reason was safety. MPD felt more comfortable with us moving it inside because they didn't have anyone in custody yet."

Cari Fealy, Cori Damron (Violence Prevention program coordinator), and Ryan Watson (Campus Events and Production manager) worked together with compassion and respect to plan the vigil and accommodate the needs of the families, students, employees, and Moscow community. People and organizations nationwide contacted Blaine's staff to offer assistance, including Alaska Airlines offering complimentary tickets to the families.

Meanwhile, MPD brought in the FBI to collaborate on the investigation and released that they knew the murderer used a bladed weapon to commit the crimes. Reporters continued to pour into town. Idaho Governor Brad Little offered assistance to the university, and Idaho State Police (ISP) came into Moscow from all over the state in a show of force.

"The governor was so supportive, immediately pledging $1 million to accommodate our response to the crime and giving the green light to the ISP to provide help," Scott recalled. "What is not widely known is that significant and visible ISP presence was a force of volunteers. They were not assigned, but officers from across the state responded to Moscow and provided security and comfort to our town and campus. We put them up in vacant dorm rooms and provided meal cards. They became a part of our community and were great with the students. There is a viral video of two officers who joined students sledding down a hill after a snowfall, to the delight of the students. That simple act of humanity demonstrated that we were all in this together. Their visibility brought solace and a sense of security to Moscow. They truly were our heroes those first few weeks in the wake of the crime."

On Wednesday, November 16, MPD held the first of many press conferences. Again, Moscow had never dealt with this type of event. The U of I lent a hand with the technology supporting the conference, which included MPD, ISP, and the U of I speaking to a press-packed room. Not all reporters could attend, but the forum was live-streamed through the university's YouTube channel.

When it came time for Scott to present, he started with condolences for the victims and their families. It was at this time that raw emotion overcame him. "I had been in reaction mode since I found out about the crimes, never taking the time or pausing to process the impact the loss of these students had on me, personally," he shared. "I started by reading, '*This crime and the loss of these young lives is beyond comprehension. While our small community is certainly not immune to such things, it is not a situation our close-knit campus is used to dealing with.*' So far, so good. Then, as soon as I started the second paragraph reading, '*First, my deepest condolences to the families,*' I was just overcome. I had to stop, compose myself, and try to get through the rest of the speech. As a father of two recent college graduates, all I could think about was the pain these families were enduring. I am not proud that I lost my composure, but the upside was that our students and their parents knew, without a doubt, that I cared deeply about them and their welfare."

Support for the president came rushing in from all over the country. It could not have come at a better time for him. "The next two days were tough for me," he shared. "Once the dam broke, it took time for all the emotional water to flow out. I knew I had to be strong for my team, so I managed it, but it was not easy."

"His vulnerability resonated with so many people," Blaine shared. "That was a powerful statement he made by being in that space like that. I told him thank you for expressing emotions that everybody is feeling."

The university kept up a constant stream of communications. The administration sent a press conference recap to students and employees and another presidential memo on Thursday, November 17, which provided the latest security response, a recap of the counseling services available to employees and students, and a reminder to watch emails over fall break for updates. Scott also sent a Friday Letter to alumni, including them in the shared grief and delivering a message of how Vandals would all get through this tragedy together. From the date of the crime on November 13 through the end of the month, the team sent 18 emails to employees, students, and alumni. Six of those messages were specifically from Scott, with one containing the president's heartfelt video.

"It was a tough week, for sure," Scott said. "The incident would continue to challenge the administration as the story spread to international tabloids and cyber-sleuths began identifying innocent people as suspects."

Law enforcement took a few punches as people wanting more information blamed them for not communicating details on the investigation.

"I'm glad they kept the investigation details to themselves," Blaine stated. "That's how you get a conviction."

MPD and the U of I held daily briefings with each other, but Blaine emphasized that the U of I had no "insider information" about the status of the investigation or leads on who committed the crime. The university provided as much information as they could to the police, working through the General Counsel's office to ensure the details shared were done so legally.

On November 30, the university held the long-promised vigil for Maddie, Kaylee, Ethan, and Xana in the Kibbie Dome on campus. A social media blast also invited anyone worldwide to join in the remembrance by turning on stadium lights, lighting candles, or holding a moment of silence.

Thousands of students, employees, community members, and family converged at the Kibbie Dome that night by walking through metal detectors and descending the stairs to the turf. In place of using candles, Cari Fealy, Cori Damron, and Ryan Watson had arranged for a scannable QR code to be available upon entering so mourners had access to a candle app on their phone or device. Dozens representing media worldwide set up cameras at a designated area on the 50-yard line. One major US network brought over a dozen media staffers to Moscow. Idaho Governor Little, Boise State University President Marlene Tromp, and representatives from Lewis Clark State College and the SBOE attended to offer support and condolences.

The victims' families were hosted in the Lighthouse Center so they could watch from a distance if they chose not to get closer. Some spoke, but they mostly stayed in their perch above the Vandal family standing crowded, side by side, from one end of the Dome to the 50-yard line where the press was set up.

The vigil lasted an hour and provided music from the university's choir, the Vandaleers, and comments by Blaine, Scott, and, most importantly, several family members of the victims who delivered memorable and touching stories of the students lost. "There was not a dry eye in the house," Scott reflected.

In Boise, approximately three hundred gathered in front of the Water Center to watch the vigil streaming live from the Kibbie Dome. "It was equally as powerful from here in Boise, and many thanked us for providing space outside of Moscow to be a part of the memorial," CEO SW Idaho Chandra Zenner Ford recalled.

Blaine invited Lutheran Campus Minister Karla Neumann Smiley to join him on stage to lead a moment of silence for each student. He then asked everyone to light up their electronic candles or phone flashlights as the house lights extinguished. Thousands of points of light began to illuminate the darkness. "In the moment, I knew the families had to see what I was seeing," Blaine shared. "I stood on stage with the sea of lights. It was like diamonds. It was just beautiful." He spontaneously said, "I would love for you all to turn your lights up to the right so the families up in the Lighthouse Suite can also see it."

The massive group of several thousand mourners turned in unison, giving the families of Xana, Ethan, Maddie, and Kaylee a glowing representation of Vandals standing in unison, hurting but filled with support and love for the four lost souls, showing they are and will continue to be the light in the families' darkness. The collective gasp in the suite said it all.

"It was one of the most powerful moments I've witnessed," shared Brenda Helbling, chief of staff for the president. "It was like a warm hug for the families. It was a beautiful moment that encapsulated the outpouring of support."

Blaine then read each name, accompanied by a bell toll. Large columns of light illuminated the ebony wall of the Kibbie Dome behind him, one for each lost Vandal. "We wanted to give a profound moment that recognized each student because we have four individuals who lost their lives," he said. "We gave them each a moment for everyone to reflect."

After a moving moment of silence, Minister Neumann Smiley led a prayer. The Vandaleers then closed the ceremony with a lovely rendition of "Let the Life I've Lived Speak for Me." "It was a beautiful tribute and an important step toward helping the community heal," Scott shared.

Schools and towns throughout Idaho, including Sandpoint, Coeur d'Alene, Post Falls, Potlatch, Lewiston, Troy, McCall, Ketchum, Kuna, Rigby, Preston, and countless others, turned on their lights to honor the four victims.

"It was an absolutely incredible outpouring of love and support," Office Manager for Division of Finance and Administration Lydia Stucki commented. "One of the most touching things for me personally was when sisters who live in Kuna and Rigby sent me pictures of their high school stadiums and shared the messages their schools had sent out. I asked my parents if the lights were on in Preston. They didn't know, so they drove to town to see. Yup. Lights were on. Then they drove to neighboring West Side High School and reported the lights were on there, too. It was extremely touching and meaningful. I'm one of the only Vandals in my extended family, so to me, it was especially obvious that this was more than just 'Vandals supporting Vandals.' It was more like 'Idaho supporting Vandals.'"

The "turn the lights on" tributes to Maddie, Xana, Ethan, and Kaylee weren't just in Idaho, either. Lights and candles in remembrance illuminated the darkness across the Pacific Northwest, nation, and world.

In the wake of the on-campus vigil, the U of I did its best to counter misinformation through some well-placed interviews. Torrey and Blaine performed most of those interviews, helping to carry the load.

"It was crazy," Blaine recounted. "For the most part, the professional media did a fine job. We notified students they were going to see media on campus. We received some complaints from students. I had the hard job of explaining that because of freedom of speech, they're allowed to be on campus, but they didn't have to talk to them. I tried to remind them that if they did participate in talking to media, to keep in mind that what they say gets back to the families and to be respectful to them and the lives lost."

In the coming weeks, social media chat board "experts" wrongly accused several students and employees of the crimes. The impact was devastating, with overwhelming scrutiny, hate mail, and harassment forcing those students into hiding. MPD publicly cleared those wrongly accused, but that meant little to those who continued to believe they knew better than the investigators.

"Those folks—with TikTok or the cyber-sleuths—were much more invasive, operating without ethics and doing it for 'likes' on their channel or social," Blaine commented. "They were much more disrespectful, especially to the students living on King Road; they're the ones who received the brunt of it."

"*The Globe* published a headline that the four students were the victims of a Manson-like cult," Scott recounted. "We learned of the story through a few alums and a relative of the Chapin family who saw the cover with photos of the victims on the magazine shelves in Boise. Chandra reached out to a top executive at the national grocery chain, Albertsons, who then had the publication voluntarily removed from their regional stores."

For weeks, there was incalculable fear in Moscow and the surrounding communities that a killer was on the loose, not to mention a media frenzy to contend with on the U of I campus. During that time, everyone ached for more details, more evidence, and more facts. MPD and their law enforcement partners released little information to preserve the investigation's integrity for trial, but when they asked people to be on the lookout for a 2011–2016 white Hyundai Elantra, hope surged that they would name a suspect soon.

Thankfully, in the early morning hours of December 30, 47 days after the murders, law enforcement informed Kent Nelson, U of I acting general counsel, that they had made an arrest. All Kent knew at that point was that they conducted the arrest outside Idaho. "We would all learn later that morning that the arrest was in Pennsylvania," Scott said.

"I was in the Minneapolis-Saint Paul airport traveling back from a holiday visit to my parents' house when I received a text message from Jodi asking if I would organize a meeting for 10 a.m. that day," Lee recalled. "I texted back, 'Sure,' but called her immediately. I was uncomfortable with the vagueness of the message, hungry for information after weeks with little, and ready to help if needed. She let me know there was movement on the case and that there would be a press conference at 1:00 p.m. We all needed to get together. As I was organizing the Zoom meeting from the airport, the reports that an arrest had been made started to hit the news outlets and popped up on my landing page feed. I ended up on the plane during the U of I's internal meeting and the press conference but asked Brian Foisy to update me via text. Halfway through the flight, I started scrolling through the various news channels via the complimentary entertainment screen on the back of the seat in front of me. One by one, they began flashing a picture of the suspect, telling what they knew about him, and showing aerial footage of his parents' home in rural Pennsylvania."

The details started to fall into place, telling a gruesome, horrific story. On early Sunday morning, sometime between approximately 4:00 a.m. and 4:20 a.m. on November 13, 2022, Bryan Christopher Kohberger, a graduate student from Pennsylvania studying criminal justice at Washington State University (eight miles west across the border from the University of Idaho), allegedly slipped into the house on King Road adjacent to the U of I campus and brutally stabbed Kaylee, Maddie, Ethan, and Xana to death.

"It was not a crime of passion, a fight with another student, or the work of a cult as many amateur Internet sleuths posited," Scott stated. "The attack appeared to be premeditated, and the perpetrator had allegedly prepared to execute his plan relying on his criminal justice education to avoid detection. He was not a known friend or close to any of the victims, which made identifying and arresting him more difficult and time-consuming."

Kohberger had driven across the country with his father from Pullman, Washington, toward Pennsylvania during the December holiday break, but law enforcement had zeroed in on him based on surveillance videos, cell phone record pings, and other evidence. After tracking him to his family's home in Albrightsville, Pennsylvania, and confirming DNA evidence, at 3:00 a.m. on December 30, Pennsylvania law enforcement entered the Kohberger home, made the arrest, and took possession of the white Hyundai Elantra that they believed the killer used to travel to and from the murder scene.

"I sat on the plane, dumbfounded by the fact that Kohberger had attended class after the murders and then traveled to his family home for what I'm sure seemed to them as a normal holiday visit—a time for family, friends, and decompression," Lee shared. "I shed a tear or two quietly, not sure if it was sadness or relief. At the same time, I could not help but draw the parallel to my family, who had woken up early to take me to the airport, a father's chore done with love after a nice visit. As stark as the comparison—the contradiction of knowing that four families had endured a much different end to 2022."

MPD hosted a press conference that day at 1:00 p.m. at Moscow City Hall, where MPD, ISP, and Scott delivered remarks. After the press conference, Scott sent out a communication to students, employees, and alumni that summed up the details of the case to that point. It read:

> Bryan Christopher Kohberger was arrested in Pennsylvania last night in connection with the King Road homicides, according to the Moscow Police Department. The U of I does not appear to have any record of Kohberger. No motive has been released by law enforcement.
>
> This is the news we have been waiting for and a relief for our community and, most importantly, the families of Kaylee Goncalves, Madison Mogen, Xana Kernodle, and Ethan Chapin. We are grateful for the hard work of law enforcement to protect our community and bring justice.
>
> It has been a stressful time for our university, but we never lost faith that this case would be solved and are grateful for the hard work of the MPD and their law enforcement partners. We appreciate the increased security presence of the Idaho State Police to bring comfort and calm to a community shocked and confused by this senseless crime. This was made possible by Gov. Brad Little's financial support. Vast and committed FBI resources brought important expertise to this complex case. Across the board, dedicated, highly competent personnel worked on this case.
>
> This crime has nevertheless left a mark on our university, our community, and our people. As such, counseling services remain available to all students over the break and when classes resume Wednesday, January 11. Employees needing assistance can use the free and confidential EAP resources available through your benefits or contact David Talbot, university ombuds, for additional support.
>
> Classes in self-defense, vigilance, stalking awareness, healthy relationships, and more, as well as the distribution of personal safety devices, will continue as planned. Additional security personnel have been added to the university's security team, and local law enforcement will increase patrols on campus and in nearby neighborhoods.
>
> The outpouring of support from across the state and nation helped sustain us during this most trying time. For the past several weeks, we were all Vandals, and that provided the strength that helped us navigate the international scrutiny visited on our students and employees. Kindness is contagious and provided light that reclaimed ground lost to evil and darkness. We are thankful for the compassion shown to our community.
>
> The care for each other and resilience of our students and employees has been remarkable. Our students come first, and that was proven each and every day of this investigation. We are committed to safely delivering the college town atmosphere, campus experience, and high-touch, quality education for which the University of Idaho is known.

While we cannot bring back Maddie, Kaylee, Xana, and Ethan, we can thoughtfully and purposefully carry their legacy forward in the work we do. The next few months will be tough on their friends and families as the legal system begins the process of publicly prosecuting these crimes to bring justice. Let's keep them in our thoughts and prayers and continue to stand #vandalstrong. (University of Idaho 2022)

"The day of the arrest, I talked to the dean of students at Washington State University four times," Blaine shared. "I told her to hang on; the tidal wave that just went through our campus was headed her way."

Shortly after the arrest, a Latah County district judge placed a non-dissemination order (gag order) on individuals involved with investigation or evidence, including law enforcement, asking them to not discuss the trial with media.

Even with the arrest, Scott knew reverberations would impact the U of I into the future, including the care of its employees and the impact on student retention and recruiting. "It was clear to me that the case would continue to be front and center in the media through trial," Scott said. "Despite the fact that the crime was committed off campus by an individual from another state, we would have to counter the view that the university is unsafe. For years, we were considered one of the safest campuses in the nation, and we will be again. But in the meantime, we prepared to respond to the inevitable questions about security and safety in our community."

The entire university would face having students directly affected by the tragedy return to campus. Any one student, or even a U of I employee, could be among those who went to the house that morning, were siblings, or were in a class with the victims. The entire campus had to consider that healing takes time, and no one grieves in quite the same way. In addition to those concerns, the president, faculty, and staff had to address the more pragmatic elements of getting back to educating students and advancing the U of I's reputation for safety and caring.

One metric that would determine how well the university handled the crisis would be spring enrollments. On January 27, 2023, the university reported that spring enrollment at the University of Idaho was up. Undergraduate enrollment increased by 3.5 percent to 6505 students over spring 2022. Graduate student enrollment declined slightly to 1929 from spring 2022's enrollment of 1938, but overall, enrollment was up 2.1 percent to 9375. This excluded dual-credit high school students and supported the notion that the largest freshman class in the U of I's history had returned to continue their studies with their Vandal family (University of Idaho 2023). Furthermore, fall acceptances also saw an increase. The early verdict was that the University of Idaho cared about its students, and they in turn wanted to complete their education at the U of I.

Time will tell if the tragedy affects long-term enrollment at the U of I. The entire Vandal family will work hard to promote a safe environment on campus, provide information so students and parents can make informed decisions, and empower students to reach out and ask for help if they need it.

Kohberger sits in the Latah County Jail, held without bail, and awaiting an October 2023 trial. A grand jury indicted him on four counts of murder and one count of burglary on May 17, 2023. At a pretrial hearing in June 2023, he stood silent when asked his plea. The judge entered a not guilty plea on Kohberger's behalf. Prosecutors will seek the death penalty if Kohberger is convicted.

"This is a unique situation for an institution of higher education to face," Blaine said. "The U of I has faced student deaths before, but this is murder—multiple murders with a knife. That's the horrific part. Every horror movie out there plays on our darkest fears of what actually happened on King Road. But I'm proud of the way our students responded and maintained their grit and resiliency. This generation gets a bad rap for being 'flakes' and not strong. But these are children of COVID. They've done the hard things. This is not what their student experience should be about, however. Their life experience shouldn't be about being on 20/20 or Dateline or talking about friends they've lost. We're going to go in the direction that moves us forward, focusing on academics and engaging in social opportunities while still remembering Ethan, Xana, Kaylee, and Maddie."

Scott's Management Insight

Unfortunately, homicides on US campuses are not uncommon. If evil visits your campus, a president must first project empathy. A family just lost a child, something none of us can imagine or would wish on anyone. Don't assume people will know how you feel. You must communicate the impact it has on you. That selfless act will bring your students, employees, and community closer, knowing that sadness, fear, and anger are normal, and we all must process these emotions. I chose to send a video to our community to explain what the university was doing to elevate security on campus and provide support services for our employees and students. I took that opportunity to express how I felt, that we all face the shock and confusion of such a crime differently, and that is okay. It is not easy for those of us raised in a time when one does not talk about their emotions, but I would strongly encourage you to make that leap for the good of your institution.

The second piece of advice is to address the hard questions up front. For this crime, it was security. How can you bring your students back to campus, and how will you keep your students and employees safe? Even though the murders didn't happen on campus, that didn't matter in our tight-knit community. No place felt safe with no one in custody. While the MPD believed the crime was a targeted attack, many were uncomfortable with that answer. We explained how we dramatically increased security through a private vendor and state, county, and local police patrols on our campus. There is no such thing as too much security. That visibility, in addition to communication, was key to assuring our community. We housed law enforcement on our campus and fed them in our dining halls. They became part of the Vandal family. We also injected flexibility in how our students attended class, permitting them to go home and Zoom remotely or continue in-person classes for those who wanted to remain on campus and grieve with their friends. By addressing the concerns head-on and providing choices, we did not spend time defending our decisions. We could focus on supporting our students and employees and the intense media scrutiny that followed.

The third action item is to overcommunicate, particularly in the early days of a crisis. We did this during the pandemic with a weekly update from the provost and me, and we also did it in response to this crime. But the comms do not have to be from the president; they can come from the provost, deans, VPs, or anyone relevant to the purpose of the communication. There will always be those who believe you do not communicate enough, so it is helpful to be prepared to remind them of all the comms you have issued. The teams accomplished this by listing a hyperlink of each communication on a purpose-built web page that the public could access.

Fourth, arm your campus leaders with talking points so the university speaks with one voice. Keep the conversation points updated as conditions on the ground change. This empowers your leadership to provide advice and direction aligned with university communications.

Fifth, hold regular meetings with law enforcement. Immediately after the incident, we set up a morning briefing and an afternoon debriefing that included our university team and law enforcement. This eventually evolved into one daily meeting. Law enforcement will not give you details about the investigation but can keep you situationally aware at a high level so that you can make decisions. When we realized how complex this case was and would not likely get solved in a matter of days, that helped us plan. These meetings allowed us to troubleshoot emergent challenges, gather input from a diverse group of stakeholders, develop and tailor communication quickly, and keep the ball moving on the daily work needed for a campus in crisis. Continue these meetings as needed, and don't deviate from their intended purpose. A clear lead and point of contact are essential. Start each discussion with a quick overview of the agenda items and allow other team members to add theirs to the list. Solicit updates regarding law enforcement, security, student support, legal, and communications. While it became moot after the arrest, we had prepared how to navigate the start of spring semester classes. We had elevated security plans for campus and were adding remote learning options for those not wanting to return to Moscow.

Finally, take care of yourself. A president cannot lead with energy and good judgment if not rested and healthy. It is easy to be overwhelmed by the crime, the media, the needs of your employees and students, and the need to communicate. Also, take care of your team. Acknowledging their efforts, thanking them, listening to and valuing their input, and creating space for them to be vulnerable and real is vital in building trust, confidence, and comradery. It also motivates and gives team members the okay to do the little things for themselves to keep the momentum for students and employees.

Part IX

Chapter 44
A University on the Rise

"He got up every morning when the whole bottom was falling out in so many ways and said we're still going to make stuff happen. And we did."
— *Chandra Zenner Ford*

One of Scott's main pillars for success as the University of Idaho president is to tell the institution's story, and in doing so, it also includes a piece of his story. He never wanted this book to be about *him*. He wanted to showcase the "Stay Calm and Vandal On" mantra utilized by the incredible faculty, staff, and students during his first three and a half years as president at his alma mater.

This story digs deep into how the University of Idaho landed in a deep financial crisis, how COVID-19 added an incalculable level of stress and severity to an already tricky situation, and how one evil person caused havoc and instilled fear in the entire Vandal family. Scott deployed his unique skill set and life experiences, looked into the box, and then thought outside it to set a course. Many heroes—tried-and-true Vandals—emerged from the trying tests.

At the end of July 2021, Scott held a Leadership Retreat at the beautiful U of I Sandpoint Organic Center in Sandpoint, Idaho. The two-day meeting revealed what his first two years as president threw at the university. Budget deficits and financial cliffs, decreased morale and increased silo mentality, spending cuts and lost institutional memory, an unprecedented pandemic, and fear. Throughout the two days utilizing Heidi Gardner's approach of Smart Collaboration (Gardner 2017), the intimate dive into the previous years exposed how the U of I took every punch, jab, and attempt at a TKO and rose stronger and more resilient under Scott's leadership.

Sometimes even the most educated, highly intellectual thinkers need education in areas outside their purview. When Scott came in as president, he shared his expertise in finance, budgeting, corporate thinking, and management. He offered a learning environment for the educators. But he was also on the receiving end of learning about the intricacies of academics, shared governance, and thinking outside the corporate mindset. He may have received his University of Idaho degree in 1984, but the university hadn't finished teaching him some invaluable lessons. The collaboration and mutual exchange of ideas didn't stop at the classroom threshold; it swirled throughout every office, conference room, public space, and hallowed hall of the grand old institution. That meeting of minds and experiences saved the University of Idaho and set it on the course to solid and continued success. Scott led the charge but couldn't have defeated the financial and pandemic foes without his Vandal tribe.

Scott recounted a list of the heavy lifts performed by the university community between July 2019 and July 2021 despite the financial and COVID-19 crises. The retreat ended with Scott presenting the list to his collaborators, his team. "It was a pretty emotional delivery," he reflected. "I was tired; I hadn't slept well the night before. I think about all the energy behind what was on that list while we had financial issues and a pandemic. It's freaking impressive."

This story mentions many smart collaborations, but those mentioned are just a sampling of what the U of I accomplished during a crisis storm.

Did Scott get everything right with the financial crisis and COVID-19? No, that would have been impossible. But, given the complexities and uncharted territory of the situation, the university is sitting in a much better position than before Scott became president.

"If we get people really working together with high productivity, there's a lot of opportunity at the U of I," Scott announced. "There's just so much potential, and I'm pretty excited about it."

Finances

The aftermath of the financial cuts lingers within some colleges and units as they struggle with the "how-to" of rebuilding while maintaining fiscal responsibility. Although the university is approaching the sweet spot of the student-to-faculty ratio, and salaries have statistically improved, they remain below regional targets, making it difficult to recruit qualified talent.

Creating a balance of revenue and expenditures is precarious but is now monitored regularly at various levels to avoid arriving at another financial cliff in the future. Scott and his team continue to work on reducing the negative unrestricted net position, replenishing cash reserves, and investing in initiatives and programs that will position the U of I to leverage its strengths.

"This is a critical phase. There are still some challenges," CALS Dean Michael Parrella shared. "We successfully cut $14 million, then $22 million, and we did it right. On top of that, there were the financial and political implications of COVID-19. We couldn't close the university down; otherwise, there probably wouldn't have been an opening day ever again. Now we're dealing with the residue of those tough decisions, whether it was people or programs. Now we have to live with the decisions, which makes the next years telling."

CFO Brian Foisy pointed out that some of the cuts during those first few years of Scott's presidency occured in areas where the U of I just happened to have the opportunity to cut. "Now we're struggling with how we build back into those areas," he shared. "I think that helps explain why administration after administration before Scott didn't immediately rush to massive budget cuts."

There was no more dramatic change factor than those monthly meetings between Scott and the deans, grinding it out, Scott showing them how to read a financial report, and familiarizing the fiscal officers with how to work from a common report that was different than they'd had before.

"We can have an academic president again after Scott," Chief of Staff Brenda Helbling stated, "but we have to be certain we never lose sight of that business side. We now have a faculty who recognizes we are a university and also a business."

The Vandal Hybrid Budget Model will be a testament to Scott's outside experience and guidance and the exceptional commitment of faculty and staff to making the changes and sticking to them.

"We will have some colleges moving the needle on undergraduate enrollment, and with the metric model, we'll reward them," Michael said. "That means taking money away maybe from the colleges that don't move the needle but are still critical to the university and what they offer. That's where there will be some tough decision-making."

Because of the dedication to cutting spending, righting the budgets, and hitting a surplus, the U of I did not increase student tuition during FY21, FY22, and FY23. Enrollment figures were up in FY22 and FY23, and budgets were increased. Fall 2022's incoming freshman class was the largest in the university's history, so large the U of I had to place over 100 students

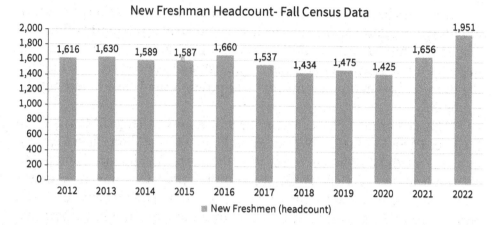

Figure 44.01   The Fall 2022 freshman class increased a whopping 17% from 2021. Overall, enrollment was up nearly 3%.

SOURCE: University of Idaho Division of Finance and Administration. Reproduced with permission of University of Idaho.

in a hotel for temporary living. That increase will benefit the FY24 budget. The university has also replaced all the investments used to fund prior deficits, cash balances are growing, and the administration is again investing in projects and people. See Figure 44.01.

COVID-19

COVID-19 is an ongoing problem. "We haven't hung the 'Mission Accomplished' sign on the aircraft carrier yet," COVID-19 Project Manager Seth Vieux shared.

The arrival of the Delta and Omicron variants in 2020, 2021, and 2022 kept the U of I faculty, staff, and students constantly on their guard.

"Control was really our objective," Scott said. "We were successful in doing that because Gritman never went to the crisis standard of care level. They never had to take that extra step. They were close a few times, but they never had to do it. It was like threading a needle. We saw COVID-19 evolve into a pandemic of the nonvaccinated. I support personal choice, but Idaho Public Health still says the vaccine is 96 percent effective against serious illness. It was an easy choice for me to receive the vaccination."

By the end of January 2022, more than 4700 U of I students had submitted proof of vaccination, and by spring 2022, the administration lifted the mask mandate, giving everyone a choice of how they wanted to handle that particular safety measure. "We've gone to optional masking on campus," Scott said. "Some people still want to be masked, and we want to be respectful of that."

Technology

"The technology revolution has completely changed how the U of I administers education," Vice President Dan Ewert expressed. "The U of I was never going to be an online institution; it has and will always be a destination campus and highly functioning research institution, and while online education is important to us, we are not set on competing with online-only schools. The U of I journey is all about receiving experiential learning and participating in research."

College of Graduate Studies Dean Jerry McMurtry shared that although graduate student programming shifted online during the pandemic, he'd like to ensure that programming can be in-person when possible. "That sense of community with our professional development initiatives was a tough shift to online. Now we have to figure out a way to make sure students are reengaged and enjoy the same kind of active discussion and participation that we had in person pre-pandemic."

"Part of the pandemic response strategy included trying not to get into a position of being a victim and then just pulling the covers over our head and hoping it all just goes away," Dean Dennis Becker said. "It was that conscious effort to determine how we could take advantage of this and turn it into a positive. Fortunately, we were already moving into online education at the time, primarily at the graduate level but some at the undergrad level. We took advantage of the COVID-19 shutdown to plug some holes in our online curriculum that we've wanted to plug for a couple of years. In many ways, COVID-19 gave us the confidence to do what we've been talking about for a few years. The 'Keep Calm and Vandal On' approach was so important."

Dan agrees that the pandemic created a paradigm shift. "We will never return to everybody having an office or space on campus," he offered. "This isn't just in my department; it's institution wide."

Enrollment and Students

Enrollment started an uptick in the fall of 2021 at the U of I, sitting at 4.7 percent higher than in 2020.

"In FY22, every college's first-year class of student enrollment was up," Scott said, beaming. "We had an incredible recruiting year. Then it happened again in FY23. We had the largest incoming freshman class in our history. Everyone on campus knew that recruiting qualified students was job #1. The Vandal hybrid was working."

Vice Provost Dean Kahler explained that in fall 2020, excluding dual-credit students, the U of I saw a dip by 3% in enrollment, but that was understandable due to COVID-19. The national average was down 6.3%. But fall 2021 saw an increase in Vandal enrollment by 16.4% in the freshman class and 4.7% overall. Then in fall 2022, the freshman class increased another whopping 17%, and overall, enrollment was up nearly 3%. "I'm going to take that and run with it all day," he said and smiled. "I'm very proud of our team. They did a great job. They shifted and worked their tails off."

A looming concern for SEM involves the decrease of students to recruit. Experts predict that enrollments will decline nationwide as early as 2025 due to the simple fact that people have fewer children. "The pure demographics of people having babies definitely can project 18 years later the number of high school graduates and the number of students that potentially would go on to college," Dean pointed out. "The competition for universities to recruit future students to maintain their enrollments is getting stiffer and stiffer as that pool gets smaller and smaller."

Scott and his team lead by example to show recruiting is everyone's job through visits, phone calls, and specific outreach to prospective and returning Vandals. Dean shared, "I tell parents they should send their son or daughter to a school where the president cares and where the people on-campus care."

The good news is that even if an enrollment cliff is imminent, the U of I's College of Graduate Studies will most likely not see a dip. "Students have to get through their undergraduate degree program to get to the grad level," Jerry said. "It'll hit us a little, but we'll work more with workforce development, professional education, and professional degree programs to fill in if we see gaps. The research degrees will always be there, but I think our real growth is going to be in professional degree programs as we build those."

Research

Research continued to funnel through the U of I during the financial crisis and COVID-19. "While other institutions were closed during COVID-19, we were writing grants," Scott said.

When Scott became president, his three pillars to success included research. The U of I was, is, and always will be built on a foundation of education and research. The goal to move the university toward R1 Carnegie Classification (very high research activity) wasn't new, but Scott established a working group to create a blueprint for action. The group encouraged a focus on new investments in postdoctoral scholar and doctoral research support and identified actions to improve research culture and incent greater research and doctoral degree productivity. All this adds up to researchers on the cutting edge of their field conducting their work at the U of I.

Carnegie R1 status is synonymous with academic and research excellence. Monies from the P3 endowment allowed for investment in research that incentivized and rewarded success.

Culture

"Everybody is maturing in their leadership in almost every area at the university because they're seeing how it can be done," Brenda Helbling said. "We're seeing a much more corporate style of distinguishing between when you manage and when you lead. Scott brought that to the front when he became president."

The outlook for the U of I is optimistic. The culture shift is noticeable; the campus community believes in itself again. The detrimental type of siloed mentality is fading. The university has unbelievable potential, and the institution is on course to realizing that potential and building a framework for future administrations to utilize. "People are putting the university first; that's something we've worked to change culturally, and I think we've been very successful," Scott said. "When you look at what people have done, it's amazing."

Provost Torrey Lawrence and U of I Ombuds Laura Smythe hosted a town hall on March 3, 2022 titled "Vandals Reflecting and Re-Building Together." Attendees were allowed to reflect on the budget crisis and COVID-19 and discuss answers to questions regarding the residue left from the cuts and pandemic response.

"We had about sixty people and maybe one hundred online," Torrey said. "Everyone was in groups of four to eight people and spent about twenty minutes on each question."

The questions included: What has been hardest for you about living and working through the pandemic during the last two years? What adaptations have you made within your role and within your unit? What has worked well? What has not worked well? What learning/lessons do you think our university should apply from this experience as we move forward?

"Each group shared their top two or three points from question number three," Torrey explained. "The responses were extremely positive. People enjoyed the opportunity to gather and discuss ideas that looked both backward and forward. We have organized a number of different events to build community following the pandemic (this one, athletic events, community BBQs). It was Laura's idea."

The groups identified five categories into which most comments fell: improved institution-wide logistics, flexibility in the workplace, emphasis on wellness, improved communication, and better pay.

"We are working on action plans to address each one and will integrate those into other workplace climate initiatives that were developed around the Great Colleges to Work For survey results," Torrey outlined. "For managers, I think the concept of paying attention to community becomes important in a crisis."

Campaign

"We have to be able to fund our strategy," Scott stated. "Fundraising and the campaign is how we'll do it. Fundraising is important at every university."

The "Brave. Bold. A Promise to Idaho's Students" campaign launched in Fall 2021, inviting alumni and donors to invest in scholarships, fellowships, experiential learning, and more to benefit students in Idaho today and for generations to come. The second phase, the "Brave. Bold. Unstoppable." campaign, launched in fall 2022 to engage alumni and donors in helping the U of I embrace its land-grant roots and continue to expand sustainable solutions and a healthy, thriving Idaho. Both phases will run concurrently.

Scott set the goal for the campaign at an arguably aggressive figure of $500 million, but the pride Vandals show for their students and campuses reflects in giving. The university had back-to-back record philanthropy years, and as of fall 2022, the U of I had raised over $100 million for student scholarships and over $350 million overall.

* * *

When Scott reflected on his first three and a half years as the U of I president, he was always overcome with deep gratitude for his Vandal family—students, faculty, staff, alumni, friends, and stakeholders. The teamwork and dedication displayed by faculty and staff stood out to him. The institution persevered through incredibly difficult and stressful situations because of its collaborative efforts. It hadn't been easy. Work to refine all that progress loomed. But when the fall semester of 2022 arrived, it seemed as if all the efforts had started to gel. Enrollment and fundraising were up, COVID-19 numbers were going down, and an air of optimism blanketed the campus and Moscow community. The Kibbie Dome was enjoying larger crowds at the football games, and students nicknamed Scott "Daddy Green," a term of endearment. He looked forward to spending time with his family over Thanksgiving break, celebrating newly graduated Vandals at winter commencement, and the Christmas holiday. He also looked forward to the Vandal tribe adding to the impressive list of smart collaborations.

Nothing could have prepared him or the entire Vandal family for what happened in the early-morning hours of November 13, 2022. The loss of Ethan Chapin, Xana Kernodle, Madison "Maddie" Mogen, and Kaylee Goncalves took the wind out of everyone's sails. Processing the murders of four Vandals seemed impossible. But it was up to Scott to show a strong face, a sense of safety and security, and empathy. It became crystal clear that his number-one job had always been and would always be keeping his students and employees safe, no matter how that looked or was defined.

To grapple with why it happened was a waste of time; instead, he spent his time with his stunned but capable teams communicating what the university was doing in the face of evil and how they would help those mourning and afraid to cope. Scott and his teams never wavered in their stance to ensure students and employees felt as safe as possible on campus.

He was mad, though. Angry at the person who took the four lives that carried so much potential. Because of his previous experience with crisis management, however, he knew to channel that negative energy into a positive.

* * *

"The University of Idaho didn't get Scott because of a career ladder," Barrie Robison stated. "He stepped down by orders of magnitude. And not because of a money thing. He stepped in because he said, 'It's my turn to contribute to the well-being of this institution that I care about.' To me, that was the difference in the last three and a half years. I'm 100 percent convinced that somebody who came in wearing a suit for a living and was looking at maybe getting a job at a big university after this, we would have been a dumpster fire if we would have hired somebody like that."

"As president, Scott had a heavier lift than others on campus," Terry Gawlik pointed out. "At least I had been in this field (athletics) for many years. He'd never done academics. What he's done managing this campus is amazing."

"We showed what we could do," Dan Ewart offered. "It was so cool to watch an organization pull this off. The ultimate goal of getting the education to the students happened during the financial crisis, budget cuts, and COVID-19. And the two reasons for that were a team that thought through the options and came up with good ones and leadership support to say, 'Go do it.'"

"As the steward of this college, I think it's a fantastic institution with so much potential moving forward," Dean Michael Parrella said. "We just need to get out of our own way to make things happen."

"Scott's already given me the permission to essentially just put the gas down," Dean Dennis Becker explained. "And that's what we're doing. I feel bullish about the future of the College of Natural Resources. We're connecting politically around the state with what we're doing."

Dennis acknowledges the U of I will face a challenging political climate for the next decade or maybe forever. "How people want to taint or what they think about higher education is something that our college can directly address through our work with our partners. Scott has been very supportive of everything we're doing, and that's just so critical."

"The U of I shows a complete shift toward believing in ourselves again and believing we're on the rise," Brenda Helbling stated. "This is a university moving up and fast, there's no doubt, and it started with Scott's credibility. The first years of his presidency—what he's accomplished—is amazing not only on a fast-paced normal scale but when you add in that it didn't always come off very elegantly, we had a few missteps and had to backtrack at times, then it becomes more impressive as you see our accomplishments."

Dean Shauna Corry expressed her feelings of optimism and confidence. "One of the main things that drew me to the University of Idaho, besides the College of Art and Architecture and the programs, was that the university always had confidence. People were confident, alums were confident, our students were confident, and faculty had confidence. But over time, I think with each successive president, and then with the rise of BSU, we lost confidence. But now I think that confidence is coming back. People have hope, and when you have hope, then all things are possible. People are hopeful because they know there's a tangible way we can get there. Before, we didn't have a pathway to getting anywhere; no one ever showed us how. It didn't exist. But now we have a path. We've seen it; we helped build it. That is the important thing about what Scott has done."

Dean Sean Quinlan also felt optimistic about the institution and moving forward. "When I came to the University of Idaho, the thing that always overwhelmed me was its alumni's love for this institution. People were incredibly proud to have gone to the University of Idaho; they loved this institution. They found that what happened to them was so personally transformative, both for their professional and personal lives. It was humbling. Scott understood that; he was a product of it. And he connected with people so deeply on that reality. He was so proud and passionate about the university. And that aura surrounded him."

"He had the right academic credentials and right work experience to become the U of I president," Interim U of I President 2013–14 Don Burnett pointed out. "But specifically, he had deep family connections to the university and the impulse to be of service to the institution—his alma mater—to establish clear visions of state leadership, academic excellence, and service to our state."

Scott held the weight of the university on his shoulders, reminiscent of the stone Idaho Vandal football gargoyles holding up Memorial Gym. Like the gargoyles, Scott wasn't alone in carrying the burdens. He had the strength from his Vandal family to take on three major crises situations that, if faced singularly, could've laid any university low.

"People are never going to understand how great of a leader Scott was during those first two years," Chandra Zenner Ford shared. "I don't think you can get your arms around it unless you look at day-to-day what he did. He got up every morning when the whole bottom was falling out in so many ways and said we're still going to make stuff happen. And we did."

Scott's Management Insight

The average tenure of a university president is dropping at a remarkable clip. It was 8.5 in 2006 and plunged to 6.5 years by 2016. My guess is that it continues to drop in the wake of the pandemic. Today, a successful candidate must prepare to add value on day one, balancing the needs of all stakeholders: students, faculty, staff, alumni, regents, legislators, and the businesses that hire your students. Candidates should be okay knowing that they cannot keep everyone happy. You will work in the shared governance model, never have complete control, and may get your way 80% of the time if you are both effective and lucky. You will see the best and worst behaviors from those you work with and have few levers to deal with those who defame you and your family. You will hand your life over to the university yet have critics at every turn. You will be overworked, presented only with difficult decisions others can't make, and then challenged for the decisions you made.

It is a job without boundaries, the work week is seven days, and there is never enough time for vacation or alone time with your family. You will be under a microscope during your entire presidency. If you are good with all that, you are ready to take on one of the most rewarding jobs available anywhere.

At the end of the day, every president is just a steward of their institution, tasked with caring for it and moving it forward. But in that time, you will work in a place where knowledge lives. You will interact with so many people at the top of their game; intelligent, engaged faculty and students solving the world's most complex problems with innovative research or advancing humanity through their creativity and contributions to the arts. You will meet some of the most interesting people in the world who will visit your campus to share their knowledge. You will rub elbows with successful alumni, from rocket scientists (literally) to poets. You will witness first-generation students who did not even know they could go to college elevate and illuminate themselves, changing the trajectory of their entire family. You will revel in music, theater, symposiums, and sporting events on your campus. Every day, you will continue to be amazed, surprised, and delighted by what is happening around you.

Yes, the job is tough, but if you are prepared and doing it for the right reasons, the rewards are well worth the sacrifice. I will be forever grateful for having the opportunity to return to my birthplace, lead my alma mater, and finish my career in the State where it began. To paraphrase Yankee great Joe DiMaggio, I like to thank the good Lord for making me a Vandal. I wish you much success in your chosen path.

Smart Collaboration

Telling the U of I's Story

One of Scott's three pillars when he first became president was to tell the University of Idaho's story. It's the institution's most valuable asset. Anyone associated with the U of I—alumni, students, faculty, staff, donors, stakeholders—has been encouraged to share their experience becoming a Vandal and how attending or associating with the university in whatever capacity changed their lives for the better.

Scott felt highly motivated to share the story after the incredible teamwork the entire university showed, recovering $50 million of deficits over three years while surviving a global pandemic of proportions *the world had never seen. And, while there is always loss, the magnitude of the tragedy the team faced in late 2022 challenged their sense of security and tested their fortitude.*

Writing articles in the magazine didn't seem big enough, and blasting out emails and links to web pages didn't seem extensive enough. This endeavor required a full-length book. Scott didn't want it to be about him but, instead, about his extended Vandal tribe. Every Vandal had to give up something during the fiscal crisis and COVID-19, and every Vandal felt loss when four students were murdered. Sacrifice and dedication from thousands of individuals with love and passion for the University of Idaho culminated in the institution remaining solvent, exceeding expectations, and enhancing its position in Idaho education, as well as the national and international educational and research scenes. Through an unthinkable crime, the Vandal family also demonstrated their capacity for grace and strength.

"I love the concept of this book," Vice President Dan Ewart stated. "I think our staff, faculty, and students deserve to have a story told around everything we did."

"This book is celebrating the University of Idaho," Dean Shauna Corry said, smiling. "It's celebrating our leadership, but it's also celebrating our faculty, staff, students, and alumni who supported us all these years."

Scott's story is every Vandal's story. Every dollar cut, every day someone had to wear a mask, every COVID-19 test administered, every student who was helped at the Counseling Center, every program cut, every early retiree, every supply chain issue, every meeting with Gritman, every daunting task to get testing equipment, every new student recruited, every win, every loss, every sleepless night about the what-ifs, every head laid on a desk in worry and anguish, every glulam beam placed in the ICCU Arena, every lonely Vandal in a dorm room or basement apartment during COVID-19, every computer enhanced for Zoom and online education, every dollar given to Idaho's land-grant institution through donations, every faculty member who pivoted on a dime to relearn how to educate their students, every gallon of hand-sanitizer made, every grant dollar earned, every email crafted to share facts and comfort, every marketing strategy to show we're closer than you think, every tear shed, every blasted Zoom

(Continued)

(Continued)

*meeting, every controversial decision, every petition disagreeing with those difficult decisions, every Grim Reaper on campus, every assurance everything would be okay, every moment from the time Scott became lead Vandal, every Vandal unwittingly crafting a story worthy of rounds of applause, every second of every hour of every day for four years, every single **thing** that wrote the university's story is worth sharing here.*

Scott's Management Insight

Never be afraid to tell your story.

References by Chapter

Vandal Tribe of Contributors

University of Idaho Special Collections. (1933). "Go, Vandals, go!" https://www.lib.uidaho.edu/special-collections/pdf/Go_Vandals_Go.pdf

Chapter 2

ESPN. (2010). "Boise State president blasts rival Idaho." https://www.espn.com/college-football/news/story?id=5417329 (accessed May 31, 2022).

US News & World Report. (2002). "University of Idaho overall rankings." https://www.usnews.com/best-colleges/university-of-idaho-1626/overall-rankings (accessed October 9, 2022).

Chapter 3

University of Idaho. (2023). "Faculty Senate." https://www.uidaho.edu/governance/faculty-senate (accessed December 10, 2021).

Chapter 4

Britannica. (n.d.). "Land-Grant College Act of 1862, United States Legislation." https://www.britannica.com/topic/Land-Grant-College-Act-of-1862 (accessed October 1, 2021).

Petersen, K. (1987). *This Crested Hill: An illustrated history of the University of Idaho.* Idaho: University of Idaho Press.

University of Idaho. (n.d.). "Nancy M. Cummings Research, Extension & Education Center." https://www.uidaho.edu/cals/nancy-m-cummings-research-extension-and-education-center (accessed October 1, 2021).

Wikipedia. (n.d.). "Idaho panhandle." https://en.wikipedia.org/wiki/Idaho_Panhandle (accessed October 1, 2021).

Chapter 6

University of Idaho. (n.d.). "University House." https://www.uidaho.edu/about/university-house (accessed November 1, 2021).

Chapter 7

University of Idaho. (n.d.). "Leadership Groups." https://www.uidaho.edu/president/leadership-groups (accessed September 1, 2021).

Chapter 8

US News & World Report. (2022). "University of Idaho overall rankings." https://www.usnews.com/best-colleges/university-of-idaho-1626/overall-rankings (accessed October 9, 2022).

Chapter 10

University of Idaho. (n.d.). "We've got WUE." https://www.uidaho.edu/ui/wue (accessed November 1, 2021).

University of Idaho McClure Center for Public Policy Research. (n.d.). "Idaho at a glance, life after high school." https://www.uidaho.edu/-/media/UIdaho-Responsive/Files/president/direct-reports/mcclure-center/Idaho-at-a-Glance/IDG-Life-After-High-School.pdf (accessed October 15, 2021).

Chapter 12

Idaho State Board of Education. (2021). "III.F. - program prioritization." https://boardofed.idaho.gov/board-policies-rules/board-policies/higher-education-affairs-section-iii/iii-f-program-prioritization (accessed October 15, 2021).

University of Idaho Office of the Provost. (2019). "Memorandum, Provost provides Academic Affairs budget update." https://www.uidaho.edu/-/media/UIdaho-Responsive/Files/provost/updates/academic-affairs-budget-update-1-30-19.pdf?la=en&hash=27C79E5FB3F193B2F4A6CF2BE161A0F684161612 (accessed January 22, 2022).

University of Idaho. (n.d.). "Update of program prioritization at the University of Idaho." https://www.uidaho.edu/-/media/UIdaho-Responsive/Files/provost/councils-committees/ipec/program-prioritization/app-taskforce-report-2020.pdf?la=en&hash=B3FFE9BBFEFB166ABDCDABEAD959FD44A9B18AAD (accessed October 1, 2022).

University of Idaho. (n.d.). "Update on program prioritization at the University of Idaho final." https://www.uidaho.edu/-/media/UIdaho-Responsive/Files/provost/councils-committees/ipec/program-prioritization/communications/update-on-program-prioritization-at-the-university-of-idaho-final.pdf?la=en&hash=AC41EACB41E2DA252C4B1EA43D14A29C4B0A9356 (accessed January 22, 2022).

Chapter 16

Idaho State Board of Education. (2019). "State board of education March 13–14, 2019, meeting minutes." https://boardofed.idaho.gov/meetings/board/archive/2019/0313-1419/03-March-13-14-2019-Special-APPROVED-minutes.pdf (accessed January 22, 2022).

University of Idaho. (2020). "First Wood column set as ICCU Arena takes shape at U of I." https://www.uidaho.edu/news/news-articles/news-releases/2020-summer/060220-iccuarena (accessed January 22, 2022).

Chapter 17

Moscow Idaho Chamber of Commerce. (2021). "Executive summary: Economic contributions of vandal athletics." https://moscowchamber.com/executive-summary-economic-contributions-of-vandal-athletics (accessed January 22, 2022).

Chapter 19

University of Idaho. (2020). "CAFE 2020 research report." https://www.uidaho.edu/research/news/research-reports/2020/cafe (accessed October 15, 2021).

University of Idaho. (2020). "Online education working group." https://www.uidaho.edu/-/media/UIdaho-Responsive/Files/president/working-groups/online-education-rprt.pdf (accessed January 22, 2022).

University of Idaho. (2020). "R1/Research working group final report." https://www.uidaho.edu/-/media/UIdaho-Responsive/Files/president/working-groups/r1_rsrchworkinggroup_rprt_vs4.pdf?la=en&hash=6AAC6A82C0EC333D5E79DDA574A95E39E40E45BF (accessed January 22, 2022).

University of Idaho. (2020). "Sustainable financial model working group white paper." https://www.uidaho.edu/-/media/UIdaho-Responsive/Files/president/working-groups/sustainable-financial-model-working-group-white-paper-oct-2020.pdf (accessed September 1, 2021).

University of Idaho. (2021). "Comprehensive campaign working group white paper." https://www.uidaho.edu/-/media/UIdaho-Responsive/Files/president/working-groups/campaign-working-group-white-paper-aug-2021.pdf (accessed January 22, 2022).

University of Idaho. (2022). "Sustainability working group: sustainable solutions for our university and for our state." https://www.uidaho.edu/-/media/UIdaho-Responsive/Files/president/working-groups/sustainability/sustainability-white-paper.pdf (accessed July 16, 2023).

University of Idaho. (n.d.). "Rinker Rock Creek Ranch." https://www.uidaho.edu/research/entities/rock-creek (accessed January 22, 2022).

University of Idaho McClure Center for Public Policy Research. (2022). "Idaho at a glance." https://www.uidaho.edu/-/media/UIdaho-Responsive/Files/president/direct-reports/mcclure-center/Idaho-at-a-Glance/idg-economy-and-climate.pdf?la=en&hash=2073D2EDAA55D570305E63F6506314621E667CD3 (accessed January 4, 2023).

Chapter 23

University of Idaho. (n.d.). "Initiative for Bioinformatics + Evolutionary Studies IBEST." https://www.iids.uidaho.edu/ibest.php (accessed October 9, 2022).

Chapter 24

Boone, K. (2020). "2020 NCAA Tournament canceled due to growing threat of coronavirus pandemic." https://www.cbssports.com/college-basketball/news/2020-ncaa-tournament-canceled-due-to-growing-threat-of-coronavirus-pandemic/ (accessed January 14, 2022).

World Health Organization. (2020). "WHO director-general's opening remarks at the media briefing on COVID-19-11 march 2020." https://www.who.int/director-general/speeches/detail/who-director-general-s-opening-remarks-at-the-media-briefing-on-covid-19---11-march-2020 (accessed October 14, 2021).

Chapter 26

University of Idaho. (2020). "Faculty Staff Handbook FSH 6990 contagious infectious disease emergency response." https://www.uidaho.edu/governance/policy/policies/fsh/6/6990 (accessed January 4, 2022).

University of Idaho. (2020). "Faculty Staff Handbook FSH 6995 face covering requirement during response to COVID-19 pandemic." https://www.uidaho.edu/-/media/UIdaho-Responsive/Files/governance/faculty-senate/emergency-presidential-actions/2020-fsh-6995-face-covering-requirement---approval-policy.pdf?la=en&hash=C725E99DED1B1B1C371A685D60DEE78AD8EFE83A (accessed January 4, 2022).

Chapter 27

Drucker, P. (n.d.). "'Culture eats strategy for breakfast' quote." https://www.manage
  mentcentre.co.uk/management-consultancy/culture-eats-strategy-
  for-breakfast (accessed January 4, 2023).
Gardner, H. (2017). *Smart Collaboration: How Professionals and Their Firms Succeed
  by Breaking Down Silos*. Boston: Harvard Business Review Press.

Chapter 28

US Geological Survey. (2020). "Magnitude 6.5 Earthquake Felt in Central
  Idaho." https://www.usgs.gov/news/featured-story/magnitude-65-
  earthquake-felt-central-idaho (accessed January 4, 2022).

Chapter 30

Lipton, J. W., & Sortwell, C. E. (2020). "Opinion: we have a coronavirus test-let us use it."
  The Wall Street Journal (15 April). https://www.wsj.com/articles/we-have-
  a-coronavirus-testlet-us-use-it-11586969078 (accessed January 4, 2022).
Nickel, A. (2020). "Purdue starts limited covid-19 testing in diagnostic lab; goal to
  expand state's capacity in serving patients." *Purdue University News* (17 April).
  https://www.purdue.edu/newsroom/releases/2020/Q2/purdue-starts-
  limited-covid-19-testing-in-diagnostic-lab-goal-to-expand-
  states-capacity-in-serving-patients.html (accessed January 4, 2022).
Sanders, R. (2020). "UC Berkeley scientists spin up a robotic COVID-19 Testing
  Lab." *Berkeley News* (7 April). https://news.berkeley.edu/2020/03/30/
  uc-berkeley-scientists-spin-up-a-robotic-covid-19-testing-lab
  (accessed January 4, 2022).

Chapter 32

Dennis, E. (2020). "UI's proposed teaching model sees pushback." https://dnews
  .com/coronavirus/ui-s-proposed-teaching-model-sees-pushback/
  article_27bf67a5-4da3-531b-bb0c-b5aaaffe9bd1.html (accessed January
  14, 2022).
Kim, H. (2020). "Sign the petition University of Idaho hold online classes for the
  safety of everyone." https://www.change.org/p/c-scott-green-the-
  university-of-idaho-needs-to-hold-online-classes-for-the-safety-
  of-everyone (accessed January 14, 2022).
University of Idaho. (2021). "Coordinated Community Response Team Resource
  Handbook." https://www.uidaho.edu/-/media/UIdaho-Responsive/Files/
  Diversity/womens-center/ccrt-resource-handbook---master.pdf
  (accessed January 25, 2022).

Chapter 34

Dawson, J. (2020). "Gov. Brad Little orders $200 million cut over Idaho's coronavirus fallout." https://www.boisestatepublicradio.org/politics-government/2020-07-07/gov-brad-little-orders-200-million-cut-over-idahos-coronavirus-fallout (accessed January 14, 2022).

Chapter 35

PotatoPro.com. (2022). "University of Idaho New Seed Potato Lab to open this year." https://www.potatopro.com/news/2021/university-idaho-new-seed-potato-lab-open-year (accessed June 10, 2022).

Staff, *East Idaho News*. (2022). "Idaho universities gain exclusive access to Idaho National Laboratory supercomputer." *East Idaho News* (28 February). https://www.eastidahonews.com/2022/02/idaho-universities-gain-exclusive-access-to-idaho-national-laboratory-supercomputer (accessed April 3, 2022).

University of Idaho. (2020). "Research activity and expenditures U of I research report 2021." https://www.uidaho.edu/research/news/research-reports/2021/activity-and-expenditures (accessed January 25, 2022).

University of Idaho. (2021). University of Idaho awarded $18.9M for deep soil research facility. https://www.uidaho.edu/news/news-articles/news-releases/2021-fall/092821-deepsoilresearch (accessed March 14, 2022).

Chapter 37

University of Idaho McCall Outdoor Science School. (n.d.). "Moss K-12 programs." https://www.uidaho.edu/cnr/mccall-field-campus/programs-and-services/moss (accessed January 4, 2022).

Chapter 38

Ellis, E. (2022). "WSU's coronavirus mandate for students will continue permanently." *Big Country News,* Pullmanradio.com. https://www.bigcountrynewsconnection.com/local/wsus-coronavirus-mandate-for-students-will-continue-permanently/article_60aed46e-9a61-11ec-9eb3-17611ff7ebbd.html (accessed June 3, 2022).

Kolpitcke, C. (2020). "Opinion: WSU vs UI: A tale of two responses." *The Argonaut* (September 23). https://www.uiargonaut.com/2020/09/22/opinion-wsu-vs-ui-a-tale-of-two-responses (accessed January 4, 2022).

Sokol, C. (2020). "WSU reverses course for fall semester, says courses will stay online due to virus surge." *Spokesman.com* (23 July). https://www.spokesman.com/stories/2020/jul/23/wsu-reverses-course-for-fall-semester-says-courses (accessed January 4, 2022).

Staff, KIRO 7 News. (2021). "WSU latest to require on-campus students to be vaccinated for covid-19." *MyNorthwest.com* (28 April). https://mynorthwest.com/2850845/wsu-latest-to-require-students-vaccinated-covid-19/amp (accessed January 4, 2022).

Washington State Governor's Office. (n.d.). "Vaccine mandate frequently asked questions." https://www.governor.wa.gov/VaccineMandateFAQ (accessed June 3, 2022).

Wolcott, R.J. (2020). "Washington National Guard buoys WSU during covid-19 storm." *WSU Insider* (18 November). https://news.wsu.edu/news/2020/11/18/washington-national-guard-buoys-wsu-covid-19-storm (accessed January 4, 2022).

Zavala, D. (2020). "WSU's first day of class a different experience for many students amid covid-19." *Spokesman.com* (24 August). https://www.spokesman.com/stories/2020/aug/25/wsu-first-day-of-class (accessed January 4, 2022).

Chapter 39

University of Idaho. (2020). "Staff Council Agenda, December 9, 2020." https://www.uidaho.edu/-/media/UIdaho-Responsive/Files/governance/Staff-Council/Minutes/2020-21/120920-sc-minutes.pdf?la=en&hash=64B725B6779600A66797759A744FB6689B9628B6 (accessed January 4, 2022).

University of Idaho. (2021). "January 4 memorandum to students, staff, and faculty." https://www.uidaho.edu/-/media/UIdaho-Responsive/Files/health-clinic/covid-19/memos/memo-210104-green-lawrence.pdf?la=en&hash=2F8FED17F38EC7B48F08002014AF53F6437F4BC1 (accessed January 4, 2022).

University of Idaho. (n.d.). "California enrollment campaign 'We're closer than you think.'" https://sway.office.com/jraPEdT5xzNhF3R6?ref=Link. (accessed June 2, 2022).

University of Idaho. (n.d.). "Common data set University of Idaho Institutional Data." https://www.uidaho.edu/provost/ir/institutional-data/common-data-set (accessed June 2, 2022).

Chapter 40

New York Times. (2021). "Tracking coronavirus in Idaho: latest map and case count." https://www.nytimes.com/interactive/2021/us/idaho-covid-cases.html (accessed March 8, 2023).

University of Idaho. (2021). "University, Gritman Medical pandemic teams awarded President's Medallion." https://www.uidaho.edu/news/news-articles/news-releases/2021-spring/051821-presidentsmedallion (accessed January 22, 2022).

Chapter 41

Bowen, W.G. (2010). *Lessons Learned: Reflections of a University President.* New Jersey: Princeton University Press.

Idaho Freedom Foundation. (2022). `https://idahofreedom.org` (accessed June 5, 2022).

Russell, B. Z. (2022). "UI Budget was cut last year based on 'false narrative,' president Scott Green tells JFAC." *Idaho Press* (1 February). `https://www.idahopress.com/eyeonboise/ui-budget-was-cut-last-year-based-on-false-narrative-president-scott-green-tells-jfac/article_f6b66467-6598-5268-9c1b-aa6b835e82a2.html` (accessed February 2, 2022).

Chapter 42

Andrews, K.R., New, D.D., Gour, D.S., et al. (2023). "Genomic surveillance identifies potential risk factors for SARS-CoV-2 transmission at a mid-sized university in a small rural town." `https://www.nature.com/articles/s41598-023-34625-7` (accessed July 9, 2023).

Goswami, S., Chakraborty, S., & Pal, S. (2022). "Spike in Mental Health issues among students due to COVID19 Pandemic." `https://www.iomcworld.org/articles/spike-in-mental-health-issues-among-students-due-to-covid19-pandemic.pdf` (accessed March 8, 2022).

University of Idaho. (2021). "Friday Letter." `https://www.uidaho.edu/president/communications/friday-letter/archive` (accessed January 4, 2022).

University of Idaho. (2021). "U of I and INBRE researchers to study coronavirus variants." `https://www.iids.uidaho.edu/news.php?newsid=103` (accessed January 22, 2021).

Chapter 43

University of Idaho. (2022). "Arrest made in King Street Homicides." `https://www.uidaho.edu/communications` (accessed January 15, 2023).

University of Idaho. (2023). "Spring 2023 Undergraduate Enrollment Rises 3.5%." `https://www.uidaho.edu/news/news-articles/news-releases/2023/012723-enrollment` (accessed July 10, 2023).

Chapter 44

Gardner, Heidi. (2017). *Smart Collaboration: How Professionals and Their Firms Succeed by Breaking Down Silos*. Boston: Harvard Business Review Press.

References A-Z

Andrews, K.R., New, D.D., Gour, D.S., et al. (2023). "Genomic surveillance identifies potential risk factors for SARS-CoV-2 transmission at a mid-sized university in a small rural town." https://www.nature.com/articles/s41598-023-34625-7 (accessed July 9, 2023).

Boone, K. (2020). "2020 NCAA Tournament canceled due to growing threat of coronavirus pandemic." https://www.cbssports.com/college-basketball/news/2020-ncaa-tournament-canceled-due-to-growing-threat-of-coronavirus-pandemic/ (accessed January 14, 2022).

Britannica. (n.d.). "Land-Grant College Act of 1862, United States Legislation." https://www.britannica.com/topic/Land-Grant-College-Act-of-1862 (accessed October 1, 2021).

Dawson, J. (2020). "Gov. Brad Little orders $200 million cut over Idaho's coronavirus fallout." https://www.boisestatepublicradio.org/politics-government/2020-07-07/gov-brad-little-orders-200-million-cut-over-idahos-coronavirus-fallout (accessed January 14, 2022).

Dennis, E. (2020). "UI's proposed teaching model sees pushback." https://dnews.com/coronavirus/ui-s-proposed-teaching-model-sees-pushback/article_27bf67a5-4da3-531b-bb0c-b5aaaffe9bd1.html (accessed January 14, 2022).

Drucker, P. (n.d.) "'Culture eats strategy for breakfast' quote." https://www.managementcentre.co.uk/management-consultancy/culture-eats-strategy-for-breakfast (accessed January 4, 2023).

Ellis, E. (2022). "WSU's coronavirus mandate for students will continue permanently." *Big Country News, Pullmanradio.com.* https://www.bigcountrynewsconnection.com/local/wsus-coronavirus-mandate-for-students-will-continue-permanently/article_60aed46e-9a61-11ec-9eb3-17611ff7ebbd.html (accessed June 3, 2022).

ESPN. (2010). "Boise State president blasts rival Idaho." `https://www.espn.com/college-football/news/story?id=5417329` (accessed May 31, 2022).

Gardner, H. (2017). *Smart Collaboration: How Professionals and Their Firms Succeed by Breaking Down Silos.* Boston: Harvard Business Review Press.

Goswami, S., Chakraborty, S., & Pal, S. (2022). "Spike in Mental Health issues among students due to COVID19 Pandemic." `https://www.iomcworld.org/articles/spike-in-mental-health-issues-among-students-due-to-covid19-pandemic.pdf` (accessed March 8, 2022).

Idaho Freedom Foundation. (2022). `https://idahofreedom.org` (accessed June 5, 2022).

Idaho State Board of Education. (2019). "State board of education March 13–14, 2019, meeting minutes." `https://boardofed.idaho.gov/meetings/board/archive/2019/0313-1419/03-March-13-14-2019-Special-APPROVED-minutes.pdf` (accessed January 22, 2022).

Idaho State Board of Education. (2021). "III.F. program prioritization." `https://boardofed.idaho.gov/board-policies-rules/board-policies/higher-education-affairs-section-iii/iii-f-program-prioritization` (accessed October 15, 2021).

Kim, H. (2020). "Sign the petition University of Idaho hold online classes for the safety of everyone." `https://www.change.org/p/c-scott-green-the-university-of-idaho-needs-to-hold-online-classes-for-the-safety-of-everyone` (accessed January 14, 2022).

Kolpitcke, C. (2020, September 23). "Opinion: WSU vs UI: A tale of two responses." *The Argonaut.* `https://www.uiargonaut.com/2020/09/22/opinion-wsu-vs-ui-a-tale-of-two-responses` (accessed January 4, 2022).

Lipton, J. W., & Sortwell, C. E. (2020). "Opinion: We have a coronavirus test—let us use it." *The Wall Street Journal* (15 April). `https://www.wsj.com/articles/we-have-a-coronavirus-testlet-us-use-it-11586969078` (accessed January 4, 2022).

Moscow Idaho Chamber of Commerce. (2021). "Executive summary: Economic contributions of Vandal athletics." `https://moscowchamber.com/executive-summary-economic-contributions-of-vandal-athletics` (accessed January 22, 2022).

New York Times. (2021). "Tracking coronavirus in Idaho: Latest map and case count." `https://www.nytimes.com/interactive/2021/us/idaho-covid-cases.html` (accessed March 8, 2023).

Nickel, A. (2020). "Purdue starts limited Covid-19 testing in diagnostic lab; goal to expand state's capacity in serving patients." *Purdue University News* (April 17). `https://www.purdue.edu/newsroom/releases/2020/Q2/purdue-starts-limited-covid-19-testing-in-diagnostic-lab-goal-to-expand-states-capacity-in-serving-patients.html` (accessed January 4, 2022).

Petersen, K. (1987). *This Crested Hill: An illustrated history of the University of Idaho.* Idaho: University of Idaho Press.

PotatoPro.com. (2022). "University of Idaho New Seed Potato Lab to open this year." `https://www.potatopro.com/news/2021/university-idaho-new-seed-potato-lab-open-year` (accessed June 10, 2022).

Russell, B. Z. (2022). "UI Budget was cut last year based on 'false narrative,' president Scott Green tells JFAC." *Idaho Press* (February 1). https://www.idahopress.com/eyeonboise/ui-budget-was-cut-last-year-based-on-false-narrative-president-scott-green-tells-jfac/article_f6b66467-6598-5268-9c1b-aa6b835e82a2.html (accessed February 2, 2022).

Sanders, R. (2020). "UC Berkeley scientists spin up a robotic COVID-19 Testing Lab." *Berkeley News* (April 7). https://news.berkeley.edu/2020/03/30/uc-berkeley-scientists-spin-up-a-robotic-covid-19-testing-lab (accessed January 4, 2022).

Sokol, C. (2020). "WSU reverses course for fall semester, says courses will stay online due to virus surge." *Spokesman.com* (July 23). https://www.spokesman.com/stories/2020/jul/23/wsu-reverses-course-for-fall-semester-says-courses (accessed January 4, 2022).

Staff, *East Idaho News*. (2022). "Idaho universities gain exclusive access to Idaho National Laboratory supercomputer." *East Idaho News* (February 28). https://www.eastidahonews.com/2022/02/idaho-universities-gain-exclusive-access-to-idaho-national-laboratory-supercomputer (accessed April 3, 2022).

Staff, KIRO 7 News. (2021). "WSU latest to require on-campus students to be vaccinated for covid-19." *MyNorthwest.com* (April 28). https://mynorthwest.com/2850845/wsu-latest-to-require-students-vaccinated-covid-19/amp (accessed January 4, 2022).

University of Idaho. (2020). "CAFE 2020 research report." https://www.uidaho.edu/research/news/research-reports/2020/cafe (accessed October 15, 2021).

University of Idaho. (2020). "Faculty Staff Handbook FSH 6990 contagious infectious disease emergency response." https://www.uidaho.edu/governance/policy/policies/fsh/6/6990 (accessed January 4, 2022).

University of Idaho. (2020). "Faculty Staff Handbook FSH 6995 face covering requirement during response to COVID-19 pandemic." https://www.uidaho.edu/-/media/UIdaho-Responsive/Files/governance/faculty-senate/emergency-presidential-actions/2020-fsh-6995-face-covering-requirement---approval-policy.pdf?la=en&hash=C725E99DED1B1B1C371A685D60DEE78AD8EFE83A (accessed January 4, 2022).

University of Idaho. (2020). "First Wood column set as ICCU Arena takes shape at U of I." https://www.uidaho.edu/news/news-articles/news-releases/2020-summer/060220-iccuarena (accessed January 22, 2022).

University of Idaho. (2020). "Online education working group." https://www.uidaho.edu/-/media/UIdaho-Responsive/Files/president/working-groups/online-education-rprt.pdf (accessed January 22, 2022).

University of Idaho. (2020). "R1/Research working group final report." https://www.uidaho.edu/-/media/UIdaho-Responsive/Files/president/working-groups/r1_rsrchworkinggroup_rprt_vs4.pdf?la=en&hash=6AAC6A82C0EC333D5E79DDA574A95E39E40E45BF (accessed January 22, 2022).

University of Idaho. (2020). "Research activity and expenditures U of I research report 2021." https://www.uidaho.edu/research/news/research-reports/2021/activity-and-expenditures (accessed January 25, 2022).

University of Idaho. (2020). "Staff Council Agenda, December 9, 2020." https://
www.uidaho.edu/-/media/UIdaho-Responsive/Files/governance/Staff-
Council/Minutes/2020-21/120920-sc-minutes.pdf?la=en&hash=64B725B
6779600A66797759A744FB6689B9628B6 (accessed January 4, 2022).

University of Idaho. (2020). "Sustainable financial model working group white
paper." https://www.uidaho.edu/-/media/UIdaho-Responsive/Files/
president/working-groups/sustainable-financial-model-working-
group-white-paper-oct-2020.pdf (accessed September 1, 2021).

University of Idaho. (2021). "Comprehensive campaign working group white
paper." https://www.uidaho.edu/-/media/UIdaho-Responsive/Files/
president/working-groups/campaign-working-group-white-paper-
aug-2021.pdf (accessed January 22, 2022).

University of Idaho. (2021). "Coordinated Community Response Team Resource
Handbook." https://www.uidaho.edu/-/media/UIdaho-Responsive/Files/
Diversity/womens-center/ccrt-resource-handbook---master.pdf
(accessed January 25, 2022).

University of Idaho. (2021). "Friday Letter." https://www.uidaho.edu/president/
communications/friday-letter/archive (accessed January 4, 2022).

University of Idaho. (2021). "January 4 memorandum to students, staff, and faculty."
https://www.uidaho.edu/-/media/UIdaho-Responsive/Files/health-
clinic/covid-19/memos/memo-210104-green-lawrence.pdf?la=en&hash=
2F8FED17F38EC7B48F08002014AF53F6437F4BC1 (accessed January 4, 2022).

University of Idaho. (2021). "U of I and INBRE researchers to study coronavirus
variants." https://www.iids.uidaho.edu/news.php?newsid=103 (accessed
January 22, 2021).

University of Idaho. (2021). "University of Idaho awarded $18.9M for deep soil
research facility." https://www.uidaho.edu/news/news-articles/news-
releases/2021-fall/092821-deepsoilresearch (accessed March 14, 2022).

University of Idaho. (2021). "University, Gritman Medical pandemic teams awarded
President's Medallion." https://www.uidaho.edu/news/news-articles/news-
releases/2021-spring/051821-presidentsmedallion (accessed January
22, 2022).

University of Idaho. (2022). "Sustainability working group: Sustainable solutions
for our university and for our state." https://www.uidaho.edu/-/media/
UIdaho-Responsive/Files/president/working-groups/sustainability/
sustainability-white-paper.pdf (accessed July 16, 2023).

University of Idaho. (2023). "Faculty Senate." https://www.uidaho.edu/
governance/faculty-senate (accessed December 10, 2021).

University of Idaho. (2023). "Spring 2023 Undergraduate Enrollment Rises 3.5%."
https://www.uidaho.edu/news/news-articles/news-releases/2023/
012723-enrollment (accessed July 10, 2023).

University of Idaho. (n.d.). "California enrollment campaign 'We're closer than you
think.'" https://sway.office.com/jraPEdT5xzNhF3R6?ref=Link (accessed
June 2, 2022).

University of Idaho. (n.d.). "Common data set University of Idaho Institutional Data."
https://www.uidaho.edu/provost/ir/institutional-data/common-
data-set (accessed June 2, 2022).

University of Idaho. (n.d.). "Initiative for Bioinformatics + Evolutionary Studies IBEST." https://www.iids.uidaho.edu/ibest.php (accessed October 9, 2022).

University of Idaho. (n.d.). "Leadership Groups." https://www.uidaho.edu/president/leadership-groups (accessed September 1, 2021).

University of Idaho. (n.d.). "Nancy M. Cummings Research, Extension & Education Center." https://www.uidaho.edu/cals/nancy-m-cummings-research-extension-and-education-center (accessed October 1, 2021).

University of Idaho. (n.d.). "Program prioritization at the University of Idaho. Update of program prioritization at the University of Idaho." https://www.uidaho.edu/-/media/UIdaho-Responsive/Files/provost/councils-committees/ipec/program-prioritization/app-taskforce-report-2020.pdf?la=en&hash=B3FFE9BBFEFB166ABDCDABEAD959FD44A9B18AAD (accessed October 1, 2022).

University of Idaho. (n.d.). "Rinker Rock Creek Ranch." https://www.uidaho.edu/research/entities/rock-creek (accessed January 22, 2022).

University of Idaho. (n.d.). "University House." https://www.uidaho.edu/about/university-house (accessed November 1, 2021).

University of Idaho. (n.d.). "Update on program prioritization at the University of Idaho final." https://www.uidaho.edu/-/media/UIdaho-Responsive/Files/provost/councils-committees/ipec/program-prioritization/communications/update-on-program-prioritization-at-the-university-of-idaho-final.pdf?la=en&hash=AC41EACB41E2DA252C4B1EA43D14A29C4B0A9356 (accessed January 22, 2022).

University of Idaho. (n.d.). "We've got WUE." https://www.uidaho.edu/ui/wue (accessed November 1, 2021).

University of Idaho McCall Outdoor Science School. (n.d.). "Moss K-12 programs." https://www.uidaho.edu/cnr/mccall-field-campus/programs-and-services/moss (accessed January 4, 2022).

University of Idaho McClure Center for Public Policy Research. (2022). "Idaho at a glance." https://www.uidaho.edu/-/media/UIdaho-Responsive/Files/president/direct-reports/mcclure-center/Idaho-at-a-Glance/idg-economy-and-climate.pdf?la=en&hash=2073D2EDAA55D570305E63F6506314621E667CD3 (accessed January 4, 2023).

University of Idaho McClure Center for Public Policy Research. (n.d.). "Idaho at a glance, life after high school." https://www.uidaho.edu/-/media/UIdaho-Responsive/Files/president/direct-reports/mcclure-center/Idaho-at-a-Glance/IDG-Life-After-High-School.pdf (accessed October 15, 2021).

University of Idaho Office of the Provost. (2019). "Memorandum, Provost provides Academic Affairs budget update." https://www.uidaho.edu/-/media/UIdaho-Responsive/Files/provost/updates/academic-affairs-budget-update-1-30-19.pdf?la=en&hash=27C79E5FB3F193B2F4A6CF2BE161A0F684161612 (accessed January 22, 2022).

University of Idaho Special Collections. (1933). "Go, Vandals, go!" https://www.lib.uidaho.edu/special-collections/pdf/Go_Vandals_Go.pdf.

US Geological Survey. (2020). "Magnitude 6.5 Earthquake Felt in Central Idaho." https://www.usgs.gov/news/featured-story/magnitude-65-earthquake-felt-central-idaho (accessed January 4, 2022).

US News & World Report. (2002). "University of Idaho overall rankings." https://www.usnews.com/best-colleges/university-of-idaho-1626/overall-rankings (accessed October 9, 2022).

Washington State Governor's Office. (n.d.). "Vaccine mandate frequently asked questions." https://www.governor.wa.gov/VaccineMandateFAQ (accessed June 3, 2022).

Wikipedia. (n.d.). "Idaho panhandle." https://en.wikipedia.org/wiki/Idaho_Panhandle (accessed October 1, 2021).

Wolcott, R.J. (2020). "Washington National Guard buoys WSU during Covid-19 storm." *WSU Insider* (November 18). https://news.wsu.edu/news/2020/11/18/washington-national-guard-buoys-wsu-covid-19-storm (accessed January 4, 2022).

World Health Organization. (2020). "WHO director-general's opening remarks at the media briefing on COVID-19—11 march 2020." https://www.who.int/director-general/speeches/detail/who-director-general-s-opening-remarks-at-the-media-briefing-on-covid-19---11-march-2020 (October 14, 2021).

Zavala, D. (2020). "WSU's first day of class a different experience for many students amid Covid-19." *Spokesman.com* (August 24). https://www.spokesman.com/stories/2020/aug/25/wsu-first-day-of-class (accessed January 4, 2022).

Resources

For links and additional information contained in the *University President's Crisis Handbook*, visit our website. There, you will find references mentioned throughout the book and other resources to enhance your reading experience.

go.uidaho.edu/presidents-crisis-handbook

About the Authors

C. Scott Green

C. Scott Green took office as the 19th president of the University of Idaho on July 1, 2019. President Green joined the U of I as a highly accomplished executive with a career in global finance, operations, and administration. He is also a proud alumnus of the university, graduating in 1984 with a bachelor of science in accounting.

He was born in Moscow, Idaho, and his family moved to Boise, Idaho, where he graduated from Boise High School. Following his degree from the University of Idaho, the third-generation Vandal went to work for Boise Cascade Corporation. He went on to attend Harvard Business School and received a master of business administration in 1989.

Green worked for Deloitte & Touche as part of its accelerated career program from 1989 to 1994. He then worked in banking, serving in various management roles for Goldman Sachs and ING Barings. He published two books on the Sarbanes-Oxley Act of 2002, which reformed regulations around auditing and financial reporting.

Green went on to leadership in global law firms, including service as CEO at Pepper Hamilton and as executive director at WilmerHale. He most recently served as the chief operating and financial officer for Hogan Lovells, one of the largest law firms in the world, with annual revenues of over $2 billion. Green led all the firm's worldwide operations, technology, conflicts, and finance functions. He has had global responsibility for more than 3,000 employees in more than 30 countries.

The first non-lawyer to run an American Lawyer 100 law firm, Green was recognized as one of the Top 50 Big Law Innovators of the Last 50 Years by *The American Lawyer* magazine in 2013. A certified public accountant, Green was inducted into the American Institute of Certified Public Accountants' Business and Industry Hall of Fame in 2006. He won the Institute of Internal Auditors Outstanding Contributor Award in 2004 and 2006.

Green's commitment to the University of Idaho over many years has included service on the U of I Alumni Association's national Board of Directors, the College of Business and Economics Advisory Board, and on the U of I Foundation Board. He is also a Vandal Scholarship Fund supporter.

Green and his wife, Gabriella, an interior design project manager, have two adult children: Nicholas and Christina.

SOURCE: Bryant Livingston Photography.

Temple Kinyon

Temple Kinyon is an author and freelance writer living in Las Vegas, Nevada. She spent her first three decades of life in Idaho, where she grew up on a wheat farm in the rural community of Potlatch. She attended the University of Idaho and received her bachelor of science in communications/advertising in 1993. While there, she worked as assistant newsletter editor at Facilities Management, where she learned the ins and outs of campus and deepened her affection for the institution and rolling hills of the Palouse.

After graduating, Kinyon worked in the real estate and hospitality industries, enhancing her marketing and communications experience before returning to her alma mater in 1997 to work at the University of Idaho Alumni Office as the off-campus events and volunteer manager. In this capacity, she met Scott Green, an alumni chapter volunteer from New York. She went on to work at University Communications and Marketing as production coordinator in 2002. Her love for the institution has never wavered, even when she and her husband, Chad, relocated to Las Vegas in 2003.

Kinyon worked at the University of Nevada Las Vegas in the President's Office as the event manager and became a certified barista for Starbucks. Her dream of becoming a published author came to fruition when she jumped into a full-time freelance writing career in 2012. She became a contributing writer for *BLVDS LV Magazine* in 2014, where she also landed her first editorial assistant position.

Kinyon published her first book, *The Button Boxes*, in 2019. Her fiction and nonfiction contributions have appeared in *Home & Harvest Magazine* and *Idaho Grain Magazine*. Kinyon considers herself a nostalgia writer; her childhood experiences continue to offer an unlimited supply of anecdotes for her varied writing projects. Writing magazine articles and books are her passions, but she also works as a freelance copywriter and editor and occasional writing mentor to young creatives.

Index

6990 COVID-19 Virus Emergency Response, adoption, 211–213

Nelson, Ann, 84–85
Nelson, Kent, 159, 351, 360
Net tuition revenue, appearance, 77
Nichols, Jake, 350–351
Nichols, Shelly, 276
Nomura, Christopher, 48, 281, 288
Nonrenewal letters, delivery, 166
Nonrenewals, 166
Non-strategic assets, lease/sale (usage), 172
Nonstrategic assets, sale/reinvestment, 160
Nontraditional president, acceptance issues, 6

O
Off-the-shelf analytical software, usage, 147
Olmstead Brothers, university master plan, 38
One-time carryover give-back, reinvestment
    purpose, 97
Online classes
    conversion, discussion, 194–195
    student usage/transition, 242, 341
Online coursework, opposition, 240–241
Online educational world, initial rollout, 243
Online education, white papers (existence), 152
Online Education Working Group, 154–155
Online initiatives, offering (increase), 155
Online offerings, development, 170
Online/remote instruction, U of I transition (imme-
    diacy), 203–204
Operating budgets, capital (difference, under-
    standing), 134
Operating Committee, establishment, 67–68
Operational budgets, 167–168
Operations, cuts (limitation), 166
Opportunities, arrival, 290
Optional Retirement Incentive Program
    (ORIP), 165
Organization (movement), trust (building), 177
Osborn, Connie, 324
Other Post Employment Benefit (OPEB), 110
Out-of-cycle pay increases process, creation, 98
Outside consultant
    hiring, 174
    usage, department management hesitancy,
    176
Outsourcing, insourcing (contrast), 171–172
Over-communication, failure, 130

P
Paid level, options, 236
Palouse area petition, 266
Parker, Daniel, 48
Parma Research and Extension Center, smart
    collaboration, 32–34
Parrella, Michael, 30–35, 43, 71, 159, 325–326
    morale (observation), Green (impact), 180
    natural environment/range practices,
    interest, 161
Partnering, factors, 171

Partnerships
    importance, 34
    leveraging, 168
Pascucci, Betsy, 53
Past. blame/lament (counterproductivity), 122
Peer data, confirmation, 72–732
Personal protective equipment (PPE), 187,
    246, 267, 271
Pfizer vaccine, usage requirements, 324
Pfund, Christopher, 304–305
Pittman Center, COVID-19 discussion, 209–210
Plexiglass, usage, 270
Position cuts, impact, 166
Postdocs, hiring, 170
Powell, Matt, 256
Presidents, fiduciary responsibility, 122
President's Leadership Breakfasts, usage, 93, 96
Presidents Leadership Council meeting (SBOE
    hosting), 198
President's Medallion, conferring, 327f
Prichard Art Gallery, 123–126
Private-sector company, collaboration, 168
Problems, breakdown, 196
Programming, impact, 156
Program Prioritization (PP), 92–93, 97
    COVID-19, relationship, 187–188
    effectiveness, 145
    funding, identification, 95
    process/discussions, 145
    process, refreshing, 144
Progress, celebration, 328–329
Pro-rata allocation method, usage, 117
Public Employee Retirement System of Idaho
    (PERSI) retirement funds, 169
Public-private partnerships (P3), 168–169,
    325, 375
    funds, allocation, 283
Purdue Research Foundation, animal testing, 248
Purdue University, P3 (usage), 168–169

Q
Quantitative polymerase chain reaction (qPCR)
    testing, analysis, 249, 260
Quinlan, Sean, 118, 201, 242, 296, 378

R
R1-2026 Research Initiative Working Group, 153
R1-2026 Working Group, 282–283
R1 Carnegie Classification, 153, 281, 285, 375
R1 research classification, path, 49
R1 status, reaching, 284
Rader, Erika, 305
Reagents, supply (obtaining), 257
Real-time data, usage, 106–107
Recruitment
    COVID-19, impact, 233–234
    remote approach, 234
Reduction in force (RIF), 167